# The Sky in
## Mayan Literature

# The Sky in Mayan Literature

Edited by

ANTHONY F. AVENI

New York • Oxford
OXFORD UNIVERSITY PRESS
1992

Oxford University Press

Oxford  New York  Toronto
Delhi  Bombay  Calcutta  Madras  Karachi
Kuala Lumpur  Singapore  Hong Kong  Tokyo
Nairobi  Dar es Salaam  Cape Town
Melbourne  Auckland

and associated companies in
Berlin  Ibadan

Copyright © 1992 by Anthony Aveni

Published by Oxford University Press, Inc.
200 Madison Avenue, New York, New York 10016

Oxford is a registered trademark of Oxford University Press

Library of Congress Cataloging-in-Publication Data
The Sky in Mayan literature / edited by Anthony F. Aveni
p. cm.  Includes bibliographical references and index.
ISBN 0-19-506844-0
1. Mayas—Writing. 2. Mayas—Astronomy. 3. Mayas—Calendar.
4. Mexico—Antiquities. 5. Guatemala—Antiquities.
I. Aveni, Anthony F.
F1435.3.W75S55  1992
972.81'016—dc20  91-17130

1 3 5 7 9 8 6 4 2

Printed in the United States of America
on acid-free paper

# PREFACE

The idea for a workshop on the astronomical content of the codices origi-
nated several years before the meeting (in November, 1989, at Colgate
University) that ultimately led to this book. The participants, in various
permutations of threes and fours, at diverse professional conferences, frequently had raised the possibility of getting together for a serious collabora-
tion on how to read the books. Thanks to the initiative of Dr. Charles G.
Trout, then Dean of Faculty at Colgate, the Colgate Cultural Center and
the Native American Studies Committee, support from the academic community of the editor of this text enabled a 4-day-long session to take place.

Our stated goal was to assess some of the recent advances in Maya
glyphic decipherment, especially those with which participants had been
intimately involved. Our focus was the understanding of the nature and
extent of Maya knowledge about the natural world, specifically the sky
environment as revealed in the codices and related texts.

Participants were asked to address the following particular themes and
questions concerning the Maya books of omen and prognostication and to
raise new questions for future research:

1. What are the layouts and calendrical structure of the almanacs and
   tables in the codices and what are some of the broader structural
   parallels among them? How were these documents composed and
   how were they used?

2. What are the references, both explicit and implicit, to astronomical
   events in the codices? What cross-references from text to text exist?

3. How are celestial events represented both iconographically and
   glyphically? Where does real time fit into the codices?

4. What evidence exists for commensuration and temporal overlap of
   astronomical events?

5. What date-reaching mechanisms were employed by the Maya astronomical "computists," and how do ephemerides in the codices differ
   from the so-called almanacs?

6. What structural parallels can be drawn between the codices and the

contemporary methods of Maya timekeeping? Can native colonial manuscripts such as the Books of Chilam Balam and the Popol Vuh help us to understand the meaning of the codices?

Maya calendrics is a difficult and demanding subject that can be engaged from a variety of disciplinary perspectives, as our list of contributors demonstrates. Sir Eric Thompson once characterized the scholarly literature pertaining to it as "arid." But I hope that the general reader will be assisted by my Introduction, in which I summarize basic themes taken up in the text, and then attempt to explain briefly what each author contributes to the broader body of ancient Maya science. If persistent readers will then explore, either selectively or completely, the many new ideas and interpretations offered by the contributors, they will discover the falsity of Thompson's statement.

I invite readers to explore the pages of this book and thus to examine the pages of those of the Maya. My wish is that readers will come away with a fuller appreciation of the literature, the mathematics, and the science of the modern West, for the mirror of Maya astronomical studies is now burnished well enough to reveal for the first time aspects of our own reflection.

*Hamilton, New York* A.F.A.
*March* 1992

# CONTENTS

# CONTRIBUTORS

ANTHONY F. AVENI Russell B. Colgate Professor of Anthropology and Astronomy at Colgate University. Author of *Skywatchers of Ancient Mexico* and *Empires of Time*.

HARVEY M. BRICKER Professor of Anthropology, Tulane University. Archaeologist specializing in use of computer in codical decipherment.

VICTORIA R. BRICKER Professor and Chair of Anthropology, Tulane University. Author of *Indian Christ, Indian King*. Ethnologist whose most recent work has been in the field of decipherment.

MICHAEL P. CLOSS Professor of Mathematics, University of Ottawa. Author of numerous articles on calendrical decipherment. Editor of *Native American Mathematics*.

CHARLES FRAKE Professor of Anthropology Emeritus, Stanford University and SUNY Buffalo. Known for his work in cognitive anthropology, particularly Polynesian seafaring and Medieval map-making.

CHARLES A. HOFLING Visiting Research Associate Professor of Anthropology at the University of Cincinnati. Currently engaged in the documentation of Itzá Maya, a dying language spoken in the Petén, Guatemala. Has recently published the volume, *Itzá Maya Texts with a Grammatical Overview* (1991) and is preparing a comprehensive grammar of that language.

FLOYD G. LOUNSBURY Professor of Anthropology Emeritus, Yale University. His seminal contributions at Palenque Round Table meetings in the 1970s led to breakthroughs in decipherment.

THOMAS O'NEIL Instructor of Biology at Fugazzi College in Lexington, Kentucky. Has studied the astronomical aspects of Mayan hieroglyphs since an introductory course under Charles Hofling taken at the University of Kentucky in 1985.

MERIDETH PAXTON Research Associate, Latin American Institute, University of New Mexico. Recently completed a Ph.D. dissertation on the Dresden Codex.

Barbara Tedlock Professor of Anthropology, SUNY Buffalo. Author of *Time & the Highland Maya*. Ethnologist working on rituals of contemporary Mexico.

Dennis Tedlock Professor of English, SUNY Buffalo. Translator of *Popul Vuh*, the Quiche Maya sacred book of creation. Working on transition from hieroglyphic to alphabetic writing after European contact.

# The Sky in
## Mayan Literature

# Introduction:
# Making Time

## ANTHONY F. AVENI

Their books were written on a large sheet doubled in folds, which was enclosed entirely between two boards which they decorated, and they wrote on both sides in columns following the order of the folds. And they made this paper of the roots of a tree and it gave it a white gloss upon which it was easy to write. And some of the principal lords learned about these sciences from curiosity and were very highly thought of on this account although they never made use of them publicly.     A. TOZZER, 1941, "Landa's Relacion de las Cosas de Yucatan" (1566?). *Papers Peabody Mus. Am. Archaeol. & Ethnol.* XVIII, pp. 28–29

These are painted on both sides with a variety of figures and characters . . . , which show not only the count of the said days, months and years, but also the ages and prophecies which their idols and images announced to them. . .

    A. AVENDAÑO Y LOYOLA, "Relación de los dos entradas que hize a la conversión de los gentiles Ytzaex," Ms. Gates, Tr., A. Tozzer *op. cit.*, pp. 28–29.

Part of our fascination with the Maya can be attributed to the fact that they were literate, at least in the most popular definition of that skill; that is, the Classic Maya possessed a visible language that consisted of letters and a grammar, and one of the products of their literacy was the book. As we can

**3**

read from the description of Bishop Landa, one of the first outsiders to see them, Mayan books distinctly resembled those developed in the Western tradition from Egyptian papyrus to Dead Sea Scrolls to Medieval Codex— in fact, today we still inappropriately call the four Maya books that survive *codices*.

The Maya also are among the ancient cultures of the world who looked up. They seem to have paid an inordinate amount of attention to the sky; therefore it comes as no surprise that their literature—in all forms—is filled with celestial knowledge. Of all of nature's periodicities, those that come from the sky are the most reliable and regular, the least inconstant. The paramount goal of the astronomically and mathematically knowledgeable scribes was to use what they saw in the sky to pattern time. They were the architects of the Maya calendar, an evolving set of formalisms whereby they canonized time. They never tired of tinkering with their creation, to speed up or slow down parts of the temporal model to keep it in tune with the pristine celestial reality from whence all human power and sustenance emanated.

Make no mistake—the written content of Maya monumental sculpture, though woven throughout by the thread of astronomical time, is concerned basically with dynastic history and political authority. It tells about marriages, alliances, accessions, captures, and battles engaged in by members of the cream of society, and there was plenty of royal history to expose to a public that worshipped the Maya king and queen as manifest divinity. Even if the public could not read every syllable, they must have understood the iconic message. The books, however, tell a different story. These were private, sacred documents, their content complex and sophisticated.

A number of citations from the post-Conquest literature—those quoted in the epigraph are examples—further fuel our fascination with these ancient people. Avendaño's statement correctly implies that the content of Mayan books is almost completely mathematical and astronomical; that is, they are calendars and almanacs designed to reach future dates. To what ends? The glyphs between the numbers give the answer: "Woe to the turtle (drought?); woe to the warrior and pregnant female; his sacrifice, his divine punishment is set; evil excessive sun; the misery of the maize seed." Unlike modern astronomical and calendrical science, the ends of such date reaching were purely astrological and, as Landa implies, confined to a very specialized literate class.

So, the Maya intrigue us because we perceive in their remains familiar aspects of our own culture—advanced writing, numeracy, and a scientific method of predicting natural events—one reason we persist in labeling that phase of the Maya culture that produced the codices "the Classical Period" (approximately A.D. 200–900). When we discover that these books contain calculations that reach into the millions, dates protracted backward toward a mythical creation era that happened 3 millennia before they were written down, and when our studies uncover Mayan predictions of the first pre-dawn appearance of the planet Venus or a total eclipse, each accurate to the day a century in advance, all without benefit of any astronomical technology and all directed towards metaphysical ends, our fascination becomes awe.

Like the monuments, so too, the books are concerned with people—with the appropriate course of human action to keep the civilized world running on sacred time. Sometimes, as the pictures that accompany the bar-and-dot numbers and calendrical day signs in the codices indicate, the ritual was related to the cycles of planting and harvesting, which the Maya believed to be microcosms of lengthier cycles related to the creation and destruction of the world, the birth of the gods and the origin of humankind. What disease or pestilence of people and crops must we act upon to ward off today? Which patron god should be paid the debt of incense; at what time is he fit to receive it and in which particular temple? What plant or animal ought we to send? These were the kinds of questions the calendrical shamans who traveled from village to village with their books of prognostications tucked under their arms were trained to formulate. The people who consulted them must have believed in their mandate in helping to run the affairs of the interlocked social and natural world. They turned out as required in the ceremonial plaza in front of the temple at the proper time to participate in re-enactments of their principles of divine sustenance. They were witnesses to the public offering of penitential blood by the king, to the parading of prisoners before the royal family and to the ceremonial ballgame between disguised representatives of the upper and lower worlds.

Knowledge of the sky set the time scale for these elaborate ritual enactments and often celestial events, like the conjunction of a triad of celestial deities, were appropriately assigned to coincide with staged celebrations of the people here on Earth.

Why the Maya became such ardent astrophiles is a problem not yet resolved. What drove them to the extreme precision we glean from the calendars and almanacs they painted in red and black glyphic day names, dots, and bars? How did the astronomers, who surely must have been careful watchers of the sky, acquire and analyze these complex data? No astronomers' notebooks survive; only fragments of the finished product, copied and recopied, have been passed down to us to decode. We try to make order out of the fragmentary chaos that remains—but is it the same order that once made sense to them?

One need not be an expert to appreciate some of the broader questions a study of Mayan astronomy can reflect upon: What was the written legacy of one of the great state societies in pre-Columbian America? What was their concept of history? What specific needs and desires did their highly sophisticated writing inform? How were their cosmological concepts and ideas influenced by European contact? What processes affected the transformation of the encoding of information from pre-Columbian picture book/codex to post-Conquest alphabetic writing?

At the comparative level we can inquire into the cultural universals implied in the observations of the natural world. Is there a singular body of astronomical data, a unique set of events that comes down from the heavens via light pulses to the human eye? Should all cultures who watch the sky know about the retrograde movement of Mars as it treks along the zodiac, or the phases of the moon and their relation to eclipses? Do they interpret these phenomena in different ways?

Such questions are important in the social sciences as well as in the sciences: in the study of anthropology and ethnology, the history of science, and in Native and Latin American studies and comparative world history. During the twentieth century, generations of scholars, from Förstemann to Morley to Spinden to Thompson expended considerable effort trying to make sense of the Maya astronomical and calendrical record. Advances in decipherment in the 1970s and 1980s have accelerated Maya scholarship to the same approximate advantage as that of the ancient Near East when at the beginning of this century Mömmsen, Langdon, Kugler, and others had finally begun to comprehend for the first time the content and process associated with omen-bearing, astronomically precise Babylonian cuneiform script.

The dramatic breakthrough in phonetic decipherment of Maya script that culminated in the mid-1970s did not result from the discovery of a Rosetta Stone in the New World. Rather, capitalizing on earlier successes in the identification of place names, deity symbols, and the titles of rulers, linguists and iconographers mounted a deliberate joint effort at reading the texts of particular carved inscriptions, especially those found at the ruins of Palenque. They succeeded in recognizing, among the 800 known hieroglyphs, a large number of pictorial or logographic equivalents of syllabic signs that are composed of consonant and vowel combinations. These glyphic types were often substituted for one another in different inscriptions. (Incidentally, for the uninitiated reader, a brief and quite readable history of this decipherment breakthrough is given by D. Stuart and S. Houston in "Maya Writing," *Sci. Am.*, August 1989, pp. 82–89.)

The 1980s saw the proliferation of a number of Maya scholarly workshops devoted to the problems of deciphering monumental inscriptions. On the other hand, those who focused attention on the books were fewer in number, and often they worked in comparative isolation. Consequently, except for a few well-known tables in the Dresden Codex (after the city where it turned up in the nineteenth century), there had been little agreement even on the most basic questions, such as: How is a given table laid out? How does it work? Is it a historical record or a predictive device—or both? Is it an almanac or an ephemeris?

Having sketched out some of the general questions and problems let us next turn to some of the major focal points of our collected works on the sky in Mayan literature.

We must constantly keep in mind that the main business of the Maya codices was to keep track of cycle upon cycle of time. On practically every page the appropriate rite, depicted pictorially, is bordered by numbers that indicate the interval that must be counted in days to pass to the next rite. The intervals are often whole multiples of periods that correspond to celestial periodicities, such as the observed cycles of Venus (584 days) and Mars (780 days). We know that at least two cycles of the moon are represented (the *sidereal*, or period relative to the stars, and the *synodic*, or the phase cycle), and we also find the year of the sun and its 364-day approximation, the so-called *computing year*, so chosen because it is readily divisible by a host of numbers that also evenly divide many other cycles. By far the most frequently utilized temporal parameter was the *tzolkin*, the "day count" of 260 or 13 × 20 days. Students of Maya culture still debate the origin of this curious time loop, which is unique to Mesoamerican calendars.

Mayan writing became thoroughly infused with principles of commensuration; that is, they were fond of discovering and rediscovering that two or more calendrical cycles could be equated to fit precisely into a larger cycle or cycles by separately multiplying each one by different small whole numbers. For example,

$$8 \times 365 = 5 \times 584 = 2920$$

relates the seasonal year to the Venus cycle, and

$$104 \times 365 = 65 \times 584 = 146 \times 260 = 37,960$$

ties both of them to the *tzolkin*.

In one very unusual case, a long-count number, which marks the time since the most recent creation, permutes a host of cycles:

$$5256 \times 260 = 3744 \times 365 = 2340 \times 584 = 1752 \times 780 = 36 \times 37960 = 1,366,560.$$

It has been labeled the *supernumber* of the Maya codices.

Such mathematical operations resemble our habit of resetting a clock to noon or midnight by making its hands point straight up when the sun crosses the meridian. The magic multipliers possess the practical value that they place the observed celestial periods on track with one another as well as with other religious cycles; for example, they can mathematically restore Mars and Venus back to the same beginning point in the sky, or they can realign eclipses with the seasons. In the last case mentioned—a super-cosmic buildup—the Mayas tried to fix a time in Maya history more than 3 millennia after creation, when Venus would repeat its first appearance as morning star, and moreover they reset the correct day name in the 260-day count to fit with that appearance. We do something similar, though far less complex, when we assign a particular Monday in February to represent the birthday anniversary of two of our favorite presidents. The Classical Maya became so carried away with finding and fitting together commensurate periods that they even concocted schemes in which they could predict the occurrences of phenomena associated with two different celestial bodies, both within the same calendrical table.

Are some of these commensuration principles the product of our own overactive imaginations? For example, Thompson believed that the number 780, which appears repeatedly in the so-called Mars Table on pp. 43b–45b of the Dresden Codex, served only as a convenient reckoning of three *tzolkin*. He argued 25 years ago that this little table had nothing to do with Mars, as the astronomers had proposed, but that instead it was a divinatory almanac. Just a few years ago, the Venus table on pp. 24, 46–50 and the Eclipse table on pp. 51–58 of Dresden would have been the only passages in all of Maya literature considered to be admitted by category of definition to the sacred scientific circle of *ephemeris*, a term that has come to mean a list that gives the positions (in time) of celestial bodies past, present, and future. Today, as the reader will learn, scholars have less difficulty equating an astronomically precise predictive table with a divinatory document; their categories of almanac and ephemeris are no longer so cleanly separable.

One very clear result that emerges from the collective research of the contributors to this volume is that many of the almanacs, regarded by Thompson and others as circular day-counting devices that possessed no point of reckoning in absolute time, do indeed contain references to specific phenomena, such as a particular eclipse or a heliacal rising of Venus, that can be anchored in real time, i.e., they are *calendars*. In fact, a major part of this text is concerned with the exploration of Maya ideas about the relation between real and canonic time, between historical events and mythic cycles.

We use a leap year to keep track of the slow slippage that happens between our own canon, the wall calendar, and natural time as reckoned by the course of the sun—now kept even more precisely by the atomic oscillator. The Maya used a different method: They kept account of the recession or advance of one calendrical period relative to another by divising clever mnemonics that are basically no different from the rule I might employ to determine the day of the week when my birthday will occur in future years: advance the day name by 1 per year, counting 2 if I pass leap day.

On the other hand, the corrections Mayan astronomers employed to update their Venus predictions were not really so different from the way Caesar in 45 B.C. and Pope Gregory XIII in 1582 reformed our own Roman calendar. To put the solar calendar on course with the sun, they called a halt to the calendar wheel, sliced a segment out of it to restore the marking of the equinox date to fit the time of year when days and nights really were equal, and then introduced a foolproof plan that would be employed thereafter to indicate far into the future when to make periodic minor adjustments to reset the canon. Caesar's scheme was clever enough to last 16 centuries before misalignment became embarrassingly obvious. Gregory's concoction, with minor alterations that came well after his time, is so effective that it exceeds the degree to which we can reckon the variable period of revolution of the Earth about the sun!

The priests who set the Maya–Venus table into real time were engaged in similar activities. They assessed single (4-day) and double (8-day) corrections to the tabulated Venus round every 104 years. The "aberrant" numbers on the introductory page of the Venus table prove it. These near-whole, large multiples of the observed Venus period were part of the grand design for making the literary script tell more precisely what Venus did in the sky. But as the perceptive reader will note, there is still disagreement about exactly in what order these aberrant numbers were employed, for how long they were effective, and even what some of them actually meant.

A final theme worth outlining, especially because it has not really been stressed before and has surfaced a number of times during our deliberations, concerns astronomical cross-referencing. In a number of cases, investigators who have studied astronomy in the codices find identical periods, even dates and pictures in different parts of a given codex, in two different codices, between codices and monuments, and even between codices and post-Conquest documents. The latter revelation is particularly exciting because it offers us keys to understanding the process of cultural transformation that pre-Columbian astronomical concepts underwent once the Spanish invaders came to the New World, bringing with them the Roman Catholic religion and Renaissance scientific and cosmological concepts.

In the post-Conquest oral and written literature, we see the syncretic byproduct of Classical Mayan astronomy, once expressed hieroglyphically in the codices, written alphabetically and today told orally by the knowledgeable shaman in highland Guatemala and the interior of Yucatan. The study of this transformation process has become an active area of study in Mayan ethnology.

Concerning my organization of the text as editor, I found that the contributions are so tightly linked by issue, theme, content, and method of argumentation that it would seem artificial to attempt to classify them in different categories or sections.

I decided to begin in the present with a paper by ethnologist Barbara Tedlock, entitled "The Road of Light." She introduces us to a living astronomy and calendrical reckoning system among contemporary Mayan people of Western Guatemala. Her many years of fieldwork among these people reveals the dramatic persistence of the kind of mathematics and astronomy as well as sacred geography that fellow investigators find in the codices; for example, the significance and uses of the basic number 20, the naming of cardinal directions as time trajectories or sides of the world along which the sun travels, rather than compass points "frozen in space," as we might regard them. The up = north, down = south equations demonstrate that the Maya were entirely capable of absorbing Western notions of how the world is arranged and assimilating them with indigenous concepts of sacred geography.

Tedlock teaches us what she learned from her informants about how the 260-day cycle still operates; she shows us that it still holds the divinatory, prognosticatory power evident from our reading of the codices. The 365-day *haab* and the year-bearer, acronic stellar risings, the day names assigned to Venus' heliacal rise, sunrise on the day the sun passes overhead—most of these phenomena and cycles were among the prominent time-marking devices of the ancient Maya, and all of them still resonate in modern calendrical shamanic practice.

So does the principle of meshing cycles. The Maya still employ a clever scheme relating space and time—a triple commensuration based upon the rotation of directional worship over the four quarters of the landscape. This principle synthesizes the seasonal cycle, a visible luni-stellar rhythmic form not yet uncovered in the codices, and the all-pervasive pulsebeat of the sacred *tzolkin*. The quarter *tzolkin* of 65 days, the third multiple of the lunar–sidereal cycle (82 days) or the time it takes the moon to return to the same constellation of the zodiac and to be visible in that constellation at the same time of the night—these two periods are rotated so that a specific set of day names will repeat at a lunar station, which is then celebrated by the opening of one of the sacred mountaintop shrines that integrates the center of Momostenango with the world quarters in the topographic periphery. This first chapter facilitates our descent into the wonderful, exotic detail that is necessary to a fuller comprehension of the Mayan way of knowing the world of nature and the sky.

The next five chapters in the volume deal directly with the problem of cross-referencing astronomical phenomena in different texts, as well as the issue of anchoring events in real time. The first by Victoria and Harvey Bricker on cross-dating almanacs begins with a clear brief overview of the basic periods that make up the Maya calendar. Intended for the uninitiated reader, it casts a comparative eye on semblances in our own Western calendar. There follows an explanation of a methodology for cross-referencing; that is, for moving in time from one almanac to another in the Dresden Codex. The principal lesson of this paper is that seasonal almanacs are not always limited to a single 260-day period of cyclic time, but that they often served as seasonal date-reaching mechanisms. In fact, some of them were destined for obsolescence after use on a one-time basis. The key to absolute time referencing is the long count that frequently appears in these almanacs.

The Brickers also uncover a clever Mayan scheme for marking the recession of the 365-day count through the actual 365.2422-day tropical year—the problem of making up for lost time that plagued all architects of the calendar. The Maya recorded the distance of the half-year mark from the summer solstice, and at different points in time they reversed the order of the pictures that refer to solstice events. Still, the purpose of the farmer's almanac was divination, particularly in the matter of planet tracking and rain prediction for irrigation. The Brickers' analysis demonstrates the role played by specific astronomical matters such as the prediction of the heliacal rise of Venus, the development of an eclipse warning system, and the marking of solstices—all related to their version of environmental sustenance.

My own contribution, which follows, deals with both the idea of commensuration and cross-referencing. In it, I point out the existence of coincidences in the Venus table in the Dresden Codex that tie together the basic periods associated with two primary celestial bodies. This arouses suspicion that a formal mechanism may have existed by which the Classic Maya kept track of lunar eclipses within the temporal reference frame of the Venus calendar. Building upon recent attempts to establish the location of the calendar round base dates of the Venus table in real time, I show that the heliacal rising of Venus following inferior conjunction, as anticipated by each of the tabulated dates in the table, always occurs after the beginning but before the termination of the next lunar cycle following a lunar eclipse that was visible in Yucatan.

I interpret this to mean that the Mayan astronomers were forcing Venus to march to the celestial beat of a lunar drummer, as opposed to the more familiar sun time that dominates our own calendar. But anyone who pays attention to the calendar of, say, Islam, which still operates on a lunar base, will not find such a timekeeping format so unusual.

The "lady with the question mark on her forehead" is the subject of the paper by Hofling & O'Neil. She fills the pictorial space of pp. 16–23 of the Dresden Codex. Always seated, she is sometimes positioned opposite gods, children, or animals, and often she carries a pack on her back. The main element in her glyph name is the moon, and the red and black numbers strung out above her carry us from given points in time (the red number coefficients of day names in the *tzolkin*) through intervals (the black distance numbers) to other points. For these reasons this portion of the Dresden book has come to be known as the *Moon Goddess Almanacs* (MGA).

This lady's function seems to have been to categorize omens about disease, seizures, skin eruptions that grow with the moon, etc., according to the day names of the 260-day cycle, but, in Hofling and O'Neil's paper, we learn that the moon's appearance was more than a descriptive metaphor for casting omens. They discover a hint of a temporal lunar element that links these pages directly to the Dresden Eclipse Table (ET) on pp. 51–58. Their method consists in mapping date sequences from the ET into the MGA. They begin with the written base dates of the ET and examine the sequences of 260-day names each of these generates; thus they find similar sequences in the MGA next to pictures that bear a counterpart in the ET. The long-count portions of the ET base dates can be used to arrive at series of actual lunar eclipses that may match up with the pictures. So, the MGA, like many other sections of the Dresden, begins to emerge as an astronomically predictive device. Two complications: First, we cannot be sure there was only one reading sequence for the tables; and, second, it is difficult to dismiss completely the possibility, as in my paper, that some of the matchups between tabulated dates and real eclipses are accidental;

nevertheless, the authors present a convincing case that there is more moontime in these tables than we had previously thought.

In another real-time study relating the Venus and Eclipse tables in the Dresden Codex, entitled "Some Parallels in the Astronomical Events Recorded in the Maya Codices and Inscriptions," Michael Closs argues that these documents do not *record* observed phenomena but instead *predict* them. He traces the occurrence of the *Ah Tsul Ahau* glyph, which he identifies as a Venus title, in both the codices and on the monuments. Specifically, Closs argues that the observational significance of this glyph is that it refers to the greatest elongation of the planet, the time in its visible cycle when it reaches its greatest angular distance from the sun in the sky. At this time it drags to a halt, reverses direction, and then plunges Earthward. In so many instances in Mayan astronomy, the *time of change* in the course of a celestial body seems to deliver the omen or message, whether the hinge in the mechanism of time be characterized by a sudden appearance or disappearance, a stoppage, or a turnaround of a celestial body.

A second contribution by the Brickers on "Zodiacal References in the Maya Codices" also offers concepts that might seem unorthodox in Western calendrics. Their meticulous detective work brings together detailed observations of a frieze on a Late Classic Period building at the ruins of Chichén Itzá with two partly effaced pages of the Paris Codex. They conclude that the Maya had indeed devised a zodiac—one like our own composed mostly of animals as signs on the celestial highway traversed by the sun, moon, and planets.

There are at least two novel developments here. First, the articulation of a scheme hidden away in an unusual set of green bar-and-dot numerals written in the table. Apparently, the astronomers used these numbers to fit the sidereal lunar calendar—the same one employed by the modern Quiché Maya of Guatemala—to the 364-day approximation of the seasonal year. Second, the Brickers offer a definite set of identifications of the constellations of the Maya zodiac, which are represented as beasts dangling from the sky band in the Codex and some of which appear carved in stone at Chichén Itzá. Unexpectedly, these star patterns are not named in the order in which the planets march across them as they traverse the ecliptic, the way the Western zodiac since Egyptian times is delineated. Instead, they are presented in an arrangement in the codex that indicates which constellation opposes another, that is, which one has just cleared the Eastern horizon as its counterpart stands above the Western horizon just after sunset.

Harvey and Victoria Bricker's chapter is sure to rekindle an old skirmish on the battleground of cultural diffusion versus independent invention. Why do so many cultures invent a zodiac, and why do they fashion it out of the constellations that straddle the ecliptic, employing 12 or 13 figural representations, usually animals? In this case, our ram is their ocelot, our lion their frog, our sea-goat one of their celestial aviary; the scorpions are exactly the same. These issues are too complex to debate here, except to say that it is quite logical for agrarian people to label the solar stations on the eliptic that correspond to the seasons and to relate them to perceptible changes in the biological cycles of animal species, of both of which they are keenly aware and which they may have purposefully connected to subsistence patterns.

One problem on which Maya researchers have made considerable headway is the correlation question: how to slide fit the Mayan long count dates so that they match the Christian chronology? Two techniques have been employed. One relies on what is written in the historical record shortly after the time of the Conquest when, in a few rare instances, Spanish chroniclers specifically stated that a certain Mayan date was the same as a given Christian one. Critics of the historical approach, however, argue that the chroniclers were not especially knowledgeable about the indigenous calendar and that they often either made mistakes or were misled. Besides, by the sixteenth century, the long count already had been out of fashion for centuries, and one could scarcely rely on an equation, the Maya side of which was a calendar round date that repeats every 52 years. It would be like offering only the information that I was born on Saturday the fifth and then asking one to find the year. There are many possible answers.

The astronomical method of solving the correlation problem proposes that one look at back-calculated significant events from modern celestial ephemerides and seek matching dates that appear juxtaposed with astronomical symbols in the corpus of Maya inscriptions. The problem here is to define which events are significant and which glyphs were deliberately intended to portray the sky events. Looking for repeatable events and inscriptions helps. Twenty years ago Mayan and Old World history were misaligned by up to 3 centuries, depending on which correlation and which method one adopted. Today an interdisciplinary merging of the historical and astronomical techniques has reduced this difference, in the eyes of most contemporary Maya scholars, to just a few days.

In Lounsbury's chapter on the Mayan–to–Julian calendar correlation, astronomy and history confront one another directly. His is a textbook lesson, written in the form of a detective story, that demonstrates how it is possible to use these two kinds of data in concert to arrive at possible answers to the correlation question. Lounsbury carefully follows the consequences of making different assumptions about the data in both the codices and the ethnohistoric record, unveiling as he goes some deep insights into the ways Maya astronomers likely manipulated and processed their data. His astronomical arguments demonstrate why even the difference between adding 584283 or 584285 days to a Mayan long count date to transpose it into our chronology is significant, for often a day or 2 shift can be used to argue that the Maya either did or did not pay attention to a particular sky phenomenon. The close reader of this text will note that the disagreement about the correlation constant among contributors persists.

In his second chapter, Lounsbury further explores the drift of real events from the canon. His principal text remains the Venus table, which, given the attention it has received in this volume, will continue to be a "hot spot" in the codices for some time to come. Lounsbury focuses on a single aberrant multiple, which reads 9100 in Arabic, 1.5.5.0 in Mayan notation. It surfaces as a mystery number in the multiplication of Venus cycles on the introductory page to the Dresden Venus table. The problem with this number is that neither is it a whole multiple of 584 days nor, like the other aberrant multiples, does it lie within a few days of being a whole multiple. How, then, could it have been part of the 4- and 8-day minor adjustment schemes used to reset the table to the real Venus? Is it a misprint—a scribal error, as Thompson suggested 30 years ago?

Lounsbury argues that it is not. He demonstrates that it could have been used instead as part of a novel mathematical operation associated with foreshortening the table to keep it in step with the actual planet in the sky. The number can be tied to the peculiar canonic station intervals of Venus written in the table—the same ones I refer to in my paper tying Venus and the lunar calendars together—to locate the starting point of the morning heliacal rise date within a synodic lunar cycle. Here is further evidence that in the Mayan version of the music of the spheres, Venus and the moon marched together.

The Books of Chilam Balam—"the sacred books of the jaguar prophet"—are nearly a dozen in number. They were all produced in the Maya language, basically European in style and script; but, as Merideth Paxton shows in her chapter on the transformation of astronomical and temporal concepts during Conquest times, these books provide a direct link to the subject matter in the codices. She has worked with the problem of connecting portions of these texts with two different sections of the Paris Codex, including the zodiacal table discussed by the Brickers. She offers a different interpretation: These zodiacs, she argues, were used exclusively to predict solar stations. She also finds in the post-Conquest texts, in addition to the eclipse half-year, some of the same calendrical cycles that Barbara Tedlock (in her opening chapter) found still to be in use today: tropical year, 360-day *tun, or year,* and *tzolkin.*

The temporal syncretism in the post-Conquest era is manifested in the conversion of *katun* (basically a score of years) prophecies into century-cycle prophecies. Though the interval may be different, it is still the turning of the temporal odometer that precipitates the need to seek omens on a grander scale, a habit that persists in Western millennialism, as some of our own twenty-first-century prophets signal the imminent termination of history and nature.

We began *The Sky in Mayan Literature* in the present, and we end it at the dawn of Maya mythic history. The closing chapter by Dennis Tedlock takes us all the way back to creation. Like Paxton, Tedlock's arguments rely heavily on the post-Conquest literature, specifically the *Popol Vuh,* or Sacred Book of Creation of the Quiché Maya. Here the Maya mythological chronology, notably the events of the birth of the triad of creator deities of the Palenque dynasty, are linked with astronomical reality through both the codices and the stucco inscriptions in the Group of the Cross at Palenque. In fact, Tedlock finds chronological compatibility via recurrent events that take place in the sky among all three diverse sets of texts.

How do we explain the fact that some of the same astronomical intervals in the Dresden Venus table turn up in the Palenque inscriptions? Tedlock gives a different interpretation from Lounsbury of a basic question on the use of astronomical tables and almanacs. Did the Venus table in the Dresden Codex provide a historical, celestially visible, commemoration of an event the Maya chronologists in seventh-century Palenque knew had happened before their time? Specifically, this was a joint heliacal rise of Venus and Mars, an event that had already acquired its mythic proportions by serving as one of the manifestations of the birth of the gods. He argues that it did.

The overview chapter is by Charles Frake, an anthropologist we chose specifically because he is not a Mayan specialist. However, he has worked extensively on problems related to timekeeping, calendars, navigation, and sacred geography, both in the Western Medieval and non-Western (Phillipine) sphere. We asked him to read the manuscripts and cast them into a more general anthropological and world-historical framework. He had also attended the workshop and participated in the discussions.

The principal reason for including such a contribution is related to my own effort to write a basic introduction to the collected set of research reports. It stems from the need to respond to a well-justified criticism made by the peripheral community concerning Mayan epigraphers, particularly those on the quantitative and calendrical end of the spectrum of the study of Maya writing: that we operate in our own closed circle and only few readers either can follow the logic of our complex discourses or judge the results. As a result, the nonspecialists are inclined either to accept blindly everything we say because they assume we all know our subject or to reject the lot on the grounds that if a modern professional in an allied field cannot comprehend with some effort what we "experts" have to say about the Mayan calendar, then surely the Maya themselves could not have understood it either.

We hope that our attempts at both ends of the text to ease the deeper descent of our readers into its intricate subject matter prove successful, for at that level one can become even more fascinated with the Maya than the aficionado and persistent visitor to the ruins. When we penetrate the cosmological meaning of the codices, we learn that here were people quite like ourselves who believed in a universe that could be conceived and described in mathematical terms—and that they could invent certain formal mechanisms capable of generating predictions of future celestial events that could be observed, contemplated, and their results used to improve and adjust their instrument to make future predictions even more precise.

Though the ends served by such predictions were founded upon religious and astrological beliefs, certain elements of the whole process begin to sound very much like what we read in the history of science in Western culture. But then, if we are willing to look back a few centuries, we discover that our own inquiry into nature possessed a similar foundation.

# I

# The Road of Light:
# Theory and Practice of
# Mayan Skywatching

## BARBARA TEDLOCK

*Chayataj qetal, qatziljel,*
*chi b'e q'ij, chi b'e saq.*

Give us our sign, our word,
on the road of the sun, on the road of light.
From a *Popol Vuh* prayer

Mayan cosmology, calendrics, and astronomy have long been flourishing areas of discussion and debate among archaeologists, linguists, epigraphers, astronomers, and ethnographers. Recent linguistic and ethnographic research has revealed an important body of cosmological, directional, calendrical, and astronomical knowledge among Mayan-speaking peoples still living in the region stretching from the Yucatán Peninsula of Mexico into Belize, through Chiapas and Guatemala, to the western regions of El Salvador and Honduras. Mayan languages as spoken today have been helpful in our understanding and conceptualization of the ancient Mayan directional system. Ongoing ritual practices have revealed a sidereal lunar cycle, together with methods of calendrical and astronomical commensuration indicating that ancient Mayans may have used celestial as well as terrestrial coordinates in their astronomy. These discoveries should prove useful in the future analysis, decipherment, and interpretation of Mayan texts.

## Cosmology

The Mayan universe in pre-Classic, Classic, post-Classic, and Colonial times was multileveled, consisting of a many-tiered upper world, a middle world, and a many-tiered underworld. The sun, moon, stars, planets, and (since the Conquest) Christian deities and saints reside in the upper worlds. Humankind, *winaq*[1] or else *winik* (also meaning "twenty") in Mayan languages, reside in the middle world. The underworld, *xib'alb'a* or "place of fear" in Quiché as well as in several other Mayan languages, is an evil location that is entered by human beings at death through a cave or the standing waters of a lake or ocean.[2] At Palenque these three worlds are represented on the sarcophagus cover of the late-Classic tomb of Pacal, located inside the Temple of the Inscriptions. They are reiterated in the stucco sculpture present at the site through the use of color coding: red indicating the world of living human beings; blue for the heavens above the Earth, together with precious things such as jade and feathers, the throne symbols, and emblems of accession of divine kings; yellow for the underworld gods and jaguars; and cross-hatched areas signifying death (Robertson 1983:52–53).

The sun is the ruler of the cosmos for ancient as well as contemporary Mayan peoples, and his two annual passages across the zenith were, and still are, used to fix dates in the agricultural calendar.[3] Today, as in the past, the eastern and western directions are established through the observation of the intersection of the daily path of the sun with the horizon, and time is marked by the sun's progress along the horizon. Further, since the movement of the sun defines both space and time in all Mayan languages, the spatial categories east and west are not distinguished from the temporal categories sunrise and sunset.

Clemency Coggins (1980) has suggested that Classic Mayan directional symbolism referred to the daily path of the sun across the sky and through the underworld (east, zenith, west, nadir) rather than to the cardinal directions (north, south, east, west). At the root of this suggestion are the twin-pyramid groups of Tikal, depicting the Maya cosmos. Each of these clusters of buildings consists of two pyramids, one in the east and one in the west; a stela enclosure to the north; and a nine-doored structure to the south. The group as a whole represents a horizontal cosmogram of the daily path of the sun in which the sun rises at the eastern pyramid, passes the zenith at the royal portrait stela in the northern enclosure, sets at the western pyramid, and passes the nadir at the nine-doored southern building.

Epigraphic support for this interpretation was given by Victoria Bricker (1983), who argued that the four directional glyphs in Classic inscriptions

*Figure 1.1* Glyph blocks on the east wall of Tomb 12.

and post-Classic codices can be read phonetically in Yucatec Maya as *lak kin*, *chik kin*, *yax*, and *mal*, which translate into English as "east, west, zenith, and nadir." Further evidence for this reading was given by a later discovery of wall paintings in a tomb at Río Azul, in which each of the four walls has a directional glyph (Adams and Mobley 1986). Directly above each of them is a glyph that has been called by epigraphers the "ben-ich superfix" and another glyph indicating day, night, moon, or Venus. The hieroglyph indicating day or sun (*kin*) is infixed in the ben-ich superfix above the directional glyph on the eastern wall (Figure 1.1), while the hieroglyph indicating night or darkness (*akbal*) is infixed in the ben-ich superfix on the western wall (Figure 1.2).

On the remaining walls, the hieroglyph indicating the moon is infixed in the ben-ich superfix above the directional glyph at the north (Figure 1.3), while the hieroglyph indicating Venus is infixed in the ben-ich super-fix above the directional glyph at the south (Figure 1.4). According to Bricker (1988), these two glyphs could represent the moon and Venus in opposition, above and below the horizon, during the night when the occupant of the tomb, Ruler 6 Sky, was buried. The fact that the tomb contains an inscription giving the date of burial as 8 Ben 16 Kayab on the calendar round, combined with the style of the painting, suggests three possible historical dates for this event. On only one of these, 6 March A.D. 502,[4]

*Figure 1.2* Glyph blocks on the west wall of Tomb 12.

*Figure 1.3* Glyph blocks on the north wall of Tomb 12.

was the moon less than 5° from true zenith and Venus within 4° of true nadir. During this particular night Venus and the moon were never visible simultaneously. Moreover, at no time was the moon in the northern part of the sky, and Venus, of course, could not have been in the south. Thus, the directional glyphs associated with the moon and Venus cannot be read as referring simply to north and south, but must involve zenith and nadir. Further, on glyphic grounds, the inscription on the northern wall (Figure 1.3) supports the Cholan reading *na-chan*, meaning "first heaven" or "zenith."

Recent evidence from other Classic Mayan inscriptions that indicate a zenithal interpretation rather than a northern interpretation of certain glyphs can be seen in texts located on northern panels in the eastern and western doors of Temple 11, situated on the northern edge of the acropolis at Copán, Honduras. In this unusual temple, consisting of two exceptionally wide noncorbelled vaults running east–west and north–south, crossing in the center, the glyphic inscription divides into two discourse sequences that begin at the north door in the front of the building (Schele, Stuart, and Grube 1989). While the subject matter located in the north–south corridor concerns the accession of the ruler and the dedication of a reviewing stand, in the east–west corridor the north panel on the east door contains the phrase *xay tu pa chan*, "crossroads of the sky," referring to the

*Figure 1.4* Glyph blocks on the south wall of Tomb 12.

dedication of the cross-corridors of Temple 11 itself (Stuart, Schele, and Grube 1989:11). In this same east–west corridor, the north panel of the west door indicates a location called *ch'ul chan*, "holy heaven" (Schele and Grube 1990:13). Both of these texts, which are located on northern panels, clearly refer to the zenith as the direction of the events in question rather than to the north.

Ethnographers and linguists have been finding that *none* of the contemporary highland or lowland Mayan directions is equivalent to our Western notion of horizontally fixed cardinal points (B. Tedlock 1983a, Watanabe 1983, Vogt 1985, Sosa 1989). Thus, for example, in Kekchí, a highland Mayan Quichean language, the terms for the directions come from intransitive verbs indicating motion. East is *releb'aal saq'e*, "sun's coming-out place," and west is *rokeb'aal saq'e*, "sun's entering place," while north is *releb'aal iq'*, "wind's coming-out place," and south is *rokeb'aal iq'*, "wind's entering place" (Haeserijn 1979:461, 467, 459, 481). In Tzeltal the important directions of orientation are east, or the "coming out of the sun," and west, or "the sleeping place of the sun" (Nash 1970:293). North and south are topographically referred to respectively as "highland" and "lowland," and north can also be called *kini ha'al*, which designates a violent wind, specifically a rain-bearing wind. In recent interviews with Cakchiquel speakers, I learned that east and west indicate the daily rising and setting motion of the sun, while north is *kaq iq'*, "violent wind," and south is *xokomil*, literally "left-handed," which is the name for the treacherous south wind that comes up suddenly each summer afternoon across Lake Atitlán, threatening boats.

The pattern is the same in the lowland Mayan languages. Today in Chol, the terms for east are *pasel k'in*, or *ba mi lok'el k'in* "sun's coming-out place," or "place where the sun is taken out," and the terms for west are *majlib k'in* or *ba mi yoche majle k'in*, "sun's going-in place," or "where the sun enters" (Aulie and Aulie 1978:92, 171; Josserand and Hopkins 1988:2). The term for north is *chak ik'lel*, "red wind," which indicates the greatest or most violent winds bringing bad weather (Aulie and Aulie 1978:51).[5] In modern Yucatec *lak'in*, "next sun," the place where the sun rises in the east, and *chik'in*, "eaten sun," the place where it sets in the west, are both considered to be located along a line between two corners of a flat, four-cornered Earth (Sosa 1985:417). Likewise, even though Colonial Spanish dictionary compilers translated the Yucatec directional terms *xaman* and *nohol* as equivalent to the European cardinal points north and south (Martínez 1930:680, 916; Barrera 1980:934), and some epigraphers and archaeologists continue to describe Mayan directions in terms of our Western compass-point tradition (Schele and Freidel 1990:66), a closer look at Colonial dictionary entries reveals that these terms, just as in the highland Mayan languages, also refer to winds. In the Motul dictionary the south wind is *nohol ik* and the north wind is *xaman ik* (Martínez 1930: 680, 916). Furthermore, recent ethnographic field work among speakers of Yucatec Maya indicate that the entire northern side of the world is referred to as *xaman* while the southern side is *nohol*; also, north is on the right-hand side of the sun god, *Hahal Dios*, while south is on his left-hand side (Sosa 1989:134).[6]

In Tzotzil, a Mayan language spoken today in highland Chiapas, the eastern and western directions do not refer to fixed cardinal points but rather to the daily motion of the sun. Thus, east is *lok'eb k'ak'al*, "rising," "appearing," or "emerging sun," and west is *maleb k'ak'al*, "setting," "disappearing," or "waning sun" (Laughlin 1975:432, 533; Vogt 1976:16). North and south are both *xokon vinahel*, "side" or "flank of the sky," which are differentiated according to whether they are on the right or left hand of the path of the sun (Laughlin 1975:474, 508; Vogt 1976:16). North can also be referred to as *xokon vinahel ta batzi k'ob*, "the edge of heaven on the right hand," with south as *xokon vinahel ta tz'et k'ob*, "the edge of heaven on the left hand" (Gossen 1974:31; 1979:119). In Mam, a highland Mayan language spoken in Guatemala, all of the directional terms are derived from intransitive verbs of motion, with east as *okni*, "to enter," or "move toward the east," and west as *elni*, "to go out," "pass in front of," or "move towards the west." The term for north is *jawni*, derived from a verb meaning "to go up," and south is *kubni*, "to go down"; both together may be referred to as *iky'ni*, "along" (Watanabe 1983:712). Since *jaa'wal*, from the intransitive verb *jaaw* "go up," refers to the termination point of the sun's ascent (England 1983:341), it might best be translated as "sun's meridian" rather than "north."

Among speakers of the highland Mayan languages Achí and Quiché, several sets of terms have been reported that can be used to translate the Spanish *norte* and *sur*; depending on the specific sociolinguistic context, they can be paired with other terms designating east and west. For example, when a Cubulco speaker of Achí is asked to name the directions—north, south, east, west—he or she calls north *ajsik*, "above" (the town center), and south *ikem*, "below" (the town center); however, if the speaker is referring to a distant place then north is *wiqab'im*, "on the right," and south is *moxim*, "on the left." East is *pa kel qa qajaw*, "where our father [the sun] comes from," and west is *pa ka qah wi qa qajaw*, "where our father descends" (Neuenswander 1981:28–29). When a speaker of Quiché is asked to name the directions, he or she may reply that east is *relëb'al q'ij*, "sun's rising place," and west is *uqajib'al q'ij*, "sun's falling place," while north is *uwiki aq'äb' relëb'al q'ij*, "right hand of the rising sun," and south is *umöx aq'äb' relëb'al q'ij*, "left hand of the rising sun." In formal discourse, however, while the east–west terms remain the same, the other pair varies: for example, *xkut ri kaj, xkut ri juyub'*, "corner of sky, corner of earth" (Schultze Jena 1954:104) and *kaj xukut kaj, kaj xukut ulew*, "four corners of sky, four corners of earth" (B. Tedlock 1983a:5). In horizontal terms, Quiché speakers think of these words as referring to the north and south, respectively, but at the same time they fit the above–below or zenith–nadir pattern found in other Mayan languages and suggest, as well, that both the sky and the Earth have four sides. Another set of contemporary Quiché terms *unik'ajal kaj, unik'ajal ulew*, "middle of sky, middle of earth," occurs together with the usual terms for east and west in the *Título C'oyoi*, an important sixteenth-century Quiché document (Carmack 1973:276, 317). Thus the pairing of terms indicating a vertical axis, with others indicating an east–west horizontal axis has considerable historical depth in Quiché.

The sun is described today, by both lowland and highland Mayan speakers, as a human or godlike figure with a brilliant round face who rises each day on the eastern horizon and faces his universe with north on his right hand and south on his left hand (Gossen 1974:31; 1979:119; B. Tedlock 1983a:5; Sosa 1989:134). After he reaches his meridian at noon, he pauses briefly, then continues across the sky, entering the Earth in the west, reaching a point opposite his meridian at midnight, remaining in the underworld until he begins his eastern rise once again. While the terms for east and west in all Mayan languages indicate a line or vector along which the sun rises and sets, depending on the season of the year, the other two directional terms indicate variously the right and left hand of the sun god, the direction of prevailing or rain-bringing winds, highland and lowland, above and below, and/or zenith and nadir. Thus, Mayan directions are *not* discrete cardinal or intercardinal compass points frozen in space but rather are sides, lines, vectors, or trajectories that are inseparable from the passage of time.

## Calendrics

The sun or day has always been the fundamental unit of timekeeping for Mayan peoples, and the road of the sun, *chi b'e q'ij, chi b'e saq* in Quiché, specifically expresses the concept of time. Calendrical and computational numerology is based on the perceived geometry and periodicites of space, the human body, and various astronomical cycles. After the Spanish Conquest, much of the original calendar system was maintained in oral tradition, in some cases with the aid of written calendar wheels and calendar boards (Berendt 1877; Bowditch 1910:326–31; Gossen 1974). Today, parts of this system exist in many communities in the Mexican states of Veracruz, Oaxaca, and Chiapas, as well as throughout the Guatemalan highlands. Suzanna Miles (1952) reported on 87 communities in these areas that were known to retain native calendars. Important cycles in several contemporary highland Guatemalan communities include a 260-day calendar, a lunar agricultural almanac, and a 365-day solar year (B. Tedlock 1983b; 1985).

The 260-day calendar has been described as closely linked either to celestial cycles, such as the interval between zenithal transits of the sun near the latitude 15° north, or else to earthly affairs, such as agricultural or midwifery practices (B. Tedlock 1985:83–87). This calendar, called the *calendar round* by students of the Classic Maya inscriptions and post-Classic codices, is a succession of day designations created by the combination of a number from 1 to 13 with one of the 20 possible names. Since 13 and 20 have no common factor, this process creates 260 unique combinations. The lunar almanac, which is much less well understood by scholars than the calendar round, is based on synodic reckoning. The 365-day solar year, consisting of 18 months of 20 days each with 5 "extra" days at the end of the year, is used in timing important political events and religious rituals in a number of contemporary Mayan communities (Lincoln 1942; B. Tedlock 1982b; Bricker 1989).

In order to illustrate current calendrical and astronomical theory and practice, I will center my discussion on the situation among the Mayans I know the best, those living in the Quiché-speaking municipality of Momostenango.[7] This community, currently consisting of approximately 72,000 persons (of whom 98% are indigenous), is located in the department of Totonicapán, Guatemala, at 15° 04′ 38″ latitude north of the equator and 91° 24′ 30″ longitude. The district is best known to travelers for its fine woolen blankets and to archaeologists and ethnographers for its celebration of the day 8 *B'atz'*, the largest ongoing Mesoamerican religious ritual scheduled according to the 260-day calendar round.

This sacred almanac, which is called both *rajilab'al q'ij*, "counting of days," and *chol q'ij*, "ordering of days," consists of a succession of day designations created by the combination of a number from 1 to 13 with the following names: No'j, Tijax, Kawuq, Junajpu, Imöx, Iq', Aq'ab'al, K'at, Kan, Kame, Kej, Q'anil, Toj, Tz'i', B'atz', E, Aj, Ix, Tz'ikin, Ajmak. Each of these day names is accompanied by a mnemonic term, phrase, or set of phrases indicating its nature, and most of these mnemonics are built on words that are phonologically or morphologically related to the name (B.

Tedlock 1982a).[8] The numbers from 1 to 13 modify the nature of the day; thus, low numbers—1, 2, and 3—are considered "gentle," high numbers—11, 12, and 13—are "violent," and middle numbers—7, 8, and 9— are "indifferent," neither gentle nor violent.

Though this is less well known to outsiders, Momostenango also reckons time by the Mayan 365-day solar calendar, called *masewal q'ij*, "common days." Each solar year begins with one of four possible year bearers— Kej, E, No'j, and Iq'—which are equivalent to the Classic and early post-Classic Yucatec year bearers Manik, Eb, Caban, and Ik. At the end of each solar year the 5 days between the last occurrence of the old *Mam*, "grandfather," or year bearer, and the entrance of the new Mam are a dangerous time when many people curtail business activity. Beginning at noon on the New Year's eve of this calendar, some people visit a local hilltop shrine and tie a red thread around their own, as well as their children's, left wrists and right ankles. The new Mam is received at midnight, *nik'aj aq'äb'*, literally "the middle of the night," on a series of local hilltops by the traditional religious and political leaders of the community, who carefully note which stars and constellations are directly overhead. Upon signal these leaders welcome the new Mam with prayers, special food, incense, bonfires, fireworks, drum-and-flute music, chanting, marimbas, and dancing. On 27 February 1990, *Mam 4 Kej* was welcomed on a series of local hilltops including Kilaja, located east of the town center.

Individuals in Momostenango who reckon time by combining observations of the sun, moon, and stars with pre-Hispanic Mayan calendars are known as *ajq'ij*, "daykeepers," and their astronomical observations are called *kajib'al ch'umil*, "descent of the stars." Daykeepers make pragmatic use of their observations and calendar keeping in many areas of their social lives, including midwifery, curing, dream interpretation, divination, and agriculture. This knowledge is considered valuable and is therefore open to individuals only through formal training.[9]

During the recent period of civil war in Guatemala (roughly 1979–83), the departments of Totonicapán (in which Momostenango is located) and Quezaltenango (in which Momostecans engage in weekly trade) were miraculously untouched by violence. However, there were serious economic consequences arising from the disruption of long-distance travel by Quiché merchants and a decline in their access to foreign markets. When conditions improved in 1983, a strong nativistic revival began among Mayan peoples. Not only did the number of individuals making the pilgrimage to Momostenango in order to celebrate 8 B'atz' increase, but Momostecan religious leaders began in 1984 to publish a mimeographed calendar book for dissemination within the community and the nation. Rigoberto Itzep

Chanchavac is the official compiler of this impressively accurate calendar, which correlates the Gregorian calendar with the 260-day Mayan calendar, titled *Rajil b'al q'ij maya*, "Mayan day count." This calendar has been so popular that it has been republished in other communities. During the summer of 1989, in the Quiché community of San Andrés Xecul, Dennis Tedlock and I were shown a version compiled locally by Juan Chuc Paxtor, who titled it *Wuj ub'eal ra qan q'ij-mayab'*, "The book of the road of the count of Mayan days." In the fall of 1990 a new, all-Mayan research organization in Quezaltenango, Centro de Investigación Social Maya, published a Quiché appointment calendar called *Cholb'äl chak: Calendario maya*, or "Instrument for ordering one's work: Mayan calendar," which is accurately correlated with the Gregorian calendar. This resurgence of interest in the ancient calendar among educated Mayans indicates an even more favorable climate for ethnoastronomical research in highland Guatemala than before.

### Celestial Lights

In Momostenango, all of the celestial bodies—sun, moon, planets, comets, meteors, stars, asterisms, constellations, and the Milky Way—constitute a single category known as *ch'umilal kaj*, "starry sky." The diurnal, monthly, and seasonal paths and positions of the sun, moon, stars, and asterisms along the horizon and across the night sky are observed and discussed by naked-eye astronomers. The daily path of the sun, known as *ub'e saq, ub'e q'ij*, "road of light, road of day," is described in Quiché as *oxib' utzuk', oxib' uxukut chupam saqil*, "three sides, three corners in the light." It is visualized as a triangle whose angles are the three transition points in diurnal time. This solar triangle stretches from the sun's rising position to its noon position to its setting position. By analogy, heavenly bodies that rise, cross the night sky, and set in opposition to the sun, in reasonable proximity to its path, are said to form *oxib' utzuk', oxib' uxukut chupam q'equm*, "three sides, three corners in the dark."

Stars are used to tell the time of night and to herald the time of year for ritual and agricultural purposes. Both the winter and summer solstice sunrise and sunset positions are called *xolkat b'e*, "change of path or road." This term, unlike our own Latin-derived term, solstice or "sun stand," stresses the back-and-forth movement of the sun. The most important change of road is the winter solstice, *raqan q'ij* or "sun's height," which annually marks the end of the high-altitude corn harvest in December (B. Tedlock 1985). At the latitude of Momostenango ($15°$ $04'$ $38''$ north of the equator), the zenith passages of the sun occur on 1 or 2 May during the sun's northward movement, and on 11 or 12 August during its southward return. The sunrise and sunset positions on both zenith passages are referred to as *jalb'al*, "place of change," indicating the location of a change in the nature of the sun's path, rather than a change of paths.

The planets, as a group, are known in Quiché as *kaq ch'umil*, "red stars." In Colonial Yucatec Maya the seven planets of medieval astronomy were also referred to as *chachac ek*, "red stars" (Roys 1967:150). Observationally, since moisture in the air causes all heavenly bodies located near the horizon to appear reddish, Mayan designation of planets in general as "red stars" may specifically refer to these planets only when they are situated near the horizon. When Venus, or any other planet that takes the role of evening star, appears in the western sky well after sunset it is called *rasq'äb*, "of the night" in Quiché. Venus in its morning-star aspect is called *Junajpu*, a day name that is also the personal name of a mythic hero in the ancient Quiché text known as the *Popol Vuh* (see D. Tedlock 1985). When Venus or any other planet appears as a bright star in the east before dawn it is referred to as *ëqo q'ij*, "sun carrier" or "sun bringer," and its path is known as *ub'eal ëqo q'ij*, "sun bringer's road." In Fray Thomás de Coto's Colonial Cakchiquel dictionary, written between 1643 and 1646, the term (rendered in modern orthography) for Venus as morning star is *iqo q'ij*, "day bringer," while Venus as evening star is *tz'etol xq'eqab'al*, "herald of darkness" (Coto 1647:223).

Comets are referred to in Quiché as *uje ch'umil*, "tail of the star," and are considered omens of massive pestilence. A shooting star or meteor is called *ch'ab'i q'aq'*, "flaming arrow." The term *ch'ab'i* refers to the tip or point of an arrow, dart, dagger, or spear, while *q'aq'* means "fire." Meteorites are thought of as the remains of falling stars, and, since it is believed that obsidian occurs wherever a meteor has landed, arrowheads, obsidian blades, and meteorites are saved and placed together in the traditional household shrine known as the *meb'il* (see B. Tedlock 1982b:40–41, 81–82). In a number of highland and lowland Mayan communities, meteors or comets are described as the cigar butts of their gods (Tozzer 1907:158; Girard 1966:74; B. Tedlock 1983a:12; D. Tedlock 1985:112), and it may well be that the cigars smoked by the hero twins of the *Popol Vuh* (D. Tedlock 1985:112) are to be understood as meteors. Throughout the Mayan area, meteors are thought to be evil omens forecasting sickness, war, and death (La Farge and Byers 1931:129; Laughlin 1975:284; Vogt 1976:217; Lamb 1981:237; Koizumi 1981:141; B. Tedlock 1983a:6; Alcorn 1984:143). A Colonial Quiché term for meteor was *ch'olanic ch'umil*, "star that makes war" (Tirado 1787:208). The cognitive connection between war, obsidian, death, and sickness is due to the past use of obsidian-tipped spears and lances in warfare and human sacrifice, together with the past and present use of obsidian blades in bleeding procedures and in surgery (Crabtree 1968; Robicsek and Hales 1984; Orellana 1987:72–75).

Some Quiché asterisms are similar to Western ones; for example, *xik*, "hawk," is recognizable as Aquila, the Eagle (B. Tedlock 1985:83). Others are not at all the same. Two or more stars or asterisms may share a single name, while single stars or asterisms may have more than one name. Individual named stars include Regulus or *jun ch'umil*, "one star," and Spica or *pix*, "spark," while Acrux (in the southern cross) and Polaris (in the Little Dipper) together are called *xukut ch'umil*, "corner stars." There are two constellations known as *ripib'al elaq'omab'*, "the thieves' cross," one of them the Southern Cross and the other a seven-star asterism in Sagittarius consisting of Sigma, Phi, Delta, Gamma, Lambda, Epsilon, and Eta (Remington 1977:85–87; B. Tedlock 1985:84). Similarly, both the Pleiades and Hyades are called *mötz*, "handful," and the Big and Little Dipper are called *paq'ab'*, "ladles" or "spoons." The Milky Way, on the other hand, has two separate designations depending on which end of it is intended. The undivided segment is *saqi b'e*, "white road," while the part with the dark cleft or Great rift is *xib'alb'a b'e*, "underworld road." The twin bright stars Castor and Pollux, in Gemini, have two designations: *kib' chuplinik*, "two shiny ones," and *kib' pix*, "two sparks." Within the constellation of Orion,[10] known as *je chi q'aq'*, "dispersed fire," there are two asterisms with a one-star overlap: Orion's Belt or *je oxib' chi q'aq' ajaw*, "tail of the three fire lords," and Alnitak, Saiph, and Rigel, called *oxib' nima ch'umil*, "three big stars." This latter asterism is also referred to as *oxib' xk'ub'*, "three hearth stones." The Great Nebula M42, located between these three stars and visible to the naked eye, is described as smoke from the celestial cooking fire.[11]

The progress of the solar year is marked by noting acronychal and cosmical risings and settings of certain key stars. Acronychal risings or settings occur at nightfall, while cosmical risings and settings occur at dawn (OED 1979:121). An acronychal star rise takes place on the eastern horizon at the moment of sunset on the western horizon, while a cosmical star set takes place on the western horizon at the moment of sunrise on the eastern horizon. In Momostenango, during the dry half of the year between harvest and planting (November through April), acronychal and cosmical risings and settings of certain key stars and asterisms are observed and used in timing ritual events. Each of six stellar events, spaced from 20 to 30 days apart, singles out a particular star or constellation as *retal aq'äb'*, "the sign of night." For example, in mid-November the Pleiades undergo an acronychal ascent during sunset twilight near the sunrise position, cross their meridian at midnight, and go down near the sunset position cosmically in the dawn twilight. Other acronychal and cosmical events occur in mid-December with Orion, in mid-January with Gemini, in the third week of February with Regulus, in mid-March with the Big Dipper, and around 1 April with Acrux.

The moon also has its own acronychal and cosmical risings and settings, but it moves according to a different temporal rhythm from the stars. At the beginning of the month, the moon is momentarily visible as a slim crescent, *ch'utin ik'*, "little moon," or *alaj ik'*, "baby moon," lying low on the western horizon at sunset. It should be noted here that according to knowledgeable Momostecans, the moon is reborn each month. When the moon reappears as a slim crescent after conjunction, they say *mix alaxik ik'*, "the moon has been born." They reckon the age of a given moon from this first appearance, but local midwives and farmers prefer to count whole months from full moon to full moon because of the comparative ease of observation.

As the month progresses, the waxing crescent moon rises in the western sky slightly east of the setting sun and edges her way slowly eastward each night, until she reaches what astronomers refer to as the first quarter, so named because the moon at this time is on the meridian one-quarter of a full circle (90°) from the sun. Momostecans, however, refer to this phase as *nik'aj ik'*, "half moon," which emphasizes the degree of the moon's illumination rather than its position in relation to the sun. The moon is on her meridian or *pa nik'aj*, "in the center," at sunset, then she sets at about midnight. For the next week, as she approaches full phase, she rises and sets later and later. During this time the waxing gibbous moon, called *chaq'a-jik*, "maturing" or "ripening," is in the eastern sky at sunset and sets after midnight. Throughout this period she is referred to as *qanan*, "our mother."

Two weeks after the new moon, the full moon or *setel ik'*, "rounded moon," is seen in the east near the sunrise point. For Momostecan observers, the true full moon is the one seen rising shortly after sunset. It travels across the night sky and sets in the west near sunrise. The night of the full moon, or *jun aq'äb' ub'e*, "one night its road," is particularly dramatic. Both the acronychal moon rise and cosmical moon set are clearly visible, and the moon's path, like that of the sun but in opposition to it, makes a complete triangle. This is the only night on which Momostecan daykeepers find the moon's movement to be similar to that of the sun. This theory may be at variance with Western astronomical knowledge that the moon, like the sun and stars, rises in the east and sets in the west every day (whether visible or not), but it fits the readily observable facts. The spectacular journey of the full moon, known as *oxib' utzuk'*, *oxib' uxucut chupam q'equm*, "three sides, three corners in the dark," is marked off by *releb'al ik'*, "moon's coming-out [or rising] place," *pa nik'aj ik'*, "at the middle of the moon" (the moon's meridian), and *uqajib'al ik'*, "moon's going-down [or falling] place." On this one night the moon takes on a male aspect and is considered the nocturnal equivalent of the sun, with its full bright disk and complete transit of the sky. It may even be referred to, figuratively, as "sun."

From its full phase until the last quarter (*nik'aj ik'* "half moon"), the moon is considered to be an old woman, referred to as "our grandmother" (*qatit*) and described as the curved surface, or back, of the moon (*rij ik'*). At this stage the moon rises quite late in the evening, until the old woman enters her final waning gibbous or shrinking, drying-up (*katzujub'ik*) phase. At the beginning of the last-quarter phase, the moon rises at midnight and is on the meridian at sunrise, remaining in the day sky until nearly noon, when the sun, at the top of his triangle, replaces the old woman. Now the waning crescent moon rises later and later and is farther and farther east when the sun rises, until near the end of her waning phase the sun begins to catch up with her. The cycle ends with the moon rising at dawn, lagging farther and farther in the east until she is buried (*muqulik*).

These descriptions of the changing age and gender identity of the moon help to explain the seeming anomaly in the *Popol Vuh*, where Xbalanque (one of the hero twins) is said to rise as the moon, although he is male. He may have corresponded to the full moon, while Blood Woman (his mother) may have been the waxing moon and Xmucane (his grandmother) the waning moon.

### Synodic and Sidereal Lunar Reckoning

In Momostenango, during our formal training in calendrics, Dennis Tedlock and I learned to make a series of five visits to a pair of low (1-day) and high (8-day) shrines stretching over a 27-day period, or 1 lunar sidereal month. We first visited Paja', "At the Water," a low, watery shrine, on 1 Kej and then 8 days later, on 8 lx, we visited a high shrine called Ch'uti Sab'al, "Little Declaration Place." This was followed by another visit to Paja', now on 1 Junajpu, followed by Ch'uti Sab'al on 8 Kej, and ending (after 27 days) on 1 lx with a final afternoon visit to Paja'. This 27-day period is called *chakalik*, "staked, stabilized, or set," and is compared with the firm place-

ment of a table on its four legs, or the firm placement of a roof on the four
forked poles at the corners of a house. The purpose of this stabilization is to
overcome illness and misfortune.

Momostecan patrilineage leaders, called *chuchqajawib' rech alaxik*,
"motherfathers of the born ones," visit a high shrine by the name of Nima
Sab'al, "Large Declaration Place," according to the following sequence of
days: 9 Kej + 13 days = 9 Junajpu + 13 days = 9 Aj + 13 = 9 Kame + 13
= 9 Kawuq + 13 = 9 E + 13 = 9 Kan + 3 = 12 Q'anil = 82 days, a sum
equivalent to three sidereal lunar months (3 × 27.32167 days = 81.96501
days). These 82-day ritual periods or triple-sidereal lunar cycles, like the 27-
day single-sidereal lunar cycles, are referred to as *chakalik*, "staked, stabilized, or set." The point of particular astronomical interest here is that
wherever the moon (if visible) might have been located among the stars on
a given 9 Kej, it will be in nearly the same position at the same time of night
82 days later on 12 Q'anil. However, since a sidereal month (27 days 7
hours 43 minutes 11.5 seconds) is shorter than a synodic month (29 days 12
hours 44 minutes 2.8 seconds), the moon will not be in the same phase
when it returns to the same position.

This 82-day *chakalik* circuit is followed in order to bring an abundant
harvest and to keep the lineage healthy. Shortly after sunset on the first day
of the series, the motherfather opens a particular altar that pertains to his
own patrilineage. Nima Sab'al belongs to a category of shrines called *tan-
ab'al*, "elevated" or "stepped place," and it offers an extensive view of the
horizon. Motherfathers remain there for some time, burning incense, praying to their deceased predecessors by name, and observing the night sky. In
their prayers they mention the specific phase of the moon and its position in
the night sky relative to certain bright stars, planets, asterisms, and constellations. They are interested in the seasonal variation in the moon's path
through the stars and across the cleft, or dark rift, in the Milky Way. Later,
at home, they make notes concerning the sky in the margins of printed
calendars and almanacs.

There are a few men in the community who are particularly well
known for predicting rain by noting the phase and position of the moon on
all 7 days of this series of *b'elejeb'*, "nine-days." The majority, however,
only observe the night sky seriously on the opening day (9 Kej) and 82 days
later (12 Q'anil), when they once again arrive at sunset to pray and burn
incense before they close the shrine for a 48-day interval that stretches from
13 Toj until 9 No'j. They begin a second 82-day period with 9 No'j + 13
days = 9 Tz'i' + 13 = 9 Aq'ab'al + 13 = 9 Toj + 13 = 9 Iq' + 13 = 9
Tz'ikin + 3 = 12 Tijax, marking another 82-day cycle. Now the shrines

remain closed for 49 days (from 12 Tijax until 9 Kej) until the first cycle, 9 Kej to 12 Q'anil, begins again.

Above the level of the patrilineage motherfathers are 14 men who head the main territorial divisions of the community. They are referred to as both *chuchqajawib' rech kanton*, "motherfathers of the canton," and *chuchqajawib' rech kalpul*, "motherfathers of the calpul."[12] Their responsibilities include greeting the Mam, or year bearer, at sunrise and sunset on each occurrence of his day name (once each 20 days), at one of four hilltop shrines located a short distance from the town center. In a Kej year, for example, a group of calpul heads led by the one from Xequemeyá will visit the hilltop shrine on Paturas once each 20 days on days named Kej. In an E year this same group will be led on each E day name to the shrine at Chuwi Aqan by the calpul head of Los Cipréses. Their dawn and dusk visits involve not only ritual activities such as praying, burning copal incense, and setting off fireworks, but also the observation of the sun's position along the horizon. This is an important task, for as Anthony Aveni and Horst Hartung (1986:58–59) have noted, observations of sunrise and sunset positions at 20-day intervals helps in properly anticipating the zenith passages of the sun.

At a still higher rank are two *chuchqajawib' rech tinimit*, "motherfathers of the town," who are selected by the calpul heads (B. Tedlock 1982b:35, 74–82). These men, together with a delegation of calpul motherfathers, greet the new Mam once a year at a shrine located on a more distant mountaintop; thus, for example, when Mam Kej first arrived in 1990, he was greeted on Kilaja, the sacred mountain of the east. In addition to this annual visit to the key mountaintop of the year, each town motherfather also visits four mountaintop shrines on a cycle of days that coordinates the four consecutive 65-day periods of the 260-day almanac with four overlapping 82-day periods (see Figure 1.5). This cycle of visits provides Momostecan calendar experts with an opportunity for observation and gives them a conceptual scheme for coordinating lunar time reckoning with the 260-day cycle and the solar year in a more orderly fashion than would be possible through synodic reckoning alone. Noting the motion of the moon against the backdrop of the stars at 82-day intervals offers the possibility of conceptually linking the course of the daytime sun with that of the nighttime stars. This, in turn, opens the conceptual pathway leading from observations of acronychal and cosmical risings and settings of the stars to the mapping of a sidereal solar path.

The commensuration of astronomical observations and calendrical cycles is accomplished in Momostenango through the use of days with the

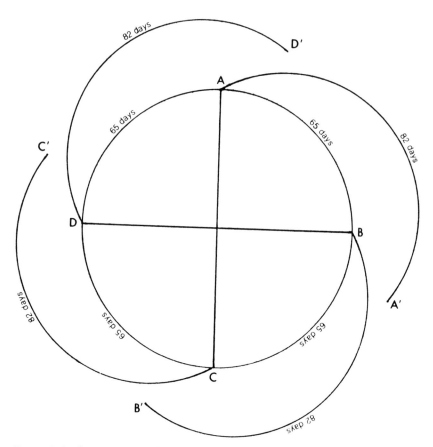

*Figure 1.5* The quartering of the 260-day almanac with overlapping sidereal lunar reckoning. On this drawing A = 9 Kej, A′ = 12 Q′anil, B = 9 E, B′ = 12 Aj, C = 9 No'j, C′ = 12 Tijax, D = 9 Iq', D′ = 12 Aq'ab'al.

same four names—Kej, E, No'j, and Iq'—to mark the beginning of the 65-day quarters of the 260-day cycle, the 82-day lunar period, and the 365-day solar cycle, or vague year. But unlike the case of solar year bearers—which occur in sequences such as 9 Kej, 10 E, 11 No'j, 12 Iq'—the prefixed number of the 4 days that mark the beginnings of 65-day and 82-day cycles stays constant; 9 Kej, 9 E, 9 No'j, 9 Iq' (see A, B, C, and D in Figure 1.5). These 4 days divide the 260-day cycle into four equal segments of 65 days each, one following the other without gaps or overlaps. On each of these days a town motherfather visits Nima Sab'al, also called B'elejeb'al or "Nine place," then he walks on to another hill closer to the town center, and finally out to one of the mountaintop shrines that lie some distance from town.

The 82-day periods, unlike the 65-day periods, overlap with one another (see Figure 1.5). Thus, after opening the shrines on Paturas and Kilaja (designated A in Figure 1.5) on 9 Kej, the motherfather returns there 80 days later in order to begin a 3-day closing ritual spanning 11 Kej, 12 Q'anil, and 13 Toj (see A' in Figure 1.5). Since the total distance from 9 Kej to 12 Q'anil is 82 days, or 3 sidereal lunar months, the opening and closing rituals permit sidereal reckoning of the moon. But the next sidereal period overlaps with the first, so that on 9 E, 15 days before the closing rituals begun on 11 Kej, he opens the second set of shrines of Chuwi Aqan and on the mountain of Tamancu, both of which are located in the south (see B in Figure 1.5). This 82-day period is then completed with the closing of these shrines on 11 E, 12 Aj, and 13 Ix (see B' in Figure 1.5). A third such period, begun 15 days before on 9 No'j, in the west at Nima Sab'al and Socop (see C in Figure 1.5), is completed on 11 No'j, 12 Tijax, and 13 Kawuq (C' in Figure 1.5). The fourth period, in the north at Cakb'ach'uy and Pipil (D in Figure 1.5), having started 15 days before on 9 Iq', is completed on 11 Iq', 12 Aq'ab'al, and 13 K'at (see D' in Figure 1.5).

Simultaneously with a sidereal rhythm these same visits contain a synodic rhythm. For any two successive mountaintop shrines A and B, the phase of the moon observed at the opening of A will repeat itself 147 days later at the closing of B (located at B' in Figure 1.5), and yet again when B is opened 178 days after it was closed, a total of 325 days after the opening of A (see Figure 1.5). Here it should be noted that the same sum is reached by adding the two canonical lunar intervals used in the Dresden eclipse table, which are 148 and 177. In Momostenango the event on the 147th day falls half a day short of 5 synodic moons, the one on the 178th day falls less than a day beyond 6 synodic moons, and the event on the 325th day falls just a little less than 4 hours beyond 11 synodic moons. Summarizing the arithmetic, we find that $147 = 65 + 82$ and $325 = 147 + 178 = 4 \times 65 + 65$. To state the pattern in another way, repetitions in phases of the moon move forward by one shrine each time around the full circle of shrines. Over a period of years the precise locations of the moon within its sidereal and synodic cycles during the shrine visits will shift, but the locations during any given visit remain good predictors of what will happen over the space of a year or more. It remains to be investigated whether the shifts might be read as auguries of changing fortunes in human affairs.

The overlapping pattern of synodic and sidereal lunar reckoning discussed here is commensurable with the 260-day cycle. Further, the selection of 4 days from this 260-day cycle that can also serve as year bearers brings this combined synodic and sidereal lunar scheme into partial alignment with the solar calendar. Thus, in any given circuit of the four shrines, three and sometimes four of the days on which openings are performed, or closings are started, will fall on days bearing the name of the current year bearer, which is itself marked by ceremonies throughout a given year. On 4 out of 52 years, spaced 13 years apart, the opening of a shrine will correspond to the first day of that year, or *nab'e mam*, "first grandfather." On another 4 years the beginning of the closing ceremony will correspond to the first day.

There is also evidence for the mixing of synodic and sidereal lunar reckoning in pre-Columbian times. As Aveni (this volume) has pointed out, the period assigned by the Dresden Codex to the visibility of Venus as the morning star, 236 days, has been rounded off so as to equal the duration of 8 synodic moons. The actual visibility of Venus as morning star averages 263 days, or 27 days longer than 8 synodic moons. Since 27 is the nearest whole-day approximation of a sidereal moon, there could have been a rule of thumb for following the progress of the morning star Venus that went something like this: Starting when it first appears, count 8 moons (of the synodic kind) and then expect Venus to disappear when the ninth moon has made one complete circuit of the zodiac. Evidence of an intricate network of multiples of synodic and triple-sidereal lunar cycles have been recently found at Palenque, El Peru, and in the almanac on pp. 23–24 of the Paris Codex (Dütting and Schramm 1988). These cycles may indicate the knowledge of celestial coordinate astronomy, one in which bodies are tracked with respect to one another rather than with respect to the horizon. The Brickers (Chapter 6 of this volume) have been able to confirm the zodiacal character of the Paris almanac and to map the approximate positions of the 13 constellations to which it refers.

## Conclusion

In all Mayan languages spoken today, the terms for east and west indicate a line or vector along which the sun rises and sets, depending on the season of the year. The other two directional terms variously indicate the right and left hand of the sun god, the direction of prevailing or rain-bringing winds, highland and lowland, above and below, and/or zenith and nadir. Thus, Classic and post-Classic Mayan directional terms ought not be ethnocentrically glossed and interpreted as though they were equivalent to our own cardinal or intercardinal compass points, which are frozen in space. Rather they ought to be described, as Mayans currently do, in terms of sides, lines, vectors, or trajectories that are inseparable from the movement of the sun and thus the passage of time.

The discovery, in a contemporary Mayan community, of the observation of acronychal and cosmical risings and settings of individual stars and asterisms, combined with the use of 82-day periods anchored to the 260-day and 365-day cycles, provides evidence that pre-Columbian Mayan society may have developed a common frame of reference for understanding the movements of the sun, moon, and stars. Although there is as yet no hard evidence of past or present angular calculations, it seems likely that Mayan peoples combined horizon with coordinate astronomy. Perhaps we will find a cache of Mayan astronomers' tools that indicate the nature and extent of their use of angular calculations. On the other hand, as Schlak (1989:271) has suggested, the Classic Maya may not have calculated anything like our own latitudes, longitudes, right ascensions, and declinations, but may rather have used iconographic compositions to record their positional astronomy.

The multimetrical temporal rituals that are described here involve dialectical thought patterns that go far beyond the simple dialectics of polarization, as exemplified in Hegelian and Marxist thought, to include the dialectics of overlapping or mutual involvement. It appears that Mayan peoples have, and had in their pre-Columbian past, differing systems of timekeeping that they used in the separate provinces of their biological, astronomical, psychological, religious, and social realities, and that these various systems underwent a process of totalization within the overlapping, intermeshing cycles of their calendars. Given the complexity of this cosmology, which is ritually re-enacted, shared, and thus maintained by contemporary Mayan peoples, their knowledge ought not be dismissed as the degenerate remains of Classic Maya glory. Rather, current cosmological theory and practice ought to be respected and studied as a precious human resource, providing key conceptual tools for understanding, reconstructing, and interpreting the hieroglyphic texts that happened to have survived.

### ACKNOWLEDGMENTS

This paper includes recent insights concerning Mayan cosmology and astronomy as well as earlier findings reported in an unpublished paper, "Earth rites and moon cycles: Mayan synodic and sidereal lunar reckoning," which was presented orally and circulated in written form during the First International Conference on Ethnoastronomy at the National Air and Space Museum, Washington, D.C., September, 1983. The ethnographic fieldwork undertaken in Momostenango, Guatemala during 1975, 1976, and 1979 was funded by the State University of New York at Albany and by Tufts University. More recent fieldwork undertaken during 1988 and 1989 in the highland Mayan communities of San Antonio Aguas Calientes, Cantel, Momostenango, Rabinal, and San Andrés Xecul was funded by research grants from the State University of New York at Buffalo.

NOTES

1. For words in highland Guatemalan languages (except proper names), I use the new alphabet decided upon by Mayan linguists who are also native speakers of those languages (see Academia de las lenguas Mayas de Guatemala 1988). The sounds are approximately as in Spanish, except that *q* is like Hebrew *qoph*, *tz* is like English *ts*, *x* is like English *sh*, and an apostrophe indicates the glottal stop when it follows a vowel and glottalization when it follows a consonant.

2. The Mayan term Xib'alb'a, Xibalbal, Xbalba, or Xibilba in Quiché (García and Yac 1980:171), Kekchí (Sedat 1955:162), Cholti (Moran 1935:38), Yucatec (Martínez 1930:920; Barrera 1980:930), and Chol (Aulie and Aulie 1978:136) is variously glossed as "the underworld," "hell," or "the devil."

3. The passage of the sun across the zenith is a phenomenon that occurs only in tropical latitudes where there are annually two such passages, equally spaced about the solstices, one occurring on the day the sun crosses the zenith as it goes northward along the ecliptic and the other as it returns southward.

4. Bricker (1988:395) used the 584,283 correlation constant in order to arrive at this date.

5. The Aulie and Aulie (1978) Cholan dictionary does not have an entry for south, and the Josserand and Hopkins (1988) Chol dictionary lack entries for either north or south. The problem of eliciting terms for north and south is such that dictionaries in several other Mayan languages also lack entries for these directions or else they simply list the Spanish terms. Thus, no terms for north or south are listed in Sedat's (1955) Kekchí dictionary, and in the Ulrich and Ulrich (1976:378) Mopan Maya dictionary the Spanish word *sur* alone is listed as the term for south.

6. Whether the directions north or south are on the right-hand or left-hand side of the sun depends upon the point of view of the observer; namely, that of a person facing the sun or that of the sun. While several ethnographers, working in both the highlands and the lowlands, have independently reported that living Mayan peoples take the sun's point of view when giving directions (Gossen 1974:31; B. Tedlock 1983a:5; Sosa 1985:420), some epigraphers and archaeologists take the point of view of a person looking at the sun (Schele and Freidel 1990:426).

7. The astronomical and calendrical information presented here is a small portion of the current knowledge in this one Quiché-speaking community. In time there may be more information available from other communities. Ethnographic descriptions of Momostenango can be found in Rodríguez (1971) and B. Tedlock (1982b).

8. This Quichean morphological patterning of mnemonic phrases, which carry the divinatory meaning of the day names, has also been found in the Mam language (Koizumi 1981:71–73).

9. My current understanding of Quiché–Maya calendars and astronomy is based on 21 months of ethnographic field research, including a formal apprenticeship in Momostenango completed during 1976 (see B. Tedlock 1982b).

10. In Kekchí the constellation of Orion is called *aj q'inb'*, "spinner," and *q'inleb' chahim*, "spindle star" (Haeserijn 1979:461).

11. Although this vast cloud of greenish glowing gases, like the Andromeda Nebula M31, is visible to the naked eye, the Orion Nebula M42 was not mentioned in any ancient or medieval records (Harrison 1984:65–70). Its European discovery in 1610 was credited to the naturalist and archaeologist Nicholas Peiresc (Burnham 1978:1320).

12. The term *kalpul*, from Nahua *calpulli*, is the name of the pre-Hispanic Mesoamerican residential land-holding unit still present today in some areas of highland Guatemala (Carrasco 1971; Carmack 1981:109–19; B. Tedlock 1982b:35, 181, 1986:125–26; Hill and Monoghan 1987:41–42).

## REFERENCES

Academia de las Lenguas Mayas de Guatemala, 1988. *Lenguas mayas de Guatemala: documentao de referencia para la pronunciación de los nuevos alfabetos oficiales* (Guatemala: Instituto Indigenista Nacional).

Adams, R. E. W., and G. F. Mobley, 1986. "Rio Azul: Lost city of the Maya." *National Geographic* **169**:420–51.

Alcorn, J. B., 1984. *Huastec Mayan Ethnobotany* (Austin: University of Texas Press).

Aulie, H. W., and E. W. de Aulie, 1978. *Diccionario ch'ol-español español-ch'ol* (México: Instituto Lingüístico de Verano).

Aveni, A. F., and H. Hartung, 1986. "Maya City Planning and the Calendar." Transactions of the American Philosophical Society, no. 76, part 7 (Philadelphia: American Philosophical Society).

Barrera Vásquez, A. 1980. *Diccionario maya cordemex, maya–español, español–maya* (Mérida: Ediciones Cordemex).

Berendt, C. H., 1877. "Calendario de los indios de Guatemala kiché (1722)." Copy of original manuscript in the Brinton Collection at the University of Pennsylvania Museum Library (Philadelphia).

Bowditch, C. P., 1910. *The Numeration, Calendar Systems and Astronomical Knowledge of the Mayas* (Cambridge: Harvard University Press).

Bricker, V. R., 1983. "Directional glyphs in Maya inscriptions and codices." *American Antiquity* **48**:347–53.

—, 1988. "A phonetic glyph for zenith: Reply to Closs." *American Antiquity* **1983**:394–400.

—, 1989. "The calendrical meaning of ritual among the Maya." In *Ethnographic Encounters in Southern Mesoamerica*, edited by V. R. Bricker and G. H. Gossen, pp. 231–49 (Albany: Institute for Mesoamerican Studies).

Burnham, R., 1978. *Burnham's Celestial Handbook*, Vol. 2 (New York: Dover).

Carmack, R. M., 1973. *Quichean Civilization: The Ethnohistoric, Ethnographic, and Archaeological Sources* (Berkeley: University of California Press).

—, 1981. *The Quiché Mayas of Utatlán: The Evolution of a Highland Guatemala Kingdom* (Norman: University of Oklahoma Press).

Carrasco, P., 1971. "Social organization of ancient Mexico." In *Handbook of Middle American Indians* 10:349–75 (Austin: University of Texas Press).

Coggins, C., 1980. "The shape of time: Some political implications of a four-part figure." *American Antiquity* 45:727–39.

Coto, Fray T. de, 1647. *Thesavrvs verborv: Vocabvlario de la lengua cakchiquel v[el] guatemalteca*, edited and introduced by R. Acuña in 1983 (México: Universidad Nacional Autónoma de México).

Crabtree, D. E., 1968. "Mesoamerican polyhedral cores and prismatic blades." *American Antiquity* 33:446–78.

Dütting, D., and M. Schramm, 1988. "The sidereal period of the moon in Maya calendrical astronomy." *Tribus* 37:139–73.

England, N. C., 1983. *A Grammar of Mam, A Mayan Language* (Austin: University of Texas Press).

García Hernández, A., and S. Y. Sam, 1980. *Diccionario quiche–español* (Guatemala: Instituto Lingüístico de Verano).

Girard, R., 1966. *Los Mayas* (México: Libro Mex).

Gossen, G. H., 1974. "A Chamula solar calendar board from Chiapas, Mexico." In *Mesoamerican Archaeology: New Approaches*, edited by N. Hammond, pp. 217–53 (London: Duckworth).

—, 1979. "Temporal and spatial equivalents in Chamula ritual symbolism." In *Reader in Comparative Religion*, edited by W. A. Lessa and E. Z. Vogt, pp. 116–29 (New York: Harper & Row).

Haeserijn V., E., 1979. *Diccionario k'ekchi' español* (Guatemala: Piedra Santa).

Harrison, T. C., 1984. "The Orion nebula: Where in history is it?" *Quarterly Journal of the Royal Astronomical Society* 25:65–79.

Hill, R. M., and J. Monaghan, 1987. *Continuities in Highland Maya Social Organization: Ethnohistory in Sacapulas, Guatemala* (Philadelphia: University of Pennsylvania Press).

Josserand, J. K., and N. A. Hopkins, 1988. "Chol (Mayan) Dictionary Database, Part III." Final Performance Report for the National Endowment for the Humanities.

Koizumi, J., 1981. "Symbol and Context: a Study of Self and Action in a Guatemalan Culture." Ph.D. Dissertation, Stanford University (Ann Arbor: University Microfilms).

La Farge, O., and D. Byers, 1931. *The Year Bearer's People*. Middle American Research Series, No. 3 (New Orleans: Tulane University).

Lamb, W. W., 1981. "Star lore in the Yucatec Maya dictionaries." In *Archaeoastronomy in the Americas*, edited by R. A. Williamson, pp. 233–48 (Los Altos, CA: Ballena Press).

Laughlin, R. M., 1975. *The Great Tzotzil Dictionary of San Lorenzo Zinacantán*. Smithsonian Contributions to Anthropology, No. 19 (Washington, D.C.: Smithsonian Institution Press).

Lincoln, S., 1942. "The Maya calendar of the Ixil of Guatemala." *Contributions to American Anthropology and History* 38:98–128.

Martínez Hernández, J., 1930. *Diccionario de Motul, maya español, atribuido a fray Antonio de Ciudad Real y arte de lengua maya por fray Juan Coronel* (Merida: Tipográfica Yucateca).

Miles, S. W., 1952. "An analysis of modern Middle American calendars: A study in conversation." In *Acculturation in the Americas*, edited by S. Tax, pp. 273–84 (New York: Cooper Square Publishers).

Moran, F., 1935. *Vocabulario en lengua cholti*. Maya Society Publication No. 9 (Baltimore: Johns Hopkins Press).

Nash, J., 1970. *In the Eyes of the Ancestors: Belief and Behavior in a Mayan Community* (New Haven: Yale University Press).

Neuenswander, H., 1981. "Glyphic implications of current time concepts of the Cubulco Achi (Maya)." Manuscript.

Orellana, S. L., 1987. *Indian Medicine in Highland Guatemala: The Pre-Hispanic and Colonial Periods* (Albuquerque: University of New Mexico Press).

Oxford English Dictionary, 1979. *Compact Edition of the Oxford English Dictionary* (New York: Oxford University Press).

Remington, J. A., 1975. "Maya Cosmology: A Pilot Study." M.A. Thesis, University of the Americas.

—, 1977. "Current astronomical practices among the Maya." In *Native American Astronomy*, edited by A. F. Aveni, pp. 75–88 (Austin: University of Texas Press).

Robertson, M. G., 1983. *The Sculpture of Palenque: The Temple of the Inscriptions* (Princeton: Princeton University Press).

Robicsek, F., and D. M. Hales, 1984. "Maya heart sacrifice: Cultural perspective and surgical technique." In *Ritual Human Sacrifice in Mesoamerica*, edited by E. H. Boone, pp. 49–90 (Washington, D.C.: Dumbarton Oaks).

Rodríguez Rouanet, F., 1971. "Monografía del Momostenango: Departamento de Totonicapán." *Guatemala Indígena* **5**:11–99.

Roys, R. L., 1967. *The Book of Chilam Balam of Chumayel* (Norman: University of Oklahoma Press).

Schele, L., and D. Freidel, 1990. *A Forest of Kings: The Untold Story of the Ancient Maya* (New York: William Morrow).

Schele, L., and N. Grube, 1990. "A Preliminary Inventory of Place Names in the Copán Inscriptions." *Copán Notes* **93**.

Schele, L., D. Stuart, and N. Grube, 1989. "A Commentary on the Restoration and Reading of the Glyphic Panels from Temple 11." *Copán Notes* **64**.

Schlak, A., 1989. "Jaguar and serpent foot: Iconography as astronomy." In *Word and Image in Maya Culture*, edited by W. F. Hanks and D. S. Rice, pp. 260–71 (Salt Lake City: University of Utah Press).

Schultze Jena, L., 1954. *La vida y las creencias de los indígenas quichés de Guatemala*. Biblioteca de Cultura Popular, Vol. 49. A. G. Carrera and H. D. Sapper, trans. (Guatemala: Ministerio de Educación Pública).

Sedat S., G., 1955. *Nuevo diccionario de las lenguas k'ekchi' y española* (Guatemala: Instituto Lingüístico de Verano).

Sosa, J. R., 1985. "The Maya Sky, the Maya World: A Symbolic Analysis of Yucatec Maya Cosmology." Ph.D. Dissertation, State University of New York at Albany (Ann Arbor: University Microfilms).

—, 1989. "Cosmological, symbolic and cultural complexity among the contemporary Maya of Yucatan." In *World Archaeoastronomy*, edited by A. F. Aveni, pp. 130–42 (Cambridge: Cambridge University Press).

Tedlock, B., 1982a. "Sound texture and metaphor in Quiché Maya ritual language." *Current Anthropology* 23(3):269–72.

—, 1982b. *Time and the Highland Maya* (Albuquerque: University of New Mexico Press).

—, 1983a. "Earth rites and moon cycles: Mayan synodic and sidereal lunar reckoning." Paper delivered at the International Conference on Ethnoastronomy, National Air and Space Museum, Washington, D.C.

—, 1983b. "Quichean time philosophy." In *Calendars in Mesoamerica and Peru: Native American Computations of Time*, edited by A. F. Aveni and Gordon Brotherston, pp. 59–72. BAR International Series (Oxford: British Archaeological Reports).

—, 1985. "Hawks, meteorology and astronomy in Quiché–Maya agriculture." *Archaeoastronomy* 8:80–88.

—, 1986. "On a mountain in the dark: Encounters with the Quiche Maya culture hero." In *Symbol and Meaning Beyond the Closed Community: Essays in Mesoamerican Ideas*, edited by G. H. Gossen, pp. 125–38 (Albany: Institute for Mesoamerican Studies).

Tedlock, D., 1985. *Popol Vuh: the Mayan Book of the Dawn of Life* (New York: Simon & Schuster).

Tirado, F. J., 1787. *Vocabulario de lengua kiche*. Photocopy of manuscript located in the Tozzer Library, Harvard University, Cambridge, Mass.

Tozzer, A. M., 1907. *A Comparative Study of the Mayas and the Lacandones* (New York: Macmillan).

Ulrich, E. M., and R. Dixon de Ulrich, 1976. *Diccionario bilingüe maya mopán y español, español y maya mopán* (Guatemala: Instituto Lingüístico de Verano).

Vogt, E. Z., 1976. *Tortillas for the Gods: A Symbolic Analysis of Zinacanteco Rituals* (Cambridge: Harvard University Press).

—, 1985. "Cardinal directions and ceremonial circuits in Mayan and Southwestern cosmology." *National Geographic Society Research Reports* 21:487–96.

Watanabe, J. M., 1983. "In the world of the sun: A cognitive model of Mayan cosmology." *Man* 18:710–28.

# 2

# A Method for
# Cross-Dating Almanacs with Tables
# in the Dresden Codex

VICTORIA R. BRICKER
HARVEY M. BRICKER

Hieroglyphic inscriptions at Classic Maya sites typically begin with one of two kinds of calendrical expressions: an initial series date in long-count or positional notation that can be correlated with a date in the Christian calendar or a calendar-round permutation that can be assigned to a position in a cycle of 52 years. Many hieroglyphic texts containing only calendar-round dates can be tied into the long count, and from there into the Christian calendar, by cross-dating them with references to related events on initial series monuments at the same or nearby sites. For example, the inscription on Lintel 2 at Yaxchilan begins with a calendar-round date, 4 Ahau 3 Zodz (Graham and von Euw 1977:15), but because it is followed by a reference to the 5-*tun* anniversary of Bird Jaguar's accession to office, it can be cross-dated with the text on the front of Stela 11. This stela commences with an initial series date, 9.16.1.0.0, referring to the day when Bird Jaguar became ruler of Yaxchilan (Schele 1982:31). The long-count position of 4 Ahau 3 Zodz is therefore 9.16.6.0.0, exactly five *tuns* after Bird Jaguar took office.

The Dresden Codex contains two kinds of hieroglyphic texts, which we call tables and almanacs. Tables are introduced by long-count dates in *pictun*, serpent, or ring-number notation, which can be correlated with dates in the Western calendar. Almanacs are introduced by *tzolkin* permutations, which can be assigned to a position in a cycle of no more than 260 days. The prefaces of almanacs are much more abbreviated than those of tables, and they do not contain sufficient information for calculating a long-count date. Until recently, scholars have focused on several astronomical tables in the Codex and, in particular, on how the base dates in the introduction to each table might be used for entering and recycling the table proper (H. Bricker and V. Bricker 1983; V. Bricker and H. Bricker 1986b, 1988; Closs 1977; Lounsbury 1983; Thompson 1972:62–64, 71–75). The texts in the Codex with only *tzolkin* permutations have been assumed by some to be divinatory almanacs (Thompson 1972:20); in any case, the question of how they might be related to the astronomical tables has not arisen.

Almanacs in the Dresden Codex are usually composed of (1) a column of day glyphs surmounted by a number in bar-and-dot notation, (2) a series of two or more clauses, and (3) a corresponding series of pictures below the clauses (Figure 2.1). Many of the pictures are repeated in different almanacs with only slight variations, suggesting that there may be some relationship among them. Furthermore, several pictures that occur with some frequency in almanacs also appear in the seasonal table on pages 65–69 of the Codex (Figure 2.2), where they can be securely dated in terms of the long count and the Christian calendar. It is, in fact, possible to use pictures for cross-dating almanacs with tables, in much the same way that textual references to events in the life of a ruler have been used for cross-dating inscriptions containing only calendar-round dates with those on initial series monuments.

*Figure 2.1* The almanac on pp. 17c and 18c of the Dresden Codex (after Villacorta C. and Villacorta 1976:44, 46).

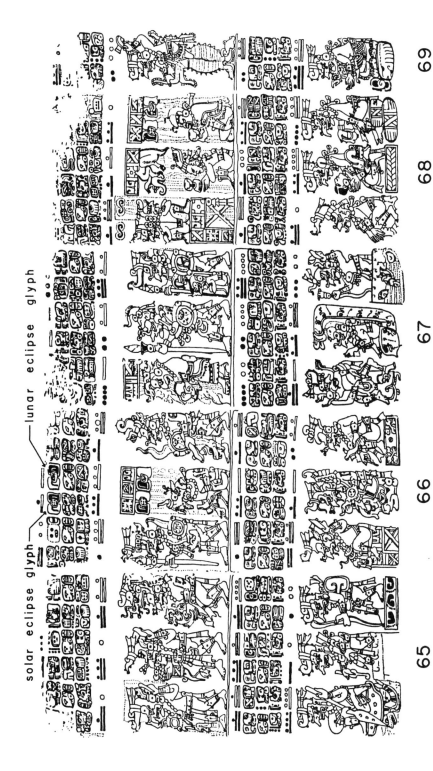

*Figure 2.2* The seasonal table on pp. 65–69 of the Dresden Codex (after Villacorta C. and Villacorta 1976:140, 142, 144, 146, 148).

solar eclipse glyph

lunar eclipse glyph

65  66  67  68  69

45

## The Maya Calendar

Before proceeding further it may be useful to review those aspects of the Classic Maya calendrical system that are necessary to an understanding of the structure of tables and almanacs in the Dresden Codex. The ancient Maya kept track of time through the use of two intermeshing calendrical cycles—the *tzolkin* of 260 days and the *haab* of 365 days—and a system of absolute or linear chronology based on the 360-day *tun* (cf. Closs 1983). The *tzolkin* cycle was itself composed of two separate subsidiary cycles, a cycle of numbers (1–13) and a cycle of 20 day names used in a constant order (Imix, Ik, Akbal, Kan, Chicchan, Cimi, Manik, Lamat, Muluc, Oc, Chuen, Eb, Ben, Ix, Men, Cib, Caban, Edznab, Cauac, Ahau). The full *tzolkin* date was a permutation of day number and day name; the first such permutation or day 1 in the *tzolkin* cycle of 260 days was the day 1 Imix, day 2 was 2 Ik, day 13 was 13 Ben, day 14 was 1 Ix, etc. The *haab* consisted of 18 20-day months (Pop, Uo, Zip, Zodz, Tzec, Xul, Yaxkin, Mol, Ch'en, Yax, Zac, Ceh, Mac, Kankin, Muan, Pax, Kayab, Cumku) plus a short intercalary month, Uayeb, having only 5 days. The 20 days in each regular month were numbered from 0 to 19; those in Uayeb were numbered from 0 to 4. The *haab* thus started with a day 0 Pop, followed by 1 Pop, 2 Pop, etc., and ended with a day 4 Uayeb. Only 4 of the 20 named days could begin the year (i.e., co-occur with 0 Pop). These ritually important days, called "year bearers," are the subject of four pages in the Dresden Codex. Ik, Manik, Eb, and Caban were the year bearers used in the Codex. The *tun* was composed of 18 months or *uinals* of 20 days each; 20 *tuns* made up a unit of time called a *katun*, and 20 *katuns* made up a *baktun*. Information about the place of a given day in all three of the major systems of time reckoning was sometimes given in the following form:

10.6.1.16.14 13 Ix 12 Mol.

The first part of this expression, the long count, states that the following temporal units of the current calendrical era have been completed: 10 *baktuns* (out of a possible 13, numbered 0 or 13 to 12 in long-count notation), 6 *katuns* (of 20, numbered 0 to 19), 1 *tun* (of 20, numbered 0 to 19), 16 *uinals* (of 18, numbered 0 to 17), and 14 *kins* or days (of 20, numbered 0 to 19). The second part of the expression is the *tzolkin* date, 3 Ix, which is day 234 of the 260-day cycle. The third part of the expression is the *haab* date, 12 Mol, the thirteenth day of the eighth month. This combination of *tzolkin* and *haab* date can occur only once in a 52-year period, the Maya "century," which is commonly referred to as the *calendar round*.

## The Structure of Almanacs in the Dresden Codex

An example of an almanac in the Dresden Codex is the one shown in Figure 2.1, which appears at the bottom of pages 17 and 18 of the Codex. The column to the left of the first picture on page 17c contains the number "4" (four red dots, shown outlined in black) and the glyphs for Ahau, Eb, Kan, Cib, and Lamat. The number serves as the coefficient of all the day names in that column. The first *tzolkin* date, 4 Ahau, introduces the first clause in the text. It is followed by a solid black distance number, "15" (3 bars), and a red *tzolkin* coefficient, "6" (one dot and one bar, shown outlined in black in Figure 2.1). The distance number links the 4 Ahau date that introduces the first clause to 6 Men, the date with which the second clause begins. The second clause is followed by the distance number, "33" (the glyph for "20" followed by two bars and three dots), and the *tzolkin* coefficient, "13" (two bars and three dots); the date 13 Lamat occurs 33 days after 6 Men and initiates the third clause. The distance number that follows that clause links 13 Lamat to 4 Eb, the second *tzolkin* date in the first column of the text (Figure 2.1). The three clauses are then recycled, with 4 Eb, 6 Manik, and 13 Ahau replacing 4 Ahau, 6 Men, and 13 Lamat, respectively. The distance number below the third clause brings the table to 4 Kan, which is the third *tzolkin* date in the first column of the almanac (Figure 2.1). The clauses are recycled three more times, and the last distance number returns the almanac to 4 Ahau, the first *tzolkin* date in the first column of the text (Figure 2.1). The structure of this almanac is summarized in Table 2.1.

It should be noted that Thompson's (1972:58) interpretation of the structure of this text is quite different from that presented here. He assumes that the calendrical information was given in tabular form, and he refers the black and red bar-and-dot numbers to the glyphs directly above them, rather than to the following clause. His scheme provides no syntactic function for the day names and number in the first column, and it places dates at the end of clauses, instead of at the beginning. The advantage of our suggested prose reading of this and other similar codical texts is that it

*Table 2.1*    The Structure of the Almanac on Pages 17c and 18c of the Dresden Codex

| Cycle | Date 1 | Date 2 | Date 3 |
|---|---|---|---|
| 1 | 4 Ahau | 6 [Men] | 13 [Lamat] |
| 2 | 4 Eb | 6 [Manik] | 13 [Ahau] |
| 3 | 4 Kan | 6 [Cauac] | 13 [Eb] |
| 4 | 4 Cib | 6 [Chuen] | 13 [Kan] |
| 5 | 4 Lamat | 6 [Akbal] | 13 [Cib] |

reveals syntactic structures that are homologous with those found in monumental texts (V. Bricker 1986). We have shown elsewhere that this reading order for almanacs can be verified by astronomical information appearing in the Mars and seasonal tables on other pages of the Codex (V. Bricker and H. Bricker 1986b, 1988; V. Bricker 1988a).

The explicit calendrical notation used in almanacs is a date in the *tzolkin*, and the same date recurs every 260 days. Although most of the almanacs in the Codex refer to a period of 260 days, a few cover much longer periods of time. The Codex contains one double-*tzolkin* almanac of 520 days (see below, one triple almanac of 780 days, one septuple almanac of 1820 days (see below), and one nine-fold almanac of 2340 days (see below). Thus, what is explicitly "the same day" may occur more than once in a long almanac or in successive runs of an almanac of any length.

On the other hand, the iconographic content of a picture, or the semantic content of the text caption to a picture, or both, may limit the reference of the explicitly expressed *tzolkin* date by relating it to a position in another cycle. The principles involved in deriving precise dating information from very abbreviated or partial calendrical notation may be illustrated by examples based on our own Western calendar.

A common notational format for our Western calendar is a series of 12 grids; each grid has 7 columns and 4 to 6 rows. The caption for a given grid (January, February, . . .), the positional information provided by the grid structure itself, the column headings (Sunday, Monday, . . . , or S, M, . . .), and the numerals within most of the cells of the grid (1, 2, . . .) serve to specify the position of a single day in the year in terms of four cycles: (1) the name and thereby the ordinal position of the month in a year of 12 months (for example, November, the eleventh month); (2) the position of the day in a month of 28, 29, 30, or 31 days (for example, the ninth day of November); (3) the name and thereby the ordinal position of the day in a 7-day week (for example, Thursday, the fifth day of a week beginning on Sunday); and (4) the ordinal position of that day in the series of all days of that name in the month in question (for example, the second Thursday in November). All days in the year may be described in terms of these four cycles, but not all days are equally significant. Certain days are ritually or historically important, and over time, they have come to be identified with distinctive emblems or iconographic themes that are widely distributed and universally recognized within our culture. The association of a certain icon with a certain day may be shown very explicitly by the presence of the icon within the cell for the day in question on the month grid of a printed calendar—for example, the picture of Santa Claus in the cell for the 25th of December, Christmas Day.

It is of course true that not all printed calendars in our culture carry such iconographic information about special days, but it is the kind of calendars that do that allow us to pursue the analogy a bit further. If, for example, we had as an object for study a small torn fragment of such a calendar printed for use in the United States, and if that fragment contained only part of one grid cell and part of a picture of Santa Claus, we would know that the cell in question was that for 25 December. If a similarly small fragment contained a jack o'lantern, we could assign it to 31 October, and if it contained a stylized heart pierced by an arrow, an assignment of 14 February would be a safe one. In all three cases, the iconography alone is sufficient to specify the month and the day of the month, but the day of the week is not determinable. A calendrical fragment containing a picture of a turkey could be diagnosed as the fourth Thursday in November, Thanksgiving day in the United States, but which day of the month it is could not be known if the numeral were missing from the fragment. In all these cases (and others that could be cited), we would need additional information in order to locate the day in question within all four of the Western calendrical cycles discussed above. If it were desired to specify the year for which the calendar was printed, or perhaps a set of several equiprobable years, additional information would certainly be needed.

The way in which information from different contexts may aid research on our own calendar can be discussed with reference to Figure 2.3, a slightly damaged sheet from the sort of printed calendar we have been considering. It is immediately apparent from the presence of the St. Valentine's Day iconography that the calendar is for the month of February. The fact that this particular February has 29 days, indicates that the year in question is a leap year. A picture of Abraham Lincoln appears in the grid cell for 12 February, and a picture of George Washington is associated with 22 February. Assuming that the pictures of the United States presidents indicate civil holidays, the conclusion is that the year predates 1970, when the U.S. Congress designated the third Monday in February as Presidents' Day to honor both Lincoln and Washington, replacing the previously separate holidays. The final icon of relevance here is a symbol of a full Moon in the grid cell for 9 February.

The calendrical grid shown in Figure 2.3 and its iconographic symbols provide enough information to determine the year in the twentieth century in which February has this particular concatenation of events. We are dealing here with a leap year in which the leap day falls on a Tuesday. This coincidence of a leap day with a particular day of the week can occur only once in a cycle of 28 years. Because of the representation of separate

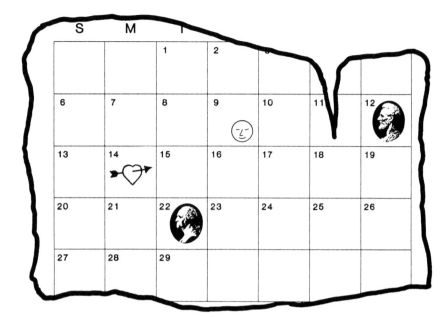

*Figure 2.3* Damaged page from a modern printed calendar (hypothetical example discussed in the text).

holidays for Washington and Lincoln, the year must be before 1970. The final limiting factor is the full moon on Wednesday, 9 February. The only year between 1901 and 1970 in which all of these events corresponded to this calendrical configuration was 1944. The determination of the date is made possible by the concurrent consideration of events having to do with the ritual of popular culture, the political history of the country, and an astronomical cycle. In this modern example, as in many examples from the Dresden Codex discussed here, it is the ability to include astronomical information in the "triangulation" that permits calendrical precision.

To return, then, to the almanacs of the Dresden Codex, it is sometimes possible to use several different kinds of iconographic information to get beyond the short *tzolkin* cycle of 260 days that forms the explicit structure of the almanacs and to locate the day in question within some longer cycle that has greater calendrical utility. There are four general kinds of iconographic information that may be useful here: (1) The picture or clause associated with the *tzolkin* date may refer it to the longer *haab* cycle of 365 days. In such cases, what is in fact "the same day" recurs every 365 days if only the (implicit) *haab* component is the referent of the text or picture (e.g., New Year's Day). (2) The picture and/or caption may limit the reference of a *tzolkin* date to the relationship between it and a day in the *haab*—in other words, to the full calendar-round permutation, like 3 Man-ik o Yax. In this case, "the same day" occurs only every 52 years, a full calendar round. (3) The content of a picture and its caption may limit the reference of a *tzolkin* date to the relationship between a date in the *haab* and a station of the tropical year (e.g., the vernal equinox). In such a case, "the same day" recurs only every 1507 tropical years (or every 1508 *haabs*). (4) The reference of a *tzolkin* date may also be constrained by references to astronomical cycles other than the tropical year, for example the synodical period of a planet or the eclipse half-year. If the planet is Venus, "the same day" recurs after two calendar rounds, or 104 *haabs*. If the planet is Mars, then "the same day" recurs after three *tzolkin* cycles, or 780 days. In the case of eclipse seasons, "the same day" recurs after two *tzolkin* cycles, or 520 days.

It is, then, apparent that the explicit *tzolkin* notation of an almanac is no guide to the function of that almanac in the absence of an understand-ing of the accompanying iconographic and/or semantic content. Such an understanding is possible only after the pictures and their captions have been placed in the chronological framework provided by the three major astronomical tables in the Codex.

## Relationship Between the Seasonal Table and Almanacs

The seasonal table on pp. 65–69 of the Dresden Codex (Figure 2.2) consists of two parts: (1) an upper table, beginning on 10.6.1.5.16 3 Cib 19 Muan, corresponding to 12 July A.D. 949 in the Gregorian calendar, and (2) a lower table, beginning 218 days later, on 10.6.1.16.14 13 Ix 12 Mol, corresponding to 17 May A.D. 950 (see V. Bricker and H. Bricker 1988 for a discussion of how the entry date for the upper table was calculated from one of the base dates given in the table's introductory section on pp. 61–64). Each part of the table covers a span of 182 days. The implied total length of the table—364 days (= 2 × 182)—is 1 day short of the 365-day *haab* and 1.2422 days short of the tropical year. The upper table correlates eclipse seasons with the vernal equinox and the Maya New Year (V. Bricker and H. Bricker 1988). The lower table is concerned primarily with the relationship between the summer solstice and the midpoint of the *haab*, as discussed below.

Two pictures in the lower part of the table are especially relevant to the question of cross-dating it with almanacs elsewhere in the Codex. The first picture on p. 66b shows the rain god Chac sitting on a sky band (Figure 2.4). The temporal interval associated with that picture is a 1-day period

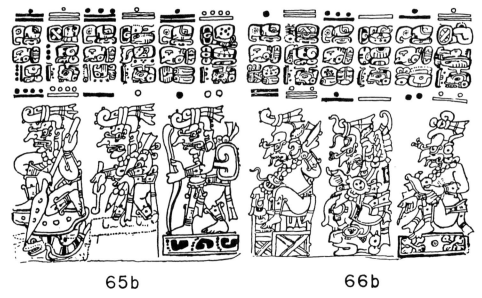

65b                          66b

*Figure* 2.4 Pages 65b and 66b in the seasonal table of the Dresden Codex (after Villacorta C. and Villacorta 1976:140, 142).

beginning on 21 June A.D. 950, 1 day before the summer solstice for that year (Kluepfel 1986b). The corresponding Maya date, 10.6.2.0.9 9 Muluc 7 Yax, is the 187th day of the *haab*. The midpoint of the *haab*, 2 Ik 0 Yax (calculated as the first day of the tenth regular month, the 181st day of the *haab*, which is the exact midpoint if one ignores the 5 nameless days of Uayeb), falls within the 11-day interval associated with the third picture on p. 65b, which depicts Chac walking on a road symbolized by three footprints heading in the same direction, from right to left (Figure 2.4). The pictures in the bottom register of the so-called New Year's pages of the same Codex also depict footprints, but oriented from left to right, instead of from right to left (e.g., Figure 2.5c).

The directional significance of the footprints in the third picture on p. 65b can be clarified by comparing it with a related picture in the table at the top of pp. 31–39 (Figure 2.6). Based on the first-appearing long-count date given in the table's introduction on p. 31, the calendar-round permutation associated with that picture, 13 Ahau 3 Yax (= 4 November A.D. 373), falls 3 days after the middle of the *haab*. Chac sits on a mat, facing left. The footprint motif appears in two contexts: along the length of his scarf and in the design of the mat. The footprints follow the weave of the mat, moving first in one direction and then doubling back in the other (Figure 2.6). The mat design is explicitly associated with time on the east face of Stela J at

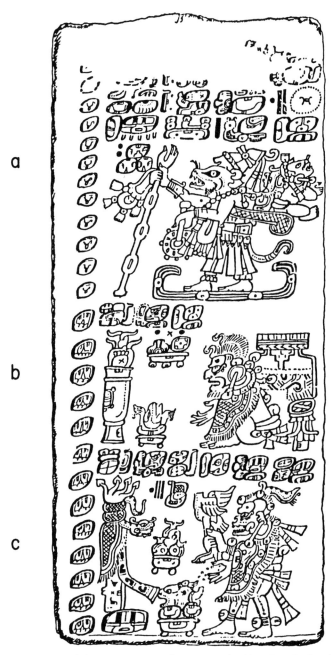

*Figure* 2.5 Page 27 of the New Year's Almanac in the Dresden Codex (after Villacorta C. and Villacorta 1976:64).

*Figure* 2.6 Page 35a of the Dresden Codex (after Villacorta C. and Villacorta 1976:80).

Copan, where long-count dates, calendar-round permutations, and distance numbers follow the course of a strand, weaving in and out and doubling back at the edges of the mat (Maudslay 1889–1902:2, Pl. 71). The colonial Books of Chilam Balam sometimes refer to the "folding" of the *katun* (e.g., Edmonson 1982:line 921; 1986:lines 3259–64), a metaphor that is consistent with the use of the mat as a symbol for the passage of time. Thus, although time in general is certainly continuous, discrete units of time have a beginning, a middle, and an end, and the middle point by analogy with the mat is the folding of time and a reverse of spatial direction. All this suggests that the third picture on p. 65b represents the middle of the year, when the year bearer reverses course and begins his journey back to his point of origin. The order of the pictures on pp. 65b and 66b— footprints before sky band—is an accurate statement of the fact that the half-year preceded the summer solstice by a few days in A.D. 950.

### RAIN-MAKING ALMANAC, PP. 29B–30B (A.D. 899)

A similar pair of pictures appears in the almanac in the middle of pp. 29 and 30 of the same Codex, but their order is reversed (Figure 2.7). This can be explained by the discrepancy between the *haab* of 365 days and the tropical year of 365.2422 days. Over time, the *haab* gradually falls behind the seasons, moving completely through the tropical year in 1508 *haabs*. Between A.D. 918 and 921, the midpoint of the year coincided with the

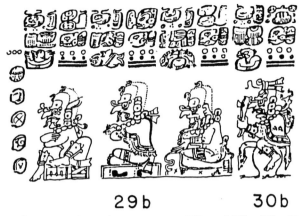

**29b**        **30b**

*Figure* 2.7 The rain-making almanac on pp. 29b and 30b of the Dresden Codex (after Villacorta C. and Villacorta 1976:68, 70).

summer solstice. The summer solstice *preceded* the half-year before A.D. 918 and *followed* it after A.D. 921. This means that the rain-making almanac must have been used before A.D. 918. The precise date of the almanac can be inferred from the *tzolkin* date associated with the second picture (3 Manik) and the 13-day interval that separates it from the *tzolkin* date associated with the first picture (3 Ix). Manik is a year-bearer day in the calendar employed by the Dresden Codex, and it is 1 of the 4 days that can co-occur with o Yax, the midpoint of the *haab*. The same is true of 8 Eb, the sixth day of the 13-day interval in question, and of 13 Caban, the eleventh day. Within the approximately 1200 years of pre-Columbian Maya history (the Classic and post-Classic), there was only one occasion each when 3 Manik o Yax, 8 Eb o Yax, and 13 Caban o Yax could follow a summer solstice by not more than 13 days. The Gregorian dates for these three occurrences are 26 June A.D. 899, 25 June A.D. 904, and 24 June A.D. 909, respectively. In both A.D. 904 and A.D. 909, both events would occur in the 13-day interval beginning with 3 Manik, thus violating the iconography of the almanac. It is, therefore, quite clear that the almanac refers uniquely to a sequence of events in A.D. 899. The date for the first picture is 10.3.10.4.14 3 Ix 7 Ch'en (= 13 June 899), 8 days before the summer solstice for that year; the date for the second picture is 10.3.10.5.7 3 Manik o Yax (= 26 June 899), 5 days after the summer solstice. The interval between successive recurrences of the same calendar-round permutation is 52 *haabs*. By A.D. 951, when 3 Manik o Yax rolled around again, the *haab* had fallen behind the tropical year by 13 days, and the pictures had to be reversed, as documented on pp. 65b and 66b of the seasonal table (Figure

2.4). Fifty-two years before A.D. 899, the summer solstice preceded the half-year by more than 13 days, and the almanac would not have been useful.

The clauses over the pictures in this almanac contain instructions for performing the rain-making ceremonies called *ch'a chac* in the Yucatan peninsula. Figure 2.8 provides an interlinear transcription and translation of the text, which are supported in V. Bricker (1991). These ceremonies are today performed on alternate Sundays during June and July in the town of Hocaba in the northwestern part of the peninsula. The 13-day intervals given by the solid black bar-and-dot numbers below each clause correspond closely to the fortnightly intervals at which the modern ceremonies take place, and the dates associated with the clauses in the almanac also fall in June and July. Four such ceremonies are performed in Hocaba every summer, the first on the eastern side of town, the second in the north, the third

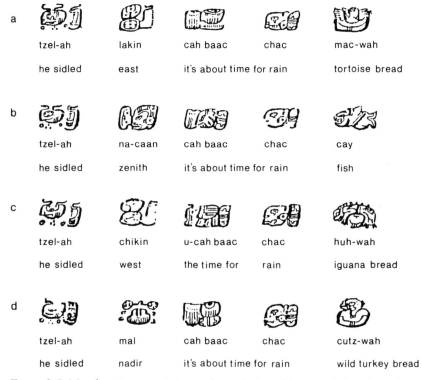

*Figure* 2.8 Morphemic transcription and translation of the text of the rain-making almanac on pp. 29b and 30b of the Dresden Codex (after Villacorta C. and Villacorta 1976:68, 70).

in the west, and the fourth in the south. The clauses in the almanac refer to the same sequence of world directions, except that zenith and nadir substitute for north and south, respectively (Figure 2.8). In other words, the text and the pictures imply the same date for the almanac. Furthermore, it is clear that the almanac was intended to be used only during a restricted portion of the *haab*, namely the months of Ch'en, Yax, and Zac. The full length of the almanac is the *tzolkin* of 260 days. Because this period is 105 days shorter than the *haab* of 365 days, the clauses are associated with a different set of *tzolkin* dates each time it is used. Table 2.2 shows that the third set of *tzolkin* dates is relevant in A.D. 900, the fifth set in A.D. 901, the second sset in A.D. 902, and the fourth set in A.D. 903, returning to the first set in A.D. 904. However, the first picture ceases to coincide with the summer solstice after A.D. 902; so the last set of dates cannot be used at all. The model we are suggesting for the use of this almanac is that its scope was not limited to a single 260-day period but was intended to serve as a "date-reaching" mechanism (Closs 1977) for determining the *tzolkin* dates of the *ch'a chac* ceremonies in successive tropical years.

*Table 2.2*   Dates for Rain-Making Ceremonies Implied by the Almanac on Pages 29b–30b of the Dresden Codex

| Year (A.D.) | First picture | Second picture | Third picture | Fourth picture |
|---|---|---|---|---|
| 899 | 3 Ix 7 Ch'en<br>10.3.10.4.14<br>13 June | 3 Manik 0 Yax<br>10.3.10.5.7<br>26 June | 3 Ahau 13 Yax<br>10.3.10.6.0<br>9 July | 3 Ben 6 Zac<br>10.3.10.6.13<br>22 July |
| 900 | 3 Edznab 6 Ch'en<br>10.3.11.4.18<br>12 June | 3 Chuen 19 Ch'en<br>10.3.11.5.11<br>25 June | 3 Kan 12 Yax<br>10.3.11.6.4<br>8 July | 3 Caban 5 Zac<br>10.3.11.6.17<br>21 July |
| 901 | 3 Ik 5 Ch'en<br>10.3.12.5.2<br>11 June | 3 Men 18 Ch'en<br>10.3.12.5.15<br>24 June | 3 Lamat 11 Yax<br>10.3.12.6.8<br>7 July | 3 Imix 4 Zac<br>10.3.12.7.1<br>20 July |
| 902 | 3 Cimi 4 Ch'en<br>10.3.13.5.6<br>10 June | 3 Cauac 17 Ch'en<br>10.3.13.5.19<br>23 June | 3 Eb 10 Yax<br>10.3.13.6.12<br>6 July | 3 Chicchan 3 Zac<br>10.3.13.7.5<br>19 July |
| 903 | 3 Oc 3 Ch'en<br>10.3.14.5.10<br>9 June | 3 Akbal 16 Ch'en<br>10.3.14.6.3<br>22 June | 3 Cib 9 Yax<br>10.3.14.6.16<br>5 July | 3 Muluc 2 Zac<br>10.3.14.7.9<br>18 July |
| 904 | 3 Ix 2 Ch'en<br>10.3.15.5.14<br>7 June | 3 Manik 15 Ch'en<br>10.3.15.6.7<br>20 June | 3 Ahau 8 Yax<br>10.3.15.7.0<br>3 July | 3 Ben 1 Zac<br>10.3.15.7.13<br>16 July |

SEASONAL ALMANAC, PP. 40C–41C (A.D. 869)

Another example of the half-year following the summer solstice appears in the almanac at the bottom of pp. 40 and 41 (Figure 2.9). The third picture in the almanac is associated with the *tzolkin* date 8 Ahau; it depicts Chac sitting on a sky band. The fourth picture is associated with the *tzolkin* date 5 Oc; it shows Chac with his feet above his head, turning a somersault over footprints heading in two directions, a clear sign that he is reversing his course. The half-year must occur during the 10-day interval beginning with 5 Oc. Following the order of days in the *tzolkin*, these days are 5 Oc, 6 Chuen, 7 Eb, 8 Ben, 9 Ix, 10 Men, 11 Cib, 12 Caban, 13 Edznab, and 1 Cauac. Of these choices, only Eb and Caban are year bearers, and it should therefore be the case that the half-year date to which the picture refers must be either 7 Eb o Yax or 12 Caban o Yax. Only the second date can be correlated with a Gregorian date falling the requisite number of days after a summer solstice. That date is 10.1.19.15.17 12 Caban o Yax (= 3 July 869). It places the date associated with the sky band picture at 10.1.19.15.0 8 Ahau 3 Ch'en (= 16 June 869), 5 days before a summer solstice. Table 2.3 shows that the almanac can also be used as a date-reaching mechanism for targeting the summer solstice and the half-year in A.D. 870 and 871. By A.D. 872, the date associated with the third picture in the almanac falls one day after the summer solstice, and the half-year coincides with the fifth picture instead of the fourth.

Another set of distance numbers is embedded in the pictures at the bottom of each page (Figure 2.9). The first, shown under the boat paddled by Chac, consists of the "moon-glyph" variant for "20" with a coefficient of

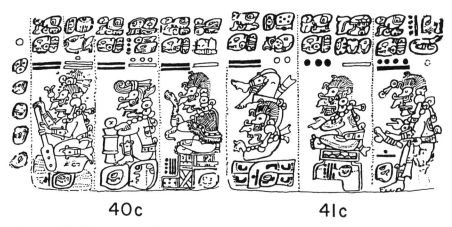

40c          41c

*Figure* 2.9 The seasonal almanac on pp. 40c and 41c of the Dresden Codex (after Villacorta C. and Villacorta 1976:90, 92).

Table 2.3  Dates for Correlation of Summer Solstice and Half-Year Implied by the Upper Set of Distance Numbers in the Seasonal Almanac on Pages 40c–41c of the Dresden Codex

| Year (A.D.) | First picture | Second picture | Third picture | Fourth picture | Fifth picture | Sixth picture |
|---|---|---|---|---|---|---|
| 869 | 1 Ahau 3 Mol<br>10.1.19.14.0<br>27 May | 11 Oc 13 Mol<br>10.1.19.14.10<br>6 June | 8 Ahau 3 Ch'en<br>10.1.19.15.0<br>16 June | 5 Oc 13 Ch'en<br>10.1.19.15.10<br>26 June | 2 Ahau 3 Yax<br>10.1.19.16.0<br>6 July | 5 Akbal 6 Yax<br>10.1.19.16.3<br>9 July |
| 870 | 1 Kan 2 Mol<br>10.2.0.14.4<br>26 May | 11 Ix 12 Mol<br>10.2.0.14.14<br>5 June | 8 Kan 2 Ch'en<br>10.2.0.15.4<br>15 June | 5 Ix 12 Ch'en<br>10.2.0.15.14<br>25 June | 2 Kan 2 Yax<br>10.2.0.16.4<br>5 July | 5 Manik 5 Yax<br>10.2.0.16.7<br>8 July |
| 871 | 1 Lamat 1 Mol<br>10.2.1.14.8<br>25 May | 11 Edznab 11 Mol<br>10.2.1.14.18<br>4 June | 8 Lamat 1 Ch'en<br>10.2.1.15.8<br>14 June | 5 Edznab 11 Ch'en<br>10.2.1.15.18<br>24 June | 2 Lamat 1 Yax<br>10.2.1.16.8<br>4 July | 5 Chuen 4 Yax<br>10.2.1.16.11<br>7 July |
| 872 | 1 Eb 0 Mol<br>10.2.2.14.12<br>23 May | 11 Ik 10 Mol<br>10.2.2.15.2<br>2 June | 8 Eb 0 Ch'en<br>10.2.2.15.12<br>12 June | 5 Ik 10 Ch'en<br>10.2.2.16.2<br>22 June | 2 Eb 0 Yax<br>10.2.2.16.12<br>2 July | 5 Men 3 Yax<br>10.2.2.16.15<br>5 July |
| 873 | 1 Cib 19 Yaxkin<br>10.2.3.14.16<br>22 May | 11 Cimi 9 Mol<br>10.2.3.15.6<br>1 June | 8 Cib 19 Mol<br>10.2.3.15.16<br>11 June | 5 Cimi 9 Ch'en<br>10.2.3.16.6<br>21 June | 2 Cib 19 Ch'en<br>10.2.3.16.16<br>1 July | 5 Cauac 2 Yax<br>10.2.3.16.19<br>4 July |
| 874 | 1 Ahau 18 Yaxkin<br>10.2.4.15.0<br>21 May | 11 Oc 8 Mol<br>10.2.4.15.10<br>31 May | 8 Ahau 18 Mol<br>10.2.4.16.0<br>10 June | 5 Oc 8 Ch'en<br>10.2.4.16.10<br>20 June | 2 Ahau 18 Ch'en<br>10.2.4.17.0<br>30 June | 5 Akbal 1 Yax<br>10.2.4.17.3<br>3 July |

"6" (one bar and one dot). The second distance number, the glyph for "20," appears directly under Chac's feet in the second picture. In the third picture, the glyph for "20" (under the sky band) has a coefficient of "19" (three bars and four dots above the *kin* glyph in the sky band). The glyphs for "20" and "6" form part of the footprint design in the fourth picture. The fifth picture shows Chac sitting on the roof of a house; the glyph for "20" with a coefficient of "19" appears in the house. And, finally, the glyphs for "20" and "6" appear above the foot of the seated Chac in the sixth picture.

The intervals given in the lower part of the almanac are, in order: 26, 20, 39, 26, 39, and 26. Twenty-six and 39 are whole multiples of 13; 20 is not, and we agree with previous scholars (e.g., Förstemann 1901:103; Thompson 1972:105) that it is an error. If it is corrected to 26 (the addition of a coefficient composed of one bar and one dot), the intervals sum to 182 days, which is equal to one-half the length of the seasonal table. This correction (which differs from those given by previous scholars) is supported by the solstitial iconography in the third picture and by the fact that the third and fourth pictures seem to correlate the summer solstice with the midpoint of the Maya solar year. The original full length of what is now the lower almanac must have been 1820 days (= 10 × 182 days or seven *tzolkin* cycles). This would have required a preface with two columns of *tzolkin* days instead of the single column appearing in the present version. Another seasonal almanac of 1820 days, based on 20 rows of 91 days, appears in the Madrid Codex, and the preface to it contains four columns of *tzolkin* days (Graff unpublished).

The intervals shown in the lower part of the almanac are several times larger than the ones appearing immediately below the captions. For example, the interval that brackets the sky band in the third picture is 39 days, whereas the interval above the picture is only 10 days. Similarly, the interval that is woven into the footprint design in the fourth picture is 26 days, whereas the interval associated with the caption is only 10 days.

There is a direct relationship between the length of these intervals and the period of time the almanac is relevant for correlating the summer solstice with the half-year. As explained above, the short intervals at the top of the page limit the almanac's utility to the years A.D. 869–71. The long intervals at the bottom of the page extend the almanac's useful life by almost 200 years, ranging from A.D. 681 to 879. Table 2.4 covers the last 9 years of that range using the lower set of distance numbers. The first four rows of Table 2.4 overlap the last four rows of Table 2.3. Note that A.D. 871, the last year when the upper set of distance numbers successfully targets a summer solstice associated with the third picture and a half-year with the fourth picture (Table 2.3), is also the first year when the lower set of distance numbers correlates the third picture with the summer solstice and the fourth picture with the half-year (Table 2.4). We suspect that the original version of the almanac contained only the lower set of distance numbers and that the upper set was added during the second half of the ninth century to focus on the period when the midpoint of the *haab* was closing in on the summer solstice.

It is clear from these examples that the ancient Maya made no effort to keep the *haab* from falling behind the tropical year by adding leap days at regular intervals. Instead, they marked the recession of the *haab* through the tropical year by recording the distance of the half-year from the summer solstice at different times, and, when necessary, they reversed the order of the pictures that referred to these events. The rain-making almanac and the seasonal almanac refer to the period before A.D. 918–21, when the summer solstice still preceded the half-year, and the lower half of the seasonal table refers to the period after those years, when the middle of the *haab* had begun to fall behind the summer solstice.

### PLANTING ALMANAC, PP. 15B–16B (A.D. 1170)

The first picture in the almanac in the middle of pp. 15 and 16 contains another example of Chac with his feet in the air (Figure 2.10). There are no footprints here to link the picture with the middle of the year. However, the column of glyphs that precedes the picture mentions only year-bearer days: 1 Ik, 1 Manik, 1 Eb, 1 Caban, and 1 Ik. These are all days that can co-occur with o Yax, the midpoint of the year. Furthermore, Chac is shown holding a maize plant in the first picture, and the clause above it refers explicitly to planting: *u-pak-ah tzen*, "he was planting food" (V. Bricker 1985). The other clauses in the almanac also refer to planting. The second upside-down figure is not Chac and therefore not a symbol of the middle of the year; it simply represents planting. The fourth collocation in the clause over the third picture is a phonetic spelling of *hinah*, "seed" (Lounsbury 1984:177), and the figure below it is holding a bowl of seeds.

The question is where, within the time period relevant to ancient Maya civilization, did the middle of the year coincide with the beginning of the planting season? The rainy season normally opens some time in May in the Yucatan peninsula and lasts through October (Page 1933:420–21). In Hocaba, Yucatan, two criteria are used in deciding when to begin planting. Some people wait until the first heavy rains have fallen, usually in the middle of May. Others prefer to begin planting just before the rains commence, usually in the last week of April. In either case, planting must be completed by the time the Pleiades reappear in the east shortly before

Table 2.4  Dates for Correlation of Summer Solstice and Half-Year Implied by the Lower Set of Distance Numbers in the Seasonal Almanac on Pages 40c–41c of the Dresden Codex

| Year (A.D.) | First picture | Second picture | Third picture | Fourth picture | Fifth picture | Sixth picture |
|---|---|---|---|---|---|---|
| 871 | 1 Cib 9 Zec 10.2.1.11.16 3 April | 1 Ik 15 Xul 10.2.1.13.2 29 April | 1 Lamat 1 Mol 10.2.1.14.8 25 May | 1 Manik 0 Yax 10.2.1.16.7 3 July | 1 Ben 6 Zac 10.2.1.17.13 29 July | 1 Eb 5 Mac 10.2.2.1.12 6 September |
| 872 | 1 Ahau 8 Zec 10.2.2.12.0 1 April | 1 Cimi 14 Xul 10.2.2.13.6 27 April | 1 Eb 0 Mol 10.2.2.14.12 23 May | 1 Chuen 19 Ch'en 10.2.2.16.11 1 July | 1 Caban 5 Zac 10.2.2.17.17 27 July | 1 Cib 4 Mac 10.2.3.1.16 4 September |
| 873 | 1 Kan 7 Zec 10.2.3.12.4 31 March | 1 Oc 13 Xul 10.2.3.13.10 26 April | 1 Cib 19 Yaxkin 10.2.3.14.16 22 May | 1 Men 18 Ch'en 10.2.3.16.15 30 June | 1 Imix 4 Zac 10.2.4.0.1 26 July | 1 Ahau 3 Mac 10.2.4.2.0 3 September |
| 874 | 1 Lamat 6 Zec 10.2.4.12.8 30 March | 1 Ix 12 Xul 10.2.4.13.14 25 April | 1 Ahau 18 Yaxkin 10.2.4.15.0 21 May | 1 Cauac 17 Ch'en 10.2.4.16.19 29 June | 1 Chicchan 3 Zac 10.2.5.0.5 25 July | 1 Kan 2 Mac 10.2.5.2.4 2 September |

| | | | | | |
|---|---|---|---|---|---|
| 875 | 1 Eb 5 Zec<br>10.2.5.12.12<br>29 March | 1 Edznab 11 Xul<br>10.2.5.13.18<br>24 April | 1 Kan 17 Yaxkin<br>10.2.5.15.4<br>20 May | 1 Akbal 16 Ch'en<br>10.2.5.17.3<br>28 June | 1 Muluc 2 Zac<br>10.2.6.0.9<br>24 July |
| | | | | | 1 Lamat 1 Mac<br>10.2.6.2.8<br>1 September |
| 876 | 1 Cib 4 Zec<br>10.2.6.12.16<br>27 March | 1 Ik 10 Xul<br>10.2.6.14.2<br>22 April | 1 Lamat 16 Yaxkin<br>10.2.6.15.8<br>18 May | 1 Manik 15 Ch'en<br>10.2.6.17.7<br>26 June | 1 Ben 1 Zac<br>10.2.7.0.13<br>22 July |
| | | | | | 1 Eb 0 Mac<br>10.2.7.2.12<br>30 August |
| 877 | 1 Ahau 3 Zec<br>10.2.7.13.0<br>26 March | 1 Cimi 9 Xul<br>10.2.7.14.6<br>21 April | 1 Eb 15 Yaxkin<br>10.2.7.15.12<br>17 May | 1 Chuen 14 Ch'en<br>10.2.7.17.11<br>25 June | 1 Caban 0 Zac<br>10.2.8.0.17<br>21 July |
| | | | | | 1 Cib 19 Ceh<br>10.2.8.2.16<br>29 August |
| 878 | 1 Kan 2 Zec<br>10.2.8.13.4<br>25 March | 1 Oc 8 Xul<br>10.2.8.14.10<br>20 April | 1 Cib 14 Yaxkin<br>10.2.8.15.16<br>16 May | 1 Men 13 Ch'en<br>10.2.8.17.15<br>24 June | 1 Imix 19 Yax<br>10.2.9.1.1<br>20 July |
| | | | | | 1 Ahau 18 Ceh<br>10.2.9.3.0<br>28 August |
| 879 | 1 Lamat 1 Zec<br>10.2.9.13.8<br>24 March | 1 Ix 7 Xul<br>10.2.9.14.14<br>19 April | 1 Ahau 13 Yaxkin<br>10.2.9.16.0<br>15 May | 1 Cauac 12 Ch'en<br>10.2.9.17.19<br>23 June | 1 Chicchan 18 Yax<br>10.2.10.1.5<br>19 July |
| | | | | | 1 Kan 17 Ceh<br>10.2.10.3.4<br>27 August |

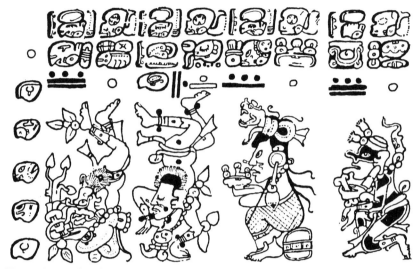

*Figure 2.10* The planting almanac on pp. 15b and 16b of the Dresden Codex (after Villacorta C. and Villacorta 1976:40, 42).

sunrise, after their period of invisibility (now around June 12). Otherwise, the seeds will be eaten by animals. This means that the 65-day period represented by the four clauses and pictures in the almanac must fall between the last week of April and the middle of June. The only year that meets these conditions is A.D. 1170, when the half-year, 1 Ik o Yax, coincided with 22 April. The fourth picture in the almanac corresponds to 13 June, which is at or near the date when the Maya try to finish planting and about 1 week before the summer solstice. Fifty-two years earlier, 1 Ik o Yax fell on 5 May 1118, and planting would have continued beyond the end of June. Fifty-two years later, 1 Ik o Yax occurred on 9 April 1222, well before it was feasible for planting to begin. Thus, although there is no explicit reference to the summer solstice in this almanac, it represents the *terminus ante quem* for the fourth planting clause and picture shown in the planting almanac.

### Relationship Between the Venus Table and Almanacs

The Venus table appears on pp. 24 and 46–50 of the Dresden Codex. It consists of two parts: (1) a preface, on pp. 24, with instructions for entering and recycling the table, and (2) the table proper on the remaining five pages. Each page of the table proper covers a period of 584 days, subdivided into smaller intervals of 236, 90, 250, and 8 days. 584 is the closest integral approximation of the mean length of a Venus synodical period, which is 583.92 days. Each row of the table correlates five Venus periods with eight *haabs* (= 2,920 days in both cases). The full length of the table is two calendar rounds (2 × 18,980 days = 37,960 days), equating 104 *haabs* with 65 Venus revolutions (Lounsbury 1983; Thompson 1972:62–64).

The *tzolkin* dates in each of the 13 rows on each page of the table (e.g., Figure 2.11a) refer to the four stations of Venus. The first column records days of last appearance as a morning star (mlast), the second and third columns deal with the first and last appearance as an evening star (efirst and elast, respectively), and the fourth column records the first appearance as a morning star (mfirst) (e.g., Figure 2.11). Only the value representing the disappearance interval before and after inferior conjunction corresponds to the true mean (8 days) (Aveni 1983); the others are canonical values for visibility as a morning star (236 days), invisibility before and after superior conjunction (90 days), and visibility as an evening star (250 days). The true means for these periods are 263 days, 50 days, and 263 days, respectively (Aveni 1980:89).

Sky bands are prominently displayed on four of the five pages of the Venus table. The uppermost picture on the first page of the table depicts a god seated on a double sky band containing two star glyphs (Figure 2.11a). The head of God K, who is shown as the patron for Eb years on the first page of the New Year's almanac on pp. 25–28, juts out from the left side of the sky bands (compare Figure 2.11a with Figure 2.12a). Floyd Lounsbury's (1983) date for entering that table, 10.5.6.4.0 1 Ahau 18 Kayab (23 November A.D. 934), leads to a date in row 1, column 3 of that page correlating three events of interest to the ancient Maya. The date in question is 10.5.7.14.16 5 Cib 4 Yax. It corresponds to 21 June A.D. 936 in the Gregorian calendar, which is the date of a summer solstice. It is also a date of Venus' last visibility as an evening star (Table 2.5). [Note that these events coincide only if one uses the 584,283 correlation constant that agrees best with historical sources. The 584,285 constant preferred by Lounsbury yields a date for that row and column 2 days after the summer solstice and after Venus has ceased to be visible as an evening star (Table 2.5).] The midpoint of the *haab* occurred 4 days earlier, on 1 Eb 0 Yax. This may be the reason why the patron associated with that year is shown peering out from the double sky band in the uppermost picture on that page (Figure 2.11a).

God K also appears in the picture at the bottom of the same page as the target of a dart hurled by the figure in the middle picture (Figure 2.11b and c). He is replaced by a jaguar in the corresponding picture on the next page of the table (Figure 2.13c). The second page of the New Year's almanac

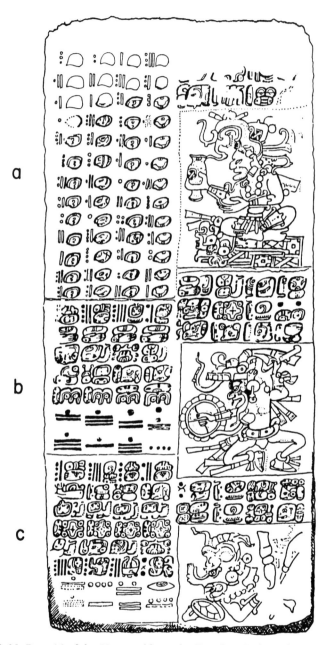

*Figure 2.11* Page 46 of the Venus table in the Dresden Codex (after Villacorta C. and Villacorta 1976:102).

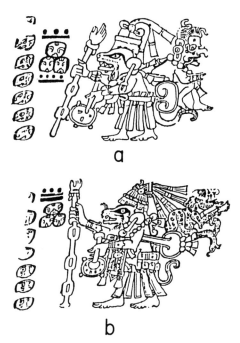

*Figure 2.12* The year bearers on pp. 25 and 26 of the New Year's Almanac in the Dresden Codex (after Villacorta C. and Villacorta 1976:60, 62). a. D. 25a. b. D. 26a.

depicts a jaguar as the patron of Caban years (compare Figures 2.12b and 2.13c), and A.D. 937, one of the years referred to on the second page of the Venus table, was a Caban year. The lower picture on the third page of the Venus table represents the maize god as the victim of the dart (Figure 2.14c); the maize god is shown as the patron of Ik years on the third page of the New Year's almanac (compare Figures 2.5a and 2.14c), and A.D. 938, one of the years implied by the third page of the Venus table, was an Ik year.

*Table 2.5* Positions of Venus and the Sun at the Moment of Sunset on 21 and 22 June A.D. 936 (Gregorian) in the Yucatan Peninsula (20°30′ North Latitude, 88°30′ West Longitude)

|  |  | Ecliptic longitude | Ecliptic latitude | Azimuth | Altitude |
|---|---|---|---|---|---|
| 21 June, 6:31 P.M. | Venus | 97.17° | −2.89° | 289.88° | 5.39° |
|  | Sun | 90.07° | 0.00° | 295.29° | −0.04° |
| 22 June, 6:32 P.M. | Venus | 96.58° | −3.12° | 290.30° | 3.67° |
|  | Sun | 91.03° | 0.00° | 295.36° | −0.21° |

*Source:* Kluepfel, 1986b.

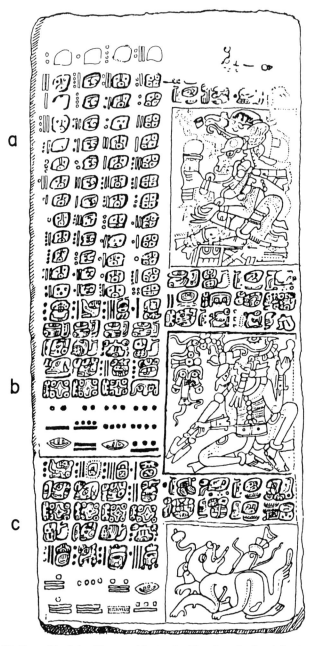

*Figure* 2.13 Page 47 of the Venus table in the Dresden Codex (after Villacorta C. and Villacorta 1976:104).

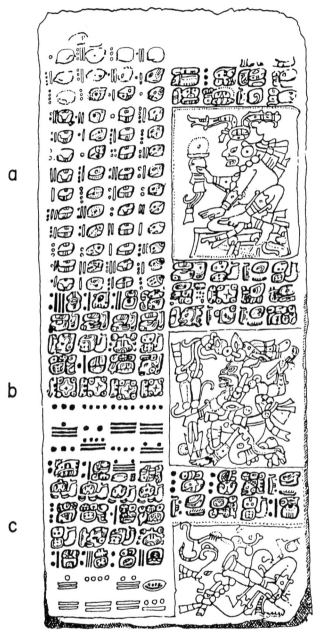

*Figure* 2.14 Page 48 of the Venus table in the Dresden Codex (after Villacorta C. and Villacorta 1976:106).

There is, then, a direct relationship between the order of pictures in the New Year's almanac on pp. 25–28 and the order of pictures at the bottom of the Venus table on pp. 46–48. The year bearer is the victim of the Venus warrior shown in the middle picture on each page.

The Venus table begins by correlating a date of heliacal rise after inferior conjunction with the *tzolkin* day, 1 Ahau. Two calendar rounds (= 104 years) must pass before 1 Ahau can coincide with the same station again. This is because the 584-day canonical value for the Venus period employed by the table is not an even multiple of the 260-day *tzolkin*, or of one of its factors, 13 or 20. The table emphasizes the relationship between Venus periods and the *haab* at the expense of the *tzolkin*.

### VENUS ALMANAC, PP. 30C–33C (A.D. 967)

The actual length of the Venus period varies between 579.6 and 588.1 days (Aveni 1980:324, n12). For some purposes, as in the Venus table, the ancient Maya found it convenient to use the 584-day value that approximates the mean. But for other purposes, a slightly higher value, 585 days, which also falls within the range of variation, was more useful because it is divisible by 13, and it is possible to correlate it with the *tzolkin* cycle in less than 7 years.

The almanac in the bottom register of pp. 30–33 covers a period of 2,340 days, which equates four Venus periods of 585 days with nine *tzolkin* cycles of 260 days (Figure 2.15). The preface to the almanac consists of four columns and five rows of glyphs. Each column has a bar-and-dot numeral at the top, which functions as the coefficient of the day glyphs below it. The almanac proper is divided into five rows of 117 days each, and the rows are further subdivided into nine 13-day intervals.

The almanac consists of nine pictures and captions (Figure 2.15). The middle picture on p. 32c contains the by now familiar scene of Chac sitting on a sky band, which we have shown is the Maya iconographic convention for the summer solstice. Here, as on the first page of the Venus table, the sky band contains a star glyph. The picture seems to be telling us that one of the *tzolkin* dates associated with it must correspond to the day of a summer solstice, when Venus or some other planet was visible.

Each picture in the almanac is associated with twenty possible *tzolkin* dates, corresponding to the twenty rows that are implied by the four columns of day glyphs in its preface. One of the *tzolkin* dates that refers explicitly to the solstitial picture on p. 32c is identical to the canonical elast date mentioned in the fifth row of the first page of the Venus table (Figure

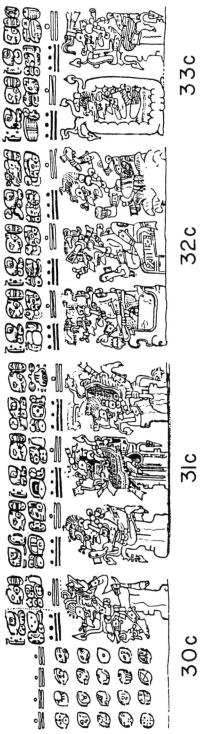

Figure 2.15 The Venus almanac on pp. 30c–33c of the Dresden Codex (after Villacorta C. and Villacorta 1976:70, 72, 74, 76).

71

*Table 2.6*   Positions of Venus and the Sun at the Moment of Sunset or Sunrise on 12, 21, and 22 June A.D. 968 (Gregorian) in the Yucatan Peninsula (20°30′ North Latitude, 88°30′ West Longitude)

|  |  | Ecliptic longitude | Ecliptic latitude | Azimuth | Altitude |
|---|---|---|---|---|---|
| 12 June, 6:30 P.M. | Venus | 88.47° | −1.70° | 291.32° | 5.49° |
|  | Sun | 81.76° | 0.00° | 295.12° | −0.29° |
| 21 June, 5:15 A.M. | Venus | 83.28° | −3.57° | 70.48° | 4.49° |
|  | Sun | 89.81° | 0.00° | 64.66° | −0.15° |
| 22 June, 5:15 A.M. | Venus | 82.69° | −3.76° | 71.20° | 5.82° |
|  | Sun | 90.76° | 0.00° | 64.65° | −0.20° |

*Source:* Kluepfel, 1986b.

2.11). That date is 11 Cib, and it appears in the fourth row of the almanac at hand (Figure 2.15). This calendrical link between the almanac and the Venus table makes it possible to correlate the almanac with the Western calendar and to explore its astronomical implications in real time.

The 11 Cib date in the fifth row of the Venus table corresponds to 13 June A.D. 968. Venus was last visible as an evening star on the previous day (Table 2.6, June 12). The summer solstice took place on 21 June, one day before Venus reappeared as a morning star (compare Table 6, June 21 and 22). The solstitial picture in the almanac suggests that the Maya astronomer had expected the solstice to coincide with the first appearance of Venus as a morning star (he was only 1 day off).

The interval associated with the solstitial picture is 13 days. Both the summer solstice and Venus' first predawn appearance after inferior conjunction occurred during that interval. The Venus table lists 6 Kan as the canonical date for mfirst in that year (the actual date was 1 day later, 7 Chicchan). If the prediction had been accurate, the summer solstice would have coincided with mfirst. The picture in the almanac is faithful to the canonical date for mfirst that is given in the Venus table. The interest in the year A.D. 968 may be a result of the fact that it is the only year during the time period covered by the Venus table when mfirst could have coincided with the summer solstice.

Thus it is possible to use a shared *tzolkin* date (11 Cib) and summer solstice iconography for cross-dating the Venus almanac with the Venus table in another part of the Codex. From it we can infer the beginning date of the almanac as 10.6.19.2.0 11 Ahau 13 Yaxkin (= 24 April A.D. 967). The almanac covers a 2,340-day period ending more than 6 years later on 18 September A.D. 973.

## Relationship Between the Eclipse Table and Almanacs

The eclipse table is spread across pp. 51–58 of the Dresden Codex. It, too, is composed of an introduction, followed by the table proper on pp. 52a–58b. The full length of the table is 11,960 days, subdivided into intervals of 178, 177, and 148 days. The table covers a period of 33 years, from 10 November A.D. 755 to 8 August A.D. 788, and it functions as a warning table for solar and lunar eclipses (H. Bricker and V. Bricker 1983).

The glyphs for solar and lunar eclipses were first identified in the context of this table. They also appear in the seasonal table on p. 66a and 68a (Figure 2.2) and the Mars table on p. 44b, where they were crucial for determining the entry dates for those tables (V. Bricker and H. Bricker 1986b, 1988).

### AGRICULTURAL ALMANAC, PP. 38B–41B (A.D. 775)

Other references to solar and lunar eclipses occur in the first and the last captions in the double *tzolkin* almanac of 520 days on pp. 38b–41b of the Codex. The 11 pictures on these pages are clearly concerned with agricultural subjects like rainfall, drought, and planting (Figure 2.16). The appearance of eclipse glyphs in an almanac 520 days in length implies that it is concerned with the correspondence between a double *tzolkin* and a triple eclipse half-year, as is the major eclipse table on pp. 51–58 (Teeple 1931:88–91; Aveni 1980:79). The eclipse half-year of 173.31 days is the periodicity of successive arrivals of the Sun (from the point of view of a terrestrial observer) at nodes of the orbit of the Moon; these nodes are the points of intersection between the ecliptic (the plane of the Earth's orbit around the Sun) and the plane of the Moon's orbit around the Earth (Aveni 1980:72–73). A node is the center of a given eclipse season, during which eclipses will occur if dates of new Moon (for solar eclipses) or full Moon (for lunar eclipses) fall close enough to the date of nodal passage—about 18 days for solar eclipses and about 12 days for lunar eclipses (Teeple 1931:90; Aveni 1980:77).

The agricultural almanac is divided into five periods of 104 days each. The caption over the first picture contains two eclipse glyphs, one for the Sun and the other for the Moon; the caption over the last picture mentions only a solar eclipse (Figure 2.16). If the eclipse glyphs over the first picture refer to an eclipse season centered close to day 1 of the 520-day period, the three subsequent eclipse seasons would be centered close to days 173, 347, and 520. On the other hand, the structure of the almanac is such that the

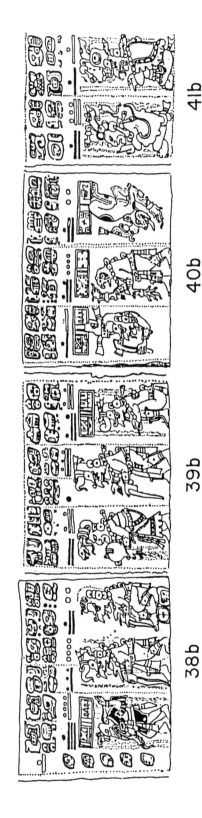

38b     39b     40b     41b

*Figure 2.16* The agricultural almanac on pp. 38b–41b of the Dresden Codex (after Villacorta C. and Villacorta 1976:86, 88, 90, 92).

eclipse glyph over the last column applies to short periods of time ending with days 104, 208, 312, 416, and 520. Because the only point of overlap between these two lists occurs at 520 days, the two eclipse seasons referred to by the almanac's captions are a full year and one-half (520 days) apart.

In order to place this almanac in real time, it is necessary to cross-date it with the eclipse table on pp. 51 to 58. The almanac begins on a day 6 Cauac. The *tzolkin* date, 6 Cauac, falls within the 30-day span of time referred to in Column 41 of the eclipse table, which begins on 6 May A.D. 775 and ends on 5 June. A solar eclipse is predicted for the first of these dates and a lunar eclipse for the midpoint of the period, 21 May. The 6 Cauac date itself falls on 20 May A.D. 775. Column 44 predicts a solar eclipse on 19 October A.D. 776, 518 days after 6 Cauac and 2 days before the 6 Cauac date that begins the next run of the almanac. This is the only set of dates in the version of the eclipse table that appears in the Dresden Codex that conforms to the conditions implied by the initial *tzolkin* date and the first and the last captions in the agricultural almanac.

Correlating the 6 Cauac date at the beginning of the almanac with 20 May 775 (= 9.17.4.6.19 6 Cauac 12 Xul) means that it coincides with the onset of the rainy season. The first picture on p. 38b depicts rain falling from a sky band onto an anthropomorphic vulture (Figure 2.16). The second picture on the same page shows the rain god Chac planting with a digging stick in the rain; Chac appears again with his digging stick in the third picture, this time without rain, walking on two glyphs, one representing the Earth. The first picture on p. 39b shows the rainbow goddess, Chac Chel, pouring water from a jug. Chac reappears in the second picture on the same page with his digging stick, but without rain; he is seated beneath a sky band from which rain is cascading in the third picture on that page. The first picture on p. 40b shows Chac hanging down from a sky band, wielding an axe. The caption above the picture states that Chac is in the sky. The second picture on that page depicts an anthropomorphized macaw brandishing two torches below a sky band. The caption above the picture refers to the macaw setting fires in heaven and ends with a *kin-tun-yabil* collocation, which signifies "drought" (Pérez 1866–77:177; Thompson 1960:269). In the third picture on the same page, a dog hangs down from a sky band holding a lighted torch. The rains reappear in the two pictures on p. 41b, signalling the end of the drought (Figure 2.16).

The pictures and several captions in the agricultural almanac seem to be describing meteorological events and agricultural activities that take place during the rainy season. What we are told is that the rains were late in A.D. 775, and planting continued until 5 July, a disastrously late date for completing planting according to modern ethnographic information. The first drought picture and caption occurred 12 days later, on 17 July. The dry spell continued for almost a month, finally breaking on 15 August. This unusual dryness is referred to as a drought by the *kin-tun-yabil* collocation at the end of the caption above the second picture on p. 40b (Figure 2.16). The pictures on p. 41b imply that once the rains had resumed, they continued for at least 17 more days, until 1 September (Figure 2.16).

There is, then, a close agreement between the date for the almanac implied by the eclipse glyphs associated with the first and last pictures and the agricultural activities represented by the remaining pictures. The almanac describes what happened during the planting season in A.D. 775, chronicling in graphic detail the drought that must have resulted in a poor harvest that year. Using the three kinds of information provided by the hieroglyphic text and the pictures—astronomical, seasonal, and cultural—it is possible to tie the almanac securely into the long count and the Gregorian calendar by cross-dating it with the eclipse table on pp. 51–58.


### BURNER ALMANAC, PP. 33C–39C (A.D. 1517)

References to eclipses appear also in the almanac at the bottom of pp. 33–39 (rearranged into rows and columns in Figure 2.17). It is the only almanac in the Codex that records *tzolkin* permutations in full form, followed by their own pictures and captions—for example, the date for the third picture in the first row is recorded as "7 Ahau," not just "7." Although the pictures in each row of a given column of the almanac have something in common, they are not identical. In particular, only the second picture in the third row of the almanac (Figure 2.17c) has clear parallels with the summer solstice picture in the seasonal table (Figure 2.4), in that Chac is shown seated on a sky band. The other pictures in that column portray Chac sitting on a sky glyph or the head of a bird, but not on a sky *band* (Figure 2.17a, b, and d). Similarly, depictions of eclipse glyphs suspended from sky bands are limited to the third and fourth rows of the third column of the almanac (Figure 2.17c and d). The third picture in the fourth row contains both solar and lunar eclipse glyphs, whereas the lunar eclipse glyph is missing from the third picture in the third row.

The four rows of the almanac begin with the *tzolkin* dates 13 Ahau, 13 Chicchan, 13 Oc, and 13 Men. We know from the colonial Books of Chilam Balam that Ahau, Chicchan, Oc, and Men belong to the "burner" set of days (Edmonson 1982:180; Long 1923). The *tzolkin* is divided into four "burner" periods of 65 days, which are further subdivided into three intervals of 20 days each and one of 5 days. The stations described in the colonial sources are the days when the Burner (*ah-toc*) takes the fire, lights

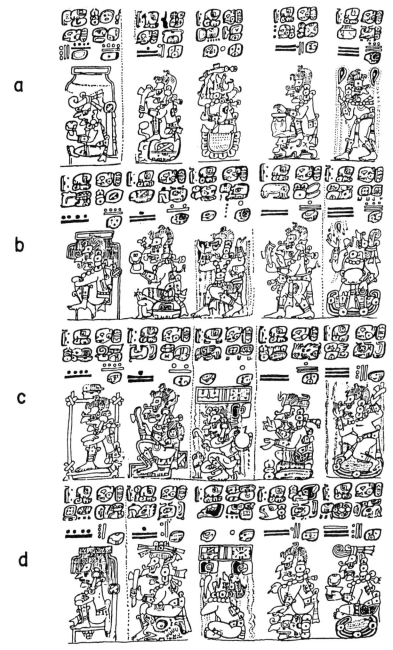

*Figure* 2.17 The burner almanac on pp. 33c–39c of the Dresden Codex (after Villacorta C. and Villacorta 1976:76, 78, 80, 82, 84, 86, 88).

the fire, names the fire, and extinguishes the fire (Long 1923). They correspond to the first, third, fourth, and fifth pictures in the burner almanac, respectively. The second picture in each row of the almanac is associated with dates that are *not* part of the burner series: 9 Muluc, 9 Ix, 9 Cauac, and 9 Kan. The picture that accompanies the 9 Cauac date in the third row, which portrays Chac seated on a sky band, suggests that it is concerned with an event in the tropical year.

Because the majority of dates in the almanac belong to the burner series, its principal function must be to determine when the different burner ceremonies were performed. On the other hand, the sky band and eclipse pictures imply that a secondary function of the almanac was to correlate burner stations with the summer solstice and eclipse seasons.

The eclipse pictures in the third and fourth rows of the almanac cannot refer to immediately successive eclipse seasons, because they are separated by only 65 days, which is not an eclipse interval. In order to approximate the periodicity of eclipse seasons implied by the pictures in the almanac, it is necessary to expand it by an additional 260 days, which suggests that it was intended to cover a double-*tzolkin* period of 520 days. On this assumption, the eclipse picture in the fourth row can be correlated with an eclipse season beginning two eclipse half-years ($2 \times 173.31$ days $= 346.62$ days) after the eclipse season implied by the eclipse picture in the third row.

Eclipse dates cluster in three restricted zones of a double *tzolkin* during any given period of several decades (Teeple 1931:90; H. Bricker and V. Bricker 1983). The *tzolkin* dates associated with the eclipse pictures in the third and fourth rows of the almanac are 7 Oc and 7 Men, respectively. Neither of these dates fell in one of these zones during the Classic period. 7 Oc entered one of the zones in A.D. 1085, but 7 Men did not fall within an eclipse zone until A.D. 1488. This means that the burner almanac became relevant for correlating the summer solstice with eclipse seasons only near the end of the fifteenth century.

The second picture in the third row of the almanac, which is associated with a day 9 Cauac, shows Chac sitting on a sky band (Figure 2.17c). The next picture in that row, which is associated with a day 7 Oc, 11 days after 9 Cauac, contains a sky band from which a solar eclipse glyph is suspended. Both types of eclipse glyphs appear in such pictures in other contexts (e.g., the upper half of p. 66 in Figure 2.2). The absence of a lunar eclipse glyph in this picture suggests that the date falls in the second half of an eclipse season, when only a solar eclipse could take place. The first year after A.D. 1488 that both satisfies this condition and correlates the second picture with a summer solstice is A.D. 1517. The summer solstice occurred on 22 June in that year, 3 days after the 9 Cauac date (11.14.17.5.2 12 Ik 5 Kayab) associated with the second picture. Seven days later, on 29 June (11.14.17.5.9 6 Muluc 12 Kayab), or one day before the 7 Oc date associated with the third picture, a solar eclipse took place, but was not visible in the Maya area (Kluepfel 1986a). This 1-day error in prediction falls within the 3-day error range permitted by the eclipse table on p. 51–58 of the same Codex (H. Bricker and V. Bricker 1983:6). No lunar eclipse occurred during the rest of that eclipse season. That must be why only a solar eclipse appears below the sky band in the second picture on that page (Figure 2.17c).

The eclipse picture in the fourth row of the almanac is associated with the date 11.14.18.3.15 7 Men 13 Muan (= 21 May A.D. 1518) (Figure 2.17d). A lunar eclipse occurred 13 days later on 3 June, which was well within the 20-day interval entailed by the black distance number above the picture. A solar eclipse took place on 18 June during the interval associated with the fourth picture in that row. Neither eclipse was visible in the Maya area (Kluepfel 1986a).

A double *tzolkin* is long enough to account for the two eclipse pictures in column 3 of the almanac, but not for three of the four pictures in column 2 (Figure 2.17). The dates in that column are the only nonburner dates in the almanac. One of them can be linked to the summer solstice in A.D. 1517, and it is reasonable to suppose that the remaining three dates refer to the other tropical year stations: the winter solstice and the vernal and autumnal equinoxes. Chac is shown sitting on either a sky band or a sky glyph in the first three pictures in column 2. The fourth picture in that column depicts him sitting on the head of a bird. That bird could be the so-called *cox* bird, which has been shown to correspond to the constellation Gemini in the zodiac almanac in the Paris Codex; Gemini was visible directly overhead on nights of the vernal equinox during the time period when the Maya codices were in use (V. Bricker and H. Bricker 1988:S38–S40). The date associated with that picture is therefore a likely candidate for the vernal equinox station of the tropical year.

That is, in fact, the case if the almanac is expanded to six *tzolkins* in length. In a sextuple almanac beginning on 11.14.16.16.0 13 Ahau 3 Yax (= 31 January A.D. 1517 Gregorian), the second picture in the first row targets the winter solstice of A.D. 1519, the corresponding picture in the second row targets the autumnal equinox of A.D. 1518, the corresponding picture in the third row targets the summer solstice of A.D. 1517, and the corresponding picture in the fourth row targets the vernal equinox of A.D. 1521 (Table 2.7 and Figure 2.17). The distance between the tropical year stations illustrated in the almanac is 15 months, or 1 ¼ tropical years. Of the 17 possible solstices or equinoxes that occur during the 1560 days of the

*Table* 2.7   Tropical Year Stations Mentioned in the Burner
Almanac on Pages 33c–39c

| Row | Calendar Round | Gregorian Date | Station |
|-----|----------------|----------------|---------|
| 1 | 9 Muluc 17 Yaxkin | 16 Dec 1519 | winter solstice |
| 2 | 1 Ix 7 Zip | 17 Sep 1518 | autumnal equinox |
| 3 | 9 Cauac 2 Kayab | 19 Jun 1517 | summer solstice |
| 4 | 9 Kan 7 Ceh | 15 Mar 1521 | vernal equinox |

almanac (= 6 × 260), these four are the only ones that can be correlated with the stations of the burner cycle and the eclipse seasons in the manner represented by the 20 pictures in the almanac. And because the total length of the almanac is equal to three double *tzolkins*, the eclipse pictures are just as relevant for the second and third double *tzolkins* as they were for the first.

Thus, in spite of the fact that this almanac contains four rows of *tzolkin* dates, pictures, and captions, it is no less abbreviated than other almanacs in the Dresden Codex. When fully expanded, the almanac would contain 24 rows of 65 days each, of which only four are actually shown. A 260-day almanac is sufficient for representing all the burner stations, but not for correlating them with eclipse seasons and the stations of the tropical year. The burner almanac provides just enough information for the reader to infer its true length of 1,560 days.

We are also now in a position to explain why the first picture in the third row is different from the other pictures in the same column (Figure 2.17). Lounsbury and Coe (1968) have pointed out that the cage-like structure in which Chac is sitting resembles a platform that is erected in the modern Maya community of Chamula in highland Chiapas each summer:

> One of the preliminaries to the celebration of the feast of San Juan involves the construction, in the yard outside the house of the alferez, of a scaffold supporting a small platform some 25 or 30 feet up in the air. The scaffold is made of four upright poles held together by cross-pieces at appropriate distances. The structure resembles a crude windmill frame. The platform on top is enclosed on three sides by bowed saplings. These are decorated with green foliage and flowers. A ladder leads from the ground to the platform. The whole thing is commonly called a *moch*, or *x-móch alperés*. As for specification of the particular kind of *moch* that this is, it is described as a *mochtée*. After the construction and decoration of this *mochtée*, on the first day of the feast—the day called 'flower-tying day' (*ta x-chuk nichim*) or the 'vesper' of the feast (*ta vixperéx*)—the alferez and his ayudantes [assistants] go to the church, get the banner of San Juan, and come on horseback to the house of the alferez. Here two ayudantes take the banner and climb up the ladder to the enclosed platform at the top of the *mochtée*, where they sit resting and drinking cane liquor.                                     Lounsbury and Coe, 1968, p. 276

Lounsbury and Coe go on to show that the glyph in the second row of the first column of the caption above the "cage" picture can be read as *ti moch-te* "on the platform" and that the caption refers explicitly to Chac sitting on it.

The people of Chamula celebrate the feast of San Juan on 24 June each year (Gossen 1974:223). The "vesper" of the feast is the preceding day, 23 June. It corresponds to St. John's Eve in the Christian calendar, which is a summer solstice festival in many parts of Europe. It is clear that the reason why the house is replaced by a "cage" in the first picture in the third row of the almanac is that the first station of the third quadrant of the burner cycle fell less than 2 weeks before the summer solstice in A.D. 1517, and the priests used the platform instead of a house or temple as the location for "taking" the fire.

There are, however, certain problems with the choice of A.D. 1517–21 as the date of the burner almanac. Not only is it the latest implied date in the Codex, but it is nearly 2 centuries later than the next most recent implied dates in the Codex (see below). On the other hand, there is the inescapable fact that the author of the almanac associated both 7 Oc and 7 Men with eclipse pictures, and that limits the date of the almanac to the period after A.D. 1488. If, for example, the intended period of use had been the thirteenth or fourteenth centuries, then the second eclipse picture should appear in the second row with the 7 Chicchan date (Figure 2.17), but it does not. It is, of course, possible that the scribe made an error, reversing the second and fourth pictures in column 3 of the almanac, but there is no additional internal evidence that would justify treating it as an error. The almanac as painted can only be dated to the years 1517–21. We will return to this question following a discussion of the age of the physical document.

## Conclusions

In this chapter we have employed iconographic parallels among six almanacs and three tables in the Dresden Codex to tie the almanacs into the long count and from there into the Gregorian calendar. The pictures used for this purpose refer to summer solstices, solar and lunar eclipses, the stations of the *haab* (its beginning, middle, and end), meteorological events (rain and drought), and agricultural activities (planting and pot irrigation). In most cases, the interaction of dates in the Maya *tzolkin* and *haab* with astronomical and seasonal events yielded unique Gregorian dates for the almanacs.

The results of the cross-dating, summarized in Table 2.8, show that the

*Table* 2.8   Chronological Relationship of Almanacs and Tables
in the Dresden Codex

| Year (A.D.) | Pages | Remarks |
|---|---|---|
| 755 | 51–58 | Eclipse table (H. Bricker and V. Bricker 1983) |
| 775 | 38b–41b | Agricultural almanac (V. Bricker and H. Bricker 1986a) |
| 818 | 43b–45b | Mars table (V. Bricker and H. Bricker 1986b) |
| 869 | 40c–41c | Seasonal almanac (V. Bricker and H. Bricker 1988) |
| 899 | 29b–30b | Rain-making almanac (V. Bricker 1991; V. Bricker and H. Bricker 1988) |
| 934 | 24, 46–50 | Venus table (Lounsbury 1983) |
| 950 | 65b–69b | Seasonal table (V. Bricker and H. Bricker 1988) |
| 967 | 30c–33c | Venus almanac (V. Bricker 1988b) |
| 1170 | 15b–16b | Planting almanac (V. Bricker 1985) |
| 1517 | 33c–39c | Burner almanac |

Dresden Codex is a collection of tables and almanacs that were composed at different times over a period of many centuries. In some of the almanacs and tables, the pictures became obsolete after just a few years. For example, the rain-making almanac in the middle of pp. 29 and 30 successfully correlated the midpoint of the *haab* with the summer solstice only between A.D. 899 and 902. Similarly, the half-year and summer solstice pictures in the seasonal table drift apart by 1.2422 days every *haab*, and they are both relevant only for the year A.D. 950. This means that the apparent redundancy of themes in the almanacs represents periodic efforts to update their contents and that the many almanacs in the Codex were not intended to be used concurrently. On the other hand, the four tables listed in Table 2.8 contain internal evidence that they could be reused at later dates, even though the pictures might not be relevant. For example, the Venus table contains an explicit reference to a later entry date, on 10.15.4.2.0 1 Ahau 18 Uo (= 11 December A.D. 1129), in the preface to the table proper (Closs 1977). The years referred to in the first row of *tzolkin* dates on pp. 46–48 do *not* agree with the patrons of the year shown as victims of darts at the bottom of those pages. Similarly, the agricultural almanac in the middle of pp. 38–41 could have been reused in A.D. 906 with no loss of fit between the dates and the pictures (V. Bricker and H. Bricker 1986a).

The centuries recorded in Table 2.8 represent most of the Classic and post-Classic periods of Maya archaeology—the "historical" epoch of the pre-Columbian Maya. The tables in the Dresden Codex, by their use of ring numbers and other devices, project statements about gods and planets far back into mythic time before the historical epoch (D. Tedlock, Chapter 10 of this volume). So the Dresden Codex purports to offer a record not merely of centuries, but of millennia, revised and recopied many times. The manuscript acquired by the Royal Library of Dresden in 1739 is the latest surviving link in a long chain, updated and copied not long before the Spanish Conquest.

Exactly when the Dresden Codex was painted is not known. Several kinds of data are relevant to the determination of the age of the physical document itself. One important source of information is internal evidence about revising the dated astronomical tables for later reuse. For example, the latest base date actually appearing in the Venus table, 1 Ahau 3 Xul, corresponds to a Gregorian date in A.D. 1324 (Thompson 1972:63; Lounsbury 1983:18); because the length of the Venus table is about 104 years, this means that the latest explicitly indicated use period of the table extends from the early fourteenth to the early fifteenth centuries A.D. For the eclipse table, we have presented evidence previously (H. Bricker and V. Bricker 1983:18) that the treatment of the table's 16th, 17th, and 18th multiples suggests that the existing version of the table was painted for use between about A.D. 1266 and A.D. 1375. Evidence from late multiples of the Mars table, on pp. 43b–45b of the Dresden Codex, is ambiguous, suggesting either ca. A.D. 1250 or A.D. 1350 as the period for which the current version of the table was constructed (V. Bricker and H. Bricker 1986b:78–79). Finally, a carefully corrected 1504th multiple of the seasonal table strongly indicates a period of contemporary use beginning in A.D. 1333 (V. Bricker and H. Bricker 1988:559).

Another important source of information about the age of the Dresden Codex comes from a comparison of ceramic vessels and other objects pictured in the Codex with actual items recovered archaeologically from dated contexts. In a recent study, Paxton (1986:229) confirmed earlier work (Thompson 1972:15) that the ceramic ties are generally with the Late post-Classic (A.D. 1200 to the Spanish Conquest) but concluded that the closest specific iconographic resemblances are with materials assigned by archaeologists to the late or Tases phase as known from Mayapan, which is conventionally dated A.D. 1300–1450. In fact, however, the terminal date of A.D. 1450 cannot be taken literally; uncertainty about the pace of changes in material culture in the very late post-Classic means that objects like those cited by Paxton may have continued to have been made until A.D. 1500 or even somewhat later (E. W. Andrews V, personal communication).

These different kinds of information about the age of the Dresden Codex have a bearing on our cross-dating of the burner almanac on pp. 33c–39c. It is perfectly possible that the Codex was painted in the early sixteenth century, shortly before the period during which the burner almanac would have been useful (A.D. 1517–21). It is, however, at least as likely that it was painted in the fourteenth century, as is indicated by the preponderance of the evidence from the dated astronomical tables. If this is true, the undeniably sixteenth-century dating of the burner almanac could be the result of scribal error, or it could be a version corrected long in advance of the need, for reasons not known to us. (Such a precocious correction, while unlikely, is not impossible; the 31st multiple of the eclipse table includes a correction to reverse cumulative error and restore the table to accuracy in the *eighteenth* century A.D.!)

Finally, it is instructive to compare, once again, the relationship between almanacs and tables in the Dresden Codex with the relationship between the two types of dated monuments found at Classic period sites. It was not necessary to expend the space needed to carve initial series dates on every stone monument at a site, because monuments with only calendar-round permutations could usually be cross-dated with those having full long-count dates. The Codex resembles the corpus of inscriptions at a site in that it contains a mixture of texts with full and abbreviated calendrical notations that can be cross-dated with each other. This is possible only because the almanacs and tables in question, like the inscriptions on stone monuments, refer to events that actually took place. They differ primarily in the types of events recorded and the purposes they served. The texts on stone monuments were intended to glorify the rulers of sites, focusing on births, marriages, accessions, military exploits, and deaths. The almanacs and tables in the Dresden Codex were used by Maya priests and astronomers to predict solar and lunar eclipses and the movements of other heavenly bodies, to determine when crops should be planted and harvested, and to schedule several kinds of rituals, including ceremonies for ensuring sufficient rainfall and others for celebrating the stations of the *tzolkin* and the *haab*. In both cases, the end result was a record of events that can be tied into the Gregorian calendar.

The method of cross-dating employed in this paper is a kind of "triangulation." Information from at least three different kinds of cycles are necessary in order to determine a unique date for an almanac. The first cycle is always the 260-day *tzolkin*, and the second is usually the 365-day *haab*. The third cycle must be astronomical—most often the tropical year or the eclipse half-year. Thus astronomy is of crucial importance for determining the meaning and function of almanacs in the Dresden Codex.

### ACKNOWLEDGMENT

We are grateful to Munro S. Edmonson for his helpful comments on earlier versions of this chapter.

### REFERENCES

Aveni, A. F., 1980. *Skywatchers of Ancient Mexico* (Austin: University of Texas Press).

—, 1983. "The Moon and the Venus Table: An Example of Commensuration in the Maya Calendar." A paper presented at the First International Conference on Ethnoastronomy: Indigenous Astronomical and Cosmological Traditions of the World, (Washington, D.C.: Smithsonian Institution, September 5–9).

Bricker, H. M., and V. R. Bricker, 1983. "Classic Maya Prediction of Solar Eclipses," *Current Anthropology* **24**(1):1–23.

Bricker, V. R., 1985. "Noun Incorporation in the Dresden Codex," *Anthropological Linguistics* **27**(4):413–23.

—, 1986. *A Grammar of Mayan Hieroglyphs.* Tulane University Middle American Research Institute Publication 56 (New Orleans).

—, 1988a. "Astronomical Syntax in the Dresden Codex," *Journal of Mayan Linguistics* **6**:55–78.

—, 1988b. "The Relationship Between the Venus Table and an Almanac in the Dresden Codex," in *New Directions in American Archaeoastronomy*, edited by Anthony F. Aveni, pp. 81–103 Oxford, England: BAR International Series 454.

—, 1991. "Faunal Offerings in the Dresden Codex," in *Sixth Palenque Roundtable, 1986*, edited by Merle Greene Robertson and Virginia M. Fields, pp. 285–92. Norman: University of Oklahoma Press.

Bricker, V. R., and H. M. Bricker, 1986a. "Archaeoastronomical Implications of an Agricultural Almanac in the Dresden Codex," *Mexicon* **8**:29–35.

—, 1986b. "The Mars Table in the Dresden Codex," in *Research and Reflections in Archaeology and History: Essays in Honor of Doris Stone*, edited by E. Wyllys Andrews V, pp. 51–80. Tulane University Middle American Research Institute Publication 57 (New Orleans).

—, 1988. "The Seasonal Table in the Dresden Codex and Related Almanacs," *Archaeoastronomy* (Supplement to the *Journal for the History of Astronomy* 19) **12**:S1–S62.

Closs, M. P., 1977. "The Date-Reaching Mechanism in the Venus Table of the Dresden Codex," in *Native American Astronomy*, edited by Anthony F. Aveni, pp. 89–99. (Austin: University of Texas Press).

—, 1983. "Comment on Harvey M. Bricker and Victoria R. Bricker, 'Classic Maya Prediction of Solar Eclipses,'" *Current Anthropology* **24**:19.

Edmonson, M. S., 1982. *The Ancient Future of the Itza: The Book of Chilam Balam of Tizimin.* (Austin: University of Texas Press).

—, 1986. *Heaven Born Merida and its Destiny: The Book of Chilam Balam of Chumayel* (Austin: University of Texas Press).

Förstemann, E. W., 1901. *Commentar zur Mayahandschrift der Königlichen öffentlichen Bibliothek zu Dresden* (Dresden: Verlag von Richard Bertling).

Gossen, G. H., 1974. *Chamulas in the World of the Sun: Time and Space in a Maya Oral Tradition* (Cambridge, Mass.: Harvard University Press).

Graff, D. H., unpublished. "Dating a Section of the Madrid Codex: Astronomical and Iconographic Evidence," in *Papers on the Madrid Codex*, edited by Victoria R. Bricker and Gabrielle Vail.

Graham, I., and E. von Euw, 1977. *Corpus of Maya Hieroglyphic Inscriptions. Volume 3, Part 1: Yaxchilan.* (Cambridge, Mass.: Peabody Museum, Harvard University).

Kluepfel, C., 1986a. *Moon & Sun* (an astronomical software package available from its author).

—, 1986b. *Planets* (an astronomical software package available from its author).

Long, R. C. E., 1923. "The Burner Period of the Mayas," *Man* 108:173–76.

Lounsbury, F. G., 1983. "The Base of the Venus Table of the Dresden Codex, and its Significance for the Calendar-Correlation Problem," in *Calendars in Mesoamerica and Peru: Native American Computations of Time*, edited by Anthony F. Aveni and Gordon Brotherston, pp. 1–26. BAR International Series 174.

—, 1984. "Glyphic Substitutions: Homophonic and Synonymic," in *Phoneticism in Mayan Hieroglyphic Writing*, edited by John S. Justeson and Lyle Campbell, pp. 167–84. Institute for Mesoamerican Studies, State University of New York at Albany 9.

Lounsbury, F. G., and M. D. Coe, 1968. "Linguistic and Ethnographic Data Pertinent to the 'Cage' Glyph of Dresden 36c," *Estudios de Cultura Maya* 7:269–84.

Maudslay, A. P., 1889–1902. *Biologia Centrali-Americana: Archaeology.* 5 vols. (1, text; 4, plates). (London: R. H. Porter and Dulau).

Morley, S. G., 1920. *The Inscriptions at Copan.* Carnegie Institution of Washington Publication 219 (Washington D.C.).

Page, J. L., 1933. "The Climate in the Yucatan Peninsula," in *The Peninsula of Yucatan: Medical, Biological, Meteorological and Sociological Studies*, edited by George Cheever Shattuck, pp. 409–22. Carnegie Institution of Washington Publication 431 (Washington D.C.).

Paxton, M. 1986. *Codex Dresden: Stylistic and Iconographic Analysis of a Maya Manuscript.* Ph.D. Dissertation (University of New Mexico).

Pérez, J. P., 1866–77. *Diccionario de la Lengua Maya.* (Mérida: Imprenta Literaria de Juan F. Molina Solís).

Schele, L., 1982. *Maya Glyphs: The Verbs.* (Austin: University of Texas Press).

Teeple, J. E., 1931. *Maya Astronomy.* Carnegie Institution of Washington, *Contributions to American Archaeology* 1:29–115 (Washington D.C.).

Thompson, J. E. S., 1960. *Maya Hieroglyphic Writing: An Introduction.* (Norman: University of Oklahoma Press).

—, 1972. *A Commentary on the Dresden Codex.* Memoirs of the American Philosophical Society 93 (Philadelphia).

Villacorta, C., J. Antonio, and C. A. Villacorta, 1976. *Códices Mayas*, 2nd ed. (Guatemala: Tipografía Nacional).

# 3

# The Moon and the Venus Table: an Example of Commensuration in the Maya Calendar

## ANTHONY F. AVENI

The Maya written calendar is a model of commensuration.[1] Its interlocking component cycles are meted against one another in precise integral ratios.

The Dresden Codex, one of four written Maya documents that survived the conquest, provides concrete evidence of the dominant theme of cyclicity in Mayan calendrics. A complete course through the Venus table on pp. 46–50 of this text neatly encapsulates whole numbers of Venus cycles, *haab* and *tzolkin*; its arrangement is geared to guarantee that the celebratory date of the morning heliacal rise of the planet following inferior conjunction shall always be the day 1 Ahau. Selected pages of the table are shown in Figures 2.11, 2.13, and 2.14.

It was typical of the Maya to impress cycles of as many celestial bodies as possible into a given time-reckoning scheme,[2] and we can be sure that the process of discovery of the relevant celestial periods and the development of a methodology for expressing the beat of the celestial harmony they perceived must have occupied the attention of Mayan astronomers during much of the pre-Classic and Early Classic periods.

The process of seeking periodic relationships among various celestial bodies is typical among cultures that sought to build a secure timekeeping mechanism so that sets of events associated with one celestial object, say the setting positions of the sun, could be employed as a check upon another (e.g., the arrival of the first crescent moon in the west after sunset). The correlation of an event of the first kind with one of the second would assure the architects of the calendar that when one phenomenon was obscured from view, a point in time still could be determined from an observation of the other. In a sense one event would speak for another, and, if neither was found to occur, then perhaps a third event might be discovered that would fill the role of marking time.

Given the power accorded commensuration in Maya calendrics, it is no surprise that events associated with one astronomical body might appear hidden away in an ephemeris that describes the motion of a completely different object. As Smiley (1973) pointed out, the three sets of calendar-round base dates running the length of lines 14, 20, and 25 of the Venus table are separated by intervals divisible almost exactly by "eclipse cycles," which may be defined as integral or half-integral multiples of both the lunar synodic and draconitic months. Thus:

Interval from line 14 to line 20—11960 days
    $= 405 \text{ LSM} + 0.1 \text{ days}$
    $= 439.5 \text{ LDM}^3 + 0.2 \text{ days}$
    $=$ length of the Eclipse table
       (pp. 51–58 of Dresden);

Interval from line 20 to line 25—9360 days
    $= 317 \text{ LSM} - 1.2 \text{ days}$
    $= 344 \text{ LDM} - 1.0 \text{ days}.$

The appearance of such numbers of lunar significance in a Venus ephemeris also may reflect the Maya astronomers' attempts to express the occurrence of lunar events in Venus time units, a habit that might seem strange to Western astronomers.

Unfortunately, having occupied himself with the task of validating his own correlation between the Maya and Christian calendars, Smiley neither developed a mechanism to explain to which lunar events the Maya might have been referring nor demonstrated how the Venus table could have functioned in practice as an eclipse predictor. Moreover, he failed to point out that several other examples of lunar–Venusian commensurabilities also reside in the pages of the Venus table.

While it is well known that Venus phenomena repeat in a seasonal cycle of 8 years, a fact clearly revealed in the basic format of the Venus table, it also should be noted that the same phenomena, taken over the same period, harmonize with the lunar measure of time. Thus, the length of one line of the Venus table:

$$2920 \text{ days} = 8.0 \text{ TY} - 1.9 \text{ days}$$
$$= 99 \text{ LSM} - 3.5 \text{ days}$$
$$= 5 \text{ VR} + 0.4 \text{ days}$$
$$= 5 \text{ VP.}[4]$$

We note that the Venus events fall back by about 4 days every 99 full moons. After 32 years, these phenomena will have shifted halfway through the lunar cycle, and, if we double this interval, they will have shifted all the way through the cycle.

There are other facts about the components and arrangement of the Venus table that further implicate the moon. The four Venus intervals repeated across line 26, which are known to be only approximations to the actual intervals of appearance and disappearance of the planet that were deliberately distorted to correspond to ritual dictates (see Gibbs 1977, especially pp. 30–35), also are approximate integral–half-integral LSM:

| (Col. A) | 236 days | = | 8.0 LSM − 0.24 days | Morning star apparition interval |
|---|---|---|---|---|
| (Col. B) | 90 days[5] | = | 3.0 LSM + 1.41 days | Disappearance interval after morning star |
| (Col. C) | 250 days | = | 8.5 LSM − 1.25 days | Evening star apparition interval |

Finally, one counts the final 8-day interval that returns Venus to morning heliacal rise. This is the only one of the four periods that closely approximates the true mean (determined in this paper to be 8.0 ± 0.3 days, p.e.). In practice this means that if, for example, a first quarter moon attends the morning heliacal rise of Venus, its phase would be the same on the last day that the morning star Venus is seen in the east. When Venus reappears as the evening star in the west, the moon will be in the opposite phase (last quarter).

One also can find among the cumulatives listed in line 19, near whole and half-integral multiples of the LDM. Such a selection and arrangement of intervals redoubles the utilitarian empirical nature of the table, for it makes it possible to know not only the lunar phase associated with a given position of Venus in its cycle, but also the likelihood that an eclipse would have occurred at the new or full moon nearest that phase.

Other lunar associations in the main body of the table include the lunar Goddess I, who appears in the top picture of p. 49 of Thompson (1972, p. 68). She emerges from a large moon sign and holds a conch-shell cup that may symbolize her birth. Her name glyph is indicated above (49E;3,4). Other lunar referents appear on p. 24, the introductory page of the Venus table. Parts of the glyphs at positions A11 and B4 contain the lunar postfix (T181), and the B6 compound incorporates the young moon goddess. While these may have functioned solely as grammatical elements, they also could have served as puns employing a lunar metaphor.

The lunar indication is far less subtle if we look at the numbers printed on p. 24. (See Figure 7.1 in Lounsbury's paper, this volume, Ch. 7). The ring number 6.2.0 (Col. A), when added to the long count (LC) date 9.9.9.16.0 (Col. C), produces the number 9.9.16.0.0 (Col. B), itself a half-integral multiple of the LSM:

$$6.2.0 - 220 \text{ days} = 74.5 \text{ LSM} - 0.03 \text{ days}.$$

Moreover, this interval is one-half of the Copan lunar count, in which lunar synodic cycles were grouped in units of 149 (79 of 30-day duration coupled with 70 of 29-day length over a 4,400-day period.) The arrangement results in a time-averaged LSM of mean length 29.530201 days.[6] The ring number, then, may have been one outcome of the attempt to align lunar phases temporarily with stations of the Venus cycle. The so-called Palenque lunar count of 405 lunations = 11,960 days, which is even more accurate than that of Copan, is also the same as the length of the Eclipse table.

Students of the codices need not be reminded that the Eclipse table immediately follows and is attached to the Venus table. Moreover, these juxtaposed tables also are related numerically:

one great cycle (GC) = 37960 days = $3 \times 11960 + 8 \times 260$ days.[7]

To summarize to this point: A set of coincidences can be found in a single Maya ephemeris between the basic periods associated with two primary celestial bodies—Venus and the moon. Such a discovery arouses suspicion that a formal mechanism might have existed by which the Maya kept track of lunar eclipse events within the reference frame of the Venus calendar. But what possible mechanisms are there, and how might they have functioned? My attempts to seek solutions to this problem were stimulated by the work of Lounsbury (1983), who offered a plausible scheme for the placement of the Venus table in the context of real time.

Before developing a hypothetical mechanism, it is necessary to review briefly Lounsbury's procedure. Essentially, he was able to resolve the discrepancy between the adoption of the Modified Thompson (584285) Correlation and the assignment of the starting LC date of the Venus table to 9.9.9.16.0[8] by showing that exactly three great cycles after this date (3 × length of the Venus table), or on 10.5.6.4.0 = 20 November A.D. 934, a Venus morning heliacal rise event occurred precisely on the acknowledged 1 Ahau 18 Kayab date.[9] This remarkable coincidence, a "unique event in historical time," as he calls it,[10] led Lounsbury to suggest that the Maya Venus table was instituted historically on the latter date. Lounsbury posited that up to that time the Maya simply had used the straight 584-day tally for the VP, not yet having discovered the shortfall between the VR and the VP of 0.08 per VP. Since the Dresden document itself dates from about 2 centuries later than the cycle-10 date and is undoubtedly a copy of a revised edition of an older ephemeris, one can imagine the problem the astronomers had been confronting for so long as they attempted to devise a reliable methodology for anticipating the all-important reappearance of Venus in the eastern predawn sky after its brief absence from view around inferior conjunction. According to Lounsbury's account, the astronomers did not recognize the need to shift bases (i.e., drop a number of days owing to the shortfall) to keep the 1 Ahau starting date in step with the real Venus events. He suggests that it was not until a full GC had elapsed since the table was instituted that Maya astronomers finally applied the first in a sequence of correction schemes.

The scenario Lounsbury lays out is satisfying because of the way it relates historical and astronomical reality.[11] If we adopt 10.5.6.4.0 1 Ahau 18 Kayab as the starting date, we find that the standard correction scheme results in three more base shifts (1 Ahau 18 Uo, 1129 December 6; 1 Ahau 13 Mac, 15 June 1227; and 1 Ahau 3 Xul, 22 December 1324), each of which brings the table almost precisely back into line with the actual occurrence of the Venus events that it allegedly was designed to commemorate. In the first base shift, a double correction of 8 days is exacted, thus reducing the tabular error from 9.4 to within 1.4 days of astronomical reality. In the second base shift a single 4-day correction is called for; this reduces the error from 6.2 to 2.2 days, and on the third occasion a 7.2-day error is reduced to 3.2 days. By this time, 4 centuries after the table had been instituted (well into the post-Classic period), the Maya evidently lost the desire to revise the table further to accommodate the ever-present, though somewhat retarded, drift.

If the Maya were interested in giving an account of lunar events in the Venus table, one way of doing so might be to incorporate within it those eclipses occurring close to the time of Venus heliacal rise events. This hypothesis suggests that one ought to search out lunar eclipses that were visible in the Yucatan peninsula in the vicinity of the tabulated base dates. Thus, I consulted Oppolzer's (1962 [1887]) tables for both lunar and solar eclipses immediately preceding and following the LC base dates of heliacal risings of Venus tabulated by Lounsbury. While I found none of the latter type, a surprising number of the former turned up. Table 3.1 is a chronological listing of the base dates A–H (in the notation of Lounsbury), in addition to the six base dates positioned at integral multiples of one GC before the first written base date.

As Table 3.1 shows, a lunar eclipse was visible on the lunar phase cycle (reckoned from the first visible crescent) immediately preceding each of the first six bases. This includes the first three base dates (A, B, and C) before the Venus correction proposed by Lounsbury was devised, an interval during which, we are led to assume, a Venus–eclipse correlation already had been recognized. For the fourth base (date D), when the table was instituted, as well as the fifth and sixth (dates E and F), one also finds an associated eclipse. Furthermore, in the last case the association could not have been recognized had the correction advocated by Lounsbury not been assessed. Finally, for the last two base dates (G and H), no association between a lunar eclipse and a heliacal rise of Venus occurs. This absence may be attributed to the decline of Maya interest in precise astronomy that also accounts for the concomitant failure of the table to anticipate Venus events. On the contrary, of the six base dates immediately preceding the table, only one is associated with a lunar eclipse.

In Table 3.2 the details of the suggested associations between Venus and the moon are examined. To determine precisely when Venus appeared or disappeared in Yucatan, one must utilize reliable values for the *arcus visionis*.[12] Schoch's limit of 5.2° for disappearance in the west and 5.7° for reappearance in the east, each derived from Babylonian observational data, were used in the present study. The actual last and first appearance dates for Venus in the vicinity of each of the base dates A through H were calculated for an assumed latitude of 20°N. The last five Venus apparitions leading up to each of the base dates are tabulated. These are the obvious dates to consider, for they fall in that time period during which the Maya most likely would have confronted the decision about whether they needed to make a correction on the next run of the table.

Quite aside from the Venus–lunar association problem, some interesting astronomical data not generally recognized in Maya studies emanated from this exercise and are worth reporting here:

1. Venus does not disappear for 8 days. The mean of the shorter disappearance intervals of Venus from 40 calculations (Column 9 of Table

Table 3.1 Lunar Eclipses Associated with Base Dates in the Venus Table

| LC date predicting inferior conjunction of venus (Lounsbury 1983) | Base date in calendar round[a] | L = visible lunar eclipse during previous lunar synodic cycle | Comments |
|---|---|---|---|
| 7.17.17. 4.0 | — | — | Six great cycles before date A |
| 8. 2. 3.12.0 | — | — | Five great cycles before date A |
| 8. 8. 8. 2.0 | — | L | Four great cycles before date A |
| 8.13.13.10.0 | — | — | Three great cycles before date A |
| 8.18.18.18.0 | — | — | Two great cycles before date A |
| 9. 4. 4. 8.0 | — | — | One great cycle before date A |
| A. 9. 9. 9.16.0 | 1 Ahau 18 Kayab | | Earliest prediction in Venus table |
| B. 9.14.15. 6.0 | 1 Ahau 18 Kayab | | |
| C. 10. 0. 0.14.0 | 1 Ahau 18 Kyab | | |
| D. 10. 5. 6. 4.0 | 1 Ahau 18 Kayab | | Historical institution of table in present form (Lounsbury 1983) |
| E. 10.10.11.12.0 | 1 Ahau 18 Kayab | | |
| F. 10.15. 4. 2.0 | 1 Ahau 18 Uo | | Base shift; no eclipse without base shift |
| G. 11. 0. 3. 1.0 | 1 Ahau 13 Mac | — | Base shift; no eclipse without base shift |
| H. 11. 5. 2. 0.0 | 1 Ahau 3 Xul | — | Base shift; no eclipse without base shift |

[a]Only dates A–H are recorded in the table.

Table 3.2  Venus and Eclipse Phenomena: Prediction by the Table versus Actual Results

| LC date[a] | A.D.[b] | Visible lunar eclipse[c] | Canonic disappearance[d] | Canonic reappearance[e] | Actual disappearance[f] | Actual reappearance[g] | Period of invisibility[h] | Error Col. 5–Col. 7[i] | Col. 6–Col. 3[i] |
|---|---|---|---|---|---|---|---|---|---|
| 9. 9. 3. 7. 4 | 616 | | 6 SEP | 14 SEP | 15 SEP | 27 SEP | 12 | −13 | |
| 9. 9. 5. 0. 8 | 618 | | 13 APR | 21 APR | 30 APR | 8 MAY | 8 | −17 | |
| 9. 9. 6.11.12 | 619 | | 18 NOV | 26 NOV | 2 DEC | 11 DEC | 9 | −15 | |
| 9. 9. 8. 4.16 | 621 | | 24 JUN | 2 JUL | 5 JUL | 17 JUL | 12 | −15 | |
| 9. 9. 9.16. 0 | A 623 | 22 JAN | 29 JAN | 6 FEB | 17 FEB | 20 FEB | 3 | −14 | 16 |
| | | | | | | | AVG. 8.8 | (−14.8) | |
| 9.14. 8.15. 4 | 720 | | 11 AUG | 19 AUG | 14 AUG | 26 AUG | 12 | −7 | |
| 9.14.10. 8. 8 | 722 | 7 MAR | 18 MAR | 26 MAR | 31 MAR | 5 APR | 5 | −10 | 24 |
| 9.14.12. 1.12 | 723 | | 23 OCT | 31 OCT | 31 OCT | 9 NOV | 9 | −9 | |
| 9.14.13.12.16 | 725 | | 29 MAY | 6 JUN | 8 JUN | 14 JUN | 6 | −8 | |
| 9.14.15. 6. 0 | B 726 | 13 DEC | 3 JAN | 11 JAN | 17 JAN | 20 JAN | 3 | −9 | 35 |
| | | | | | | | AVG. 7.0 | (−8.6) | |
| 9.19.14. 5. 4 | 824 | | 16 JUL | 24 JUL | 13 JUL | 28 JUL | 15 | −4 | |
| 9.19.15.16. 8 | 826 | | 20 FEB | 28 FEB | 27 FEB | 3 MAR | 4 | −3 | |
| 9.19.17. 9.12 | 827 | | 27 SEP | 5 OCT | 26 SEP | 8 OCT | 12 | −3 | |
| 9.19.19. 2.16 | 829 | | 3 MAY | 11 MAY | 10 MAY | 16 MAY | 6 | −5 | |
| 10. 0. 0.14. 0 | C 830 | 3 NOV | 8 DEC | 16 DEC | 15 DEC | 21 DEC | 6 | −5 | 42 |
| | | | | | | | AVG. 8.6 | (−4.0) | |
| 10. 4.19.13. 4 | 928 | | 20 JUN | 28 JUN | 19 JUN | 28 JUN | 9 | 0 | |
| 10. 5. 1. 6. 8 | 930 | 17 JAN | 25 JAN | 2 FEB | 29 JAN | 31 JAN | 2 | +2 | 12 |
| 10. 5. 2.17.12 | 931 | | 1 SEP | 9 SEP | 24 AUG | 6 SEP | 13 | +3 | |

| | | | | | | | | | |
|---|---|---|---|---|---|---|---|---|---|
| 10. 5. 4.10.16 | 933 | | 7 APR | 15 APR | 9 APR | 15 APR | 6 | 0 | |
| 10. 5. 6. 4. 0 | D 934 | 25 OCT | 12 NOV | 20 NOV | 11 NOV | 19 NOV | 8 | +1 | **17** |
| | | | | | | AVG. | 7.6 | (+1.2) | |

Calendar instituted

| | | | | | | | | | |
|---|---|---|---|---|---|---|---|---|---|
| 10.10. 5. 3. 4 | 1032 | | 25 MAY | 2 JUN | 20 MAY | 29 MAY | 9 | +4 | |
| 10.10. 6.14. 8 | 1033 | 8 DEC | 30 DEC | 7 JAN | 28 DEC | 1 JAN | 4 | +6 | 20 |
| 10.10. 8. 7.12 | 1035 | | 6 AUG | 14 AUG | 26 JUL | 7 AUG | 12 | +7 | |
| 10.10.10. 0.16 | 1037 | | 12 MAR | 20 MAR | 7 MAR | 13 MAR | 6 | +7 | |
| 10.10.11.12. 0 | E 1038 | 16 SEP | 17 OCT | 25 OCT | 6 OCT | 18 OCT | 12 | +7 | **20** |
| | | | | | | AVG. | 8.6 | (+6.2) | |
| 10.14.17.11. 4 | 1123 | | 7 JUL | 15 JUL | 2 JUL | 9 JUL | 7 | +6 | |
| 10.14.19. 4. 8 | 1125 | 21 JAN | 10 FEB | 18 FEB | 11 FEB | 15 FEB | 4 | +3 | 21 |
| 10.15. 0.15.12 | 1126 | | 17 SEP | 25 SEP | 8 SEP | 21 SEP | 13 | +4 | |
| 10.15. 2. 8.16 | 1128 | | 23 APR | 1 MAY | 23 APR | 30 APR | 7 | +1 | |
| 10.15. 4. 2. 0 | F 1129 | 29 OCT | 28 NOV | 6 DEC | 29 NOV | 4 DEC | 5 | +2 | **31** |
| | | | | | | AVG. | 6.8 | (+3.2) | |

First correction instituted between
E and F

| | | | | | | | | | |
|---|---|---|---|---|---|---|---|---|---|
| 10.19.16.10. 4 | 1121 | | 13 JAN | 21 JAN | 13 JAN | 19 JAN | 6 | +2 | |
| 10.19.18. 3. 8 | 1222 | | 20 AUG | 28 AUG | 10 AUG | 24 AUG | 14 | +4 | |
| 10.19.19.14.12 | 1224 | | 26 MAR | 3 APR | 25 MAR | 30 MAR | 5 | +4 | |
| 11. 0. 1. 7.16 | 1225 | | 31 OCT | 8 NOV | 27 OCT | 4 NOV | 8 | +4 | |
| 11. 0. 3. 1. 0 | G 1227 | — | 7 JUN | 15 JUN | 4 JUN | 13 JUN | 9 | +2 | |
| | | | | | | AVG. | 8.4 | (+3.2) | |

*(continued)*

Table 3.2  Venus and Eclipse Phenomena: Prediction by the Table versus Actual Results (*Continued*)

| LC date[a] | A.D.[b] | Visible lunar eclipse[c] | Canonic disappearance[d] | Canonic reappearance[e] | Actual disappearance[f] | Actual reappearance[g] | Period of invisibility[h] | Error Col. 5–Col. 7[i] | Col. 6–Col. 3[j] |
|---|---|---|---|---|---|---|---|---|---|
| Second correction instituted between F and G | | | | | | | | | |
| 11. 4.15. 9. 4 | 1318 | | 23 JUL | 31 JUL | 18 JUL | 28 JUL | 10 | +3 | |
| 11. 4.17. 2. 8 | 1320 | 26 JAN | 26 FEB | 6 MAR | 26 FEB | 1 MAR | 3 | +5 | 31 |
| 11. 4.18. 3.12 | 1321 | | 30 OCT | 11 OCT | 23 SEP | 5 OCT | 12 | +6 | |
| 11. 5. 0. 6.16 | 1323 | | 10 MAY | 18 MAY | 8 MAY | 15 MAY | 7 | +3 | |
| 11. 5. 2. 0. 0 | H 1324 | — | 14 DEC | 22 DEC | 12 DEC | 19 DEC | 7 | +3 | |
| | | | | | | AVG. | 7.8 | (+4.0) | |
| Third correction instituted between G and H | | | | | | | | | |
| 10.15.17. 2. 0 | F' 1142 | — | 25 SEP | 3 OCT | 3 SEP | 15 SEP | 12 | +18 | |
| 11. 1. 2.10. 0 | G' 1246 | — | 30 AUG | 7 SEP | 4 AUG | 17 AUG | 13 | +21 | |
| 11. 6. 8. 0. 0 | H' 1350 | — | 4 AUG | 12 AUG | 7 JUL | 19 JUL | 12 | +24 | |

[a] The LC dates of the reappearance of Venus as predicted by the Venus table. The base dates are labeled A–H. Entries F', G', H' are those that would result had no correction been applied.

[b] The date A.D. in the Christian calendar.

[c] The Christian date of the last visible lunar eclipse preceding the Venus canonic disappearance date.

[d] Canonic disappearance expressed in the Christian calendar.

[e] Canonic reappearance expressed in the Christian calendar.

[f] Actual disappearance date of Venus as calculated. Late limit assumes clear skies.

[g] Actual reappearance date of Venus, also calculated. Early limit assumes clear skies.

[h] The difference of Col. g and Col. e, or the actual disappearance interval. Means of groups of five also are tallied.

[i] The difference of Col. e and Col. g, or the error of the prediction, which expresses the number of days by which the table anticipates reality. Means of groups of five also are tabulated.

[j] The difference of Col. f and Col. c, or the longest possible interval between the occurrence of a visible lunar eclipse and the actual disappearance of Venus following. Bold face indicates eclipse was likely linked to Venus disappearance.

3.2) is 8.0 ± 0.3 days (probable error), the shortest interval being 3 days and the longest 16 days.[13]

2. A seasonal rhythm to these disappearance intervals exists. As Figure 3.1 shows, the shortest intervals around inferior conjunction are confined to late January and early February, when, in this latitude, the ecliptic lies nearly in the vertical relative to the western horizon after sunset. The greatest delay in reappearance occurs during the late July–early August period, when the ecliptic is at its shallowest incline relative to the western horizon at twilight. One factor that controls the length of the disappearance period is the celestial latitude of Venus at the time of disappearance or reappearance, which can be as large as 9°.

The latter result offers an observable seasonal correlate for Venus references to rain and maize planting that appear in Mayan texts and iconography (see, e.g., Closs, Aveni, and Crowley 1984).

Column j of Table 3.2 tabulates the interval between the last visible lunar eclipse and the latest actual disappearance of the planet in the west. The latter event associated with this time difference is rather fundamental because it could be used to interpret, given the season of the year, how much time would need to pass before Venus arrived at its visible morning heliacal rise station, which the table is fundamentally geared to anticipate (Column e). This event is found *always to take place after the beginning but before the termination of the next lunar cycle* (i.e., between 15 and 45 days after the visible eclipsed full moon). To illustrate, in the vicinity of base date A (6 Feb 623), a lunar eclipse was visible in Yucatan on 22 Jan (Col. c). Not more than 16 days later, or 1 day into the cycle of the next moon, Venus disappeared (Col. f). Typical for a February disappearance, the planet was absent from view for at least 3 days (Col. h),[14] returning to

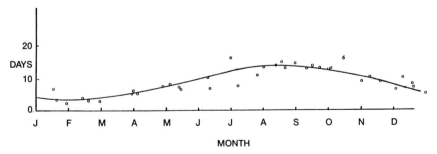

*Figure 3.1* Venus disappearance interval at inferior conjunction.

view on 20 Feb (Col. g). The reappearance date anticipated by the table was
6 Feb (Col. e), or 14 days before the event. For Lounsbury's base date B
(canonic heliacal rise 11 Jan 727) the visible lunar eclipse of 13 Dec
preceded the last disappearance of Venus in the west after sunset on the
evening of 17 Jan, 20 days into the next lunar synodic month. The reappearance, again hastened, occurred on 20 Jan, 9 days after the tabular
date.[15]

For each succeeding base date, the apparition of Venus and the eclipse
attending it experience a 1-month fallback per GC, receding from mid-
February to mid-January, etc., through to mid-October as the table progresses from bases A to E. The institution of the correction scheme after
date E results in a shift that not only shortens the disappearance interval
associated with the new base (cf. F', G', H',[16] with F, G, H entries of
Table 3.2), but also picks up an eclipse for the terminal base date after the
first correction, which an uncorrected version of the table fails to do (cf. F
and F' entries). A shorter interval, one that reduces the anticipation of the
recurrence of the heliacal rising of Venus, might have been deemed desir-
able by the Maya to reckon with. In any event the Maya calendar keepers
made their corrections, and, as has been demonstrated, the capacity of the
table to match eclipse phenomena with the stations of Venus also began to
weaken as the post-Classic period advanced, and with it Maya acuity in
astronomical matters became dulled.

In sum, Maya calendar keepers were attracted to formalizing their
timekeeping according to principles of commensuration. The distortion of
real events to fit the ritual calendar is well documented in Mayan culture,
but, as we have seen, real astronomical observing lies at the base of their
calendar; however, the basic astronomy one needs to learn to penetrate the
Maya scientific mentality does not necessarily consist of the phenomena
perceived by people of Western culture. For example, who could have
imagined the Maya would concoct 236/250/90-day intervals for Venus? I
believe they did it because they thought the significance of Venus omens
could not be discussed without reference to the moon. While we would
scarcely think of dreaming up a principle that associates morning and
evening stars with lunar phasing and lunar eclipses, such a concept appears
to have been an integral part of Maya calendrical common sense.

ACKNOWLEDGMENT

I am indebted to V. Bricker, W. Lamb, I. Sprajc, and M. Paxton for their comments on an earlier draft of this chapter.

NOTES

1. For two excellent reviews of the contents of Maya calendars, see (Closs 1989; Justeson 1989). A summary of Maya calendrics at a more elementary level is given in Aveni (1980).

2. Though they will not be dealt with in this paper, cycles that are concerned with nonastronomical phenomena were also a vital component of Maya ephemerides. Maya astrologers devoted a good deal of attention to synthesizing periods of astronomical and numerological significance to form great periods as long as several centuries. In this regard, see McCluskey (1983).

3. One lunar synodic month = 29.530589 days, hereinafter LSM; one lunar draconitic month = 27.212220 days, hereinafter LDM.

4. VR, hereinafter one true Venus revolution = one Venus synodic period = 583.92 days (average of 5 cycles). This should be distinguished from VP, the canonic Venus period, which is reckoned in the table as 584 days. TY = tropical year = 365.2422 days.

5. 89 days would have been a more accurate choice; likewise 251 days would have been better for the entry in Column C; however, neither of these accommodates the appropriate celebratory set of dates in the *tzolkin*. On the lunar coincidence, see also Justeson (1989, p. 94).

6. Lounsbury (1978) (see especially p. 775). Like many of the numbers the Maya tabulated, 2200 also refers to another period, as Thompson (*op. cit.* 1972, p. 62) pointed out; namely 4 VP + 4 days − 140 days, or 4 days fewer than the distance forward from 4 Ahau to 1 Ahau (i.e., 2340 days less 140), which *tzolkin* entries appear below the ring number. D. Dütting's (1984) recent work also discloses the intermingling of lunar and Venus numbers in the Dresden Codex.

7. While this chapter has focuses solely upon the incorporation of lunar matters in the Venus table, it is worth mentioning that the inverse problem ought to be worthy of some future attention. References to Venus in the Eclipse table are somewhat more tenuous save for one very obvious example. The 10th picture, p. 58b, shows a human figure of which the head is completely replaced by a Venus glyph. "The figure dives downward from a celestial band, his feet touching sun and moon signs enclosed in affix 326 (Thompson 1972, p. 77). His glyphs are rendered adjacent to the figure, though Thompson prefers to assign only a general stellar association to them, suggesting that they represent the stars that become visible during a solar eclipse. On the other hand, the author believes it is more likely that this table is concerned with lunar rather than solar eclipses (Aveni 1983). Venus references also occur adjacent to pictures 5 and 9, but no Venus cycles or parts thereof have been recognized among the intervals over which the Venus glyph is represented in the lunar tables.

8. The discrepancy results from the fact that the date (6 February A.D. 623) occurs 17 days before a Venus heliacal rise.

9. Lounsbury gave only an approximation to the heliacal rise date by adding 4 days to the date of inferior conjunction, without consideration of the *arcus visionis* (see Note 12). However, his results are completely validated in the present chapter.

10. Lounsbury *op. cit.* 1983, p. 9. The correction discussed by Thompson (*op. cit.* 1972, pp. 62–63, which is accepted by most Mayan scholars, is adopted in the present chapter. It consists of a program that calls for truncating runs through the table at certain stated points shortly before completion of a GC, deleting either 4 or 8 days, and then returning to the beginning of the table. A completely different type of correction scheme that transcends the notion of base shifting has been offered by Closs (1977). After my data were assembled, V. Bricker (personal communication) kindly pointed out that the mean error in our Table 3.2 between the canonical and actual reappearance is reduced (from 4.1 to 2.1 days) if one uses the 584283 rather than the 584285 correlation constant. She favors the former constant because it correlates better with the astronomical data in other instances. She also demonstrated, to my satisfaction, that the argument given in the present chapter for correlating visible lunar eclipses with Venus heliacal rise events works for Closs's entry date to the table as well as Lounsbury's.

11. In fact the whole problem resembles that that long confronted Western timekeepers and ultimately resulted in the Julian and Gregorian calendar reforms. In each instance a base date shift was accompanied by the development of a scheme designed to reduce further the drift between canonic and real time (see Aveni, 1987).

12. The *arcus visionis* is defined as the altitude of the sun below the astronomical horizon when Venus is barely visible on that horizon. For a full discussion of the problem see Huber (1977).

13. Sometimes the limits may be even greater than this. In January 1982 the author observed, in latitude 15°S, the first appearance of Venus as morning star on the day *prior* to last disappearance as evening star. T. Settle (1976) has suggested Renaissance astronomers in northern Italy (latitude 40°N) had done the same, though telescopically. Thus Venus can be evening and morning star on the same day.

14. Note that the calculated disappearance and reappearance times must be regarded as the latest and earliest, respectively, because we assume excellent observing conditions on every night of the year.

15. Lunar eclipses also precede a few other dates in the table. In the other five instances that appear in Table 3.2, the third date before the concluding base date is found to be preceded by an eclipse. In all but one of these cases, the rule that the Venus apparition occurs during the next lunar phase cycle is obeyed. Whether this less firm correlation between Venus and lunar events also was recognized by the Maya seems more doubtful. A systematic study of the entire table for other possible associated eclipse–Venus dates should be conducted.

16. The primed entries correspond to what the base dates would have been in the absence of Lounsbury's correction program.

REFERENCES

Aveni, A., 1980. *Skywatchers of Ancient Mexico* (Austin: Univ. Texas Press).
Aveni, A., 1983. "Comment on V. Bricker and H. Bricker, 'Classic Maya Prediction of Solar Eclipses,'" *Current Anthropology* **24**:1–23.

Aveni, A., 1987. "Some Parallels in the Development of Maya and Roman Calendars," *Interciencia* **12**(3):108–116.

Closs, M., 1977. "The Date-Reaching Mechanism in the Venus Table of the Dresden Codex," in *Native American Astronomy*, edited by A. Aveni, pp. 89–99 (Austin: University of Texas Press).

Closs, M., 1989. "Cognitive Aspects of Mayan Eclipse Theory," in *World Archaeoastronomy*, edited by A. Aveni, pp. 389–415 (Cambridge, CUP).

Closs, M., A. Aveni, and B. Crowley, 1984. "The Planet Venus & Temple 22 at Copan," *Indiana* **9**:221–47.

Dütting, D., 1984. "Venus, the Moon and the Gods of the Palenque Triad," Z. *für Ethnologie* **109**:7–74.

Gibbs, S., 1977. "Mesoamerican Calendrics as Evidence of Astronomical Activity," in *Native American Astronomy*, edited by A. Aveni, pp. 21–36 (Austin: University of Texas Press).

Huber, P., 1977. "Early Cuneiform Evidence for the Existence of the Planet Venus," in *Scientists Confront Velikovsky*, edited by D. Goldsmith, pp. 21–36 (Ithaca: Cornell University Press).

Justeson, J., 1989. "Ancient Maya Astronomy: An Overview of Hieroglyphic Sources," in *World Archaeoastronomy*, edited by A. Aveni, pp. 76–129 (Cambridge: CUP).

Lounsbury, F., 1978. "Maya Numeration, Computation, and Calendrical Astronomy," in *Dictionary of Scientific Biography*, Vol. 15, pp. 759–818 (N.Y.: C. Scribner and Sons).

Lounsbury, F., 1983. "The Base of the Venus Table of the Dresden Codex and its Significance for the Calendar-Correlation Problem," in *Calendars in Mesoamerica and Peru: Native American Computations of Time*, edited by A. Aveni and G. Brotherston, British Archaeol. Reports, International Series No. 174, pp. 1–26.

McCluskey, S., 1983. "Maya Observations of Very Long Periods of Venus," *Jour. for the Hist. of Astr.* **14**:92–101.

Oppolzer, T. von, 1962 (1887). *Canon der Finsternisse (Canon of Eclipses)*, trans. O. Gingerich (N.Y.: Dover).

Settle, T., 1976. "Giovanni Alfonso Borelli e la Visibilitá di Venere," *Ann. dell'Istituto e Museo di Storia della Scienza di Firenze*, Facs. 2, pp. 37–56.

Smiley, C., 1973. "The Thix and the Fox, Mayan Solar Eclipse Intervals," *Royal Astr. Soc. Jour.* **76**(4):175–82.

Teeple, J., 1930. "Maya Astronomy" *CIW* I(1):*Contr. to Am. Arch.*, 29–115.

Thompson, J. E. S., 1962. A Catalog of Maya Hieroglyphic Writing (Norman: University of Oklahoma Press).

Thompson, J. E. S., 1971. *Maya Hieroglyphic Writing* (Norman: University of Oklahoma Press).

Thompson, J. E. S., 1972. *A Commentary on the Dresden Codex, A Maya Hieroglyphic Book*. (Philadelphia: Am. Phil. Soc.).

# 4

# Eclipse Cycles in the Moon Goddess Almanacs in the Dresden Codex

## CHARLES A. HOFLING
## THOMAS O'NEIL

In his 1972 commentary on the Dresden Codex, J. Eric S. Thompson devotes considerable attention to a group of almanacs appearing on pp. 16–23 of the Codex, which he calls the Moon Goddess almanacs. These almanacs are dominated by portraits of a female figure now identified as the Moon Goddess, Ix Chel, who is also consistently named in the glyphic text appearing above the portraits (Hofling 1989; Figure 4.1). Thompson (1972:72) also identifies a portrait of a hanging woman in the eclipse table as a variant of the Moon Goddess named Ix Tab, "She of the Cord" (Figure 4.2), an interpretation supported by Kelley (1980:S37–38). In this chapter we hope to demonstrate that there are calendric as well as iconographic connections between the Moon Goddess almanacs and the eclipse table, and that these almanacs also reflect eclipse cycles. The eclipse cycles embedded in the calendrical information in these almanacs provide structural underpinnings for interalmanac relations. Astronomical cycles thus function as a cohesive device linking Moon Goddess almanacs to one another.[1]

## The Eclipse Table

The eclipse table appears on pp. 51–58 of the Dresden Codex. In this table, series of intervals of 177 or 178 days (approximately 6 lunations) and intervals of 148 days (approximately 5 lunations) appear between pictures with prominent eclipse iconography. A total of 11959 days, a period of 405 lunations or nearly 46 × 260 days, are recorded (Thompson 1972:72–73; see Table 4.1), reflecting a typical Maya concern for commensurating different astronomical and ritual cycles (Teeple 1931; Lounsbury 1978; H. Bricker and V. Bricker 1983; Aveni 1980 and Chapter 3, this volume; Justeson 1989). Several base dates, separated by 15 days, enable the table to be used successfully to predict both lunar and solar eclipses (H. Bricker and V. Bricker 1983; Aveni 1980) The first three base dates are:

| | | |
|---|---|---|
| Base A: | 9.16.4.10.8 | 12 Lamat (1 Muan) |
| Base B: | 9.16.4.11.3 | 1 Akbal (16 Muan) |
| Base C: | 9.16.4.11.18 | 3 Etz'nab (11 Pax) |

Bases A and C predict solar eclipses, while Base B predicts lunar eclipses. The eclipse table also allows 1 day's leeway on either side of a target date. Its utility for predicting both lunar and solar eclipses is indicated in Table 4.1, which compares predicted eclipse dates with dates on which eclipses actually occurred somewhere in the world according to Oppolzer's *Canon of Eclipses* (1887).

The pictures in the eclipse table include representations of the Sun God, a death god, Venus, and the goddess Ix Tab, who is portrayed hanging from a sky band in the lower section of p. 53 (Figure 4.2). The goddess, with her eye closed, is marked by black spots on her cheek and nipple, iconography associated with death and eclipses (Closs 1989). In Yucatec Maya, the eclipsed body (sun or moon) is said to have its eye extinguished or blinded (Barrera Vasquez 1980:824), echoing the closed-eyed portraits of the Moon Goddess in the Dresden Codex.

## Moon Goddess Almanac Structure

The pages on which the Moon Goddess almanacs appear (pp. 16–23) are uniformly divided into three horizontal sections, labeled a, b, and c, from top to bottom respectively. Throughout the discussion of the Moon Goddess almanacs, the reader is encouraged to refer to the illustration in Figure 4.1. These almanacs, like almanacs in other sections of the Codex, usually entail 260-day cycles of the sacred calendar or *tzolkin*.[2] Almanacs begin with a column of day signs, often with a numeral coefficient above, and vertical intra-almanac sections are separated by calendric intervals or distance numbers (Figure 4.1).

For example, Almanac 48 begins at the bottom of p. 17 (pp. 17c–18c;

Almanac 33 (5 × 52 days)

| kan | +21= chi | +31= cib |
|-----|----------|----------|
| cib | cab | lam |
| lam | mul | aha |
| ahau | imi | eb |
| eb | ben | kan |

Almanac 34

| men |
|-----|
| cib |
| cab |
| etz |
| cau |

Almanac 39 (5 × 52 days)

| mul | +13= ik | +4= cim |
|-----|---------|---------|
| imi | ix | etz |
| ben | cim | oc |
| chi | etz | ik |
| cab | oc | ix |

Almanac 47 (4 × 65 days; intervals uncertain)

| mul | +8= cab | +13= oc | +13= akb |
|-----|---------|---------|----------|
| ix | ik | men | lam |
| cau | man | aha | ben |
| kan | eb | chi | etz |

Figure 4.1 Moon Goddess almanacs on pp. 16–23 of the Dresden Codex (after Anders 1975).

**Almanac 34 cont.**

| aha | chi | oc |
|-----|-----|-----|
| imi | cim | chu |
| ik | man | eb |
| akb | lam | ben |
| kan | mul | ix |

**Almanac 39 cont.**

| +20= cim | +15= imi |
|----------|----------|
| etz | ben |
| oc | chi |
| ik | cab |
| ix | mul |

**Almanac 40 (5 × 52 days)**

| eb | +11= akb | +7= oc | +6= cib |
|-----|----------|--------|---------|
| kan | men | ik | lam |
| cib | man | ix | aha |
| lam | cau | cim | eb |
| aha | chu | etz | kan |

**Almanac 47 cont.**

| +13= cib | +8= kan | +10= ix |
|----------|---------|---------|
| imi | mul | cau |
| cim | ix | kan |
| chu | cau | mul |

**Almanac 48 (5 × 52)**

| 4aha | +15 = 6men |
|------|------------|
| eb | man |
| kan | cau |
| cib | chu |
| lam | akb |

*Figure 4.1 (Continued)*

Almanac 35 (5 × 52 days)

| 8ik | +12= 7ix | +12 = 6cim | +9= 2men |
|---|---|---|---|
| ix | cim | etz | man |
| cim | etz | oc | cau |
| etz | oc | ik | chu |
| oc | ik | ix | akb |

Almanac 40 cont.

| +16= eb | +8= aha | +4= kan |
|---|---|---|
| kan | eb | cib |
| cib | kan | lam |
| lam | cib | aha |
| aha | lam | eb |

Almanac 48 cont.

| +33= 13lam | +4= 4eb |
|---|---|
| aha | kan |
| eb | cib |
| kan | lam |
| cib | aha |

Almanac 49 (5 × 52 days)

| 13aha | +32= 6eb |
|---|---|
| eb | kan |
| kan | cib |
| cib | lam |
| lam | aha |

Figure 4.1 (Continued)

| Almanac 35 cont. | | Almanac 36 (4 × 65 days) | |
|---|---|---|---|
| +10= 12chi | +9= 8ix | 11aha | +13= 11ben |
| cab | cim | chi | etz |
| mul | etz | ok | akb |
| imi | oc | men | lam |
| ben | ik | | |

| Almanac 41 (5 × 52 days) | | | Almanac 42 (5 × 52) | |
|---|---|---|---|---|
| 10ik | +29= 13chu | +23= 10ix | 6cib | +28= 8kan |
| ix | akb | cim | lam | cib |
| cim | men | etz | aha | lam |
| etz | man | oc | eb | aha |
| oc | cau | ik | kan | eb |

| Almanac 49 cont. | Almanac 50 (5 × 52 days) | | |
|---|---|---|---|
| +20= 13eb | 13aha | +11= 11chu | +11= 9ik |
| kan | eb | akb | ix |
| cib | kan | men | cim |
| lam | cib | man | etz |
| aha | lam | cau | oc |

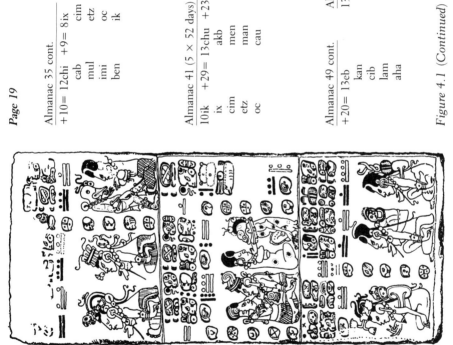

*Figure 4.1 (Continued)*

Almanac 36 cont.

| +13= 11cim | +13 = 11cau | +13= 11eb |
|---|---|---|
| chu | kan | cab |
| cib | mul | ik |
| imi | ix | man |

Almanac 43 (5 × 52 days)

Alm. 42 cont.

| +24= 6lam | 2cau | +20= 9cau | +19= 2etz | +13= 2chu |
|---|---|---|---|---|
| aha | chu | chu | oc | akb |
| eb | akb | akb | ik | men |
| kan | men | men | ix | man |
| cib | man | man | cim | cau |

Almanac 50 cont.

| +11= 7ben | +10= 4akb | +9= 13eb |
|---|---|---|
| chi | men | kan |
| cab | man | cib |
| mul | cau | lam |
| imi | chu | aha |

Figure 4.1 (Continued)

**Almanac 36 cont.**

| +13= 11chi |
| --- |
| oc |
| men |
| aha |

**Alm 37 (10 × 26 days)**

| 7aha | + 3 = 10akb | +2 = 12chi |
| --- | --- | --- |
| cim | mul | chu |
| eb | men | cab |
| etz | imi | akb |
| kan | man | mul |
| oc | ben | men |
| cib | cau | imi |
| ik | chi | man |
| lam | chu | ben |
| ix | cab | cau |

**Almanac 44 (10 × 26 days)**

| 7aha | +7= 1man | +7= 8ix | +7= 2imi | +5= 7cim |
| --- | --- | --- | --- | --- |
| cim | ben | aha | man | eb |
| eb | cau | cim | ben | etz |
| etz | chi | eb | cau | kan |
| kan | chu | etz | chi | oc |
| oc | cab | kan | chu | cib |
| cib | akb | oc | cab | ik |
| ik | mul | cib | akb | lam |
| lam | men | ik | mul | ix |
| ix | imi | lam | men | aha |

**Almanac 51 (5 × 52 days)**

| cab | +5= ik | +21= akb | +16= cau |
| --- | --- | --- | --- |
| mul | ix | men | chu |
| imi | cim | man | akb |
| ben | etz | cau | men |
| chi | oc | chu | man |

*Figure 4.1 (Continued)*

**Almanac 37 cont.**

| +7= 6eb | +9= 2imi | +3= 5kan | +2= 7cim |
|---|---|---|---|
| etz | man | oc | eb |
| kan | ben | cib | etz |
| oc | cau | ik | kan |
| cib | chi | lam | oc |
| ik | chu | ix | cib |
| lam | cab | aha | ik |
| ix | akb | cim | lam |
| aha | mul | eb | ix |
| cim | men | etz | aha |

**Almanac 38 (20 × 39 days)**

| 2etz | cab |
|---|---|
| | men |
| | ix |
| | ben |
| | eb |
| | chu |
| . | . . |

**Almanac 45 (5 × 52 days)**

| 3akb | +13= 3cib | +13= 3mul | +13= 3ik | +13= 3men |
|---|---|---|---|---|
| men | lam | imi | ix | man |
| man | aha | ben | cim | cau |
| cau | eb | chi | etz | chu |
| chu | kan | cab | oc | akb |

**Almanac 51 cont.**

| +10= mul |
|---|
| imi |
| ben |
| chi |
| cab |

**Almanac 52 (5 × 52 days)**

| 2oc | +10= 12aha | +12= 11eb | +9= 7imi |
|---|---|---|---|
| ik | eb | kan | ben |
| ix | kan | cib | chi |
| cim | cib | lam | cab |
| etz | lam | aha | mul |

*Figure 4.1 (Continued)*

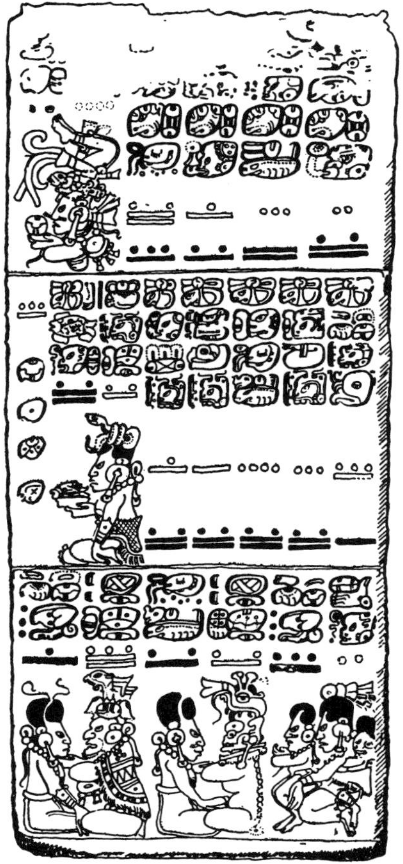

Almanac 38 cont.

| +2= 4aha | +8= 12lam | +7= 6men | +10= 3chi | +12= 2cab |
|---|---|---|---|---|
| cau | man | ix | kan | cib |
| etz | cim | ben | akb | men |
| cab | chi | eb | ik | ix |
| cib | kan | chu | imi | ben |
| men | akb | oc | aha | eb |
| ix | ik | mul | cau | chu |
| · | · | · | · | · |
| · | · | · | · | · |

Almanac 46 (4 × 65 days)

| 8 kan | +12= 7cib | +12= 6lam | +12= 5aha | +12= 4eb | +12= 3kan | +5= 8mul |
|---|---|---|---|---|---|---|
| mul | imi | ben | chi | cab | mul | ix |
| ix | cim | etz | oc | ik | ix | cau |
| cau | chu | akb | men | man | cau | kan |

Almanac 52 cont.

| +6= 13man | +7= 7ix | +8= 2ik |
|---|---|---|
| cau | cim | ix |
| chu | etz | cim |
| akb | oc | etz |
| men | ik | oc |

*Figure 4.1 (Continued)*

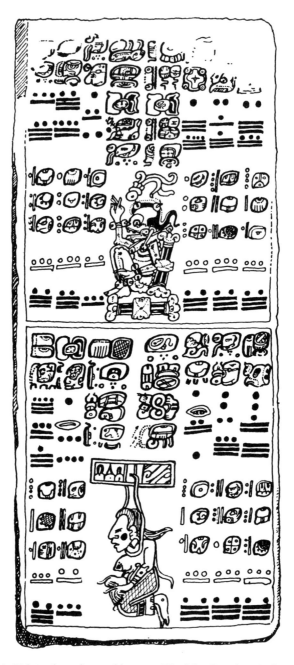

*Figure* 4.2 Ix Tab in the eclipse table on p. 53 of the Dresden Codex (after Anders 1975).

*Table 4.1*  Predicted Eclipse Dates from the Dresden Eclipse Tables and Actual Eclipse Dates According to Oppolzer (1887) (p = partial eclipse; r = annular eclipse; t = total eclipse)

| | Base A Solar Predict | Actual | Base B Lunar Predict | Actual | Base C Solar Predict | Actual |
|---|---|---|---|---|---|---|
| Julian day | 1997131 | | 1997146 | 1997148:17 | 1997161 | 1997163:p |
| 0 | 12 lam | | 1 akb | 3 chi | 3 etz | 5 cau |
| 1 + 177 = | 1997308 | 1997311:p | 1997323 | 1997325:17 | 1997338 | |
| | 7 chi | 10 lam | 9 aha | 11 ik | 11 men | |
| 2 + 177 = | 1997485 | 1997488:t | 1997500 | 1997502:12 | 1997515 | |
| | 2 ik | 5 chi | 4 cab | 6 cau | 6 eb | |
| 3 + 148 = | 1997633 | | 1997648 | | 1997663 | 1997665:r |
| | 7 oc | | 9 chi | | 11 aha | 13 ik |
| | picture | | | | | |
| 4 + 177 = | 1997810 | | 1997825 | | 1997840 | 1997842:r |
| | 2 man | | 4 ik | | 6 cab | 8 cau |
| 5 + 177 = | 1997987 | | 1998002 | 1998005:2 | 1998017 | 1998019:t |
| | 10 kan | | 12 cau | 2 ik | 1 ix | 3 cib |
| 6 + 177 = | 1998164 | | 1998179 | 1998181:2 | 1998194 | 1998197:r |
| | 5 imi | | 7 cib | 9 etz | 9 chu | 12 ix |
| 7 + 178 = | 1998342 | 1998344:p | 1998357 | 1998359:18 | 1998372 | 1998374:p |
| | 1 cau | 3 imi | 3 ix | 5 cib | 5 mul | 7 chu |
| 8 + 177 = | 1998519 | | 1998534 | 1998536:18 | 1998549 | 1998551:p |
| | 9 cib | | 11 chu | 13 ben | 13 cim | 2 lam |
| 9 + 177 = | 1998696 | 1998699:t | 1998711 | 1998713:10 | 1998726 | |
| | 4 ben | 7 cib | 6 lam | 8 oc | 8 akb | |
| 10 + 177 = | 1998873 | 1998875:r | 1998888 | 1998891:11 | 1998903 | |
| | 12 oc | 1 eb | 1 chi | 4 lam | 3 aha | |
| 11 + 177 = | 1999050 | 1999053:r | 1999065 | | 1999080 | |
| | 7 man | 10 oc | 9 ik | | 11 cab | |
| 12 + 177 = | 1999227 | 1999230:t | 1999242 | | 1999257 | |
| | 2 kan | 5 man | 4 cau | | 6 ix | |
| 13 + 148 = | 1999375 | | 1999390 | 1999393:4 | 1999405 | |
| | 7 eb | | 9 man | 12 oc | 11 ik | |
| | picture | | | | | |
| 14 + 178 = | 1999553 | | 1999568 | 1999569:4 | 1999583 | 1999584:t |
| | 3 oc | | 5 chi | 6 cim | 7 aha | 8 imi |
| 15 + 177 = | 1999730 | | 1999745 | 1999747:20 | 1999760 | 1999762:p |
| | 11 man | | 13 ik | 2 kan | 2 cab | 4 cau |
| 16 + 177 = | 1999907 | 1999910 | 1999922 | 1999924 | 1999937 | 1999939:p |
| | 6 kan | 9 man | 8 cau | 10 imi | 10 ix | 12 cib |
| 17 + 177 = | 2000084 | 2000086:r | 2000099 | 2000102:10 | 2000114 | |
| | 1 imi | 3 akb | 3 cib | 6 cau | 5 chu | |
| 18 + 177 = | 2000261 | 2000264:r | 2000276 | 2000278:6 | 2000291 | |
| | 9 etz | 12 imi | 11 ben | 13 men | 13 lam | |
| 19 + 148 = | 2000409 | | 2000424 | | 2000439 | 2000441:t |
| | 1 cim | | 3 imi | | 5 cib | 7 etz |

(*continued*)

*Table 4.1*  Predicted Eclipse Dates from the Dresden Eclipse Tables and Actual Eclipse Dates According to Oppolzer (1887) (p = partial eclipse; r = annular eclipse; t = total eclipse) (*Continued*)

| Base A Solar Predict | Actual | Base B Lunar Predict | Actual | Base C Solar Predict | Actual |
|---|---|---|---|---|---|
| picture | | | | | |
| 20 + 177 = 2000586<br>9 akb | | 2000601<br>11 etz | 2000603:.3<br>13 aha | 2000616<br>13 ben | 2000618:r<br>2 men |
| 21 + 177 = 2000763<br>4 aha | | 2000778<br>6 men | | 2000793<br>8 oc | 2000795:t<br>10 eb |
| 22 + 177 = 2000940<br>12 cab | | 2000955<br>1 eb | 2000958:16<br>4 men | 2000970<br>3 man | 2000972:r<br>5 mul |
| 23 + 178 = 2001118<br>8 men | | 2001133<br>10 oc | 2001134:15<br>11 chu | 2001148<br>12 chi | 2001150:p<br>1 man |
| 24 + 177 = 2001295<br>3 eb | 2001297:t<br>5 ix | 2001310<br>5 man | 2001312:12<br>7 mul | 2001325<br>7 ik | |
| 25 + 177 = 2001472<br>11 mul | 2001474:r<br>13 chu | 2001487<br>13 kan | 2001489:6<br>2 cim | 2001502<br>2 cau | |
| 26 + 148 = 2001620<br>3 cab | | 2001635<br>5 eb | | 2001650<br>7 man | 2001652<br>9 mul |
| picture | | | | | |
| 27 + 177 = 2001797<br>11 ix | | 2001812<br>13 mul | | 2001827<br>2 kan | 2001828:r<br>3 chi |
| 28 + 177 = 2001974<br>6 chu | | 2001989<br>8 cim | 2001991<br>10 lam | 2002004<br>10 imi | 2002006:t<br>12 akb |
| 29 + 178 = 2002152<br>2 mul | | 2002167<br>4 kan | 2002169:3<br>6 cim | 2002182<br>6 cau | 2002183:r<br>7 aha |
| 30 + 177 = 2002329<br>10 cim | 2002331:p<br>12 lam | 2002344<br>12 imi | 2002345:19<br>13 ik | 2002359<br>1 cib | 2002361:p<br>3 etz |
| 31 + 177 = 2002506<br>5 akb | 2002508:p<br>7 chi | 2002521<br>7 etz | 2002523:19<br>9 aha | 2002536<br>9 ben | 2002537:p<br>10 ix |
| 32 + 177 = 2002683<br>13 aha | 2002685:r<br>2 ik | 2002698<br>2 men | 2002700:11<br>4 cab | 2002713<br>4 oc | |
| 33 + 177 = 2002860<br>8 cab | 2002862:t<br>10 cau | 2002875<br>10 eb | 2002877:8<br>12 ix | 2002890<br>12 man | |
| 34 + 177 = 2003037<br>3 ix | 2003039:r<br>5 cib | 2003052<br>5 mul | | 2003067<br>7 kan | |
| 35 + 177 = 2003214<br>11 chu | 2003217:t<br>1 ix | 2003229<br>13 chu | | 2003244<br>2 imi | |
| 36 + 148 = 2003362<br>3 cau | | 2003377<br>5 ix | 2003380:3<br>8 cab | 2003392<br>7 mul | 2003394:r<br>9 chu |
| picture | | | | | |
| 37 + 178 = 2003540<br>12 cab | | 2003555<br>1 eb | 2003556:10<br>2 ben | 2003570<br>3 man | 2003571:r<br>4 lam |
| 38 + 177 = 2003717<br>7 ix | | 2003732<br>9 mul | 2003734:17<br>11 chu | 2003747<br>11 kan | 2003748:p<br>12 chi |
| 39 + 177 = 2003894<br>2 chu | 2003896:p<br>4 ben | 2003909<br>4 cim | 2003911:19<br>6 lam | 2003924<br>6 imi | |
| 40 + 177 = 2004071<br>10 lam | 2004073:t<br>12 oc | 2004086<br>12 akb | 2004088:12<br>1 chi | 2004101<br>1 etz | |

*Table 4.1*  (*Continued*)

| | Base A Solar Predict | Actual | Base B Lunar Predict | Actual | Base C Solar Predict | Actual |
|---|---|---|---|---|---|---|
| 41 + 177 = | 2004248 | 2004250:r | 2004263 | 2004265:2 | 2004278 | |
| 42 + 148 = | 5 chi | 7 man | 7 aha | 9 ik | 9 men | |
| | 2004396 | | 2004411 | | 2004426 | 2004428:r |
| | 10 ben | | 12 lam | | 1 akb | 3 chi |
| picture | | | | | | |
| 43 + 177 = | 2004573 | | 2004588 | 2004590:1 | 2004603 | 2004604:t |
| | 5 oc | | 7 chi | 9 man | 9 aha | 10 imi |
| 44 + 177 = | 2004750 | | 2004765 | 2004767:2 | 2004780 | 2004782:r |
| | 13 man | | 2 ik | 4 kan | 4 cab | 6 cau |
| 45 + 177 = | 2004927 | 2004930:p | 2004942 | 2004944:17 | 2004957 | 2004959:p |
| | 8 kan | 11 man | 10 cau | 12 imi | 12 ix | 1 cib |
| 46 + 177 = | 2005104 | | 2005119 | 2005121:17 | 2005134 | 2005136:p |
| | 3 imi | | 5 cib | 7 etz | 7 chu | 9 ben |
| 47 + 177 = | 2005281 | 2005284:t | 2005296 | 2005298:12 | 2005311 | |
| | 11 etz | 1 imi | 13 ben | 2 men | 2 lam | |
| 48 + 177 = | 2005458 | 2005460:r | 2005473 | 2005476:12 | 2005488 | |
| | 6 men | 8 cab | 8 oc | 11 ben | 10 chi | |
| 49 + 148 = | 2005606 | | 2005621 | | 2005636 | 2005639:r |
| | 11 akb | | 13 etz | | 2 ben | 5 cib |
| picture | | | | | | |
| 50 + 177 = | 2005783 | | 2005798 | | 2005813 | 2005815:t |
| | 6 aha | | 8 men | | 10 oc | 12 eb |
| 51 + 177 = | 2005960 | | 2005975 | 2005978:5 | 2005990 | 2005993:r |
| | 1 cab | | 3 eb | 6 men | 5 man | 8 oc |
| 52 + 178 = | 2006138 | | 2006153 | 2006155:3 | 2006168 | 2006170:t |
| | 10 men | | 12 oc | 1 eb | 1 chi | 3 man |
| 53 + 177 = | 2006315 | | 2006330 | 2006333:19 | 2006345 | 2006347:p |
| | 5 eb | | 7 man | 10 oc | 9 ik | 11 kan |
| 54 + 177 = | 2006492 | 2006495:p | 2006507 | 2006509:20 | 2006522 | 2006524:p |
| | 13 mul | 3 eb | 2 kan | 4 cimi | 4 cau | 6 imi |
| 55 + 177 = | 2006669 | 2006671:r | 2006684 | 2006687:10 | 2006699 | |
| | 8 cim | 10 lam | 10 imi | 13 kan | 12 cib | |
| 56 + 177 = | 2006846 | 2006849:r | 2006861 | 2006863:8 | 2006876 | |
| | 3 akb | 6 cimi | 5 etz | 7 aha | 7 ben | |
| 57 + 177 = | 2007023 | 2007026:t | 2007038 | | 2007053 | |
| | 11 aha | 1 akb | 13 men | | 2 oc | |
| 58 + 148 = | 2007171 | | 2007186 | | 2007201 | 2007203:r |
| | 3 lam | | 5 akb | | 7 etz | 9 aha |
| picture | | | | | | |
| 59 + 177 = | 2007348 | | 2007363 | | 2007378 | 2007381:t |
| | 11 chi | | 13 aha | | 2 men | 5 etz |
| 60 + 178 = | 2007526 | | 2007541 | 2007543:14 | 2007556 | 2007557:r |
| | 7 akb | | 9 etz | 11 aha | 11 ben | 12 ix |

(*continued*)

**115**

*Table 4.1* Predicted Eclipse Dates from the Dresden Eclipse Tables
and Actual Eclipse Dates According to Oppolzer (1887) (p = partial eclipse;
r = annular eclipse; t = total eclipse) (*Continued*)

| | Base A Solar | | Base B Lunar | | Base C Solar | |
|---|---|---|---|---|---|---|
| | Predict | Actual | Predict | Actual | Predict | Actual |
| 61 + 177 = | 2007703 | | 2007718 | 2007720:15 | 2007733 | 2007735:p |
| | 2 aha | | 4 men | 6 cab | 6 oc | 8 eb |
| 62 + 177 = | 2007880 | 2007882:t | 2007895 | 2007898:14 | 2007910 | |
| | 10 cab | 12 cau | 12 eb | 2 men | 1 man | |
| 63 + 177 = | 2008057 | 2008060:p | 2008072 | 2008074:14 | 2008087 | |
| | 5 ix | 8 cab | 7 mul | 9 chu | 9 kan | |
| 64 + 177 = | 2008234 | 2008237:t | 2008249 | | 2008264 | |
| | 13 chu | 3 ix | 2 cim | | 4 imi | |
| 65 + 148 = | 2008382 | | 2008397 | | 2008412 | 2008414:r |
| | 5 cau | | 7 ix | | 9 mul | 11 chu |
| | | | | | | |
| picture | | | | | | |
| | | | | | | |
| 66 + 177 = | 2008559 | | 2008574 | 2008576:1 | 2008589 | 2008592:t |
| | 13 cib | | 2 chu | 4 ben | 4 cim | 7 mul |
| 67 + 177 = | 2008736 | | 2008751 | 2008754:2 | 2008766 | 2009768:r |
| | 8 ben | | 10 lam | 13 chu | 12 akb | 1 chi |
| 68 + 177 = | 2008913 | | 2008928 | 2008931:18 | 2008943 | 2008946:p |
| | 3 oc | | 5 chi | 8 lam | 7 aha | 10 akb |
| 69 + 177 = | 2009090 | 2009093:p | 2009105 | 2009108:17 | 2009120 | 2009122:p |
| | 11 man | 1 oc | 13 ik | 3 chic | 2 cab | 4 cau |

Figure 4.1) with the day 4 Ahau, indicated by the numeral 4 above the
column of day signs headed by Ahau. Black distance numbers indicate the
number of days to advance, while outlined or red numerals indicate the
coefficients of day signs reached by such advances. Almanac-internal day
signs are implicit but unexpressed. In the case of Almanac 48, the three
black bars in the first section indicate that one advances fifteen days from 4
Ahau to arrive at 6 Men, indicated by the outlined numeral 6 (a bar and a
dot). As just mentioned, the day sign Men is implicit but unexpressed. The
next black numeral (on p. 18c) indicates an advance of 33 days to arrive at
13 Lamat, and in the last section the black numeral 4 indicates an advance
of 4 days to arrive at 4 Eb, a day appearing as the second glyph in the initial
column of day signs on p. 17c. Thus, after 52 days (15 + 33 + 4), one
returns to the first section of the almanac and cycles through again. After
cycling through five times (indicated by the five day signs in the initial
column), an entire cycle of 260 days is completed, and one returns to the
starting point of 4 Ahau. Typically, each section is associated with five
dates, one for each run of 52 days.

In Almanac 48 (pp. 17c–18c; Figure 4.1), each section is marked by a picture of the Moon Goddess, seated carrying a load on her back, and by a hieroglyphic caption above. Following V. Bricker (1988a), we assume that the initial column of dates headed by Ahau is associated with the first section, and that the dates appearing between the portrait of the Moon Goddess and the hieroglyphic caption in each section are associated with the following portrait and caption. Thus, in Almanac 48, 4 Ahau is a date for the first section, 6 Men for the second, 13 Lamat for the third, and 4 Eb returning to the first caption.

There are three major types of Moon Goddess Almanacs (Thompson 1972; Hofling 1989), based on patterned differences in the portraits and the accompanying captions. In almanacs such as 48, where the Moon Goddess carries a burden on her back, the *cuch* ("burden") hieroglyph regularly appears in the caption above. In almanacs where the Moon Goddess carries a bird on her shoulder, such as Almanacs 40 (pp. 17b–18b) and 47 (pp. 16c–17c), the *mut* ("bird" or "omen") hieroglyph regularly appears above, and in almanacs where the Moon Goddess is seated facing another protagonist (e. g., Almanac 41, p. 19b), the *yatan* ("wife") hieroglyph regularly appears (Hofling 1989). Thompson (1972:48–49) suggests that the latter *yatan* almanacs refer to conjunctions of the moon with other celestial bodies. While Thompson proposes that the *cuch* and *mut* almanacs refer to associations of the Moon Goddess to diseases, these almanacs might also relate to observable celestial phenomena.

## Eclipse Cycles in the Moon Goddess Almanacs

Until now, no rationale has been proposed in any detail for why the particular dates and intervals recorded in the Moon Goddess almanacs are what they are and not some other set of dates and intervals. The only constraint that has been generally recognized is that well-formed almanacs be composed of 260 days or some multiple therof, and it has been mentioned in passing that presumably the dates are astronomically or ritually significant. We propose that dates and intervals recorded in the eclipse tables also appear in the Moon Goddess almanacs, again reflecting the Maya interest in the commensuration of the 260-day sacred year with lunar cycles. The much larger eclipse cycles provide structural underpinnings linking almanacs to one another and show that these almanacs are cohesive calendrically as well as iconographically and in their noncalendric glyphic content. Undoubtedly, the dates recorded in the Moon Goddess almanacs are motivated by other factors as well, but eclipse cycles appear to be a major consideration.

While our current focus is on the calendrical content of these almanacs, and how it reflects eclipse cycles, some mention should be made of iconographic evidence suggesting lunar eclipses. As noted above, a closed eye and black (death) spots are common eclipse symbolism, and death and eclipses are closely linked conceptually for the Maya, who thought that the eclipsed body was dying (Closs 1989). These same signs of death/eclipse are commonly present in portraits of the Moon Goddess in these almanacs. In the first section of the first Moon Goddess almanac (Almanac 33, p. 16a), her burden is a skull. In Almanac 35 (pp. 18a–19a) the nipple of the Moon Goddess is blackened in the second section, while her eye is closed in the fourth. In Almanac 37, (pp. 21a–22a) her leg is blackened. In Almanac 39 (pp. 16b–17b) she bears a skeletal death figure in the second section. In Almanac 40 (pp. 17b–18b), her eye is again closed in the second portrait as a skeleton is perched on her shoulder, and black (death) spots appear on her in the fourth. She has both the closed eye and spots in the second portrait of Almanac 41 (pp. 19b), where she sits facing a similarly spotted death figure. Her nipple is again blackened in Almanac 46 (p. 23b). In Almanac 48 (pp. 17c–18c) she carries death on her back in the first portrait, and her nipple is blackened in both the first and third portraits. Likewise, her nipple is blackened in Almanac 49 (pp. 18c–19c). Finally, in Almanac 52 (pp. 22c–23c) she is united with death figures in the first, second, and fourth portraits, with her nipple also blackened in the fourth. From this listing it should be clear that the Moon Goddess is frequently marked by death iconography, suggesting eclipses.[3]

Calendric evidence indicating eclipse cycles includes both the dates recorded and the intervals between them. While intervals are recorded in all but Almanac 34 (pp. 16a–17a), numeral coefficients for day signs are missing in several of the almanacs, particularly those appearing at the beginning of the Moon Goddess section on pp. 16 and 17. The significance of this is not clear, but we doubt that it is accidental and suspect a recycling function, whereby different numeral coefficients could be provided for these almanacs. It is also worth noting that at the end of the Moon Goddess section (pp. 22–23), the almanacs become increasingly abbreviated and tabular (cf. Figure 4.1). In fact, Thompson (1972:60–61) does not consider Almanacs 38 (pp. 22–23a), 45 (p. 22b), and 46 (p. 23b) to be Moon Goddess almanacs. We do not think their presence on these pages is accidental and include them in our considerations, but we do have reservations and recognize that they are different in some ways.

As mentioned, the key intervals in the eclipse table are most frequently periods of 177 days, with occasional intervals of 178 and 148 days. A single run through most almanacs covers an interval of 52 days, with five runs completing the cycle (5 × 52 = 260). To cover an interval of 177 days in a typical almanac, one would cycle through three periods of 52 days (156 days) plus 21 days; an interval of 178 days could be covered by three cycles of 52 days plus 22 days; and an interval of 148 days by 2 cycles of 52 days (104 days) plus 44 days. Thus the key interval numbers suggesting eclipse cycles are (or add up to) 21, 22, and 44. These are recorded in the Moon Goddess almanacs, and, indeed, one need look no further than the first section of the first almanac (Almanac 33, p. 16a) to find the interval 21 recorded.

## Almanac-Internal Eclipse Intervals

Although one cannot match particular eclipse interval series to almanacs in which the numeral coefficients are missing, many of these almanacs do have appropriate distance numbers to calculate eclipse intervals. The reader is again encouraged to refer to the illustrations in Figure 4.1 with regard to the almanacs mentioned in the following discussion. As noted, 21 is the first interval recorded in Almanac 33 (p. 16a), allowing one to link dates 177 days apart. In Almanac 40 (pp. 17b–18b) two sets of columns of days are 22 days apart, allowing intervals of 178 days to be calculated. Adding 22 (6 + 16) days to a position in the third column headed by Oc one arrives in the fifth column, headed by Eb. By adding 22 (4 + 11 + 7) days to a date in column 6 headed by Ahau, one arrives back at the third column.

Almanac 47 (pp. 16c–17c) is a 4 × 65 days almanac, which requires different intervals in order to mark eclipse spans. In such almanacs, intervals of 47, 48, and 18 days would be useful for eclipse calculations [177 = (2 × 65) + 47; 178 = (2 × 65) + 48; 148 = (2 × 65) + 18]. There is clearly an error in one of the intervals marked in the Dresden Almanac 47. We follow the correction suggested by Förstemann (Thompson 1972:57). With the corrected intervals, the days in column five occur 47 (8 + 13 + 13 + 13) days after those in column one, those in column six occur 47 (13 + 13 + 13 + 8) days after those in column two, and days in column six are separated from days in column two by 18 (10 + 8) days.

Almanacs 37 (pp. 21a–22a) and 44 (p. 22b) record 10 × 26 day cycles, and the relevant intervals for them are 21, 22, and 18 (177 = 6 × 26 + 21; 178 = 6 × 26 + 22; 148 = 5 × 26 + 18). Almanac 38 (pp. 22a–23a) is a unique (20 × 39)-day almanac, for which the intervals 21 and 22 are again relevant, as well as 31 [148 = (3 × 39) + 31].

A listing of useful intervals recorded in the Moon Goddess almanacs is given in Table 4.2 (cf. Fig. 4.1). As shown in Table 4.2, intervals relevant to eclipse calculations are common in almanacs with and without numeral

*Table 4.2*   Possible Eclipse Intervals within Moon Goddess Almanacs (Example Days in Parentheses)

| | |
|---|---|
| Almanac 33: | Column 1 (+3 × 52) + 21 = Column 2 |
| Almanac 34: | No intervals given |
| Almanac 35: | Column 2 (7 Ix) (+3 × 52) + 21 = Column 4 (2 Chuen) |
| | Column 5 (12 Chicchan) (+3 × 52) + 21 = Column 2 (7 Ik) |
| Almanac 36: | None |
| Almanac 37: | Column 1 (7 Ahau) (+6 × 26) + 21 = Column 5 (2 Caban) |
| | Column 2 (10 Akbal) (+6 × 26) + 21 = Column 6 (5 Ahau) |
| | Column 2 (10 Akbal) (+5 × 26) + 18 = Column 5 (2 Chuen) |
| | Column 3 (12 Chicchan) + 21 = Column 7/1 (7 Cimi) |
| Almanac 38: | Column 4 (6 Men) (+4 × 39) + 22 = Column 6/1 (2 Ben) |
| | Column 5 (3 Chicchan) (+4 × 39) + 22 = Column 3 (12 Akbal) |
| Almanac 39: | None |
| Almanac 40: | Column 3 (+3 × 52) + 22 = Column 5 |
| | Column 6 (+3 × 52) + 22 = Column 3 |
| | Column 6 (+3 × 52) + 44 = Column 5 |
| Almanac 41: | None |
| Almanac 42: | None |
| Almanac 43: | None |
| Almanac 44: | Column 1 (7 Ahau) (+6 × 26) + 21 = Column 4 (2 Caban) |
| Almanac 45: | None |
| Almanac 46: | Column 1 (8 Kan) (+2 × 65) + 48 = Column 5 (4 Ik) |
| Almanac 47: | Column 1 (+2 × 65) + 47 = Column 5 |
| | Column 2 (+2 × 65) + 47 = Column 6 |
| | Column 5 (+2 × 65) + 18 = Column 7/1 |
| Almanac 48: | None |
| Almanac 49: | None |
| Almanac 50: | Column 1 (13 Ahau) (+3 × 52) + 22 = Column 3 (9 Etz'nab) |
| | Column 2 (11 Chuen) (+3 × 52) + 22 = Column 4 (7 Muluc) |
| | Column 3 (9 Ik) (+3 × 52) + 21 = Column 5 (4 Cauac) |
| Almanac 51: | Column 2 (+3 × 52) + 21 = Column 3 |
| Almanac 52: | Column 1 (2 Oc) (+2 × 52) + 44 = Column 6 (7 Etz'nab) |
| | Column 2 (12 Ahau) (+3 × 52) + 21 = Column 4 (7 Caban) |
| | Column 4 (7 Imix) (+3 × 52) + 21 = Column 7/1 (2 Etz'nab) |

coefficients. As we would expect, 177-day intervals are the most common. One may also note that the intervals are concentrated in particular almanacs, allowing multiple intervals to be calculated almanac internally. There is no striking correlation between almanac type and density of eclipse intervals. The *mut* almanacs (40 and 47) both lack numeral coefficients and are dense with eclipse intervals. There is considerable variation among *cuch* and *yatan* almanacs in this regard.

## Interalmanac Eclipse Intervals

Eclipse intervals are also common between different almanacs. In addition, many dates are repeated in more than one almanac, further suggesting

interalmanac relations. For example, all of the dates recorded in columns
2–5 of Almanac 35 (pp. 18a–19a) also occur in Almanac 37 (pp. 21a–22a)
(cf. Figure 4.1). This extensive overlap means that intervals could be calculated between these almanacs as well as within each of them. For example,
the dates in the second column of Almanac 35 (35:2) also appear in the first
column of Almanac 37 (37:1). By adding 177 days, one might arrive either
at 35:4 or 37:5 (cf. Table 4.2). Almanac 36 (pp. 19a–20a) also has connections to both Almanacs 35 and 37. Almanac 36 is designed so that all of its
numeral coefficients are 11. Adding 177 days to any of these dates, one
arrives at days with the coefficient 6, most of which are present in 37:4.
Moreover, by adding an additional 148 days, one may return to Almanac
36. For example, 36:1 (e.g., 11 Men) + 177 = 37:4 (6 Eb) + 148 = 36:1
(11 Ahau). Similar links join Almanac 36 to Almanac 35. 36:5 (e.g., 11
Caban) + 177 = 35:3 or 37:4 (6 Ix) + 148 = 36:5 (11 Ik); 35:4 (e.g., 2
Men) + 177 = 36:2 (11 Ben). Possible connections with Almanac 38 (p.
23a) are numerous, but problematic, because one would expect some simply by chance due to the large number of days recorded (100).[4]

The almanacs in the middle section (b) are also linked to horizontally
contiguous almanacs by eclipse intervals (example dates are again in parentheses): 41:2 (13 Manik) + 177 = 42:2 (8 Kan); 43:2 (9 Men) + 148 = 44:2
(1 Akbal); 44:1 (7 Ix) + 177 = 43:1 (2 Chuen); 44:3 (8 Kan) + 177 = 45:3
(3 Imix); 46:1 (8 Cauac) + 177 = 45:2 (3 Cib); 46:2 (7 Cib) + 177 = 45:4
(3 Ix).

In the bottom section (c), Almanacs 48, 49, and 50 are connected less
by intervals than by shared dates (see Figure 4.1). Each almanac includes
13 Ahau, Eb, Kan, Cib, Lamat as a column of dates. By adding 178 days to
dates in any of these columns, one arrives at dates in 50:3. Almanacs 50
and 52 are also linked by eclipse intervals (recall that Almanac 51 lacks
numeral coefficients, and so is not considered here with regard to interalmanac intervals). Adding 177 days to a date in 50:5 (e.g., 4 Akbal), one
arrives at 52:2 (12 Ahau); and adding another 177 days brings one to a date
recorded in both 50:4 and 52:4 (7 Caban). Also interesting, are the interalmanac links between Almanac 52 (pp. 22c–23c) and Almanac 35 (p.
18a), the first almanac in Section a with numeral coefficients recorded.
Adding 148 days to the dates recorded in 52:1 (e.g., 2 Oc), one arrives at a
date recorded both in 52:6 and 35:2 (e.g., 7 Etz'nab), and, adding another
177 days, one arrives at dates recorded in 35:4 (e.g., 2 Men). This connection suggests a reading order among almanacs that is analogous to the order
within an almanac; that is, after reaching the end of a cycle at the bottom
right, one returns to the top left to start again.

In addition to horizontal connections between almanacs, as given in
the examples above, there appear to be vertical linkages. For example,

intervals between Almanac 37 (pp. 21a–22a) and Almanac 41 (p. 19b) allow one to move naturally from the end of Section a to the first almanac with numeral coefficients in Section b (see Figure 4.1). Adding 177 days to dates in 37:5 (or 38:1) (e.g., 2 Imix) leads to dates in 41:1 (e.g., 10 Etz'nab). Likewise, adding 177 days to certain dates in 37:6 (e.g., 5 Oc) leads to dates in 41:2 (e.g., 13 Manik). Similarly, an eclipse interval linking Almanac 44 (p. 21b) to Almanac 48 (p. 17c) allows one to move from the end of Section b [excluding the problematic Almanacs 45 (p. 22b) and 46 (p. 23b)] to the beginning of Section c (44:3 + 178 days leads to 48:1). Almanac 44 may also have linkages to Almanac 50 (pp. 19c–20c) (44:2 + 177 = 50:3; 44:4 + 148 = 50:4).

There is also the suggestion of direct vertical linkages as in the connections between Almanacs 37 (pp. 21a–22a) and Almanac 44 (p. 21b), which share two columns of day signs as well as eclipse intervals [37:1 or 44:1 (e.g., 7 Kan) + 177 = 37:5 or 44:4 (2 Imix); 37:4 (e.g., 6 Oc) + 177 = 44:2 (1 Manik)]. On p. 22, Almanac 45 (p. 22b) is linked to Almanac 52 (p. 22c): 45:1 (e.g., 3 Akbal) + 177 = 52:3 (11 Ahau) + 148 = 45:2 (3 Lamat). Almanacs 36 (pp. 19a–20a), 42 (pp. 19b–20b), and 50 (pp. 19–20c) have similar links: 50:2 (e.g., 11 Men) + 177 = 42:1 (6 Eb) + 148 = 36:1 (11 Ahau). The full range of possible interalmanac relations is suggested in the following direct comparison of the eclipse table with the Moon Goddess almanacs.

### Comparison of the Eclipse Table and the Moon Goddess Almanacs

In attempting to relate the eclipse cycles recorded in the table on Dresden Codex pp. 51–58 to the Moon Goddess almanacs, a number of issues of method and of principles of interpretation demand attention (cf. Hofling 1988). First, we are now limiting our investigation to the relationship of the Moon Goddess almanacs to the particular cycles recorded in the eclipse table. One might also examine the possibility of a different set of eclipse predictions or records, but we have not done so. As we hope to have shown, the ample presence of the key intervals within and among almanacs suggests that eclipse intervals are significant, but in itself does not favor one set or time period over another. A related issue is whether the Moon Goddess almanacs were predictive, based on actual observations, or both.

Because of the large number of days recorded in both the eclipse tables and the Moon Goddess almanacs, one would expect considerable overlap in the dates recorded simply by chance. Also recall that in the eclipse tables there is one day's leeway on either side of the target date, significantly increasing the number of relevant days that might be used for eclipse intervals. In this study we do not consider days immediately ahead of or behind a target date, but only the target dates themselves. This constraint may well be too rigid, but we prefer to be conservative in this initial investigation. Moreover, we do not consider identical dates alone as evidence of a relationship, but look for identical sequences of dates.

Because we insist on sequences of dates, and believe that one of the functions of the eclipse cycles is to provide cohesion within and among almanacs, we require criteria on which to base decisions about acceptable reading orders. Without such criteria, the evidence of sequentiality might be quite weak. If two dates that occur in sequence in the eclipse table appear at all in the Moon Goddess almanacs, one might claim that they form a sequence. However, we do not consider them to be a sequence unless they appear in a reasonable reading order in the Moon Goddess almanacs as well. As suggested, this generally requires that they occur in either horizontally or vertically contiguous almanacs. A glance at these pages indicates that pages are divided into three sections horizontally, and that almanacs can extend across page boundaries. As the almanac numbers imply, Thompson (1972) suggests first reading the top section from left to right, then the middle section, and finally the bottom section. We are not convinced that the almanacs must be read from left to right, top to bottom. In fact, our research suggests that there may be a number of ways these almanacs might be read and that there may not be a single correct reading order.

In order to test the hypothesis that eclipse cycles are embedded in the Moon Goddess almanacs further, we compared the dates recorded in the eclipse tables with those in the relevant almanacs. Identities between the two sets of dates are extensive, as shown in Table 4.3. It is clear that the overlap is similar (but usually not identical) for all three of the series (starting from base dates A, B, and C) due to the structure of the table, and often involves the same Moon Goddess almanacs. For example, the sequences (12 Oc–)7 Manik–2 Kan(–10 Imix) occur with Base A (without 10 Imix, dates 10–12, Table 4.3), Base B (dates 52–55, Table 4.3), and Base C (without 12 Oc, dates 26–28, Table 4.3); the sequence 7 Ix–2 Chuen–10 Lamat–5 Chicchan occurs with Base A (dates 38–41, Table 4.3) and Base B (dates 65–68, Table 4.3); the sequence 1 Akbal–9 Ahau–4 Caban occurs with Base B (dates 1–3, Table 4.3) and Base C (dates 42–44, Table 4.3). While such exact overlaps are considerable, especially for Base B, correspondences of identical numeral sequences with equivalent day signs (day signs appearing in the same columns in the almanacs) are extremely common. As a result, the Moon Goddess almanacs appear to correspond rea-

Table 4.3  Correspondences of Dates in the Eclipse Table and the Moon Goddess Almanacs

| Date No. | Base A | | | Base B | | | Base C | | |
|---|---|---|---|---|---|---|---|---|---|
| 0 | 12 lam | (38:3) | 52:2 | 1 akb | 44:2 | | 3 etz | (38:5) | 45:4 |
| 1  + 177 = | 7 chi | 50:4 | 52:4 | 9 aha | | | 11 men | 36:1 | 50:2 |
| 2  + 177 = | 2 ik | (38:1) 52:1 | 43:3 | 4 cab | (38:2) | | 6 eb | 37:4 42:1 | (38:4) 49:2 |
| 3  + 148 = | 7 oc | 35:2 44:1 | 37:1 52:6 | 9 chi | | | 11 aha | 36:1 | 52:3 |
| picture | | | | | | | | | |
| 4  + 177 = | 2 man | 35:4 (38:1) 44:4 | 37:5 43:1 | 4 ik | (38:2) | 46:5 | 6 cab | 38:4 | |
| 5  + 177 = | 10 kan | | | 12 cau | 37:3 | (38:3) | 1 ix | | |
| 6  + 177 = | 5 imi | | | 7 cib | 46:2 | | 9 chu | 43:2 | |
| 7  + 178 = | 1 cau | 44:2 | | 3 ix | (38:5) | 45:4 | 5 mul | | |
| 8  + 177 = | 9 cib | | | 11 chu | 36:3 | 50:2 | 13 cim | | |
| 9  + 177 = | 4 ben | (38:2) | | 6 lam | 37:4 | (38:4) | 8 akb | | |
| 10  + 177 = | 12 oc | (38:3) | | 1 chi | 44:2 | | 3 aha | (38:5) | 45:2 |
| 11  + 177 = | 7 man | | | 9 ik | 50:3 | | 11 cab | 36:5 | |
| 12  + 177 = | 2 kan | (38:1) | | 4 cau | (38:2) | 50:5 | 6 ix | 35:3 (38:4) | 37:4 |
| 13  + 148 = | 7 eb | 37:1 | 44:1 | 9 man | | | 11 ik | 36:5 | |
| picture | | | | | | | | | |
| 14  + 178 = | 3 oc | (38:5) | 45:4 | 5 chi | 46:4 | | 7 aha | 37:1 46:2 | 44:1 |
| 15  + 177 = | 11 man | 36:5 | 50:2 | 13 ik | | | 2 cab | 37:5 44:4 | (38:1) |
| 16  + 177 = | 6 kan | 37:4 49:2 | 42:1 | 8 cau | 46:1 | | 10 ix | 41:1 | |
| 17  + 177 = | 1 imi | | | 3 cib | (38:5) | 45:2 | 5 chu | | |
| 18  + 177 = | 9 etz | 50:3 | | 11 ben | 36:2 | | 13 lam | 48:3 50:1 | 59:1 |
| 19  + 148 = | 1 cim | | | 3 imi | (38:5) | 45:3 | 5 cib | 37:6 | |
| picture | | | | | | | | | |
| 20  + 177 = | 9 akb | 43:2 | | 11 etz | 36:2 | | 13 ben | | |
| 21  + 177 = | 4 aha | (38:2) | 48:1 | 6 men | (37:4) 48:2 | 38:4 | 8 oc | 35:1 | 44:3 |

Table 4.3   (Continued)

| Date No. | Base A | | | Base B | | | Base C | | |
|---|---|---|---|---|---|---|---|---|---|
| 22 + 177 = | 12 cab | 35:5 (38:3) | 37:3 | 1 eb | | | 3 man | 38:5 | 45:1 |
| 23 + 178 = | 8 men | | | 10 oc | | | 12 chi | 35:5 (38:3) | 37:3 |
| 24 + 177 = | 3 eb | (38:5) | 45:2 | 5 man | | | 7 ik | 35:2 44:1 | 37:1 52:6 |
| 25 + 177 = | 11 mul | 36:4 | | 13 kan | 48:3 50:1 | 49:1 | 2 cau | 35:4 (38:1) | 37:5 44:4 |
| 26 + 148 = | 3 cab | (38:5) | 45:3 | 5 eb | 37:6 | | 7 man | | |
| | picture | | | | | | | | |
| 27 + 177 = | 11 ix | 36:4 | | 13 mul | | | 2 kan | (38:1) | |
| 28 + 177 = | 6 chu | (38:4) | 48:2 | 8 cim | 35:1 | 44:3 | 10 imi | 37:2 | |
| 29 + 178 = | 2 mul | 37:5 44:4 | (38:1) | 4 kan | (38:2) | 48:1 | 6 cau | (38:4) | 48:2 |
| 30 + 177 = | 10 cim | 41:1 | | 12 imi | 37:3 | (38:3) | 1 cib | | |
| 31 + 177 = | 5 akb | | | 7 etz | 35:2 44:1 | 37:1 52:6 | 9 ben | | |
| 32 + 177 = | 13 aha | 48:3 50:1 | 49:1 | 2 men | 35:4 (38:1) 44:4 | 37:5 43:1 | 4 oc | (38:2) | |
| 33 + 177 = | 8 cab | | | 10 eb | | | 12 man | 37:3 | (38:3) |
| 34 + 177 = | 3 ix | (38:5) 46:6 | 45:4 | 5 mul | | | 7 kan | 37:1 | 44:1 |
| 35 + 177 = | 11 chu | 36:3 | 50:2 | 13 cim | | | 2 imi | 37:5 44:4 | (38:1) |
| 36 + 148 = | 3 cau | (38:5) | 45:1 | 5 ix | 37:6 | | 7 mul | 50:4 | 52:4 |
| | picture | | | | | | | | |
| 37 + 178 = | 12 cab | 35:5 (38:3) | 37:3 | 1 eb | | | 3 man | (38:5) | 45:1 |
| 38 + 177 = | 7 ix | 35:2 44:1 | 37:1 52:6 | 9 mul | | | 11 kan | 36:4 | 52:3 |
| 39 + 177 = | 2 chu | 35:4 (38:1) 44:4 | 37:5 43:1 | 4 cim | (38:2) | | 6 imi | (38:4) | |
| 40 + 177 = | 10 lam | | | 12 akb | 37:3 | (38:3) | 1 etz | | |
| 41 + 177 = | 5 chi | 46:4 | | 7 aha | 37:1 | 44:1 | 9 men | 43:2 | |
| 42 + 148 = | 10 ben | 37:2 | | 12 lam | (38:3) | 52:2 | 1 akb | 44:2 | |

(continued)

| Date No. | Base A | | | Base B | | | Base C | | |
|---|---|---|---|---|---|---|---|---|---|
| | picture | | | | | | | | |
| 43  + 177 = | 5 oc | 37:6 | 46:4 | 7 chi | 50:4 | 52:4 | 9 aha | | |
| 44  + 177 = | 13 man | 41:2 | 52:5 | 2 ik | (38:1) 52:1 | 43:3 | 4 cab | (38:2) | 46:5 |
| 45  + 177 = | 8 kan | 42:2 46:1 | 44:3 | 10 cau | 37:2 | | 12 ix | (38:3) | |
| 46  + 177 = | 3 imi | (38:5) | 45:3 | 5 cib | 37:6 | | 7 chu | 46:2 | |
| 47  + 177 = | 11 etz | 36:2 | | 13 ben | | | 2 lam | (38:1) | |
| 48  + 177 = | 6 men | 37:4 48:2 | (38:4) | 8 oc | 35:1 | | 10 chi | 37:2 | |
| 49  + 148 = | 11 akb | 36:2 | 50:2 | 13 etz | | | 2 ben | 37:5 | (38:1) |
| | picture | | | | | | | | |
| 50  + 177 = | 6 aha | 37:4 42:1 | (38:4) 49:2 | 8 men | | | 10 oc | 41:1 | |
| 51  + 177 = | 1 cab | 44:2 | | 3 eb | (38:5) | 45:2 | 5 man | | |
| 52  + 178 = | 10 men | 37:2 | | 12 oc | (38:3) | | 1 chi | 44:2 | |
| 53  + 177 = | 5 eb | 37:6 | | 7 man | | | 9 ik | 50:3 | |
| 54  + 177 = | 13 mul | | | 2 kan | (38:1) | | 4 cau | (38:2) | 50:5 |
| 55  + 177 = | 8 cim | 35:1 | 44:3 | 10 imi | 37:2 | | 12 cib | (38:3) | 52:2 |
| 56  + 177 = | 3 akb | (38:5) | 45:1 | 5 etz | 37:6 | | 7 ben | 50:4 | 52:4 |
| 57  + 177 = | 11 aha | 36:1 | 52:3 | 13 men | 41:2 | 52:5 | 2 oc | (38:1) 52:1 | 43:3 |
| 58  + 148 = | 3 lam | (38:5) 46:6 | 45:2 | 5 akb | | | 7 etz | 35:2 44:1 | 37:1 52:6 |
| | picture | | | | | | | | |
| 59  + 177 = | 11 chi | 36:1 | | 13 aha | 48:3 50:1 | 49:1 | 2 men | 35:4 43:1 | (38:1) |
| 60  + 178 = | 7 akb | | | 9 etz | 50:3 | | 11 ben | 36:2 | |
| 61  + 177 = | 2 aha | (38:1) | | 4 men | (38:2) | 50:5 | 6 oc | 35:3 (38:4) | 37:4 |
| 62  + 177 = | 10 cab | 37:2 | | 12 eb | (38:3) | 52:2 | 1 man | 44:2 | |
| 63  + 177 = | 5 ix | 37:6 | | 7 mul | 50:4 | 52:4 | 9 kan | | |
| 64  + 177 = | 13 chu | 41:2 | 52:5 | 2 cim | (38:1) 52:1 | 43:3 | 4 imi | (38:2) | |
| 65  + 148 = | 5 cau | | | 7 ix | 35:2 44:1 | 37:1 52:6 | 9 mul | | |

*Table 4.3* (*Continued*)

| Date No. | | Base A | | | Base B | | | Base C | | |
|---|---|---|---|---|---|---|---|---|---|---|
| | picture | | | | | | | | | |
| 66 | + 177 = | 13 cib | 48:3 50:1 | 49:1 | 2 chu | 35:4 (38:1) 44:4 | 37:5 43:1 | 4 cim | (38:2) | |
| 67 | + 177 = | 8 ben | | | 10 lam | | | 12 akb | 37:3 | (38:3) |
| 68 | + 177 = | 3 oc | (38:5) | 45:4 | 5 chi | 46:4 | | 7 aha | 37:1 | 44:1 |
| 69 | + 177 = | 11 man | 36:5 | 50:2 | 13 ik | | | 2 cab | 37:5 44:4 | (38:1) |

sonably well to the sequences of all three bases. In the following discussion, we will examine some of the series indicated in Table 4.3.

Let us begin with Base A, 9.16.4.10.8 12 Lamat (1 Muan). As indicated in Table 4.3, the base date 12 Lamat is recorded in the second section of Almanac 52 (pp. 22c–23c) (see Figure 4.1). Adding 177 days, one arrives at 7 Chicchan, recorded in section 4 of Almanac 52 (52:4). Adding another 177 days, one arrives at 2 Ik, recorded in 52:1. Thus, the first three *tzolkin* dates recorded in the eclipse table are also recorded in Almanac 52. The portraits in Almanac 52 are also appropriate for eclipses, as this is a *yatan* almanac in which the Moon Goddess is paired with death deities.

In order to continue with the series of dates recorded in the eclipse tables, one adds 148 days to arrive at 7 Oc, recorded in 35:2, 37:1, 44:1, and 52:6; and then 177 days to arrive at 2 Manik, recorded in 35:4, 37:5, 43:1, and 44:4. One is thus confronted with several calendrically parallel paths, and no clear reasons for choosing among them, though the simplest solution would be to stay in Almanac 35.

Basically equivalent, but somewhat longer series appear for Base B dates 59–66 and Base C dates 53–62 (c.f. Figure 4.1). In the Base B series one starts with 13 Ahau recorded in 48:3, 49:1, and 50:1, + 178 days = 9 Etz'nab (50:3), + 177 days = 4 Men (50:5), + 177 days = 12 Eb (52:2), + 177 days = 7 Mul (52:4) + 177 = 2 Cimi (52:1) + 148 = 7 Ix (35:2) + 177 days = 2 Chuen (35:4). The Base C sequence (dates 53–62, Table 4.3) is parallel but extends further. By adding 178 days to 2 Men (35:4), one arrives at 11 Ben (36:2) + 177 days = 6 Oc (35:3, 37:4) + 177 = 1 Manik (44:2). If vertical moves between almanacs were not permitted, the last step would be omitted.

Another Base C series links dates 11–15 as follows: 11 Caban (36:5) + 177 days = 6 Ix (35:3 or 37:4) + 148 days = 11 Ik (36:5) + 178 days = 7 Ahau (37:1 or 44:1) + 177 days = 2 Caban (37:5 or 44:4) [+ 177 = 10 Ix

(41:1) ?]. Many, if not all, of the dates 43–51 in the Base A series also appear to be linked in the Moon Goddess almanacs: 5 Oc (37:6) + 177 days = 13 Manik (41:2) + 177 days = 8 Kan (42:2 or 44:3) + 177 days = 3 Imix (45:3) + 177 days = 11 Etz'nab (36:2) + 177 = 6 Men (37:4) + 148 = 11 Akbal (36:2) + 177 = 6 Ahau (37:4) + 177 = 1 Caban (44:2).

Clearly, long series of eclipse intervals from each of the bases can be traced through the Moon Goddess almanacs. What appear to be repetitions of dates in different almanacs might actually reflect different sequences for the different bases. As an examination of Table 4.3 reveals, many plausible sequences can be mapped onto the Moon Goddess almanacs, and, if one were to allow the one day period before and after the target date, many of the gaps could be filled.

## Conclusion

We hope to have demonstrated that there is strong evidence indicating that eclipse intervals are a structuring mechanism in the Moon Goddess almanacs. The evidence presented is of several types. If one agrees with the identification of the female figure dominating these almanacs as the Moon Goddess, it would be natural to expect astronomically significant events involving the moon to be recorded. It has long been supposed that at least some of the pairings of the female figure with other characters represent celestial events. Iconographic evidence supports such expectations. Death symbolism associated with eclipses, which were conceived as deaths of the eclipsed body, are common throughout the Moon Goddess almanacs, closely matching the iconography associated with Ix Tab in the eclipse table.

Calendric evidence also strongly indicates the relevance of eclipse intervals. Many of the distance numbers recorded are shown to function in eclipse interval calculations almanac internally. Intervals between almanacs are likewise useful for calculating eclipse intervals.

More particularly, we investigated the relationship between the dates and intervals recorded in the Dresden eclipse table with the Moon Goddess almanacs. Other astronomical tables in the Dresden Codex have been shown to relate to almanacs elsewhere (V. Bricker 1988b; V. Bricker and H. Bricker 1986), suggesting such a hypothesis. Results are encouraging, but not conclusive. We find that many of the dates and intervals appearing in the table are found in the almanacs, and that, allowing the one day period of leeway, even more could be identified. However, we encountered methodological problems that persuade us to be cautious in our conclusions.

One difficulty is that different series of eclipse intervals may look alike, as noted in the overlaps in the series with Bases A, B, and C. A related problem is that of determining acceptable reading orders among almanacs.

As we noted, the Moon Goddess almanacs differ in structure as they progress from p. 16, where the day signs lack numeral coefficients, to p. 23, where they are increasingly tabular. Such differences might relate to differences in the relationship of the text to oral performance. As the ethnographic record indicates (e.g., Tedlock 1982), modern Mayan shamans have a complex set of mnemonics relating to the calendar and divination, independent of writing. Perhaps the relationship of these almanacs, particularly the more tabular ones, to oral performance is similarly indirect. However, the structure and content of the hieroglyphic captions accompanying portraits of the Moon Goddess do have features of parallelism and redundancy characteristic of chants (cf. Hofling 1989) and might have been related directly to oral performance. In either case, but especially if chanted, the practitioner would need rules for proceeding from one almanac to another. Iconographic and calendric evidence suggest the familiar conventions of horizontal and vertical moves, as well as cyclic moves linking the end to the beginning (e.g., links between Almanac 52, pp. 22c–23c to Almanac 35, pp. 18a–19a). Eclipse intervals provide a structure for numerous interalmanac linkages and might well have guided oral performance.

There are several possible avenues for determining more precisely which series of eclipse intervals is recorded in the Moon Goddess almanacs. First, attention to the iconography and glyphic passages associated with each date can provide valuable clues. For example, death iconography associated with the Moon Goddess suggests lunar rather than solar eclipses, while the presence of the Sun God in one of his guises might suggest a solar eclipse. Ideally, Moon Goddess almanac events could be firmly cross-dated, providing an absolute chronology, as the Brickers have done so impressively for almanacs elsewhere (V. Bricker 1988b; V. Bricker and H. Bricker 1986, 1988).[5] In the absence of firm cross-dating, we simply note that the eclipse table provides a good match for the Moon Goddess almanacs with Base dates A, B, and C.

A final point also concerns how these almanacs were used. First, we would like to emphasize that we neither claim nor believe that eclipse information is all that is recorded in these almanacs. Many other kinds of information about the moon are known to have been important to the Maya, and likely are included in these almanacs.[6] Our investigation raises questions about likely reading orders and suggests that there may have been more than one possible order. Indeed, one might speculate that different orders are appropriate for different functions (i.e., the almanacs, and sections within almanacs, are multifunctional and meaningfully related to one another in a variety of ways (cf. V. Bricker unpublished). It appears that one of the ways in which these almanacs relate to one another is based on eclipse intervals, quite likely the same ones recorded in the eclipse table.

NOTES

1. In a similar vein, Hofling (1988) suggests connections between the Venus tables and the so-called miscellaneous almanacs at the beginning of the Dresden Codex.

2. Because our focus in this chapter is the astronomical significance of the calendrics in the Moon Goddess Almanacs, the noncalendric hieroglyphic passages are mentioned only briefly. The interested reader is referred to Hofling (1989) and Thompson (1972) for a more complete discussion of them.

3. In examining the iconography of the Moon Goddess portraits, we were struck by what appear to be meaningful variations in her hand and arm positions. As Neuenswander (1981) pointed out, hand positions may be used to communicate information about astronomical phenomena in contemporary Maya communities. Of particular relevance is their use to indicate lunar phases. We suspect a similar function to the alternation of hand positions in the Moon Goddess almanacs.

4. Because of the problematic nature of Almanac 38, we largely omit it from discussion of interalmanac eclipse intervals. However, it is included in Tables 4.2 and 4.3, and in Figure 4.1.

5. Several possibilities for cross-dating Moon Goddess almanacs were checked, but unfortunately none has given definitive results. Specifically, in the third section of Almanac 52 (p. 22c), the first glyph resembling two human figures seated back to back has been identified by V. Bricker and H. Bricker (1988) as a sign of equinox and solstice. If the assumption that these dates relate to the eclipse table is correct, this might refer to a Spring equinox occurring on 21 March, 786 (9.17.15.6.17 12 Caban, 15 Zip), 1 day after the 11 Cib date recorded in 52:3. Other evidence possibly supporting interpreting the Moon Goddess almanac dates as those recorded in the eclipse table involve Venus events. V. Bricker and H. Bricker (1986) identified occasions involving lunar and solar eclipses and lunar conjunction with Venus in the eclipse table and in an agricultural almanac. A vulture is associated in both contexts. What appears to be the same vulture appears in the first section of Almanac 36. Dates identified involving the conjunction of Venus and the Moon do not suggest an obvious match to 36:1, but one of them (3 August, 775, Julian Day 2,004,337, 3 Ix) may be recorded in 46:6, also associated with a vulture.

6. For example, lunar phase, position in lunar semester, and occultations of planets and stars by the moon might well be relevant (see Meeus and Smith 1985 on occultations of Venus by the moon).

## REFERENCES

Anders, F., 1975. *Codex Dresdensis Maya: Sachsische Landesbibliothek Dresden.* (Graz: Akademische Druckund Verlagsanstalt).

Aveni, F., 1980. *Skywatchers of Ancient Mexico* (Austin and London: University of Texas Press).

Barrera Vasquez, A., J. R. B. Manzano, and W. B. Sansores, 1980. *Diccionario Maya Cordemex: Maya–Español, Español–Maya* (Merida: Ediciones Cordemex).

Bricker, H. M., and V. R. Bricker, 1983. "Classic Maya Prediction of Solar Eclipses," *Current Anthropology* **24**:1–24.

Bricker, V. R., 1988a. "Astronomical Syntax in the Dresden Codex," *Journal of Mayan Linguistics* 6:55–78.

—, 1988b. "The Relationship Between the Venus Table and an Almanac in the Dresden Codex," in *New Directions in American Archaeoastronomy*, edited by Anthony F. Aveni, pp. 81–103. BAR International Series 454.

—, unpublished. "What Constitutes Discourse in the Maya Codices?" Paper presented at the conference on "The Language of Maya Hieroglyphs," University of California at Santa Barbara, February, 1989.

Bricker, V. R., and H. M. Bricker, 1986. "Archaeoastronomical Implications of an Agricultural Almanac in the Dresden Codex," *Mexicon* 8:29–35.

—, 1988. "The Seasonal Table in the Dresden Codex and Related Almanacs," *Archaeoastronomy* (Supplement to the *Journal for the History of Astronomy* 19) **12**:S1–S62.

Closs, M. P., 1989. "Cognitive Aspects of Ancient Maya Eclipse Theory," in *World Archaeoastronomy*, edited by Anthony F. Aveni, pp. 389–415 (Cambridge: Cambridge University Press).

Hofling, C. A., 1988. "Venus and the Miscellaneous Almanacs in the Dresden Codex," *Journal of Mayan Linguistics* 6:79–102.

—, 1989. "The Morphosyntactic Basis of Discourse Structure in Glyphic Text in the Dresden Codex," In *World and Image in Maya Culture*, edited by William F. Hanks and Don S. Rice, pp. 51–71. (Salt Lake City: University of Utah Press).

Justeson, J. S., 1989. "Ancient Maya Ethnoastronomy: An Overview of Hieroglyphic Sources," In *World Archaeoastronomy*, edited by Anthony F. Aveni, pp. 76–129. (Cambridge: Cambridge University Press).

Kelley, D. H., 1980. "Astronomical Identities of Mesoamerican Gods," *Contributions to Mesoamerican Anthropology* 2:S1–54. (Miami: Institute of Maya Studies, Inc.).

Lounsbury, F. G., 1978. "Maya Numeration, Computation, and Calendrical Astronomy," in *Dictionary of Scientific Biography*, Vol. 15, Suppl. 1, pp. 759–818 (New York: Scribner's).

Meeus, J., and V. G. Smith, 1985. "A New Test for Maya Astronomical Observation: Occultations of Venus by the Moon," *Archaeoastronomy* 9:S97–101.

Neuenswander, H., 1981. "Vestiges of Early Maya Time Concepts in a Contemporary Maya (Cubulco Achi) Community: Implications for Epigraphy." *Estudios de Cultura Maya*, Vol. XIII, pp. 125–163. (Mexico: UNAM).

Oppolzer, T., 1987. *Canon der Finsternisse*. Kaiserliche Akademie der Wissenschaften, Mathematisch–Naturwissenschaftliche Classe, Denkschriften 52 (Wien: Kaiserliche–Königliche Hof-und Staatsdruckerei).

Tedlock, B., 1982. *Time and the Highland Maya* (Albuquerque: University of New Mexico Press).

Teeple, J. E., 1931. *Maya Astronomy*, Contributions to American Anthropology 1 (2) (Washington: Carnegie Institute of Washington).

Thompson, J. E., 1972. *A Commentary on the Dresden Codex*. (Philadelphia: American Philosophical Society).

Willson, R. W., 1924. *Astronomical Notes on the Maya Codices*, Papers of the Peabody Museum, **vi**(3) (Cambridge, Mass.: Harvard University).

# 5

# Some Parallels in the Astronomical Events Recorded in the Maya Codices and Inscriptions

MICHAEL P. CLOSS

The Dresden Codex contains two excellent examples of astronomical tables, one dedicated to the planet Venus and the other to solar and lunar eclipses. It has been proposed that the canonical base date of the Venus table reflects a real astronomical event (Lounsbury 1983). On the other hand, the canonical base date of the eclipse table reflects a theoretical eclipse station that was not an actual eclipse visible in the Maya area (Closs in press). In any case, scholars agree that many dates in the two tables do not refer to observed astronomical phenomena but are intended to predict significant stations in the astronomical cycles described. The tables are chronologically anchored in real time but are not embedded within the secular history of the Maya. In general, dynastic information on Maya rulership is not recorded in any of the surviving codices.

By contrast, most of the dates recorded in the monumental inscriptions are related to events in the lives of the Maya kings who commissioned the monuments. Nevertheless, it is not unusual to find that some of these dates are glyphically marked with astronomical references. The most common of these pertain to the moon and to Venus, and the references are usually incidental to the main events described, these being of a nonastronomical nature.

Despite the divergence in the content of the codices and the inscriptions, the moon ages in the latter are dated in a manner consistent with the moon ages predicted in the Dresden eclipse table (Closs in press). Similarly, the phenomena associated with references to Venus in the inscriptions are significant in relation to the expected Venus ages based on the Dresden Venus table (Closs 1979, 1981; Lounsbury 1982; Justeson 1989). It will be seen in this chapter that there are additional astronomical parallels in the events recorded in the inscriptions and codices.

## (Ah) Tsul Ahaw

In an earlier work (Closs in press), I have discussed 16 examples of a glyph I have read as *(Ah) Tsul Ahaw* (Figure 5.1). The essential components of the glyph consist of a T168, *ahaw* ("lord") superfix and a T559, *tsul* ("spine, dog") as the main sign. In addition, it may take an optional T12/229, *ah*, agentive prefix and/or a T130, *wa*, phonetic complement. The whole signifies "(He, the) Spine Lord," or "(He, the) Dog Lord." It is the name or title of a deity of the planet Venus, primarily associated with the evening star. The term *tsul* ("spine, dog") also reflects both the skeletal and canine attributes of the evening star (Closs 1979:158–162; 1989:409–11).

The reading of T559 as the logograph *tsul* is recommended by its iconic form in the codices, where it represents the fleshless ribcage together with the spine and pelvic region. It is also used as a rebus for *tsul* ("dog") in the iconography of the codices. Moreover, in these sources it is known to have phonetic value *tsu*. In one example, in the inscriptions, the T559 sign is replaced by T753, the head of a dog, recognizable as such by its characteristic ragged, or torn, ear. The same substitution occurs in the glyph for the month Kankin/Uniw.

In seven examples, the (Ah) Tsul Ahaw glyph is preceded by a Sky-in-Hand glyph taking a variety of prefixes: 1, *wi*, *ta*, or *ti*. Two of these are found in the inscriptions (Palenque, Temple of the Inscriptions, East Panel, P10–O11; Copan, Stela F, A10–B10), one is found in the Venus table of the Dresden Codex (Dresden 24, A15–16), two are found in the eclipse table for the Dresden Codex (Dresden 53a; Dresden 58b), and two are found in the *katun* pages of the Paris Codex (Paris 5, C11–B12; Paris 6, C11–B12).

In my previous study of the (Ah) Tsul Ahaw glyph (Closs in press), I was able to assign firm dates to 11 of the 16 examples. In the case of the text from the Middle Panel of the Temple of the Inscriptions, there are two examples of the glyph in a single text unit. On the other hand, on Dresden 58b, while there is only one example of the glyph, it is also the implied

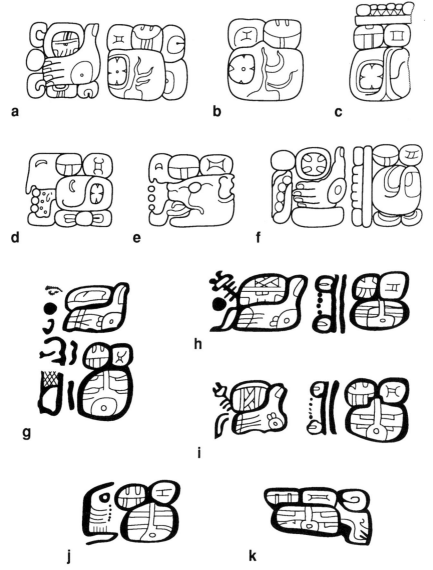

*Figure 5.1* Some (Ah) Tsul Ahaw glyphs and Sky-in-Hand (Ah) Tsul Ahaw phrases in Maya writing: a. Palenque, Temple of the Inscriptions, East Panel, P10–O11 (after a drawing of L. Schele); b. Palenque, Temple of the Inscriptions, Middle Panel, G8 (after a drawing of L. Schele); c. Dos Pilas, Stela 8, I16a (after a drawing of I. Graham); d. Quirigua, Structure 1,J' (after Morley 1935:Fig. 33); e. Quirigua, Structure 1,U' (after Morley 1935:Fig. 33); f. Copan, Stela F, A10–B10 (after Maudslay 1889–1902, Vol. 1, Pl. 52); g. Dresden 24, A15–A16 (drawing by the author); h. Dresden 53a (drawing by the author); i. Dresden 58b (drawing by the author); j. Dresden 47f (drawing by the author); k. Madrid 37d (drawing by the author).

135

*Table 5.1* Souces, Dates, and Venus Associations of (Ah) Tsul Ahaw Texts[a]

| Location of text | LC position | Julian date | Venus data |
|---|---|---|---|
| Palenque, Inscr. E, P10–011 | 9. 9. 0. 0. 0 | 9 May 613 | −66 (me) |
| Dresden 24, A15–A16 | 9. 9. 9.16. 0 | 6 Feb 623 | −13 |
| Palenque, Inscr. Mid, H6–H9 | 9.12. 0. 0. 0 | 28 Jun 672 | −70 (me) |
| Copan, Stela F, A10–B10 | 9.14.10. 0. 0 | 9 Oct 721 | −175 |
| Dos Pilas, Stela 8, H16–I16a | 9.14.15. 2. 3 | 26 Oct 726 | −84 (me) |
| Dresden 53a | 9.16. 5.17.10 | 24 Mar 757 | −70 (me) |
| Quirigua, Stela E, C20b–D20 | 9.17. 0. 0. 0 | 20 Jan 771 | −274 |
| Quirigua, Str. 1, U′ | 9.18.19.16. 0 | 15 May 810 | +68 (me) |
| Quirigua, Str. 1, J′ | 9.19. 0. 0. 0 | 24 Jun 810 | +108 |
| Dresden 58b (Picture text Date B) | 10.19.19. 1. 8 | 14 Jul 1223 | −259 |
| Dresden 58b (Picture text Date C) | 11. 0. 6. 1. 8 | 7 Jun 1230 | −71 (me) |

[a]Legend: − indicates days before inferior conjunction; + indicates days after inferior conjunction; LC = long count; me = approximate maximum elongation; correlation constant = 584285.

subject of the succeeding text unit. Thus, the results of the earlier study yield 11 dated passages. These results are summarized in Table 5.1.

In Table 5.1, the Venus data column lists the number of days before (−) or after (+) the nearest inferior conjunction of Venus as computed using the tables of Tuckerman (1964). The calculations are reliable only up to about 1 day, which is adequate for the present purposes. Maximum elongations of Venus occur about 72 days before and after inferior conjunction. Justeson (1989:125) allots a span of about 20–24 days as an approximate period for both maximum eastern elongation and maximum western elongation in a given Venus year. This is the time during which motion to and from maximum elongation would not be perceived. I expect that the Maya would have been aware of this and would have estimated the mid-point of such a span to create a canonical value for maximum elongations within a mean Venus cycle of 584 days. In fact, the data suggest that some of the records of maximum elongation were calculated by such a procedure, since the discrepancies with precise maximum elongations are considerably less than would otherwise be expected.

It is interesting to see that six of the eleven records occur near maximum elongations of Venus. Since the eighth and ninth dates, as well as the tenth and eleventh dates, occur in the same inscription, these are best treated as single items. This would imply that six of nine (Ah) Tsul Ahaw references occur near maximum elongations of the planet Venus. Two of these are found in the Dresden Codex and four in the inscriptions.

## Ah Tsul Ahaw in the Madrid Codex

There are five examples of the Ah Tsul Ahaw glyph for which I did not assign dates in my previous study. One of these is a variant form of the name with a distinctive prefix, found on Dresden 47f. This is the page of the Venus table in which the Venus god Lahum Chan is illustrated with a fleshless spine and ribcage, marking him as a god of the evening star. The context is one which suggests that it is to be considered typical of the evening star. Two other examples are from the Paris Codex; these can now be dated and will be considered later. The remaining two examples occur in the New Year pages of the Madrid Codex. Since these pages are not fixed in the long count, it is not possible to assign unique dates to them.

One of these examples is found on Madrid 34. The last two glyphs in the text are the sign for west and the name glyph of Tsul Ahaw. Directly below this glyph pair is a black deity sowing grains of maize (Figure 5.2). Since black is the color of the direction west, it is likely that the black deity depicted here is the West Tsul Ahaw named previously. This identification

*Figure* 5.2 Detail from Madrid 34, showing the name and figure of the West Tsul Ahaw.

is supported by the other three New Year pages. Each of these illustrates a deity sowing maize in the same location on the page. Moreover, each figure is situated beneath a direction sign and a presumed name that terminate the respective text. None of these is painted black; so the correspondence between the West Tsul Ahaw and the pictured deity seems secure. The god is wearing a jaguar headdress with crossed bands and other elements above it and also a large pectoral.

Of the corresponding deities on the other New Year pages, only one wears a similar pectoral and headdress (but without the jaguar head). This is the deity on Madrid 37 who is named in the text above as the North Tsul Ahaw (Figure 5.3). The deity is white, the color of north, but this is surely not significant since the deities on the east and south pages are also painted white. However, in this instance, the deity is face to face with a dog playing a drum. The dog is conspicuously marked with the bared ribs signifying *tsul* ("dog, spine"). This is the same symbol found in the name glyph of Tsul Ahaw and in the illustration of the Venus god Lahun Chan on Dresden 47.

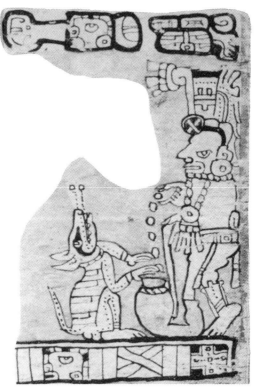

*Figure* 5.3 Detail from Madrid 37 showing the name and figure of the North Tsul Ahaw and the *tsul* dog playing a drum.

It is the feature that marks Lahun Chan as a god of the evening star. The presence of the *tsul* dog here is entirely gratuitous and is simply an iconic allusion to the identity of the Venus god, who is depicted and named on this page.

The four New Year pages of the Madrid Codex are divided into upper and lower sections by horizontal sky bands. The Tsul Ahaw figures and the other directional deities are shown standing upon the right half (Figure 5.2) or center right half (Figure 5.3) portions of these bands. The sky bands on the four pages make use of a very limited set of those elements that are known to occur in such contexts. The signs, in their order of appearance on the different pages, are given in Table 5.2.

The crossed bands have the linguistic value *ta* ("in, on, at"), *akbal* signifies "night", and God C represents *k'u* ("god, deity") (Kurbjuhn 1989:63, 73; Ringle 1988). The mat sign is a symbol of power or rule. The set of signs appearing in these sky bands form a coherent complex of elements relating to gods and the night sky. In fact, from its iconic form and the present context, I would suggest that the dotted cross offset on a black field represents the starry night sky itself. With this understanding, the signs under the West Tsul Ahaw may refer to him as "the god (of the) starry night sky" (Figure 5.2). Similarly, the signs under the North Tsul Ahaw may refer to him as "the god in the starry night sky" (Figure 5.3).

When Venus is the evening star, it is visible in the western sky shortly after sunset. Thus, the association of the direction west with the evening star is natural. The association of north with the evening star is less well known. It was first brought to notice by Closs, Aveni, and Crowley (1984). In this work, it was argued that there was an intimate relationship between Venus, the rains, and the coming of the maize. One element of the relationship involved an astronomical interest in northern extremes of Venus as an indicator of the coming of the rains. It was also noted that the direction north is explicitly associated with the coming of the rains in ethnohistorical accounts. Mention was also made that, in the Moran vocabulary of Manche Chol, north is rendered as *no ec*, that is *Noh Ek* ("Great Star"), the Manche Chol term for Venus. These ideas have been further developed

*Table 5.2*   The Elements Appearing in the Sky Bands in the New Year Pages of the Madrid Codex

| | |
|---|---|
| Madrid 34 | Crossed bands, *akbal*, God C, dotted cross offset on a black field |
| Madrid 35 | Dotted cross offset on a black field, mat, God C, crossed bands, *akbal* |
| Madrid 36 | Crossed bands, dotted Venus sign, *akbal*, dotted cross offset on a black field, mat |
| Madrid 37 | Dotted Venus sign?, *akbal*, God C, crossed bands, dotted cross offset on a black field |

and treated by Ivan Sprajc (1989) in his thesis *Venus, Lluvia y Maiz: Simbolismo y Astronomia en la Cosmovisión Mesoamericana*.


## The Eclipse of 9.17.0.0.0

Kelley (1977) observed a tentative correspondence between the first glyph in a zero moon-age record at 9.17.0.0.0 on Stela E from Quirigua and the first glyph in the 32nd eclipse station in the eclipse table of the Dresden Codex. He also noted that if the initial run of the eclipse table counts from the table base date of 12 Lamat 1 Muan at 9.16.4.10.8, then the 32nd eclipse possibility is fixed at 9.17.0.0.0, at which time, according to the 584285 correlation, there occurred Oppolzer eclipse 4724, an annular eclipse visible in the Yucatan. My earlier work has shown that the initial run of the eclipse table did count from that base date (Closs in press).

Kelley also proposed that a sentence at the end of the inscription, on the east face of Stela E, might be a reference to the same eclipse. Again, I have shown that the subject of this final sentence is Ah Tsul Ahaw (Closs in press) and that he was regarded as an eclipse agent (Closs 1989:409–11). In this case (see Table 5.1), Venus is about 10–15 days prior to its first appearance as the evening star and normally would not be visible. However, I have also pointed out that the verb in the final sentence suggests that the Maya anticipated the evening star would become visible for a brief time if the projected eclipse did materialize (Closs in press).

The preceding information suggests that the Maya did take notice of the eclipse possibility at 9.17.0.0.0, both on Quirigua Stela E and in the eclipse table. It may be objected that the latter reference is coincidental since it is only one station among many. Even so, other evidence has now come to light that reveals an explicit reference to this particular eclipse in the Paris Codex.

Hannelore Treiber (1987) has given a detailed analysis of the cycle of *katun* pages in the Paris Codex. Among her findings, she presents a chronological reading of the sequence from G1 to G2 on Paris 4 (Figure 5.4) as 5 Akbal 16 Zac in Katun 11 Ahau. She places this date in the long count at 9.17.16.15.3. Although other placements are possible, such as 9.4.13.4.3, these can be eliminated by the astronomical evidence that is to be discussed. With this information, Paris 4 can be assigned to the *katun* that runs from 9.17.0.0.0 (13 Ahau) to 9.18.0.0.0 (11 Ahau), the *katun* being named after its ending day.

The initial clause of the prophecy pertains to the seating of the lords of Katun 11 Ahau at 9.17.0.0.0 and also contains the opening augury for the *katun*. This sequence runs from B1 to C11, at which point a distance

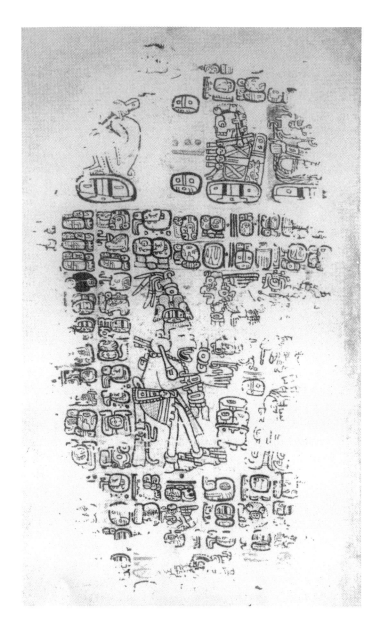

*Figure* 5.4 Paris 4.

number leads one to a later point in the *katun*. Following the work of Treiber (1987:68), with some modifications by the author, the first clause can be paraphrased as follows:

| | | | |
|---|---|---|---|
| B1 | The successor lord (is) | C1 | the divine god [God C]; |
| B2 | the successor lord (is) | C2 | K'awil [God K]; |
| B3 | the successor lord (is) | C3 | the successor lord. |
| B4 | The sun is darkened (?) [possible solar eclipse reference] | C4 | ? [a glyph which ends phrases]. |
| B5 | Pawatun | C5 | *tok' - te' – ?* |
| B6 | *? - tun* | C6 | *sak tun* |
| B7 | north | C7 | west |
| B8 | 6 *pistun* (?) | C8 | Death (to the) |
| B9 | maize god [God E]; | C9 | death (to) |
| B10 | mankind. | C10 | Eclipse of sun, |
| B11 | eclipse of moon; | C11 | the underworld Venus lord plunges Earthwards. |

The paraphrase permits a clearer understanding of the syntactic structure of the clause and its interpretation. The clause begins with a triplet construction, from B1 to C3, marking the change to a new rule. The glyph at B4 is a unique glyph that, from its appearance, may refer to the darkening of the sun at the beginning of Katun 11 Ahau. The sign at B4 appears to occur at the end of phrases in the *katun* pages; its meaning is opaque. There follow at least four couplets running from B6 to C6, from B7 to C7, from C8 to B10, and from C10 to B11. The emphasis in this initial augury is on terrible calamities (C8–B10) that are related to the eclipse mentioned from C10 to C11. The directional couplet at B7–C7 is associated with the Venus god of the underworld, who is regarded as the causative agent of Maya eclipses (Closs 1989). This was seen in the preceding section, where the Ah Tsul Ahaw deity is named and depicted in the New Year pages of the Madrid Codex in association with these two directions. The glyph at C11 refers to the same Venus deity, who following an eclipse, was expected to descend to the Earth to devour mankind. This apocalyptic prophecy is the glyphic analog of the ominous scene on Dresden 58b showing the Venus eclipse god, plunging Earthwards from paired eclipse symbols attached to a skyband, ready to devour the human race.

The fearful nature of the prophecy at the beginning of Katun 11 Ahau is related to its placement, in agreement with Treiber, as the one that runs from 9.17.0.0.0 to 9.18.0.0.0. As noted earlier, the seating day of this *katun* was the day of a solar eclipse visible in the Maya area. It is the 32nd eclipse station in the Dresden eclipse table and is also anticipated on Quirigua Stela E. It is the most important eclipse in Maya history, since it is the only one known to have occurred on a *katun* ending.

### Ah Tsul Ahaw in the Paris Codex

An Ah Tsul Ahaw glyph is found at B12 on Paris 5 (Figure 5.5). It is preceded by a *ta*-Sky-in-Hand glyph at C11 and followed by a distance number that marks the beginning of the next sentence. The sentence that concerns us gives the prophecy for the seating of Katun 9 Ahau at 9.18.0.0.0. The structure of the text is similar to that found on Paris 4. It begins by mentioning the seating of the lords of Katun 9 Ahau at 9.18.0.0.0 and ends with an astronomical phrase. In this case, that phrase refers to Venus, which was approximately 10 days before its maximum eastern elongation, a point when the evening star was entering its more or less stationary period.

This astronomical reference is parallel to similar records on the Temple of the Inscriptions at Palenque (East Panel, P10–O11; Middle Panel, G6–H9). The first of these marks 9.9.0.0.0, when Venus was about 5 days past maximum eastern elongation, and the second marks 9.12.0.0.0, when Venus was at precise maximum eastern elongation. The Maya seemed to have been interested in the near coincidence of Venus phenomena every three *katuns* and likely were aware of the corresponding 5-day shift in Venus positions. It seems clear that the Maya were prompted to make these records because of the coincidence of chronological (*katun* endings) and astronomical events (maximum elongations of Venus). This same motivation can be seen in the reference to the eclipse of 9.17.0.0.0 on Paris 4.

It may be observed that at 9.15.0.0.0 Venus was about 5 days before maximum eastern elongation. Although we have no instance of this phenomenon being marked in the inscriptions, it is interesting to note that the ruler Eighteen Rabbit of Copan erected Stela F during the *katun* ending at 9.15.0.0.0. In the inscription on Stela F, he specifically mentions the current *katun* (Copan Stela F, B3) and seems to have appropriated the Sky-in-Hand Ah Tsul Ahaw phrase as a title in his nominal phrase. This may have been motivated by the approximate maximum elongation of Venus, which would occur on the name day of the current *katun*. If so, it may explain the anomalous Venus record for Stela F noted in Table 5.1.

A second Ah Tsul Ahaw glyph is found at B12 on Paris 6 (Figure 5.6). It

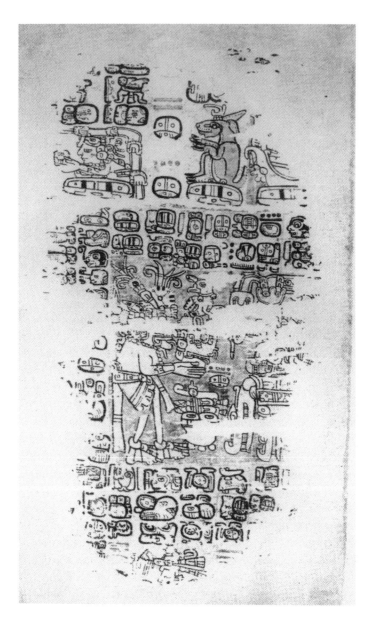

*Figure* 5.5 Paris 5.

*Figure* 5.6 Paris 6.

is preceded by a *ti*-Sky-in-Hand glyph at C11. The glyphic phrase occurs at the end of the initial sentence of the prophecy for Katun 7 Ahau, since the next glyph at C12 is a distance number. The opening sentence in the prophecy begins with the seating of the lords of Katun 7 Ahau at 9.19.0.0.0 and ends with the phrase referring to Venus. In this case, the planet is in its morning star phase about 111 days after inferior conjunction. The astronomical position of Venus seems anomalous, but it is exactly 40 days (or one footstep, in Maya parlance) after maximum western elongation. Another Venus record for the *katun* ending at 9.19.0.0.0 is found on Quirigua Structure 1. In the latter case, both the *katun* ending and the maximum elongation date 40 days earlier are recorded in successive sentences with the same Venus reference (see Table 5.1).

## A Probability Estimate

Let us consider the question of whether or not the Venus positions that occur in relationship to the Tsul Ahaw glyph may be due to chance behavior. In this paper, the stationary period near maximum elongation has been maximally estimated as 24 days. This means that there are 48 of 584 days during which an approximate maximum elongation could occur in a random selection of dates. The likelihood of this happening is given by $p = 48/584 \approx 0.082$.

We have nine independent dated text references associated with (Ah) Tsul Ahaw glyphs in Table 5.1, and we have two such references from the Paris Codex. In eight of these cases (nine if we accept the notion that the record on Copan Stela F is related to the *katun* ending at 9.15.0.0.0 rather than to the date of erection of the monument), the dates are associated with approximate maximum elongations of Venus. We can then determine the likelihood that at least eight of the eleven texts should yield such results based on chance behavior. A suitable model for this problem is to consider the Venus records as a sequence of 11 Bernoulli trials, each having success probability $p = 0.082$. In such a case, we find that $P$ (at least 8 successes in 11 trials) $\approx 0.0000003$. Therefore, there is less than one chance in two million that these results are coincidental. The results are highly statistically significant.

### ACKNOWLEDGMENT

The author thanks Hannelore Treiber for stimulating discussions that led to this paper. This work has been supported by a research grant (410-89-0451) from the Social Sciences and Humanities Research Council of Canada.

REFERENCES

Closs, M. P., 1979. "Venus in the Maya World: Glyphs, Gods and Associated Astronomical Phenomena," in *Tercera Mesa Redonda de Planenque*, Vol. 4, edited by Merle Greene Robertson and Donnan Call Jeffers, pp. 147–65. (Monterey, Calif.: Pre-Columbian Art Research, Herald Printers).

—, 1981. "Venus dates revisited," *Archaeoastronomy: The Bulletin of the Center for Archaeoastronomy* 4(4):38–41.

—, 1989. "Cognitive Aspects of Ancient Maya Eclipse Theory," in *World Archaeoastronomy*, edited by A. F. Aveni, pp. 389–415. (Cambridge: Cambridge University Press).

—, in press. "A Glyph for Venus as Evening Star," to appear in a volume of selected papers from the *Septima Mesa Redonda de Palenque* held in Palenque, Chiapas, Mexico, June, 1989.

Closs, M. P., A. F. Aveni, and B. Crowley, 1984. "The Planet Venus and Temple 22 at Copan," *Indiana* 9:221–47.

Justeson, J. S., 1989. "Ancient Maya Ethnoastronomy: An Overview of Hieroglyphic Sources," in *World Archaeoastronomy*, edited by A. F. Aveni, pp. 76–129 (Cambridge: Cambridge University Press).

Kelley, D. H., 1977. "A Possible Maya Eclipse Record," in *Social Process in Maya Prehistory*, edited by Norman Hammond, pp. 405–8 (London: Academic Press).

Kurbjuhn, K., 1989. *Maya: The Complete Catalogue of Glyph Readings* (Kassel, Germany: Schneider & Weber).

Lounsbury, F. G., 1982. "Astronomical Knowledge and its Uses at Bonampak, Mexico," in *Archaeoastronomy in the New World*, edited by Anthony F. Aveni, pp. 143–68 (Cambridge: Cambridge University Press).

—, 1983. "The Base of the Venus Table of the Dresden Codex, and its Significance for the Calendar-Correlation Problem," in *Calendars in Mesoamerica and Peru: Native American Computations of Time*, edited by Anthony F. Aveni and Gordon Brotherston, pp. 1–26. BAR International Series 174 (Proceedings of the 44th International Congress of Americanists).

Ringle, W. M., 1988. "Of Mice and Monkeys: The Value and Meaning of the God C Hieroglyph." Research Reports on Ancient Maya Writing, 18 (Washington, D.C.: Center for Maya Research).

Sprajc, I., 1989. *Venus, Lluvia y Maiz: Simbolismo y Astronomia en la Cosmovision Mesoamericana*. Tesis que para optar por el titulo de Maestro en Historia y Etnohistoria, Escuela Nacional de Antropologia e Historia, Mexico, D.F.

Treiber, H., 1987. *Studien zur Katunserie der Pariser Mayahandschriften*. Acta Mesoamericana, Band 2. (Berlin: Verlag Von Flemming).

Tuckerman, G., 1964. *Planetary, Lunar, and Solar Positions* A.D. 2 to A.D. 1649 *at Five-Day and Ten-Day Intervals* (Philadelphia: The American Philosophical Society).

# 6

# Zodiacal References
# in the Maya Codices

HARVEY M. BRICKER
VICTORIA R. BRICKER

Previous scholarship on the astronomical content of the Maya codices has demonstrated that pre-Columbian astronomers were concerned with recording and predicting such cyclically recurring events as the synodic stations of the planets Venus (Closs 1977; Lounsbury 1978, 1983; Aveni, Chapter 3 of this volume; Justeson 1989) and Mars (Willson 1924:22–25; Aveni 1980:195–99; V. Bricker and H. Bricker 1986), solar and lunar eclipses (H. Bricker and V. Bricker 1983), and the stations of the synodic or tropical year (V. Bricker and H. Bricker 1988, 1989). In all these cases, systems of commensuration were developed that related individual astronomical cycles to others as well as to the principal calendrical cycles of the Maya—always to the 260-day *tzolkin* and sometimes to the 364-day "computing year" (Thompson 1941, 1960:256) or the 365-day *haab*. This chapter examines the evidence for the proposition, long entertained (for example, Förstemann 1903:30; Spinden 1916, 1924:55–56) but not satisfactorily demonstrated, that the pre-Columbian Maya were concerned also with recording the stations of the sidereal year and commensurating these stations with their calendrical cycles.

The stations of the sidereal year must be defined with reference to the fixed stars, and there is every reason to expect that for the Maya, as for other prescientific peoples in both hemispheres, what was most salient was the patterning of bright stars within a few degrees of the ecliptic. In other

148

words, what this chapter is concerned with is evidence that the pre-Columbian Maya recognized zodiacal constellations and related the cyclical pattern of their appearance and disappearance to other astronomical or calendrical cycles of interest.

The most important evidence bearing on a Maya zodiac has long been recognized (Spinden 1916, 1924:56) to be an almanac in the Paris Codex (*Codex Peresianus* 1968), and our model of the stations of the sidereal year is based primarily on this document. It is, however, additionally informed by inscriptional evidence from the Las Monjas complex at Chichén Itzá, which has also long been recognized as relevant (Spinden 1916, 1924:56). The model we develop, which suggests correspondences between Maya constellations and those of traditional Western astronomy and specifies how the zodiacal cycle was commensurated with the Maya calendar, is tested against the evidence provided by zodiacal references in the Dresden Codex (*Codex Dresdensis* 1975), the Madrid Codex (*Codex Tro-Cortesianus* 1967), and the murals of Bonampak (Miller 1986). The test results strongly support a view of pre-Columbian Maya concern with the stations of the sidereal year that is quite consistent with current understanding of their treatment of other astronomical cycles.

### Calendrical Structure of the Paris Zodiacal Almanac

Pages 23 and 24 of the Paris Codex (*Codex Peresianus* 1968), a pre-Columbian Maya hieroglyphic book, contain an 1820-day almanac composed of five rows of 364 days, each of which is divided into 13 smaller intervals of 28 days (Figure 6.1). The almanac occupies the lower half of the middle register of the pages in question. The upper half of the middle register contains a sky band and a row of solar eclipse glyphs from which seven zoomorphic figures are suspended. In the lower register of these pages, what were once six more zoomorphic figures are suspended from another row of solar eclipse glyphs. The upper register consists of a 13-column hieroglyphic text.

Previous scholars, beginning with Herbert Spinden in 1916, have suggested that the zoomorphic figures on these pages represent the constellations of a Maya zodiac; recent treatments of the subject include those of Kelley (1976:45–50), Aveni (1980:199–202), Severin (1981), Dütting and Schramm (1988), Brotherston (1989), and Justeson (1989). The 364-day length of the rows in the almanac is only 1.2564 days short of the sidereal year, and the 28-day intervals that make up each row are appropriate for a zodiac composed of 13 constellations, which is almost certainly the number

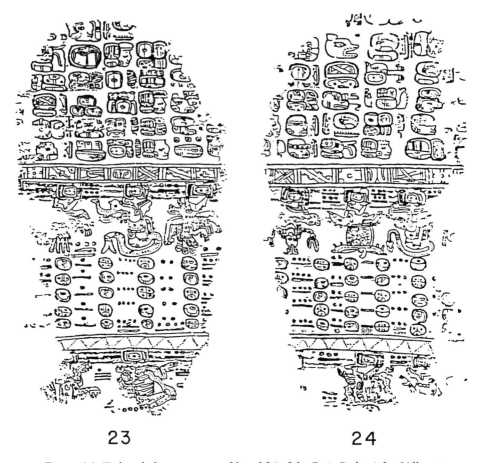

*Figure 6.1* Zodiacal almanac on pp. 23 and 24 of the Paris Codex (after Villacorta C. and Villacorta 1976:220, 222).

of dangling zoomorphic figures shown in the second and third registers. In order to demonstrate that this is, in fact, a zodiacal almanac, it is necessary to determine how the almanac could have been used and recycled and to specify the constellational referents of the zoomorphic figures. Our solutions to these problems are different from those offered by other scholars.

The calendrical component of the zodiacal almanac consists of five rows and thirteen columns of dates in *tzolkin* notation. The head glyphs shown in profile in the upper register face the right, instead of the left, as is usual for the writing system, and so do the zoomorphic figures in the second and third registers. This suggests that the almanac is to be read from right to left, which is the reverse of the normal reading order (Figure 6.1).

Because of damage to the edges of the pages, only seven columns of dates are shown in full, but the other six columns can be reconstructed from the information that is given (Table 6.1a).

The almanac contains two kinds of coefficients differentiated by color. Red bar-and-dot numbers to the left of the day glyphs represent the coefficients of the *tzolkin* date to which they refer. Green bar-and-dot numbers appear just above or just below each extant column of red numbers. The distance between the last red number in a given column and the green number immediately below it is 7 days, whereas the distance between the green number above a column and the first red number immediately beneath it is 6 days. For example, the coefficient of the last day in the tenth column of Table 6.1a is "4" (four red dots), and the green number below it is "11" (two green bars and one green dot), which is 4 + 7. Similarly, immediately above the eleventh column in Table 6.1a is a green "13" (two bars and three dots), and the coefficient of the first *tzolkin* date in that column is a red "6" (one bar and one dot), which is 13 + 6 modulo 13.

The period covered by the almanac, 1820 days or 5 computing years, is 6.282 days short of 5 sidereal years. We believe that the green numbers in the almanac are corrected values that, if employed in recycling, allow for more accurate commensuration of the Maya calendar and the sidereal year. Just how the corrections are to be made is not stated explicitly on the surviving pages of the almanac (perhaps some introductory material once existed on the page immediately to its right, the contents of which are now completely effaced), but the structure of the almanac itself suggests a probable answer based on the relationship:

$$n + 7 + 6 = n \text{ modulo } 13$$

After one full 1820-day run through the almanac has been completed, ending on a day with a *tzolkin* coefficient of 11, the next day, which would be the first day of a second run through the almanac were no correction applied, has a *tzolkin* coefficient of 12. If, however, a 7-day positive correction is applied at this point, the second run through the table then begins on a day with a *tzolkin* coefficient of 6, which is the value that can be reconstructed for the green coefficient in column 1 of the almanac, now effaced. The corresponding *tzolkin* coefficients for columns 2 through 13 of the corrected almanac are 8, 10, 12, 1, 3, 5, 7, 9, 11, 13, 2, and 4, respectively. The majority of this series of coefficients, painted in green, is clearly legible in columns 2–5 and 7–10 of the almanac. The second run of the almanac so corrected ends on a day with a *tzolkin* coefficient of 5. If, instead of beginning a third run with the next day, which would have a coefficient of 6, a 6-day positive correction is applied, the third run then

Table 6.1  Part a. The Calendrical Structure of the Zodiacal Almanac on Pages 23 and 24 of the Paris Codex; Numbers in Italics Above and Below the *Tzolkin* Dates Represent Green Numbers. Parts b and c. A Model for recycling the Zodiacal Almanac

**a. 12 Lamat Original**

| (13) | (12) | (11) | (10) | (9) | (8) | (7) | (6) | (5) | (4) | (3) | (2) | (1) |
|---|---|---|---|---|---|---|---|---|---|---|---|---|
|  | *13* |  |  |  | *7* |  |  |  |  |  |  |  |
| 10 Kan | 8 Cib | 6 Lamat | 4 Ahau | 2 Eb | 13 Kan | 11 Cib | 9 Lamat | 7 Ahau | 5 Eb | 3 Kan | 1 Cib | 12 Lamat |
| 10 Lamat | 8 Ahau | 6 Eb | 4 Kan | 2 Cib | 13 Lamat | 11 Ahau | 9 Eb | 7 Kan | 5 Cib | 3 Lamat | 1 Ahau | 12 Eb |
| 10 Eb | 8 Kan | 6 Cib | 4 Lamat | 2 Ahau | 13 Eb | 11 Kan | 9 Cib | 7 Lamat | 5 Ahau | 3 Eb | 1 Kan | 12 Cib |
| 10 Cib | 8 Lamat | 6 Ahau | 4 Eb | 2 Kan | 13 Cib | 11 Lamat | 9 Ahau | 7 Eb | 5 Kan | 3 Cib | 1 Lamat | 12 Ahau |
| 10 Ahau | 8 Eb | 6 Kan | 4 Cib | 2 Lamat | 13 Ahau | 11 Eb | 9 Kan | 7 Cib | 5 Lamat | 3 Ahau | 1 Eb | 12 Kan |
|  |  | *11* |  | *9* |  |  | *3* | *1* | *12* | *10* |  |  |

**b. 6 Men Corrected Multiple**

| (13) | (12) | (11) | (10) | (9) | (8) | (7) | (6) | (5) | (4) | (3) | (2) | (1) |
|---|---|---|---|---|---|---|---|---|---|---|---|---|
| 4 Chuen | 2 Akbal | 13 Men | 11 Manik | 9 Cauac | 7 Chuen | 5 Akbal | 3 Men | 1 Manik | 12 Cauac | 10 Chuen | 8 Akbal | 6 Men |
| 4 Men | 2 Manik | 13 Cauac | 11 Chuen | 9 Akbal | 7 Men | 5 Manik | 3 Cauac | 1 Chuen | 12 Akbal | 10 Men | 8 Manik | 6 Cauac |
| 4 Cauac | 2 Chuen | 13 Akbal | 11 Men | 9 Manik | 7 Cauac | 5 Chuen | 3 Akbal | 1 Men | 12 Manik | 10 Cauac | 8 Chuen | 6 Akbal |
| 4 Akbal | 2 Men | 13 Manik | 11 Cauac | 9 Chuen | 7 Akbal | 5 Men | 3 Manik | 1 Cauac | 12 Chuen | 10 Akbal | 8 Men | 6 Manik |
| 4 Manik | 2 Cauac | 13 Chuen | 11 Akbal | 9 Men | 7 Manik | 5 Cauac | 3 Chuen | 1 Akbal | 12 Men | 10 Manik | 8 Cauac | 6 Chuen |

**c. 12 Imix Corrected Multiple**

| (13) | (12) | (11) | (10) | (9) | (8) | (7) | (6) | (5) | (4) | (3) | (2) | (1) |
|---|---|---|---|---|---|---|---|---|---|---|---|---|
| 10 Caban | 8 Muluc | 6 Imix | 4 Ben | 2 Chicchan | 13 Caban | 11 Muluc | 9 Imix | 7 Ben | 5 Chicchan | 3 Caban | 1 Muluc | 12 Imix |
| 10 Imix | 8 Ben | 6 Chicchan | 4 Caban | 2 Muluc | 13 Imix | 11 Ben | 9 Chicchan | 7 Caban | 5 Muluc | 3 Imix | 1 Ben | 12 Chicchan |
| 10 Chicchan | 8 Caban | 6 Muluc | 4 Imix | 2 Ben | 13 Chicchan | 11 Caban | 9 Muluc | 7 Imix | 5 Ben | 3 Chicchan | 1 Caban | 12 Muluc |
| 10 Muluc | 8 Imix | 6 Ben | 4 Chicchan | 2 Caban | 13 Muluc | 11 Imix | 9 Ben | 7 Chicchan | 5 Caban | 3 Muluc | 1 Imix | 12 Ben |
| 10 Ben | 8 Chicchan | 6 Caban | 4 Muluc | 2 Imix | 13 Ben | 11 Chicchan | 9 Caban | 7 Muluc | 5 Imix | 3 Ben | 1 Chicchan | 12 Caban |

152

begins on a day with a coefficient of 12, the value of all the red coefficients that can be reconstructed for column 1 of the almanac.

Our model for recycling the almanac specifies, then, that the two sets of *tzolkin* coefficients, red and green, are used in alternating runs of the almanac. The red coefficients, appropriate to the first, third, fifth, etc. runs, are shown five times, once for every row of the almanac. The green coefficients, used in the second, fourth, etc. runs, are shown only once, either just above or just below each column. The full structure of the model may be seen by comparing Figure 6.1 and Table 6.1. The original run (Table 6.1a) begins on a day 12 Lamat; the starting day of each 28-day period is specified completely by the glyph for the *tzolkin* day and a red coefficient. After a 7-day correction, the second run (Table 6.1b) begins on a day 6 Men; the *tzolkin* coefficients for the start of each 28-day period are shown in green above or below each column, but the appropriate day glyphs are not shown. Following a 6-day correction, the third run (Table 6.1c) begins on a day 12 Imix; the original coefficient of 12 and all others of the set shown in red have been recovered, but the appropriate day glyphs are again not represented.

Use of the almanac in the way we suggest would allow its structure to fit quite well, for about a century, with the sidereal year. After one run of the almanac (5 computing years), it is 6.282 days behind the sidereal cycle (1820 days is 6.282 days less than 5 sidereal years). The use of a 7-day correction at this point creates an overcorrection of just less than 1 day ($7 - 6.282 = 0.718$) for starting the second run. By the end of the second run, the accumulated shortfall is 5.564 days ($+0.718 - 6.282$), but the application of a 6-day correction here means that the third run is begun with another slight overcorrection ($-5.564 + 6.000 = 0.436$ days). After 110 computing years or 22 full runs of the almanac, accumulating overcorrection would have caused the almanac's structure to be almost 5 days (4.796) ahead of the sidereal cycle. In the absence of any explicit indications in the almanac itself, we offer no speculations about other corrections that might have made it useful over longer periods of time.

Further understanding of the zodiacal almanac in the Paris Codex depends upon placing it in real time. Unlike the astronomical tables in the Dresden Codex (*Codex Dresdensis* 1975), the almanac in the Paris Codex does not have a preface or introduction with a base date in long-count notation that would permit it to be tied directly into the Western calendar. It is, however, possible to supply a base date for the almanac by cross-dating it with the eclipse table in the Dresden Codex. Two circumstances allow us to use this procedure here with great confidence. First, of the several hundred separate almanacs or tables appearing in the four surviving Maya codices, only these two documents have a 12 Lamat base date. Second, there are clear thematic ties between the two documents. Both have solar eclipse glyphs associated with zoomorphic figures, and at least two of the specific zoomorphic figures in the zodiacal almanac appear also in the eclipse table (the skeleton on Paris 23c and the rattlesnake on Paris 24b—compare Figures 6.2a and 6.2b with Figure 6.1).

The base date of the eclipse table is 9.16.10.4.8 12 Lamat 1 Muan, which corresponds to 10 November A.D. 755 in the Gregorian calendar (H. Bricker and V. Bricker 1983). Using the same base date for the zodiacal almanac allows us to specify the Gregorian month and day equivalents for each of the *tzolkin* dates in the first three runs of the almanac (Table 6.2). If we look at the Gregorian date of the first day of each row (or computing year) in the first run of the almanac (Table 6.2a, column 1), we see that the date in the first row is 10 November. After 364 days, it has recessed by two days to 8 November, and it continues to move backward in each of the following rows by 1 or 2 days, reaching 5 November in the fifth row. If not corrected, it would drift back to 3 November at the beginning of the second run through the almanac. However, the effect of the 7-day correction at the end of the first run through the almanac is to return the beginning date for the second run to 10 November (Table 6.2b, column 1). This date then recesses by 1 or 2 days in the subsequent rows of the almanac until the second correction, this time of 6 days, brings the date back to 10 November to start the third run through the almanac (Table 6.2c, column 1). The recession of the 364-day computing year with respect to the sidereal year was, therefore, overcome by alternating between 7-day and 6-day corrections every 5 years.

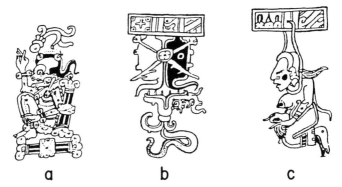

a          b          c

*Figure* 6.2 Zoomorphic figures in the eclipse table of the Dresden Codex. a. From p. 53a; b. from p. 56b; c. from p. 53b (after Villacorta C. and Villacorta 1976:116, 122).

*Table 6.2* Gregorian Equivalents of Dates in the Original and Corrected Multiples of the Zodiacal Almanac on Pages 23 and 24 of the Paris Codex

| (13) | (12) | (11) | (10) | (9) | (8) | (7) | (6) | (5) | (4) | (3) | (2) | (1) |
|---|---|---|---|---|---|---|---|---|---|---|---|---|
| **a.  12 Lamat Original (A.D. 755–760)** | | | | | | | | | | | | |
| 11 Oct | 13 Sep | 16 Aug | 19 Jul | 21 Jun | 24 May | 26 Apr | 29 Mar | 1 Mar | 2 Feb | 5 Jan | 8 Dec | 10 Nov |
| 10 Oct | 12 Sep | 15 Aug | 18 Jul | 20 Jun | 23 May | 25 Apr | 28 Mar | 28 Feb | 31 Jan | 3 Jan | 6 Dec | 8 Nov |
| 9 Oct | 11 Sep | 14 Aug | 17 Jul | 19 Jun | 22 May | 24 Apr | 27 Mar | 27 Feb | 30 Jan | 2 Jan | 5 Dec | 7 Nov |
| 8 Oct | 10 Sep | 13 Aug | 16 Jul | 18 Jun | 21 May | 23 Apr | 26 Mar | 26 Feb | 29 Jan | 1 Jan | 4 Dec | 6 Nov |
| 6 Oct | 8 Sep | 11 Aug | 14 Jul | 16 Jun | 19 May | 21 Apr | 24 Mar | 25 Feb | 28 Jan | 31 Dec | 3 Dec | 5 Nov |
| **b.  6 Men Corrected Multiple (A.D. 760–765)** | | | | | | | | | | | | |
| 12 Oct | 14 Sep | 17 Aug | 20 Jul | 22 Jun | 25 May | 27 Apr | 30 Mar | 2 Mar | 2 Feb | 5 Jan | 8 Dec | 10 Nov |
| 11 Oct | 13 Sep | 16 Aug | 19 Jul | 21 Jun | 24 May | 26 Apr | 29 Mar | 1 Mar | 1 Feb | 4 Jan | 7 Dec | 9 Nov |
| 10 Oct | 12 Sep | 15 Aug | 18 Jul | 20 Jun | 23 May | 25 Apr | 28 Mar | 28 Feb | 31 Jan | 3 Jan | 6 Dec | 8 Nov |
| 8 Oct | 10 Sep | 13 Aug | 16 Jul | 18 Jun | 21 May | 23 Apr | 26 Mar | 27 Feb | 30 Jan | 2 Jan | 5 Dec | 7 Nov |
| 7 Oct | 9 Sep | 12 Aug | 15 Jul | 17 Jun | 20 May | 22 Apr | 25 Mar | 25 Feb | 28 Jan | 31 Dec | 3 Dec | 5 Nov |
| **c.  12 Imix Corrected Multiple (A.D. 765–770)** | | | | | | | | | | | | |
| 12 Oct | 14 Sep | 17 Aug | 20 Jul | 22 Jun | 25 May | 27 Apr | 30 Mar | 2 Mar | 2 Feb | 5 Jan | 8 Dec | 10 Nov |
| 11 Oct | 13 Sep | 16 Aug | 19 Jul | 21 Jun | 24 May | 26 Apr | 29 Mar | 1 Mar | 1 Feb | 4 Jan | 7 Dec | 9 Nov |
| 9 Oct | 11 Sep | 14 Aug | 17 Jul | 19 Jun | 22 May | 24 Apr | 27 Mar | 28 Feb | 31 Jan | 3 Jan | 6 Dec | 8 Nov |
| 8 Oct | 10 Sep | 13 Aug | 16 Jul | 18 Jun | 21 May | 23 Apr | 26 Mar | 26 Feb | 29 Jan | 1 Jan | 4 Dec | 6 Nov |
| 7 Oct | 9 Sep | 12 Aug | 15 Jul | 17 Jun | 20 May | 22 Apr | 25 Mar | 25 Feb | 28 Jan | 31 Dec | 3 Dec | 5 Nov |

The sort of correction called for by our model of the zodiacal almanac may be quite relevantly considered as the pre-Columbian Maya counterpart of our leap-year correction, but it was employed at 5-year instead of 4-year intervals, and, because the Maya computing year was only 364 days, it required corrections of 6 or 7 days rather than of only 1 day. It is important to emphasize that this correction did not affect the 365-day *haab*, the Maya counterpart of our vague year. They were apparently more concerned about keeping their computing year from falling behind the sidereal year than about synchronizing the *haab* with the tropical year.

## The Maya Constellations

### EVIDENCE FROM THE PARIS CODEX

The middle and lower registers of pp. 23 and 24 of the Paris Codex (*Codex Peresianus* 1968) contain nine completely or partially identifiable zoomorphic figures, remnants of two others, and space for two more (Figure 6.1). For this reason, it has generally been considered that the zodiacal almanac originally had thirteen such figures that must be related in some way to the thirteen columns of *tzolkin* day glyphs in the middle register (Spinden 1916, 1924:55–56; Kelley 1976:45), which we have just discussed. The figures are arranged in two rows, the top seven in the middle register and the bottom six in the lower register. All are suspended in one way or another from solar eclipse glyphs. In all legible examples except one, the figure in question grasps an eclipse glyph in its jaws; the exception, a scorpion, is suspended from an eclipse glyph by its tail. The seven eclipse glyphs in the top row are attached to the bottom border of a sky band, which appears to have continued originally down the left side of the middle register of p. 23. The six eclipse glyphs in the bottom row are attached to the lower border of a different kind of horizontal band, filled in this case with a dotted zigzag motif. As mentioned earlier in this chapter, previous scholars have long considered the zoomorphic figures on these pages to be what we may call zodiacal beasts that represent the constellations of a Maya zodiac.

Very little remains of the first zodiacal beast, which, following the right-to-left reading order, is located in the middle register on the right side of p. 24 (Figure 6.1). What is left may well be part of the wing of a bird (which we will refer to as "bird 1"), but it is not possible to be more precise.

The second beast, to the left of the first, is clearly a rattlesnake. According to the Motul Dictionary, which was probably compiled during the sixteenth century, the Yucatecan Maya equate the snake's rattle with the Pleiades, referring to both as *tzab* (Martínez Hernández 1929:254).

The third beast is a turtle, which is *ac* in Yucatec Maya (Martínez Hernández 1929:66). Kelley (1976:45) has noted that the "Motul dictionary identified the Maya turtle constellation as coinciding, in part, with our Gemini." However, Lounsbury (1982:166–67) has pointed out that "by the sixteenth century, when the Motul Dictionary was being assembled, the constellation of Gemini, because of precession, was mostly in the 'sign' of Cancer, and the stars in the 'sign' of Gemini included those of Orion and much of Taurus." As we will discuss later, evidence from Bonampak provides strong support for the identification of Orion as the turtle constellation in pre-Columbian times.

A scorpion suspended from the eclipse glyph by its tail is the fourth zodiacal beast. Scorpion is *sinaan* in Yucatecan Maya, and the same word is used for constellation Scorpio in the Motul Dictionary (Martínez Hernández 1929:237). This does not necessarily mean that the Maya scorpion constellation corresponded exactly to the Western constellation named Scorpio, but it may mean just that. The Yucatec terms for other Western zodiacal beasts with which the early post-Conquest Maya were familiar— for example, the fish—appear in the dictionary as names for animals only, not constellations. It would be a mistake to reject this possible correspondence out of hand just because it seems too obvious.

The fifth beast (on the right side of p. 23) is a bird of some sort ("bird 2" of the series). This particular bird is a distinctive component of the faunistic iconography of the Dresden, Madrid, and Paris Codices, but previous scholars have provided various specific identifications. In agreement with Kelley (1976:47), we call this beast the *cox* bird, adopting the terminology of Seler (1961:631–42), who identified it as the crested guan (*Penelope purpurascens*).

The sixth beast may be a fantastic composite rather than a real animal. Its snakelike body ends in a bifurcate, fishlike tail, but its head, vaguely reptilian, corresponds to no known animal. We follow Kelley (1976:50) in calling this beast the fish–snake.

The seventh beast is another bird ("bird 3"), whose wing and tail feathers have different markings from those of the *cox* bird. This is the last zodiacal beast in the top row.

The eighth zodiacal beast, the rightmost in the lower register on p. 24, has been almost completely effaced. Kelley (1976:47, 49–50) identifies it as a peccary on the basis of seeing a hoof on the one forelimb that remains visible. In our opinion, the limb terminates in what is probably a humanlike hand, but in any case is certainly not a hoof. We follow the suggestion of Spinden (1916:77) that the beast is a frog. Severin (1981:11), who also regards it as a frog, points out similarities with undoubted frogs on pp. 31 and 101 of the Madrid Codex, which we find very convincing.

The ninth beast is almost certainly a leaf-nosed bat, as argued convincingly by Kelley (1976:47, 49), rather than a butterfly, as suggested by Seler (1961:728).

The tenth beast is completely effaced, and of the eleventh only an indecipherable squiggle remains. Severin (1981:12) suggests that the squiggle may be the cloven hoof of a deer or peccary, but we regard this as reading too much into too little.

The twelfth beast is a humanlike figure with a skeletal ribcage and the head and fleshless mandible of God A.

The thirteenth and last zodiacal beast, the head of which is completely effaced, has a spotted trunk and forelimbs, which bear prominent claws. Following Kelley (1976:49), we regard this as an ocelot or jaguar.

In both the middle and lower registers, the spaces between the solar eclipse glyphs are occupied by black bar-and-dot numbers in positional notation (as is the space to the left of "bird 2"). The color of these numbers and the use of positional notation suggest that they are distance numbers, representing intervals separating the constellations. Depending on how one interprets or reconstructs damaged areas, five, six, or all seven of these numbers in the middle register are composed of two sets of one bar and three dots each, which can be written as 8.8 ( = 168 days or six sidereal periods of 28 days) in Maya long-count notation. The separation of solar eclipse glyphs by 168-day intervals strongly suggests that the almanac has something to do with eclipse seasons. The distance between sequential eclipse seasons (known as the eclipse half-year) is 173.31 days (Teeple 1931:90), or 5.31 days more than the intervals separating the zodiacal beasts in the middle register.

Although we have little doubt that one function of the zodiacal almanac was to commensurate eclipse seasons with other cycles of interest to the Maya, the current state of our research does not satisfactorily address this question. Among other difficulties is the fact that the eclipse glyphs in the lower register are separated by black distance numbers also, but only one of the four legible examples is 168 days (8.8 in long-count notation). The other three distance numbers appear to total 8 days only—a single set of one bar and three dots. What this may mean we cannot suggest.

Setting aside for the moment any attempt to relate the distance numbers to eclipse half-years, we may nevertheless consider on its own merits the proposition that zodiacal constellations (or at least those in the middle register) are separated by distances of 168 days. If this were true, the constellations associated with the solar eclipse glyphs could not be adjacent to each other, or 28 days apart, but would have to be at opposite ends of the sky, roughly 6 months apart. This is essentially the position taken by Kelley (1976:49–50), who concludes from the fact that the beasts in the zodiacal almanac are separated by distance numbers of 168 days that they do not represent the constellations in their normal positions in the sky. He believes, rather, that "alternate pictures are one-half to one-third of the sky apart and should roughly correspond to successive zodiacal constellations, in the reverse of the normal order" (1976:49). In other words, his position is that *adjacent* figures in the almanac represent constellations at *opposite* sides of the sky. Our own position, which we will explain more fully later, is that *some* beasts that are adjacent in the almanac do, in fact, represent adjacent constellations [as Spinden (1924:55, Figure 25) originally proposed], whereas *other* adjacent beasts represent constellations at opposite ends of the sky, as Kelley proposes.

Before considering evidence relevant to the Maya zodiac from Chichén Itzá, it is perhaps useful to recapitulate here what the almanac in the Paris Codex tells us about the corpus of zodiacal beasts and their sequential ordering. The thirteen zodiacal elements as known from the Paris Codex are: bird 1, rattlesnake, turtle, scorpion, *cox* bird or bird 2, fish–snake, bird 3, frog, bat, unknown, unknown, skeleton, and ocelot. External evidence—namely, data from the Motul dictionary and Lounsbury's analysis of them—indicates that the rattlesnake and turtle constellations are to be identified with the Pleiades and Orion, respectively. The same sort of evidence suggests that the Maya and Western scorpion constellations may be essentially the same.

## EVIDENCE FROM CHICHÉN ITZÁ

The second major source of information on a pre-Columbian Maya zodiac is a bas-relief inscription on one of the buildings of the architectural complex at Chichén Itzá known as Las Monjas. The inscription is a sky band located in the center of the eastern facade of the East Wing of the complex. Drawings of this spectacular and well-preserved facade were included in some of the earliest published accounts of Chichén Itzá [for example, a Catherwood drawing published by Stephens in 1843 (Stephens 1963, Vol. 2:194, Pl. 29)], but the first adequate drawing of the sky band was made by Hunter from plaster casts and published by Maudslay (1889–1902, Vol. III, Pl. 13b). The Maudslay rendition, which has served as the basis of all subsequent scholarship, shows the sky band as composed of 24 rectangular fields or segments, 22 of which are well preserved and completely legible. Twelve of the legible segments contain crossed-bands signs, and ten contain other objects, most commonly an animal figure resting upon a star glyph. The contents of the leftmost segment published by Maudslay are completely effaced, and, in the segment immediately to its right, only a star glyph at the bottom of the field can be read.

Because of the need to compare the sky band from Las Monjas with pp. 23 and 24 of the Paris Codex, the adequacy of the Maudslay rendition, including the question of just how much is now missing from the sky band as a result of physical damage to the left end of the inscription, is of critical importance. We have concluded that the Maudslay rendition has misled later scholars in several small but crucial details. Our reinterpretation was based originally on the examination of published photographs (Maudslay 1889–1902, Vol. III, Pl. 11b) and architectural drawings (Bolles 1977:114) and of some unpublished photographs of Horst Hartung; the conclusions we reached were then verified and further documented photographically at Chichén Itzá in August, 1990.

The sky band of Las Monjas is carved on nine separate tabular stones, which we have lettered A–I in Figure 6.3. Stones B–D and F–I are of nearly identical size, and each contains three segments of the sky band. Stone E, which is in the center of the sky band and, indeed, the central axis of the facade, is much shorter, and it contains only one sky-band element. Stone A, the leftmost component of the row, is badly damaged (Figure 6.4). The drawing published by Maudslay includes only the rightmost two-thirds of the stone, but Stone A is, in fact, the same size as all the others except the short central stone (Stone E). The lower framing border of the sky band [the lower horizontal reglet in the terminology of Bolles (1977:125)] continues to the extreme left end of Stone A, and, in its original condition, the stone contained three sky-band elements, not just the two shown by the Maudsley rendition. The rightmost element of Stone A (Figure 6.4) contains a heavily damaged and therefore illegible figure of some sort resting upon a star glyph. More than half of the middle element has been destroyed by the exfoliation of the carved surface, but enough is left to indicate clearly that it is a crossed-bands sign. The leftmost element is almost totally effaced by exfoliation and gross fractures, but it is certain that whatever is there is *not* a crossed-bands sign.

Doubt has been expressed in earlier literature about the north end of the sky band (the rightmost end of Stone I in our terminology). Bolles (1977:125) states that the north end is "broken off," seeming to imply that the original length of Stone I was greater than all the other stones (except E) and that it may have contained more than three sky-band elements. This is,

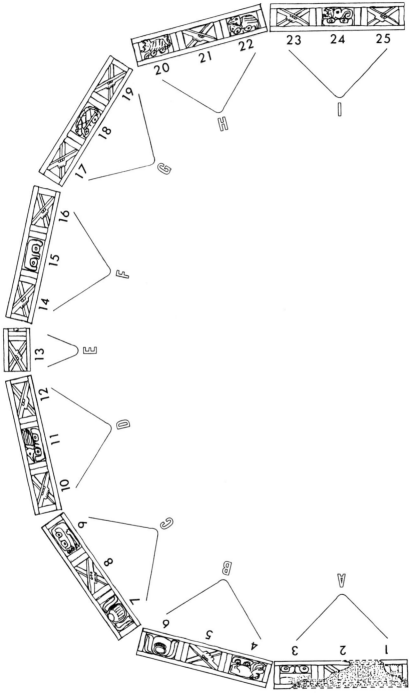

*Figure 6.3* The Las Monjas sky band as interpreted by the authors (based on drawings published by Maudsley 1889–1902, Vol. III, Pl. 13b, and photographs by Donald Bradburn, 24 August 1990).

*Figure 6.4* Stone A, at the left end of the Las Monjas sky band (photograph by Donald Bradburn, 24 August 1990).

however, not the case. The extreme right end of Stone I is split from top to bottom, but it is not "broken off" or missing. The stone's rightmost element, a crossed-bands sign, is framed normally by two vertical reglets, and the present length of the stone is the same as all others except Stone E. Under the circumstances, we consider Stone I to be complete with three elements.

As we have reinterpreted it, the Las Monjas sky band is composed, then, of 25 elements (Figure 6.3), whose order from left to right is given in Table 6.3. The depictions that may represent zodiacal constellations include a peccary, variants of the glyphs for Moon and Imix, a human skull, a bird (without any distinct identifying characteristics), a large star or Venus glyph, a turtle, a scorpion, a bird identified variously as a vulture (Kelley 1976:47) or *cox* bird (Seler 1961:642), and a composite beast described as a

*Table 6.3* Elements of the Sky Band on the Eastern Facade of the East Wing of Las Monjas at Chichén Itzá, Listed from Left to Right. The Numbering and Lettering Systems for the Elements and Stones are Those of the Authors

| Element | Stone | Iconography/epigraphy |
|---------|-------|----------------------|
| 1 | A | (Effaced figure?) |
| 2 | | Crossed bands; crossing pattern indeterminate |
| 3 | | (Effaced figure?) upon star glyph |
| 4 | B | PECCARY upon star glyph |
| 5 | | Crossed bands; crossing pattern #1[a] |
| 6 | | Moon glyph with wings |
| 7 | C | Imix glyph with wings |
| 8 | | Crossed bands; crossing pattern #1 |
| 9 | | HUMAN SKULL with infixed star glyph |
| 10 | D | Crossed bands; crossing pattern #1 |
| 11 | | BIRD upon star glyph |
| 12 | | Crossed bands; crossing pattern #1 |
| 13 | E | Crossed bands; crossing pattern #2[a] |
| 14 | F | Crossed bands; crossing pattern #1 |
| 15 | | Star glyph |
| 16 | | Crossed bands; crossing pattern #1 |
| 17 | G | Crossed bands; crossing pattern #1 |
| 18 | | TURTLE upon star glyph |
| 19 | | Crossed bands; crossing pattern #1 |
| 20 | H | SCORPION upon star glyph |
| 21 | | Crossed bands; crossing pattern #1 |
| 22 | | BIRD (vulture or *cox*) upon star glyph |
| 23 | I | Crossed bands; crossing pattern #1 |
| 24 | | REPTILIAN MONSTER (FISH–SNAKE) upon star glyph |
| 25 | | Crossed bands; crossing pattern #1 |

[a] In crossing pattern #1, the band extending from the upper left corner of the field to the lower right corner covers the band extending from upper right to lower left. In crossing pattern #2, the band extending from the upper right corner to the lower left corner covers the band extending from upper left to lower right.

reptilian monster (Kelley 1976:47), a fish–snake (Kelley 1976:50), or perhaps some kind of worm (Seler 1961:642). It is immediately apparent that there are significant differences between the iconographic content of this sky band and that of the almanac in the Paris Codex. Any attempt to interpret these differences and therefore to use the data from Chichén Itzá to elucidate the nature of the pre-Columbian Maya zodiac must take into account strong evidence casting doubt on the textual integrity of the Las Monjas sky band.

There are several indications that some or all of the sky band of Las Monjas may be composed of reused stones moved to the facade of the East Wing from some other architectural context or, more likely, two separate contexts. Bolles' architectural study of the eastern facade raises this possibility without endorsing it (Bolles 1977:125):

> [I]t was impossible to determine whether the constellation was of full length or was merely a borrowed section from another structure. The central stone and the ill-fitting stones next to each end pointed toward this possibility of borrowing, but it would have been counter to the general feeling of the entire facade, in which everything seemed carved for the position it occupied.

Despite Bolles' ambivalence, it is highly unlikely that Stone E, in the center of the sky band, was carved for the position it occupies in the eastern facade (Figure 6.5). The crossed-bands glyph it contains is typologically different (crossing pattern #2; Figure 6.3, element 13) from all determinable examples on other stones (crossing pattern #1; Figure 6.3, elements 5, 8, 10, 12, 14, 16, 17, 19, 21, 23, and 25). The horizontal reglets on Stone E are only about two-thirds as wide as those on all other stones. Furthermore, it is quite clear that the typologically aberrant crossed-bands glyph on Stone E lacks the framing bar or vertical reglet to its left, whereas there are to its right two vertical reglets. One of these reglets is the right framing bar for the glyph in question, but the other is the left framing bar for some adjacent depiction of which only a small and totally illegible fragment remains. Stone E should almost certainly be seen as a not very carefully bitruncated fragment of a larger stone that originally contained at least two sky-band elements. Its typological differences from all other crossed-bands elements makes it highly unlikely that its original provenience was the same as that of the rest of the sky band.

If it is true, as we have reason to believe, that the sky band of Las Monjas is a composite construct of diverse proveniences assembled to fit within the spatial and thematic restrictions of the eastern facade, it is unwise to regard it as a complete and textually integral rendition of Maya

*Figure 6.5* Center of the sky band at Las Monjas, showing the short Stone E (photograph by Donald Bradburn, 24 August 1990).

zodiacal iconography. Rather, any comparison of Las Monjas with the zodiacal almanac of the Paris Codex should be based, very conservatively, on the evidence provided by individual stones of the Las Monjas sky band, without reference to how these stones were combined. Such an approach does not assume that the order of assembly has any necessary significance or that all of the stones from the original provenience or proveniences were incorporated into the eastern facade of the East Wing.

Excluding Stone E from further consideration, the eight remaining stones fall into two patterns (Figure 6.3). Stones D, F, G, and I contain one zodiacal beast or other iconic depiction as a central element bracketed by crossed-bands glyphs. These stones cannot be used in a strictly conservative investigation of the ordering of the Maya zodiac. Stones A, B, C, and H have one crossed-bands glyph as a central element bracketed by other glyphs or zodiacal beasts. Only on Stone H are the two non-crossed-bands elements—scorpion and vulture/*cox* bird—directly comparable to two of the zodiacal beasts in the Paris almanac, and they are shown as adjacent in both contexts. This is, very strictly speaking, the only point of comparison that can be made between the order of elements of Las Monjas and the Paris Codex, and the results of the comparison are mutually confirmatory. The other two extant pairings of individual stones at Las Monjas (peccary and Moon on Stone B and Imix and skull on Stone C) do not provide points of comparison, because neither Moon nor Imix is present in the Paris almanac.

Previous scholars have accepted longer lists of corresponding sequences for Las Monjas and the Paris Codex. For example, Kelley (1976:49) mentions the sequence including skull (on Stone C), bird (Stone D), star/Venus/rattlesnake (Stone F), and turtle (Stone G). Following this line of argumentation, one could certainly continue the sequence with scorpion and vulture/*cox* bird (both on Stone H). However, any such attempt quickly reveals noncorrespondences. For example, as Kelley (1976:49) points out in criticism of his own interpretation, the absence of a jaguar or ocelot from Las Monjas means that the sequences are, in fact, not the same (skeleton–ocelot–bird in the Paris almanac and skull–bird at Las Monjas). Without taking time here for an extended discussion of the problems, we can report simply that no scheme of rearrangement of the stones of the Las Monjas sky band—even allowing complete freedom in reconstructing the original contents of Stone A—can produce an extensive correspondence with the order of zodiacal elements in the Paris almanac. At best, one would have to specify the content of one or more missing stones, and such untestable hypotheses are of no great utility.

In summary, then, the contribution of the Las Monjas sky band to an understanding of the Maya zodiac appears to be quite limited if one accepts that the primary documentation on the matter is the Paris almanac, the textual integrity of which is not in doubt. Specifically, Las Monjas makes three contributions: First, it confirms the evidence of the Paris Codex for the existence of skull or skeleton, bird (either bird 1 or bird 3), turtle, scorpion, vulture or *cox* bird, and reptilian monster or fish–snake as zodiacal beasts. Second, it confirms that scorpion and vulture or *cox* bird are directly sequential without the interpolation of any other beast. Third, it adds the peccary to the list of zodiacal beasts. None of the evidence from Las Monjas in any way disconfirms or challenges the model of the Maya zodiac developed from the evidence of the Paris Codex.

## A Model of the Maya Zodiac

### RELATIONSHIP BETWEEN THE CONSTELLATIONS AND THE ZODIACAL ALMANAC

The 12 constellations of the Western zodiac, a 16-degree-wide zone centered on the ecliptic, are each identified with a different month-long period of the year. The relationship between the constellations and the months was defined by astrologers at the beginning of the Christian Era. At that time, the vernal equinox was "in the sign" of Aries. What this meant was that Aries was invisible on the night of the spring equinox and for approximately 30 days thereafter. When Aries reappeared, it was said that the Sun had moved into the sign of Taurus, and so on through the sidereal year.

Western astrologers still use the same zodiac, equating the vernal equinox with "the first point of Aries," even though the spring equinox is now in the sign of Pisces. The vernal equinox moves or *precesses* "in a westerly direction along the ecliptic amounting to about 50 seconds of arc per year" (Aveni 1980:101). By A.D. 755, the date of the eclipse table in the Dresden Codex, the vernal equinox had slipped out of Aries and was moving into Pisces.

In relating a constellation to one of the months of the year, Western astrologers chose the period when it could not be seen. Based on information available from various ethnographic studies (for example, B. Tedlock unpublished:13–14 and this volume, Chapter 1), studies of astronomical tables in the codices (for example, Closs 1977, Lounsbury 1978, and Aveni, Chapter 3 of this volume, for the Venus table of the Dresden Codex), and studies of architectural alignments at archaeological sites (for example, Aveni 1977 and Aveni and Hartung 1986), we think it far more likely that the pre-Columbian Maya were interested in the *visibility* of their zodiacal constellations, most probably at the horizon, at Sunrise or Sunset or both. This guess about which aspect of the annual cycle of variation in the fixed stars would have been cognitively salient is the foundation upon which our model of the Maya zodiac is built. We interpret visibility at the horizon in broad terms—a significant part of the constellation either was or was not visible. Except for the Pleiades, the constellations of known or suspected relevance cover so much area that the more precise concepts of heliacal and achronic rising or setting seem inappropriate unless one is prepared to construct a model based on the movements of individual stars, which we are not.

If one is concerned with the visibility of constellations at the horizon, there are then two observations to be made at both Sunrise and Sunset, one at the eastern end of the ecliptic (the rising constellation) and one at its western end (the setting constellation). The "Sunrise" portion of Table 6.4 specifies the constellations in question at Sunrise for 1 year beginning on 10 November A.D. 755 (Gregorian), the starting date for the Paris almanac that we have derived by cross-dating it with the Dresden eclipse table.[1] The "Sunrise" portion of Table 6.4 proceeds by the 28-day intervals determined by the almanac's structure, and it has, therefore, 13 divisions. The constellations dealt with by the table are, with two exceptions, the zodiacal constellations of Western astronomy. First, we list the asterism, Pleiades, rather than the constellation, Taurus, of which it is a part. Second, we insert the constellation, Orion, between Pleiades and Gemini. The "Sun-

*Table 6.4*   The Sky at Sunrise and Sunset in A.D. 755–56 using the Maya Divisions of the Sidereal Year[a]

|        | Sunrise | | Sunset | |
|--------|-----------------|-----------------|-----------------|-----------------|
|        | Western ecliptic | Eastern ecliptic | Western ecliptic | Eastern ecliptic |
| 10 Nov | Pleiades | Libra | Scorpio | Aries |
| 8 Dec  | Orion | Scorpio | Sagittarius | Pleiades |
| 5 Jan  | Gemini | Sagittarius | Capricorn | Gemini |
| 2 Feb  | Leo (western) | Capricorn | Aquarius | Cancer |
| 1 Mar  | Leo (eastern) | Aquarius | Aquarius | Leo |
| 29 Mar | Virgo | Pisces | Pisces | Virgo (western) |
| 26 Apr | Libra (+ Virgo) | Aries | Aries | Virgo (eastern) |
| 24 May | Scorpio | Pleiades | Pleiades | Libra |
| 21 Jun | Sagittarius | Orion | Gemini | Scorpio |
| 19 Jul | Capricorn | Gemini | Cancer | Sagittarius |
| 16 Aug | Aquarius | Leo (western) | Leo | Capricorn |
| 13 Sep | Pisces | Leo (eastern) | Virgo (western) | Aquarius |
| 11 Oct | Aries | Virgo | Virgo (eastern) | Pisces |

[a] After 7 sidereal months, constellations at the western end of the ecliptic at Sunrise appear at the eastern end and vice versa. After 8 sidereal months, constellations at the western end of the ecliptic at Sunset appear at the eastern end, and vice versa.

set" portion of Table 6.4, constructed in the same fashion, shows the rising and setting constellations at Sunset.

It can be seen from Table 6.4 that, after about seven 28-day periods (or eight periods for the Sunset sequence), the constellations that were at the western end of the ecliptic have moved to the eastern end. For example, in Table 6.4, Sunrise, Orion, which is setting at the western end of the ecliptic at Sunrise on 8 December, is rising just ahead of the Sun at the eastern end of the ecliptic on 21 June. The other pattern that can be seen in Table 6.4 is that after six (not seven) 28-day periods, the rising constellation on a given day becomes the setting constellation. For example, referring again to the Sunrise data of Table 6.4, Scorpio, which is rising with the Sun on 8 December, is setting at Sunrise on 24 May. All of this suggests that the 28-day sidereal months of the year can be defined in terms of *pairs* of constellations that bracket the ecliptic at Sunrise and Sunset and that these pairs reverse their positions in an asymmetrically patterned fashion. The asymmetrical patterning, "at sixes and sevens," is reminiscent of the physical layout of the 13 zodiacal beasts in the Paris almanac and the alternation of correction factors implied by its green numbers.

The beginning of the sequence of constellations on Paris 23–24 (bird 1–rattlesnake–turtle–scorpion) has a better fit with the Sunrise model in Table 6.4 than with the Sunset model in Table 6.4. If we follow all the suggestions of the Motul dictionary, we can read this sequence as unknown constellation–Pleiades–Orion–Scorpio. Table 6.4, Sunset, places Scorpio in first or second position and associates it with 10 November; Table 6.4, Sunrise, places it in the third or fourth position and associates it with 8 December. The Maya scorpion occupies the fourth position in the almanac, which is consistent with Table 6.4, Sunrise. Table 6.4, Sunset, places the Pleiades in the third or fourth position; Table 6.4, Sunrise places it in the first or second position. The rattlesnake figure appears in the second position in the almanac, which is consistent with the Sunrise column. The Sunset column has no place for Orion; the Sunrise column locates Orion in the third or fourth position. The turtle is the third figure in the almanac sequences, which is consistent with its placement in the Sunrise column. It is therefore more likely that the zodiacal beasts in the almanac on Paris 23–24 represent pairs of constellations at Sunrise than at Sunset.[2]

According to this reasoning, the bird 1 constellation at the beginning of the almanac sequence must represent Libra, which was rising in the east at Sunrise on 10 November A.D. 755. The Pleiades would have been seen setting at the western end of the ecliptic on that date. After 28 days, Libra was replaced by Scorpio and the Pleiades by Orion at the two ends of the ecliptic. At this point, 4 of the 13 zodiacal beasts in the almanac have been assigned to constellations of European astronomy, and the ordering of these four in the almanac may be seen to occur in a patterned fashion. The four constellations are grouped into two pairs, one pair for each of two successive 28-day sidereal months. The order of appearance of the four is:

1. Rising constellation (for month 1), then
2. Setting constellation (for month 1), then
3. Setting constellation (for month 2), then
4. Rising constellation (for month 2).

Another element of the pattern is defined by the three boundaries between the four constellations in the set. That pattern is "opposite–adjacent–opposite," in the sense that Pleiades is at the opposite end of the sky from Libra, Orion is adjacent to Pleiades, and Scorpio is opposite to Orion.

Our attempts to build a more complete model of the almanac based on the structure of the first four elements were constrained by the need to pair the thirteenth zodiacal beast (ocelot) with the first (bird 1) in such a way as to provide an accurate description of the rising and setting constellations during the seventh sidereal month (beginning on 26 April A.D. 756 using our starting date). If each sidereal month is represented by a *pair* of zodiacal beasts, a set of thirteen pictures will, obviously, take one only halfway through a sidereal year. Within this constraint, the best constructed model is that shown in Figure 6.6, which shows an alternating inversion of the

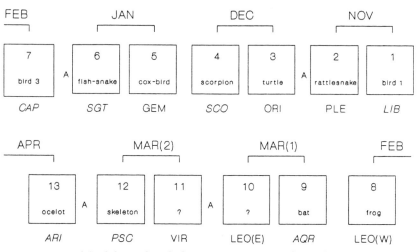

*Figure* 6.6 Model of the zodiacal almanac on pp. 23 and 24 of the Paris Codex. Abbreviated names of constellations on the eastern horizon at Sunrise are italicized; constellations on the western horizon are not italicized. Numbers in the boxes represent the order of appearance of zodiacal beasts in the Paris almanac. The letter A between boxes indicates constellations that are adjacent to each other in the sky.

horizon patterning derived from the first four elements. In other words, the first and third sets of four have identical patterns (rising–setting–setting–rising), whereas the second set of four has the inverse of this pattern (setting–rising–rising–setting). The patterning of location in the sky, opposite–adjacent–opposite, remains a constant for the boundaries within each set of four. The boundaries between four-element sets are of the "opposite" variety except for what we may call the recycling shift from the complete third to the incomplete fourth set.

One final comment on our model concerns the constellational equivalent of the eighth beast, the frog. In terms of the European zodiacal constellations, the expected equivalent would be Cancer. However, Cancer is a very narrow constellation whose four brightest stars are not very bright, and at Sunrise on the day in question, it has already disappeared below the western horizon. Although we do not wish to insist strongly on the point, it seems to us to be rather likely that the Maya frog constellation was composed, at least in part, of some of the bright stars in the western portion of Leo, and we have constructed our tables and figures to reflect this likelihood.

WESTERN EQUIVALENTS OF THE MAYA CONSTELLATIONS

The full sequence of zodiacal beasts in the Paris almanac and their approximate Western zodiacal equivalents are shown in Table 6.5. The tenth and eleventh beasts, completely effaced in the Paris, must represent, according to our model, the eastern stars of Leo and some or all of the stars of Virgo, respectively. The sky band of Las Monjas strongly suggests that one of the

*Table 6.5*  Western Zodiacal Equivalents of the Constellations Pictured in the Zodiacal Almanac on Pages 23–24 of the Paris Codex

| Paris | Western |
|---|---|
| 1. Bird 1 | Libra |
| 2. Rattlesnake | Pleiades |
| 3. Turtle | Orion |
| 4. Scorpion | Scorpio |
| 5. Bird 2 or *cox* bird | Gemini |
| 6. Fish–snake | Sagittarius |
| 7. Bird 3 | Capricorn |
| 8. Frog | Leo (western) |
| 9. Bat | Aquarius |
| 10. ? (Peccary) | Leo (eastern) |
| 11. ? | Virgo |
| 12. Skeleton | Pisces |
| 13. Ocelot | Aries |

*Table 6.6*  The Maya Zodiac

| Paris | Western |
|---|---|
| 2. Rattlesnake (*tzab*) | Pleiades |
| 3. Turtle (*ac*) | Orion |
| 5. Bird 2 or *cox* bird | Gemini |
| 8. Frog | Leo (western) |
| 10. ? (Peccary) | Leo (eastern) |
| 11. ? | Virgo |
| 1. Bird 1 | Libra |
| 4. Scorpion (*sinaan*) | Scorpio |
| 6. Fish–snake | Sagittarius |
| 7. Bird 3 | Capricorn |
| 9. Bat | Aquarius |
| 12. Skeleton | Pisces |
| 13. Ocelot | Aries |

beasts missing from the Paris is the peccary. Our suggested placement of the peccary in the tenth position is based on evidence from Bonampak, as discussed below. The actual sequence of the constellations in the sky is given in Table 6.6

As we have already mentioned, our model of the Maya zodiac implies that the arrangement of signs on Paris 23 and 24 accounts for only half the sidereal year, from 10 November to 26 April. The second half of the year would require a different sequence of signs, which would begin with ocelot, as shown in a hypothetical model (Figure 6.7) patterned on the sequence for the first half of the year that is actually given in the Paris Codex.

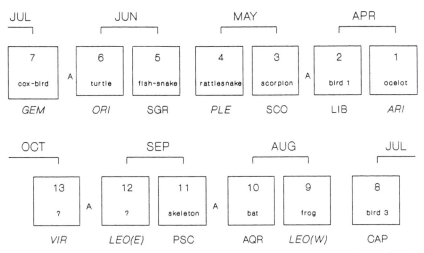

*Figure 6.7* Model of a hypothetical almanac for the second half of the sidereal year; graphic conventions are the same as in Figure 6.6.

## Testing the Model of the Maya Zodiac

EVIDENCE FROM THE DRESDEN CODEX

Because we obtained a starting date for the zodiacal almanac in the Paris Codex by cross-dating it with the eclipse table in the Dresden Codex, the zodiacal iconography in the latter cannot be used as a fully independent test of our model of the Maya zodiac. However, because the evidence used in cross-dating did *not* take into account the intervals separating the examples of zodiacal iconography in the eclipse table, our model could be disconfirmed by such a test. This does not happen; indeed the eclipse table provides additional support for the model.

The first picture in the eclipse table, a seated skeleton below a caption containing both solar and lunar eclipse glyphs, is very similar to the skeleton in the Paris almanac that we have identified with Pisces (compare Figure 6.1 and 6.2a). The dates associated with the eclipse table's skeleton run from 26 March until 25 April A.D. 757. Table 6.4, Sunrise, shows that skeleton (Pisces) would have been visible rising in the east at Sunrise on 29 March and several weeks thereafter.

The eclipse table contains three more pictures with possible zodiacal connections. Two of them represent serpents, which we believe correspond to the rattlesnake constellation (e.g., Figure 6.2b). The first is associated with dates running from 7 May to 6 June A.D. 783. Table 6.4, Sunrise, shows that the Pleiades were rising in the east at Sunrise toward the end of this period. The second serpent picture is not relevant during the first run through the eclipse table. It becomes relevant only during the second run through the table, where it is associated with dates from 29 May to 28 June A.D. 819. This also encompasses the period when the Pleiades are rising with the Sun (Table 6.4 Sunrise).

The third picture that may represent a constellation is of the so-called Moon Goddess, who is pictured suspended from a sky band on p. 53b of the eclipse table (Figure 6.2c). It is associated with dates from the beginning to the end of October A.D. 775. This is the period when the constellation Virgo would have been visible rising in the east before Sunrise (Table 6.4 Sunrise). The figure corresponding to Virgo on p. 24b of the Paris Codex has been almost completely destroyed (Figure 6.1). We wonder if it could have been the woman shown in the eclipse table of the Dresden Codex (Figure 6.2c) and if the stars in Virgo were also interpreted as forming the body of a woman by the ancient Maya. Our curiosity on this point must, of course, remain unsatisfied.

The pictures in the Paris zodiacal almanac and in the Dresden eclipse table depict the eclipsed Sun in the jaws of rising constellations. The Sun appears to be moving with the relevant constellation at Sunrise. If it is then eclipsed during the daytime, the visual metaphor of the constellation devouring the Sun would be appropriate. The Book of Chilam Balam of Chumayel refers quite explicitly to the Sun being "bitten" during a solar eclipse: *ca chiibi u uich kine* ("then the face of the Sun was bitten") (Gordon 1913:12). It is therefore likely that the conventional representation of a zodiacal constellation in the Maya codices was a sign in which a solar eclipse might take place.

### EVIDENCE FROM THE MADRID CODEX

The almanac on pp. 65a–72b and 73b of the Madrid Codex contains the only occurrence in that Codex of a calendar-round date (13 Ahau 13 Cumku). This calendar-round almanac contains, as well, several examples of zodiacal iconography. The left-hand picture on p. 71a depicts a turtle suspended from two solar eclipse glyphs located below a sky band (Figure 6.8a). The turtle is weighted down by three Cauac glyphs, which probably represent stones [*tun*, "stone," is one of the attested readings of the Cauac glyph (Fox and Justeson 1984:48–49)]. The picture on the right-hand side of p. 67b portrays one solar eclipse glyph suspended from a sky band in the jaws of a serpent (Figure 6.8b). What seems to be the same kind of serpent appears in another picture, which is associated with a date 2 days earlier in

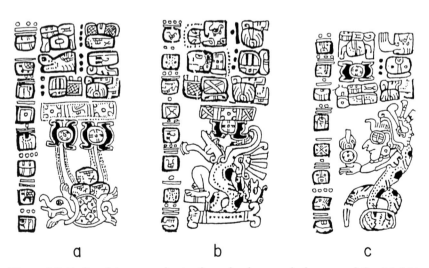

a                    b                    c

*Figure* 6.8 Zodiacal iconography in the calendar-round almanac of the Madrid Codex. a. From p. 17a; b. from p. 67b; c. from p. 66b (after Villacorta C. and Villacorta 1976:356, 358, 366).

the almanac. The second serpent is shown resting on a Caban glyph, the glyph for "Earth," with a head variant of the glyph for the Sun emerging from its jaws (Figure 6.8c). The serpent's tail does not end in a rattle; so it cannot represent the Pleiades. Its most likely referent is the so-called fish–snake in the Maya zodiac, which we have identified as Sagittarius. The bifurcation of the tail is suggested by the vertical line at the end of it. The first glyph in the second row of the caption above that picture refers to a solar eclipse.

If the model of the Maya zodiac we have presented is correct, the turtle in the first of the three pictures (Figure 6.8a) would represent the constellation Orion rising in the east shortly before Sunrise, and the serpent in the second picture (Figure 6.8b) would represent Sagittarius rising in the east just before dawn. The reference to a solar eclipse in the caption above the third picture (Figure 6.8c) raises the possibility of determining unique dates for all three pictures and thus being able to perform truly independent tests of our model of the Maya zodiac.

In a separate study to be published elsewhere, Victoria Bricker (unpublished) has shown that the calendar-round almanac of the Madrid Codex can be successfully cross-dated using only the interactions of the *tzolkin* cycle, the eclipse cycle, and the *haab*. The unambiguously best fit with these kinds of data places the 260-day original run of the almanac within the Christian years A.D. 1451 and 1452. The choice of this fifteenth-century date means that the eclipse reference in the caption on p. 66b fits appropriately with modern astronomical data not only for the original run of the almanac, but for the two succeeding 260-day runs as well. The calendar-round almanac, which internal evidence suggests was meant to be recycled at least several times, offers a period of at least 780 days in the mid-fifteenth century within which we can test our zodiacal model.

The results of such testing show our model to be completely consistent with the data from the Madrid almanac. The serpent picture on p. 67b would correspond to 2 January A.D. 1452, or 11.11.10.15.10 7 Oc 18 Yaxkin in the Maya calendar. The date, 7 Oc, is the fifth of the 8 days in the column of *tzolkin* days to the left of the picture and caption in Figure 6.8b. On this day, Sagittarius was indeed rising at Sunrise (Figure 6.9). This was 2 days after the solar eclipse pictured on p. 66b, which was not visible in the Maya area (Oppolzer 1887:254). The first of the three zodiacal pictures in the almanac, the turtle, would then be associated with a Gregorian date of 11 June A.D. 1451, corresponding to a Maya date of 11.11.10.2.2 10 Chicchan 18 Muan. The *tzolkin* date, 10 Chicchan, is the seventh of the 8 days in the column to the left of the picture and caption in Figure 6.8a. As called for by our model, Orion was rising at Sunrise on

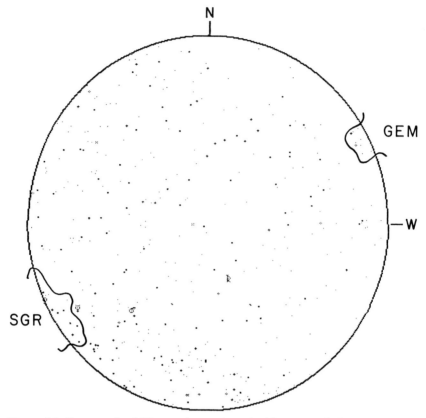

*Figure 6.9* Sky map for 6:23 A.M. (approximately 10 minutes before Sunrise), 2 January A.D. 1452, at 20° 30′ north latitude, 80° 30′ west longitude, showing the positions of Sagittarius, the rising zodiacal constellation, and Gemini, the setting zodiacal constellation.

this day. These two tests against completely independent data provide strong confirmation of our model of the Maya zodiac.

### EVIDENCE FROM THE BONAMPAK MURALS

One small portion of the murals from Bonampak is relevant to any investigation of a pre-Columbian Maya zodiac. The depictions in question are located on the sloping north wall of the vault of Room 2, directly beneath the capstone of the vault. Their relevance as iconographic representations of constellations of stars has been understood in general terms for nearly half a century (Miller 1986:47–48 provides a brief summary of early scholarship), but it was the insight offered by Lounsbury (1982) that has provided the key for further understanding of the Bonampak evidence and, indeed, the evidence offered by Chichén Itzá and the Paris Codex.

The Bonampak evidence in question consists of four subrectangular cartouches set above a narrow sky band (Miller 1986:Pls. 16–19). This sky band is, however, very incomplete. Miller (1986:48) describes the sky band as being "now fragmentary," seeming to imply that painting once present has been effaced, but the photographs published by her (1986:Pls. 17 and 18) suggest rather that the painting was never completed. However this may be, the sky band in its present form appears to have ten rectangular fields or segments. Both the leftmost two and the rightmost two segments contain crossed-bands signs similar to those in the sky band of Las Monjas at Chichén Itzá. The central six segments of the Bonampak sky band are empty.

Each of the four cartouches above the sky band contains a combination of star glyphs and anthropomorphic or zoomorphic figures. The figures depicted are, from right to left, a turtle, a human male holding a lance, a second human male holding a dish and an unidentified object, and two copulating peccaries. These figures are described in detail by Miller (1986:48) and Lounsbury (1982:147–48). The extant sky band extends from just beneath the turtle, the rightmost figure, to just beneath the second human, the third figure from the right. Our concern here is with only the turtle and the peccaries, animals that are documented as "zodiacal beasts" by the context of their occurrence in the almanac of the Paris Codex, the sky band of Las Monjas at Chichén Itzá, or both. For both the turtle and the peccaries, the star glyphs are superposed, in whole or in part, upon the bodies of the beasts in question, which is not the case for the two cartouches containing human figures (*pace* Lounsbury 1982:167, Figure 3).

Based on information in the sixteenth-century Motul dictionary (Martínez Hernández 1929) as interpreted in the light of both sixteenth-century European astrological practice and the results of the precession of the equinoxes, Lounsbury (1982:167–68) has shown very convincingly that the turtle constellation of the pre-Columbian Maya should be equated with a portion of the Western constellation, Orion. Specifically, the three star glyphs on the carapace of the turtle at Bonampak (Figure 6.10) can be seen as the three bright stars in the belt of Orion [from left to right, Alnitak (magnitude 2.05), Alnilam (1.70), and Mintaka (2.23)]. Accepting this identification as correct (as we do), it is of further interest to note that the alignment of the three star glyphs, slanting upward from left to right, mimics quite faithfully the orientation of the line of stars as they appear in the sky.

Previous discussions of the peccaries of Bonampak have not included their identification with any specific constellation of the Western zodiac

*Figure 6.10* Cartouche containing star glyphs and a turtle at Bonampak (drawn from a photograph published by Miller 1986:Pl. 19).

(Lounsbury 1982:167; Miller 1986:49–50). The system of correspondences suggested by us in this paper for the zodiacal beasts of the Paris almanac equates the tenth beast, now effaced, with the eastern part of the European constellation, Leo. Evidence from Las Monjas suggests that either the tenth or eleventh beast in the Paris series was a peccary. Further examination of the Bonampak peccaries appears to us to disambiguate the sequential ordering and to confirm the identification of peccaries with Leo. Both the text description of Miller (1986:48) and the photograph published by her (1986:Pl. 17) indicate that the cartouche in question (Figure 6.11a) contains, in addition to the two animals themselves, either three or, more probably, four star glyphs, arranged as in Figure 6.11b. The constellation Leo, as viewed directly overhead, contains seven bright stars, and there is a remarkable concordance between the pattern formed by four of them and the pattern of the star glyphs associated with the peccaries (Figure 6.11c). If the evidence of the Bonampak turtle may be taken to indicate a geometrically accurate pictograph of three bright stars in Orion, the peccaries seem to be offering us an equally accurate pictograph of four of the bright stars in Leo—Denebola (magnitude 2.14), Zosma (2.56), Chertan (3.34), and Regulus (1.35). Although such pattern matching would certainly not be convincing in and of itself, the way in which its results conform with and further clarify a model developed from quite different data is very encouraging.

## Conclusions

Our work with zodiacal references in the Maya codices, although very much still in progress, has produced some very promising results. We think

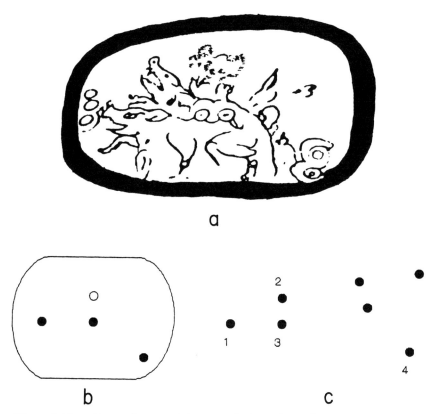

*Figure 6.11* a. Cartouche containing star glyphs and copulating peccaries at Bonampak (drawn from a photograph published by Miller 1986:Pl. 17); b. arrangement of the star glyphs in the peccary cartouche; c. seven bright stars of Leo, including Denebola (1), Zosma (2), Chertan (3), and Regulus (4).

we have elucidated several of the important structural characteristics of the zodiacal almanac in the Paris Codex, including how the green numbers function as corrections to permit reasonably accurate commensuration of the Maya computing year and the sidereal year over long periods of time. Our reexamination of the sky band from Las Monjas has shown that its utility for the study of the Maya zodiac is not as great as previous scholarship has assumed. Building on the previous work of Lounsbury with entries in the Motul dictionary and with certain of the Bonampak murals, we have been able to construct a coherent and testable model of the Maya zodiac. Data that can be used for such testing are very few, but we have been able to perform several meaningful tests against data from the Dresden and Madrid Codices. Although many elements of our model remain untested, all tests that we have been able to perform have produced results confirming the model. We shall continue this line of research in the belief that we have achieved at least partial understanding of this aspect of pre-Columbian Maya astronomy.

## ACKNOWLEDGMENTS

We acknowledge with gratitude both the opportunity to participate in the "Colgate Round Table on Astronomy," for which the original version of this paper was written, and the very useful comments on the research we received from Anthony Aveni and other participants during that conference. We have benefitted as well from the comments and criticisms of our colleagues Gary Urton at Colgate and Robert D. Purrington and Munro S. Edmonson at Tulane. Our special thanks are extended to Horst Hartung and Anthony Aveni for making available to us un-published photographs of the Monjas sky band taken by them during previous fieldwork at Chichén Itzá. We thank Anne and Donald Bradburn for bringing to our attention the computer planetarium software upon which this research has so heavily depended. Finally, we are very grateful to Donald Bradburn for his as-sistance at Chichén Itzá in August 1990, for his excellent photographic documenta-tion of the Monjas sky band, and for his authorization to publish his photos here.

## NOTES

1. In the construction of Table 6.4 and in the research reported in the re-mainder of this chapter, we have used the software of Davis (1985) to produce sky maps for the Yucatan peninsula on the dates in question. Of the scores of sky maps used in the research, only one (Figure 6.9) is reproduced here as an example.

2. Gary Urton (1981:113–18) reports that, in Andean astronomy, the pair of constellations that appear at the eastern and western horizons on the morning of the winter solstice (June 21 in the southern hemisphere) are treated as equivalent in the sense of being given the same name. Therefore, the pre-Columbian Maya were not alone in the New World in having an interest in the pairing of constellations in opposition to each other at both ends of the ecliptic at Sunrise. Other examples of the "terminological equation of opposing stars" have been found in Indian and Coptic astronomy (Urton 1981:213n2).

## REFERENCES

Aveni, A. F., 1977. "Concepts of Positional Astronomy Employed in Ancient Mesoamerican Architecture," in *Native American Astronomy*, edited by A. F. Aveni, pp. 3–19 (Austin and London: University of Texas Press).

—, 1980. *Skywatchers of Ancient Mexico* (Austin and London: University of Texas Press).

Aveni, A. F., and H. Hartung, 1986. "Maya City Planning and the Calendar,"

*Transactions of the American Philosophical Society* **76**(7) (Philadelphia: American Philosophical Society).

Bolles, J. S., 1977. *Las Monjas: A Major Pre-Mexican Architectural Complex at Chichén Itzá* (Norman: University of Oklahoma Press).

Bricker, H. M., and V. R. Bricker, 1983. "Classic Maya Prediction of Solar Eclipses," *Current Anthropology* **24**:1–24.

Bricker, V. R., unpublished. "The 'Calendar Round' Almanac in the Madrid Codex," *Papers on the Madrid Codex*, edited by V. R. Bricker and G. Vail.

Bricker, V. R., and H. M. Bricker, 1986. "The Mars Table in the Dresden Codex," in *Research and Reflections in Archaeology and History: Essays in Honor of Doris Stone*, edited by E. W. Andrews, pp. 51–80. Tulane University, Middle American Research Institute, Publication 57 (New Orleans).

—, 1988. "The Seasonal Table in the Dresden Codex and Related Almanacs," *Archaeoastronomy* **12**:S1–S62 (Supplement to *Journal for the History of Astronomy*, **19**).

—, 1989. "Astronomical References in the Table on Pages 61 to 69 of the Dresden Codex," in *World Archaeoastronomy*, edited by A. F. Aveni, pp. 232–45. (Cambridge: Cambridge University Press).

Brotherston, G., 1989. "Zodiac Signs, Number Sets, and Astronomical Cycles in Mesoamerica," in *World Archaeoastronomy*, edited by A. F. Aveni, pp. 276–88. (Cambridge: Cambridge University Press).

Closs, M. P., 1977. "The Date-Reaching Mechanism in the Venus Table of the Dresden Codex," in *Native American Astronomy*, edited by A. F. Aveni, pp. 89–99 (Austin and London: University of Texas Press).

*Codex Dresdensis*, 1975. *Codex Dresdensis: Sächsische Landesbibliothek Dresden, Mscr. Dresd. R 310 (Faksimile-Ausgabe des Codex mit Kommentar von Helmut Deckert und Ferdinand Anders)*, Codices Selecti 54 (Graz: Akademische Druck- und Verlagsanstalt).

*Codex Peresianus*, 1968. *Codex Peresianus (Codex Paris): Bibliothèque Nationale Paris (mit Einleitung und Summary von Ferdinand Anders*, Codices Selecti 9 (Graz: Akademische Druck- und Verlagsanstalt).

*Codex Tro-Cortesianus*, 1967. *Codex Tro-Cortesianus (Codex Madrid): Museo de América Madrid (mit Einleitung und Summary von Ferdinand Anders)*, Codices Selecti 7 (Graz: Akademische Druck- und Verlagsanstalt).

Davis, M., 1985. P. C. Planetarium (an astronomical software package).

Dütting, D., and M. Schramm, 1988. "The Sidereal Period of the Moon in Maya Calendrical Astronomy," *Tribus* **37**:139–73.

Förstemann, E., 1903. *Commentar zur Pariser Mayahandschrift (Codex Peresianus)* (Danzig: Verlag von L. Sauniers Buchhandlung, G. Horn).

Fox, J. A., and J. S. Justeson, 1984. "Polyvalence in Mayan Hieroglyphic Writing," In *Phoneticism in Mayan Hieroglyphic Writing*, edited by J. S. Justeson and L. Campbell, pp. 17–76. (Albany: State University of New York at Albany, Institute for Mesoamerican Studies, Publication 9).

Gordon, G. B., 1913. *The Book of Chilam Balam of Chumayel*. University of

Pennsylvania Museum Anthropological Publications 5 (Philadelphia: University Museum).

Justeson, J. S., 1989. "Ancient Maya Ethnoastronomy: An Overview of Hieroglyphic Sources," in *World Archaeoastronomy*, edited by A. F. Aveni, pp. 76–129. (Cambridge: Cambridge University Press).

Kelley, D. H., 1976. *Deciphering the Maya Script* (Austin and London: University of Texas Press).

Lounsbury, F. G., 1978. "Maya Numeration, Computation, and Calendrical Astronomy," in *Dictionary of Scientific Biography*, Vol. 15, suppl. 1, pp. 759–818 (New York: Scribner's).

—, 1982. "Astronomical Knowledge and Its Uses at Bonampak, Mexico," in *Archaeoastronomy in the New World*, edited by A. F. Aveni, pp. 143–68 (Cambridge: Cambridge University Press).

—, 1983. "The Base of the Venus Table of the Dresden Codex, and Its Significance for the Calendar-Correlation Problem," in *Calendars in Mesoamerica and Peru: Native American Computations of Time*, edited by A. F. Aveni and G. Brotherston, pp. 1–26. BAR International Series, 174 (Oxford).

Martínez Hernández, J., 1929. *Diccionario de Motul maya–español atribuido a Fray Antonio de Ciudad Real y arte de lengua maya por Fray Juan Coronel* (Mérida: Talleres de la Compañia Tipográfica Yucateca).

Maudslay, A. P., 1889–1902. *Biologia Centrali-Americana; or, Contributions to the Knowledge of the Fauna and Flora of Mexico and Central America. Archaeology.* Vols. III and IV (Plates) (London: Porter and Dulau).

Miller, M. E., 1986. *The Murals of Bonampak* (Princeton: Princeton University Press).

Oppolzer, T., 1887. *Canon der Finsternisse.* Kaiserliche Akademie der Wissenschaften, Mathematisch-Naturwissenschaftliche Class, Denkschriften 52 (Wien: Kaiserliche-Königliche Hof- und Staatsdruckerei).

Seler, E., 1961. "Die Tierbilder der mexikanischen und der Maya-Handschriften," in *Gesammelte Abhandlungen zur Amerikanischen Sprach- und Altertumskunde*, Band 4, pp. 458–758. (Graz: Akademische Druck- und Verlagsanstalt). (originally published in 1909 and 1910 in *Zeitschrift für Ethnologie*).

Severin, G. M., 1981. *The Paris Codex: Decoding an Astronomical Ephemeris.* Transactions of the American Philosophical Society, Vol. 71, pt. 5 (Philadelphia: American Philosophical Society).

Spinden, H. J., 1916. "The Question of the Zodiac in America," *American Anthropologist* 18:53–80.

—, 1924. *The Reduction of Maya Dates.* Harvard University, Peabody Museum of American Archaeology and Ethnology, Papers, Vol. 6, no. 4 (Cambridge: Peabody Museum).

Stephens, J. L., 1963. *Incidents of Travel in Yucatan.* 2 vols. (New York: Dover) (originally published in 1843 by Harper and Brothers).

Tedlock, B., unpublished. "Mayan Cosmology and Astronomical Commensuration." Paper presented to the University Museum Centennial Symposium, "New Theories on the Ancient Maya," Philadelphia, PA, April 1987. 1987.

Teeple, J. E., 1931. *Maya Astronomy*. Carnegie Institution of Washington, Publication 403; Contributions to American Anthropology and History (Washington, D.C.: Carnegie Institution).

Thompson, J. E. S., 1941. *Maya Arithmetic*. Carnegie Institution of Washington, Publication 528; Contributions to American Anthropology and History 36 (Washington, D.C.: Carnegie Institution).

—, 1960. *Maya Hieroglyphic Writing*, 2nd ed. (Norman: University of Oklahoma Press).

Urton, G., 1981. *At the Crossroads of the Earth and the Sky* (Austin: University of Texas Press).

Villacorta C., J. Antonio, and C. A. Villacorta, 1976. *Códices mayas*, 2nd ed. (Guatemala: Tipografía Nacional).

Willson, R. W., 1924. *Astronomical Notes on the Maya Codices*. Harvard University, Peabody Museum of American Archaeology and Ethnology, Papers, Vol. 6, no. 3 (Cambridge: Peabody Museum).

# 7

# A Derivation of the Mayan–to–Julian Calendar Correlation from the Dresden Codex Venus Chronology

## FLOYD G. LOUNSBURY

### Mayan Venus Chronology

Chronological data derived from the Venus auxiliary table of p. 24 of the Dresden Codex,[1] taken together with astronomical data pertaining to the planet, are employed here to derive the correlation between the Mayan and the Julian calendars and the respective associated day counts.

The Mayan chronology is outlined in Table 7.1. The items in boldface type are among those that appear on p. 24 of the Codex (Figure 7.1). They include the first two dates, namely R, the "ring number" base in mythological time,[2] and A, the earliest base in historical time, together with the long interval between them; and they include, after these, a series of seven shorter intervals for reckoning either from date A or from a subsequent base, date E. The other numbers in the tabulation (in plain type) are derived from these. One of the dates, F, occurs twice, inasmuch as its derivation is given twice in the codex table, once with reference to date A, and once with reference to date E.

Table 7.2 presents the same chronology, chaining the dates by means of the separate intervals that relate each date to its immediately adjacent predecessor and/or successor. The intervals employed for that purpose are derived from the cumulative intervals recorded on p. 24 of the Codex, which are those listed in boldface in Table 7.1.

*Table 7.1* Chronology of the Bases of the Venus Table of the Dresden Codex, Stated in Terms of the Cumulative Intervals Recorded on Page 24 of the Codex[a]

|  |  |  |  |  |  |  |
|---|---|---|---|---|---|---|
|  |  |  |  | −6. 2.0, | 1 Ahau 18 Kayab | (R) |
| −6. 2.0 | + | 9. 9.16. 0.0 | = | 9. 9. 9.16.0, | 1 Ahau 18 Kayab | (A) |
| 9. 9. 9.16.0 | + | 5. 5. 8.0 | = | 9.14.15. 6.0, | 1 Ahau 18 Kayab | (B) |
| 9. 9. 9.16.0 | + | 10.10.16.0 | = | 10. 0. 0.14.0, | 1 Ahau 18 Kayab | (C) |
| 9. 9. 9.16.0 | + | 15.16. 6.0 | = | 10. 5. 6. 4.0, | 1 Ahau 18 Kayab | (D) |
| 9. 9. 9.16.0 | + | 1. 1. 1.14.0 | = | 10.10.11.12.0, | 1 Ahau 18 Kayab | (E) |
| 9. 9. 9.16.0 | + | 1. 5.14. 4.0 | = | 10.15. 4. 2.0, | 1 Ahau 18 Uo | (F) |
| 10.10.11.12.0 | + | 4.12. 8.0 | = | 10.15. 4. 2.0, | 1 Ahau 18 Uo | (F) |
| 10.10.11.12.0 | + | 9.11. 7.0 | = | 11. 0. 3. 1.0, | 1 Ahau 13 Mac | (G) |
| 10.10.11.12.0 | + | 14.10. 6.0 | = | 11. 5. 2. 0.0, | 1 Ahau 3 Xul | (H) |

[a] Dates and intervals in boldface print are from page 24 of the Codex. Other data are implied by them and/or are recorded on page 50 of the Codex.

Other numbers in p. 24 of the Codex, but not listed in Tables 7.1 and 7.2, include the first twelve multiples of 8.2.0, that is, of 2920, which lead up to the thirteenth multiple, 5.5.8.0, equal to 37960, or two calendar rounds. This thirteenth multiple is the length of a full run of the main Venus table of pp. 46–50 of the Codex. The number 8.2.0, or 2920, is the length of any one of the 13 lines of that table, and it is the lowest common multiple of 584 and 365, the whole-number approximation to the mean synodic period of Venus and the length of the Mayan calendar year or *haab*, respectively, being equal to five of the former and eight of the latter.

## The Landa Equation

The date most often used as a starting point in historically based attempts to determine the Mayan–Julian correlation is that of the Mayan new-year day given by Diego de Landa in his outline of a Mayan year, halved and

*Table 7.2* Chronology of the Bases of the Venus Table of the Dresden Codex, Restated in Terms of Successive Base-to-Base Intervals[a]

|  |  |  |  |  |  |  |
|---|---|---|---|---|---|---|
|  |  |  |  | −6. 2.0, | 1 Ahau 18 Kayab | (R) |
| −6. 2.0 | + | 9. 9.16. 0.0 | = | 9. 9. 9.16.0, | 1 Ahau 18 Kayab | (A) |
| 9. 9. 9.16.0 | + | 5. 5. 8.0 | = | 9.14.15. 6.0, | 1 Ahau 18 Kayab | (B) |
| 9.14.15. 6.0 | + | 5. 5. 8.0 | = | 10. 0. 0.14.0, | 1 Ahau 18 Kayab | (C) |
| 10. 0. 0.14.0 | + | 5. 5. 8.0 | = | 10. 5. 6. 4.0, | 1 Ahau 18 Kayab | (D) |
| 10. 5. 6. 4 0 | + | 5. 5. 8.0 | = | 10.10.11.12.0, | 1 Ahau 18 Kayab | (E) |
| 10.10.11.12.0 | + | 4.12. 8.0 | = | 10.15. 4. 2.0, | 1 Ahau 18 Uo | (F) |
| 10.15. 4. 2.0 | + | 4.18.17.0 | = | 11. 0. 3. 1.0, | 1 Ahau 13 Mac | (G) |
| 11. 0. 3. 1.0 | + | 4.18.17.0 | = | 11. 5. 2. 0.0, | 1 Ahau 3 Xul | (H) |

[a] The intervals between successive bases are derived from the cumulative values recorded on page 24 of the Codex, as outlined in Table 7.1.

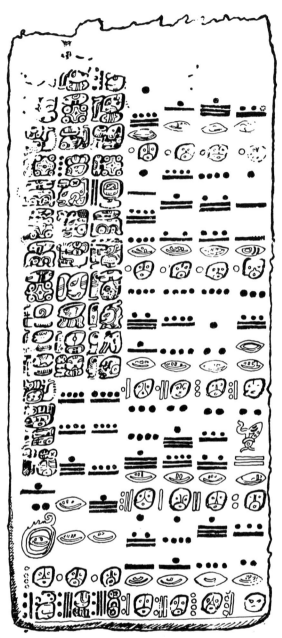

*Figure* 7.1 Page 24 of the Dresden Maya Hieroglyphic Codex. Drawing by Carlos A. Villacorta (Villacorta and Villacorta 1930:58). The obliterated higher-order digits of the numerals in the top tier can be determined from the surviving lower-order digits, the indicated *tzolkin* days 1 Ahau, and the structure of the table; those numbers, right to left, should read 5.5.8.0, 10.10.16.0, 15.16.6.0, and 1.1.1.14.0 (see Teeple 1931:95; Thompson 1950:225; and Thompson 1972:62). (The number 1.12.5.0 of the bottom tier lacks 3 dots over the bar; the 7 Ahau below it, and the progression of multiples of 8.2.0, require it to have been 1.12.8.0.)

overlaid in two parts onto a year of the Julian calendar, in his *Relacion de las cosas de Yucatan*. After reordering the halves so that they fit together properly, and determining the Christian year to which the date pertained, the Landa equation is the following[3]:

$$16 \text{ July } 1553 \text{ (Julian)} = 12 \text{ Kan } 1 \text{ Pop (Puuc)} \qquad (1)$$

Because of the 1-day dislocation in the relation between the almanac day and the year day in the Puuc system as compared with their relation in Classic Mayan dates, this equation has been subject to two different interpretations when translated for use with these, either

$$16 \text{ July } 1553 \text{ (Julian)} = 11 \text{ Akbal } 1 \text{ Pop (Classic)} \qquad (1a)$$

or

$$16 \text{ July } 1553 \text{ (Julian)} = 12 \text{ Kan } 2 \text{ Pop (Classic)} \qquad (1b)$$

And for another reason a third possibility has also been posited,

$$15 \text{ July } 1553 \text{ (Julian)} = 12 \text{ Kan } 2 \text{ Pop (Classic)}^4 \qquad (1c)$$

Of these three alternatives I shall choose the first, at least as a working hypothesis, remaining ready to switch to one of the others should the result of the investigation appear to call for it.

The value of the left-hand member of this equation (1a) is unique; that of the right-hand member, as it stands, is not. Since such a calendar-round day recurs every 18980 days, we should rewrite the left-hand member so as to make it similarly unspecific:

$$16 \text{ July } 1553 \text{ (Julian)} + 18980n = 11 \text{ Akbal } 1 \text{ Pop (Classic)} \qquad (2)$$

where $n$ is any integer, positive or negative.

For the date in the left-hand member of Eq. 2 we may substitute its corresponding Julian day number,[5] attaining the convenient formulation,

$$\text{JD } 2288488 + 18980n = 11 \text{ Akbal } 1 \text{ Pop (Classic)} \qquad (3)$$

which we can utilize in what follows.

### Deriving the Correlation

Since the initial base of the Mayan Venus table was a day 1 Ahau 18 Kayab, we begin our inquiry by asking, "When was the most recent 1 Ahau 18 Kayab in modern times?" To answer the question we need only an unspecific equation such as Eq. 3 above, derived from Landa's new-year date.

The interval from 11 Akbal 1 Pop to the *next* 1 Ahau 18 Kayab thereafter is 1797 days, or 4.17.17 in Maya notation. Adding this to both sides of Eq. 3, and understanding that all calendar-round dates henceforth will be given in their Classic form, we have

$$\text{JD } 2290285 + 18980n = 1 \text{ Ahau } 18 \text{ Kayab} \qquad (4)$$

Choosing now the value of $n$ that will yield the most recent possible such date, viz., letting $n = 8$, we have

$$\text{JD } 2442125 = 1 \text{ Ahau } 18 \text{ Kayab}$$

which, restated in terms of our calendar, "old style" and "new style," is

$$5 \text{ March } 1974 \text{ (Julian)} = 1 \text{ Ahau } 18 \text{ Kayab}$$

or

$$18 \text{ March } 1974 \text{ (Gregorian)} = 1 \text{ Ahau } 18 \text{ Kayab}$$

Our next question is, "What was the age of Venus on that date?"

That can be answered simply by consulting a table of dates of inferior conjunctions of Venus, such as that of Meeus (1983:7.21–25), where we find that the most recent inferior conjunction of Venus, prior to 1974 March 18, was on January 23 of the same year. The planet's "age" on March 18, then, was 54 days.

Next we ask, "What was the age of Venus on the date of the 1 Ahau 18 Kayab base of the table in the Dresden Codex?"

Given the structure of the table, it must be inferred that the 8-day period before the 1 Ahau 18 Kayab base was intended to represent the period of invisibility of the planet between last-of-evening-star and first-of-morning-star, 8 days being the best whole-day approximation to the mean duration for such periods. With the inferior conjunction falling approximately midway into the period, the canonical age of Venus at its end must be taken as 4 days. On the date of institution of that base, the age of the planet can be assumed actually to have been reasonably close to that figure, that is, to within a day or two, or at most 3 days, one side or the other.

Now we can ask, "How many Mayan calendar rounds must have elapsed between these two 1 Ahau 18 Kayab dates in order for the age of Venus on such a day to have increased from 4 days to 54 days, that is, for an increase of 50 days?"

The full length of the grand Venus cycle of the codex table is two calendar rounds (i.e., 37,960 days), as, for example, from a day 1 Ahau 18 Kayab to the second-next day of that same name. It contains 65 canonical Venus periods of 584 days each. The closest approximation to a true mean synodic period of that planet, however, is 583.92, a difference of 0.08 days.

In 65 such periods (i.e., in two calendar rounds) this accumulates to a shortfall of 5.2 days; that is, heliacal risings of Venus as morning star, after two calendar rounds, are coming—on an average—about 5.2 days earlier than canonically scheduled. For a difference of approximately 50 days to have accumulated, as between the 1 Ahau 18 Kayab base of the codex table and the 1 Ahau 18 Kayab of 1974, the number of two-calendar-round periods separating them must have been either nine or ten. (50 divided by 5.2 is equal to a little over 9.6, but since we require whole periods, of two calendar rounds each, their number must have been 9 or 10.) We must try both, checking their results against computed astronomical tables in order to make a choice, if possible, between them.

We reckon from the most recent 1 Ahau 18 Kayab, using its Julian date:

$$5 \text{ March } 1974 \text{ (Julian)} = \text{JD } 2442125$$

Let the number of intervening two-calendar-round periods be ten:

$$\text{JD } 2442125 - 10(37960) = \text{JD } 2062525$$
$$= 20 \text{ November A.D. } 934$$
$$\text{(Julian)}$$

Let the number of intervening two-calendar-round periods be nine:

$$\text{JD } 2442125 - 9(37960) = \text{JD } 2100485$$
$$= 25 \text{ October A.D. } 1038$$
$$\text{(Julian)}$$

These, then, are the two apparent candidates for the Julian date of a Maya day 1 Ahau 18 Kayab on which the age of Venus was approximately 4 days.

According to astronomical tables, the inferior conjunction of Venus next prior to the *earlier* of these two dates was on 16 November of that year, at around 3:30 a.m., 90th-meridian time, west. The age of Venus at sunrise, at this longitude, on the morning of the 1 Ahau 18 Kayab of 20 November A.D. 934, was therefore about 4.1 days.

The inferior conjunction of Venus next prior to the *later* of the two dates under consideration was on October 14 at approximately 8:24 p.m., same time zone. The age of Venus at sunrise on the morning of the 1 Ahau 18 Kayab of 25 October A.D. 1038, was therefore approximately 10.4 days.

The choice is clear. The Julian date on which the 1 Ahau 18 Kayab base of the table conformed to the astronomical circumstance there ascribed to it was A.D. 934 November 20.

This, however, does not yet give us the correlation that we seek. Although the date is specific in Julian chronology, it is not so in Mayan chronology, because at this point in the argument we do not yet know which of the five possible days 1 Ahau 18 Kayab on p. 24 of the codex (dates A–E in Tables 7.1 and 7.2) was the 1 Ahau 18 Kayab depicted as a base of the table on p. 50 of the Codex in the position to which a 4-day Venus age is ascribable. To remove this ambiguity we must turn to the later bases that were ingeniously made to replace 1 Ahau 18 Kayab, and to replace one another in turn, so as to keep the table from getting too far out of step with reality.

## 1 Ahau 18 Uo

We can repeat the same question-and-answer process now for the calendar-round day 1 Ahau 18 Uo, but we need here only to summarize the answers. These are as follows:

The most recent occurrence of a day 1 Ahau 18 Uo was JD 2437445, which was 25 May 1961 (Gregorian), 12 May (Julian). The age of Venus on that date was 45 days.

The canonical age of Venus for the tabular position to which 1 Ahau 18 Uo was assigned when it was made the first replacement base of the Maya table was 4 days. It can be assumed that the actual age of Venus on that day was reasonably close to that figure, that is, deviating from it by not more than 3 days.

The difference between the ages of Venus on these two days 1 Ahau 18 Uo, then, was the difference between 45 and approximately 4, or about 41 days. 41 divided by 5.2 is equal to about 7.88. Therefore the number of intervening 2CR periods necessary to accumulate a difference of that magnitude was either 7 or 8.

Possibilities for the date of the 1 Ahau 18 Uo base of the table can then be determined as follows: The most recent 1 Ahau 18 Uo, expressed in terms of its Julian date, was

$$12 \text{ May } 1961 \text{ (Julian)}, = \text{JD } 2437445$$

If the number of intervening 2CR periods was 8, we have:

$$\text{JD } 2437445 - 8(37960) = \text{JD } 2133765$$
$$= 6 \text{ December A.D. } 1129$$
$$\text{(Julian)}$$

If the number of intervening 2CR periods was 7, we have:

$$\text{JD } 2437445 - 7(37960) = \text{JD } 2171725,$$
$$= 10 \text{ November A.D. } 1233$$
$$\text{(Julian)}$$

The choice between the two possibilities rests on their relative astronomical qualifications for occupying the position in the table that prescribes a Venus age of 4 days, with but little leeway.

The inferior conjunction of Venus just prior to the *earlier* of these two dates was 1129 December 1 (Julian), at around 1 a.m. in the time zone of the Maya (90th-meridian time, west; i.e., North American CST). The age of Venus just before sunrise on the 1 Ahau 18 Uo of December 6 was therefore about 5.2 days.

The inferior conjunction of Venus just prior to the *later* of these two dates was 29 October 1233 (Julian), at around 3:30 p.m. in this same time zone. The age of Venus just before sunrise on the 1 Ahau 18 Uo of November 10 of that year was therefore about 11.6 days.

The choice is clear: the 1 Ahau 18 Uo of the table has to have been the earlier date, 6 December 1129 (Julian). Its age on this date was only about 1 day more than the canonical age for its position in the table. On the later of the two dates the difference would have been about 7 or 8 days more.

With this determination, we have an unambiguous chronological equation for date F of Tables 7.1 and 7.2:

$$10.15.4.2.0, 1 \text{ Ahau } 18 \text{ Uo} = 1129 \text{ December } 6 \text{ (Julian)}$$

or

$$\text{Maya day } 1549480 = \text{Julian day } 2133765$$

The correlation constant that we seek is that number which, added to a Maya day number, yields a value that is equal to the corresponding historical Julian day number. We have therefore:

$$\text{Correlation constant} = 2133765 - 1549480$$
$$= 584285$$

## 1 Ahau 13 Mac

We repeat this process also for the two remaining Mayan dates that appear as bases of the Venus table (Dresden Codex, p. 50:D), viz., 1 Ahau 13 Mac and 1 Ahau 3 Xul. We begin with the first of these.

The most recent occurrence of a day 1 Ahau 13 Mac was JD 2435105, which was 28 December 1954 (Gregorian), December 15 (Julian). The age of Venus on that most recent return of 1 Ahau 13 Mac was 43 days.

The canonical age of Venus for the tabular position to which 1 Ahau 13 Mac was assigned when it was made the second replacement base of the Maya table was 4 days, and it can be assumed that the actual age of Venus on that day was reasonably close to that figure, that is, deviating from it by not more than 3 days.

The difference between the ages of Venus on these two days 1 Ahau 13 Mac was thus the difference between 43 and approximately 4, or about 39 days. 39 divided by 5.2 is equal to 7.5. Therefore, the number of intervening 2CR periods necessary to accumulate a difference of about 39 days was either 7 or 8, seemingly with about equal probability.

Possibilities for the date of the 1 Ahau 13 Mac base of the table are then determined as follows: The most recent 1 Ahau 13 Mac, expressed in terms of its Julian date, was

$$\text{15 December 1954 (Julian)}, = \text{JD 2435105}$$

If the number of intervening 2CR periods was 8, we have:

$$\text{JD 2435105} - 8(37960) = \text{JD 2131425}$$
$$= \text{11 July A.D. 1123 (Julian)}$$

If the number of intervening 2CR periods was 7, we have:

$$\text{JD 2435105} - 7(37960) = \text{JD 2169385}$$
$$= \text{15 June A.D. 1227 (Julian)}$$

The inferior conjunction of Venus just prior to the *earlier* of these two dates was 8 July 1123 (Julian), at about 6 p.m. in the time zone of the Maya. The age of Venus just before sunrise on the 1 Ahau 13 Mac of 11 July was therefore about 2.5 days.

The inferior conjunction of Venus just prior to the *later* of these two dates was 8 June 1227 (Julian), at around 1:00 p.m. in this same time zone. The age of Venus just before sunrise on the 1 Ahau 13 Mac of June 15 of that year was therefore about 6.7 days.

The choice this time is less clear; both are within the permitted range, whether early or tardy. If the 1 Ahau 13 Mac of the table was the earlier date, then its age on this date was about 1.5 days less than the canonical age for its position in the table. If it was the later of the two dates, then its age on that date was about 2.7 days more than the canonical age. We have other clear evidence, however, on which to base the choice. If the choice were to be the earlier of these two alternatives, then the 1 Ahau 13 Mac base of the table would fall on a date *earlier* than the 1 Ahau 18 Uo base. But that is contradicted by the intervals recorded in the second tier from the top on p. 24 of the Codex, and by the chronology they determine. The 1 Ahau 13 Mac base (date G in Tables 7.1 and 7.2) was a *later* base than the 1 Ahau 18 Uo base (date F). It is therefore the later of the two alternative possibilities for 1 Ahau 13 Mac that is required.

With this, we have an equation for date G and a unique solution:

$$11.0.3.1.0, \ 1 \text{ Ahau } 13 \text{ Mac } = 15 \text{ June } 1227 \text{ (Julian)}$$
$$\text{Maya day } 1585100 = \text{Julian day } 2169385$$
$$\text{Correlation constant } = 2169385 - 1585100$$
$$= 584285$$

## 1 Ahau 3 Xul

We turn to the last of the bases of the Venus table indicated on p. 50 of the Codex.

The most recent occurrence of a day 1 Ahau 3 Xul was JD 2432765, which was 1 August 1948 (Gregorian), 19 July (Julian). The age of Venus on that most recent return of 1 Ahau 3 Xul was 38 days.

The canonical age of Venus for the tabular position to which 1 Ahau 3 Xul was assigned when it was made the third replacement base of the Maya table was 4 days, and it can be assumed that the actual age of Venus on that day was reasonably close to that figure, that is, deviating from it by not more than 3 days.

The difference between the ages of Venus on these two 1 Ahau 3 Xul days, then, was the difference between 38 and approximately 4, or about 34 days. 34 divided by 5.2 is equal to 6.54. Therefore, the number of intervening 2CR periods necessary to accumulate a difference of about 34 days was either 6 or 7.

We have then the following: The most recent 1 Ahau 3 Xul, expressed in terms of its Julian date, was

$$19 \text{ July } 1948 \text{ (Julian)} = \text{JD } 2432765$$

If the number of intervening 2CR periods was 7, we have:

$$\text{JD } 2432765 - 7(37960) = \text{JD } 2167045$$
$$= 17 \text{ January A.D. } 1221$$
$$\text{(Julian)}$$

If the number of intervening 2CR periods was 6, we have:

$$\text{JD } 2432765 - 6(37960) = \text{JD } 2205005$$
$$= 22 \text{ December A.D. } 1324$$
$$\text{(Julian)}$$

The inferior conjunction of Venus nearest to the *earlier* of these two dates was on that very day itself, 17 January 1221 at about 1:00 a.m., in the time zone of the Maya. The age of Venus just before sunrise on that 1 Ahau 3 Xul of 17 January 1221 was therefore about 0.2 days.

The inferior conjunction of Venus nearest to the *later* of these two dates was 15 December 1324 (Julian), very shortly before midnight, in this same time zone. The age of Venus just before sunrise on the 1 Ahau 3 Xul of 22 December of that year was therefore about 6.25 days.

The choice is quite clear. If the 1 Ahau 3 Xul of the table was the earlier date, then the age of Venus on this date was about 3.8 days less than the canonical age for its position in the table, which is a negative deviation outside the reasonable range. If it was the later of the two dates, then its age on that date was about 2.25 days more than the canonical age, a positive deviation within the acceptable range. The later of the two alternative possibilities for 1 Ahau 3 Xul is therefore the more appropriate. That it is also a necessary choice is guaranteed by the fact that the structure of the Venus table implies that the 1 Ahau 3 Xul base was a *later* base than that of 1 Ahau 13 Mac. If the earlier of the two possibilities here were chosen, it would reverse that relationship. We can be sure, then, that the correct choice is the later of the two, viz. 22 December 1324, JD 2205005.

With this, we have an equation for date H of Tables 7.1 and 7.2:

$$11.5.2.0.0, \text{ 1 Ahau 3 Xul} = 22 \text{ December } 1324 \text{ (Julian)}$$
$$\text{Maya day } 1620720 = \text{Julian day } 2205005$$
$$\text{Correlation constant} = 2205005 - 1620720$$
$$= 584285$$

## 1 Ahau 18 Kayab

The calculations carried out in the section on Deriving the Correlation yielded a 1 Ahau 18 Kayab date that was specific in Julian chronology and that satisfied exactly the requirement imposed by its location in a base position in the Venus table of the Codex (Dresden 50:D13, D22), viz., occurring 4 days after an inferior conjunction of the planet. Its place in Mayan chronology, however, was determined only to within a set of five alternative long-count dates at successive two-calendar-round intervals. The resulting 1 Ahau 18 Kayab equation is:

$$9.9.9.16.0 + x(5.5.8.0) = 20 \text{ November A.D. } 934 \text{ (Julian)}$$

where $x$ is one of the integers in the range from 0 to 4. This can be re-stated as:

$$\text{Maya day } 1364360 + x(37960) = \text{Julian day } 2062525$$

with the same limitation on $x$.

This yields the following five alternative solutions for a correlation constant:

If $x = 0$, then the correlation constant $= 698165$
If $x = 1$, then the correlation constant $= 660205$
If $x = 2$, then the correlation constant $= 622245$
If $x = 3$, then the correlation constant $= 584285$
If $x = 4$, then the correlation constant $= 546325$

The previous derivations, from the 1 Ahau bases of 18 Uo, 18 Mac, and 3 Xul, respectively, all yielded a consistent result, viz.,

correlation constant $= 584285$.

Of the five tentative possibilities just derived from the alternatives for a 1 Ahau 18 Kayab base, only the fourth, with $x = 3$, is consistent with the three-times-previously attested solution. This points to the Maya date D of Tables 7.1 and 7.2 as the one—the only one—that satisfied the condition that it be a day 1 Ahau 18 Kayab that occurred 4 days after an inferior conjunction of Venus. This now removes the ambiguity from the above equation and we have instead:

20 November A.D. 934 (Julian) $= 9.9.9.16.0 + 3(5.5.8.0)$
$= 9.9.9.16.0 + 15.16.6.0$
$= 10.5.6.4.0,$ 1 Ahau 18 Kayab

This presents us with an apparent anomaly, for it is clear that the 1 Ahau 18 Kayab *reckoning* bases were dates A (9.9.9.16.0) and E (10.10.11.12.0), separated from each other by an interval of 4(5.5.8.0), or 1.1.1.14.0. This is indicated, for example, by the recorded intervals 1.5.14.4.0 and 4.12.8.0, which differ by that same amount, the first deriving 1 Ahau 18 Uo (10.15.4.2.0) from date A (9.9.9.16.0), and the second deriving it from date E (10.10.11.12.0).

The anomaly is only "apparent," however; there is no real inconsistency. The relationship between the dates of Tables 7.1 and 7.2 and their loci in time vis-à-vis adjacent inferior conjunctions of Venus is as shown in Table 7.3.

In this table the columns at the left give the dates of the bases and potential bases as indicated either on p. 24 of the Codex or in the final column of p. 50, or in both places. The Mayan long-count positions and the 1 Ahau *haab* positions are as in Tables 7.1 and 7.2. The Julian dates are those determined in the preceding parts of this discussion for dates D, F, G, and H, with equivalents for the other dates as determined by the correlation thereby established. (The appended decimal fractions will be explained shortly.)

*Table 7.3*  The Ages of Venus on the Base Dates of the Dresden Codex Venus Table (by the 584285 Correlation), and Their Deviations from the Canonical Age Prescribed for the Bases

| Base dates of the Venus table | | | | Inferior conjunction of Venus (UT) | Age of Venus on base day | Deviation from canon |
|---|---|---|---|---|---|---|
| Base | Long Count | 1 Ahau | Julian (UT) | | | |
| (A) | 9. 9. 9.16.0 | 18 Kayab | 6.5 Feb 623 | 20.1 Feb | −13.6 | −17.6 |
| (B) | 9.14.15. 6.0 | 18 Kayab | 11.5 Jan 727 | 19.8 Jan | − 8.3 | −12.3 |
| (C) | 10. 0. 0.14.0 | 18 Kayab | 16.5 Dec 830 | 18.8 Dec | − 2.3 | − 6.3 |
| (D) | 10. 5. 6. 4.0 | 18 Kayab | 20.5 Nov 934 | 16.4 Nov | + 4.1 | + 0.1 |
| (E) | 10.10.11.12.0 | 18 Kayab | 25.5 Oct 1038 | 15.1 Oct | +10.4 | + 6.4 |
| (F) | 10.15. 4. 2.0 | 18 Uo | 6.5 Dec 1129 | 1.3 Dec | + 5.2 | + 1.2 |
| (G) | 11. 0. 3. 1.0 | 13 Mac | 15.5 Jun 1227 | 8.8 Jun | + 6.7 | + 2.7 |
| (H) | 11. 5. 2. 0.0 | 3 Xul | 22.5 Dec 1324 | 16.2 Dec | + 6.3 | + 2.3 |

In the third column from the right are given the dates and times of the adjacent inferior conjunctions of Venus as these are listed in Jean Meeus' *Astronomical Tables of the Sun, Moon, and Planets* (1983:7.21–25, Table VII). The decimal fractions indicate the times of the respective conjunctions, rounded off to the nearest tenth of a day, in Universal Time (i.e., Greenwich Mean Time). For purposes of computation it has been convenient simply to leave them in that form, even though we are interested in phenomena and their timings at roughly 90 degrees west longitude (a quarter of a day earlier, North American Central Standard Time). It is for this reason, namely, to simplify computation, that the Julian equivalents of the Mayan Venus-table base dates all have the decimal fraction 0.5 appended to them. This indicates Greenwich noon, which is 6:00 a.m. in North American CST, the approximate time for a *heliacal* rising of Venus in the Mayan area (rounded off, again, to the nearest tenth of a day).

The ages of Venus on the several 1 Ahau base dates, as given in the penultimate column of the table, are the differences obtained by subtracting the inferior-conjunction dates (and times) from the respective base dates (and times), with all timings to the nearest tenth of a day. The final column of the table lists the deviations between these ages and the canonical age of 4 days that is ascribed by the Mayan Venus table to its 1 Ahau base position. Thus, for example, for date A it is the difference between the actual age of −13.6 days and the tabular age of +4 days, amounting to −17.6 days. And for date H it is the difference between the actual +6.3 and the tabular +4, amounting to +2.3 days.

It is obvious, to begin with, that not more than one of the five 1 Ahau 18 Kayab dates (A–E) can have articulated with astronomical reality in the manner prescribed by the Mayan table, and that all of the others must have deviated from that condition, in one direction or the other, by amounts that approximate to integral multiples of 5.2. Table 7.3 shows clearly which one of the five 1 Ahau 18 Kayab dates that was: It was date "D," 10.5.6.4.0 (20 November A.D. 934).

It is equally clear, however, that 10.10.11.12.0 was the reference date and reckoning base for the corrective intervals 4.12.8.0 and 9.11.7.0 recorded in the second tier of numbers on p. 24 of the Codex. (This is secured, for example, by the double derivation of the 1 Ahau 18 Uo date, first by application of the interval 1.5.14.4.0 from that same tier of numbers to the earlier reference date 9.9.9.16.0, and then by application of the interval 4.12.8.0 to this later reference date 10.10.11.12.0, which is eight calendar rounds later, and by the fact that no other motivation can be found for those two recorded intervals that differ from each other by that same amount.)

One will ask, then, why this later reference date, 10.10.11.12.0, rather than the astronomically more appropriate 10.5.6.4.0 of two calendar rounds earlier, became the reckoning base for application of the corrective intervals. The answer, I believe, consists essentially in the following points:

1. The 1 Ahau 18 Kayab base of the Venus table was instituted as of the date on which it was astronomically appropriate, viz. 10.5.6.4.0, which was 20 November A.D. 934.

2. It was projected backward in time by an amount equal to three runs of the table (six calendar rounds), to 9.9.9.16.0, for reasons having to do with a simultaneous phenomenon of Mars on 10.5.6.4.0, and with the commensurability of the reckoning periods of Venus and Mars (six calendar rounds is the lowest common multiple of 584 and 780). It was projected backward even further, to −6.2.0 in mythic time, for the same reason and in conformity with Mayan practice in astronomical and related mythologizing.

3. A complete historical run of the Maya table brought it from 10.5.6.4.0, its initial date, to 10.10.11.12.0, its terminal date. Note that the 1 Ahau 18 Kayab base on p. 50 of the Codex is a terminal date. On this date a second run of the table, with the same base, was begun.

4. By this time, however, the prescriptions of the table were beginning to lag noticeably behind the astronomical phenomena they were designed to indicate, and during this second run it became increasingly apparent that the discrepancy would continue to grow in magnitude.

5. In response to the problem posed by this growing discrepancy, the procedure for corrective adjustments was invented. This procedure achieved its end by truncating runs of the table in such a way as to locate potential 1 Ahau bases that were closer to their target. It required foreshor-

tenings in the amount of integral multiples of 6.9.0 (2340 days, a multiple of the *tzolkin*, thus preserving 1 Ahau), each of which effected a 4-day correction [2340 = 4(584) + 4].

6. The current second run of the table was truncated in this manner, effecting a double adjustment of 8 days, and instituting a new base on 1 Ahau 18 Uo. The fact that this was a double correction shows that the drift it corrected was the product of close to *two* runs of the table, not just one. This constitutes confirming evidence that their starting date was that of the *previous* run, 10.5.6.4.0, not that of the current run, 10.10.11.12.0. But it was the *current* run that was subjected to the foreshortening; hence it was *its* starting date, 10.10.11.12.0, that became the reckoning base for these adjustments.

The astronomical circumstances attending the institution of the 1 Ahau 18 Kayab base, apparently motivating its retrospective projections to 9.9.9.16.0 and −6.2.0, and those attending the institution of the corrective mechanism and the 1 Ahau 18 Uo base, have been described in ample detail in a previous publication (Lounsbury 1983); they need not be repeated here.

## Interpretations of the Landa Equation

In the discussion of the Landa equation there were listed three alternative Classic conversions of Landa's Puuc-style calendaric equation, viz.,

$$16 \text{ July } 1553 \text{ (Julian)} = 11 \text{ Akbal } 1 \text{ Pop (Classic)} \qquad (1a)$$
$$16 \text{ July } 1553 \text{ (Julian)} = 12 \text{ Kan } 2 \text{ Pop (Classic)} \qquad (1b)$$
$$15 \text{ July } 1558 \text{ (Julian)} = 12 \text{ Kan } 2 \text{ Pop (Classic)} \qquad (1c)$$

Of these, the first was chosen, tentatively, for the above derivations of a Classic–to–Julian correlation constant. It remains to consider what would have been the results of the other alternatives, and what desiderata may determine a final choice from among them.

The first of these, Eq. (1a), implies that it was in the *tzolkin* (e.g., with its 12 Kan here in place of 11 Akbal) that the Puuc calendar differed from the Classic. But since Puuc *katun* endings, like Classic, are on days Ahau, and since known examples of Initial Series dates with Puuc-style calendar-round days show no difference from the Classic in their relationship between *tzolkin* days and *kin* digits, this interpretation makes it necessary to posit a 1-day discontinuity in the long count (skipping a day number, or counting two day numbers on one day) coeval with the posited Puuc shift in the tzolkin.

The consequences of this first interpretation of the Landa equation are as here derived. The resulting correlation constant is 584285.

The second interpretation, Eq. (1b), implies instead that it was in the *haab* (with 2 Pop here rather than 1 Pop) that the Puuc calendar differed from the Classic. It is, in a way, a simpler assumption than the first, involving only one of the three Mayan variables (the *haab*), rather than two of them (the *tzolkin* and the long count).

The consequence of this interpretation of Landa's Puuc date is a correlation constant of 584284 rather than 584285. Applied to a Maya day number, it determines a Julian day number and a Julian or Gregorian calendar date 1 day earlier in time than that determined by 584285. Applied to a Julian day number, it determines a Maya day number and calendar-round day 1 day later than those determined by 584285.

The third interpretation, Eq. (1c), is the same as the second, Eq. (1b), insofar as the nature of the Puuc shift is concerned; but it makes a different assumption about Landa's Julian date, supposing that it was, or should have been, 15 July rather than 16 July of the year 1553. Possibilities suggested by proponents of this interpretation, to explain how the hypothetic error in Landa's date might have come about, include the following:

1. Although the year in Landa's example was definitely 1553, his information that the Maya new year began on 16 July may not have been of that year, but from an earlier year (before the leap year of 1552), there being "no reason why Landa should not have witnessed the year-bearer celebrations in some heathen community in 1550 or 1551, or casually heard of it from one of his colleagues, and made a note of the date in the European calendar" (Thompson 1950:304).

2. The "freeze" of the Maya *haab*, locking it into fixed position in the Julian calendar year, may have taken place before the leap-year day of 1552, fixing the beginning of the Maya year at 16 July for all time to come. In that case, Landa's year bearer would have been an anachronism. Had the freeze not been forced onto the Maya before that year, the 1st of Pop in 1553 would—by this hypothesis—have fallen on 15 July (Satterthwaite 1965:613).

The consequence of this interpretation, had it been employed in the above derivations, would be a correlation constant of 584283 rather than 584284 or 584285. Applied to a Maya day number, it would determine a Julian day number and a Julian or Gregorian calendar date 2 days earlier than by 584285. Applied to a Julian day number, it would determine a Maya day number and calendar-round day 2 days later than by 584285.

There is no *direct* evidence to support this revision of Landa's Julian date or any of the speculative explanations offered for it; but there is an important item of *indirect* evidence that has motivated it. It is the fact that the historically surviving almanacs in Highland Guatemala—almost all of them—agree with the predictions of a 584283 correlation, as do the most secure of the Axtec double dates from the Conquest period in Central Mexico. This fact, together with the belief, or hope, that the Meso-american 260-day almanacs may all have been synchronous, has led some chronologists to assume the third interpretation of Landa's double date.

We are concerned here with the astronomical implications of the three different interpretations, first as regards Venus, and then (in the next section) as regards the moon. Some of the consequences for Venus on the four fundamental base dates (D, F, G, and H), as determined by each of the three interpretations of the Landa equation, may be seen in Table 7.4. The pertinent items for comparison are the Venus age on these dates (in days since inferior conjunction) and the *arcus visionis* (the sun's depression, or negative altitude, when Venus appears at the horizon). The canonical prescription for Venus age on these dates, as implied by the scheme of the Codex table, is 4 days. The critical *arcus visionis* for a heliacal rising of Venus is variable, ranging from about eight or nine degrees down to about four or three degrees, depending on the time of the year, the latitude of observation, the celestial latitude of the planet, and yet other factors.

It is date D whose astronomical circumstances are the most critical for an evaluation of the relative merits of the three interpretations of Landa's double date. Dates A, B, and C are backward projections from that base, with Venus ages that depart widely from the prescription of the Codex. Date E is a repeat base, also with a discrepant Venus age. Dates F, G, and H are the better approximations to the prescription of the Codex that were made

*Table 7.4*  Venus Age and *Arcus Visionis* on the Base Dates D, F, G, and H, as Determined by the Interpretations 1a, 1b, and 1c of the Landa Equation and the Corresponding Correlation Constants 584285, 584284, and 584283

| Base | Long count | 1 Ahau | Landa | Julian | Venus age (days) | Arcus visionis (degrees) |
|------|-----------|--------|-------|--------|------------------|--------------------------|
| (D) | 10. 5.6.4.0 | 18 Kayab | (1a) | 20 Nov 934 | 4.1 | 7.0 |
|     |            |          | (1b) | 19 | 3.1 | 5.4 |
|     |            |          | (1c) | 18 | 2.1 | 3.7 |
| (F) | 10.15.4.2.0 | 18 Uo | (1a) | 6 Dec 1129 | 5.2 | 9.2 |
|     |            |          | (1b) | 5 | 4.2 | 7.6 |
|     |            |          | (1c) | 4 | 3.2 | 6.0 |
| (G) | 11. 0.3.1.0 | 13 Mac | (1a) | 15 Jun 1227 | 6.7 | 8.3 |
|     |            |          | (1b) | 14 | 5.7 | 7.0 |
|     |            |          | (1c) | 13 | 4.7 | 5.7 |
| (H) | 11. 5.2.0.0 | 3 Xul | (1a) | 22 Dec 1324 | 6.3 | 11.5 |
|     |            |          | (1b) | 21 | 5.3 | 10.0 |
|     |            |          | (1c) | 20 | 4.3 | 8.5 |

possible by application of the corrective foreshortening, but they are artifacts of calculation, limited by the constraints of that method, which required corrections in 4-day modules and preservation of the *tzolkin* day 1 Ahau. On the basis of the data for date D presented in Table 7.4 (last two columns), interpretation 1a appears best to qualify, 1b appears also to be a fair possibility, while 1c appears least likely. However, none of these can definitely be excluded on the basis of the above Venus data at this point. The matter requires evaluation by an astronomer who has the appropriate theoretical knowledge and experience with observation of horizon phenomena.

## A Lunar Test

The derivations of the correlation presented here have been completely independent of any data or considerations involving the moon. It is therefore appropriate to subject their result to a lunar test. A correlation that is to be entertained as historically true must necessarily predict moon ages that agree with those of both Mayan and Old World lunar records for any given date.

Mayan sources for lunar chronology are of two main varieties: (1) the eclipse table of the Dresden Codex, in particular its initial reference date of 9.16.4.10.8, 12 Lamat 1 Muan, commonly understood to be a date of astronomical new moon, that is, of lunar–solar conjunction, and (2) the records of moon ages for initial-series dates in Mayan monumental inscriptions. Those of the latter variety are numerous, but not entirely consistent, this being due in part to the fact that some may have been based on current observations while others, retrospective in nature, must have been products of computation; and apparently due also in part to local differences in the concept of moon age, that is, whether it was counted from first visibility of the new crescent moon or from calculated conjunction date; or, alternatively, whether from conjunction date or from disappearance of the old moon.

By the 584285 correlation that was derived here from the Venus-table data with Landa's new-year date, taking the latter in its first interpretation (1a), we have the following equivalence for the initial reference date of the eclipse table:

$$9.16.4.10.8 \; (12 \; \text{Lamat} \; 1 \; \text{Muan}) = \text{Mayan day} \; 1412848$$
$$= \text{Julian day} \; 1997133$$
$$= 8 \; \text{November A.D.} \; 755$$
$$(\text{Julian})$$

According to the Goldstine lunar tables (1973), this Julian date was a date of an astronomical new moon, with lunar–solar conjunction occurring at 11:08 a.m. in the time zone of the Maya (90 degrees west).[6]

The 584285 correlation thus satisfies our presumed prime lunar requirement of a true correlation, viz., that 9.16.4.10.8 (12 Lamat 1 Muan) should be a date of lunar–solar conjunction. If that presumption is legitimate, then this is the correct correlation. But the legitimacy of that assumption may still bear inquiry.

In the above derivations, it will be remembered, there were two candidates for each crucial date. The choice between them was determined by the degree to which they approximated the canonical Venus age prescribed for them in the Codex, and, in a single case of possible ambivalence in this regard, on the temporal order of the bases as determined by the distance numbers on p. 24 of the Codex and as listed in Tables 7.1 and 7.2. A different choice in any one of these cases would have either increased or decreased the value of the derived correlation constant by an amount of 37960 days. It can be noted now that, had such a different choice been made, it would also have either increased or decreased the predicted moon age for the Julian or Gregorian equivalent of a Mayan date by the amount of 13.2 days, causing a gross discrepancy in every recorded moon age in Mayan inscriptions, and in every moon age prescribed or implied in the codices. This can be taken as confirming evidence that the choices made were the correct ones.

That the initial reference date of the eclipse table, 9.16.4.10.8, must have been a date of astronomical new moon (as presumed above), or at least within a day or two of such a date, cannot be doubted; for if that were not the case, then not a single one of the 69 solar eclipse stations in that table would ever have had any validity within a time span of several millenia either side of any reasonable Mayan time horizon. The table does, however, by virtue of its three lines of successive *tzolkin* days, allow for a leeway of 1 or 2 days. In the present lunar test we have assumed that 9.16.4.10.8 represented a date of astronomical new moon, because that has appeared to be the implication of the table. And if that assumption is valid, then 584285 is the appropriate correlation constant and the first interpretation (1a) of the Landa equation can be presumed to be the correct one. Nevertheless, we are obliged to inquire whether that commonly held assumption about 9.16.4.10.8 is indeed precisely valid.

There is, in fact, another assumption that can be made about that date, and it has certain advantages over the commonly accepted one. Under this alternative, the 9.16.4.10.8 date would not be supposed to have been the historical base of the Codex table, nor would it have been the date of the institution of "12 Lamat" bases for the eclipse cycle. Rather, these would have been some nine or ten eclipse cycles later. The 9.16.4.10.8 date would be—like its 9.9.9.16.0 counterpart in the Venus table—an invented "throwback" base, projected backwards from the actual historical base for a theoretical reason.[7] For the actual historical base, a date that is ten eclipse cycles later, *less 1 day*, is an especially attractive possibility. But because of the "less 1 day," this would be an "11 Manik" by the 584285 correlation and the first interpretation of Landa. For it to be a "12 Lamat," a correlation constant of 584284 would be required, which is obtainable only under the second interpretation (1b). The Julian date is 19 April A.D. 1083 which then, by 584284, would be 10.12.16.14.8, 12 Lamat 1 Ch'en. This is the date that Maud Makemson (1943) proposed for the start of the eclipse calendar of the Dresden codex (see also Thompson 1950:235).

The advantages of this alternative are (1) that the locations of the eclipse seasons and the nodes in the existing codical version of the eclipse table are actually in agreement with those of eleventh-century dates, whereas they are 15 to 17 days out of phase for the eighth century; and (2) the historical "12 Lamat" starting date of the Codex table could then have been the date of an impressive near-total annular eclipse, optimally observable mid to late afternoon throughout the Maya area, whereas the earlier base could not have been an eclipse date, whether under the correlation derived here from Venus data, or under any other hypothetical correlation that takes account of pertinent historical data.

These considerations cause us then to take seriously also the possibility of a 584284 correlation, and with it, the second interpretation (1b) of the Landa equation. Still to be evaluated are the third interpretation (1c) and the 584283 value of the constant that it determines.

The astronomical length of the Maya eclipse cycle (405 lunations = 11959.89 days) is about one-ninth of a day less than its calendrical length (46 *tzolkins*). This is the reason for the "less 1 day" after nine or ten lengths of the cycle, requiring a 1-day decrement in the correlation constant if the attained new-moon date is to be a "12 Lamat." Moreover, the corresponding nodical cycle (69 nodical half-years = 11958.39 days) is about 1.61 days less than the calendrical cycle. And this is the reason for the 15- to 17-day difference in the positions of the nodes and the eclipse seasons after the passage of nine, ten, or eleven Mayan eclipse cycles.

There are many other multiples of the *tzolkin*, of various magnitudes, that approximate eclipse intervals but exceed their lunar requirement by 1 day, and would thus require a 1-day diminution of the correlation constant in order to place "12 Lamat" on the attained new-moon date. For example, a familiar short one is the 9360-day period, 1.6.0.0, which is approximately a day short of 317 lunations, and of 54 internodal intervals. This is 10 *tzolkins* less than the full Mayan cycle of 11960 days.

The 10-tzolkin interval is itself about 1.31 days more than one of the natural subdivisions of the saros, 88 lunations. And it is about 0.35 days short of the corresponding 15 internodal intervals. Subtraction of 2600 days from any "12 Lamat" new-moon date will locate another 12 Lamat date that is usually about a day prior to another new-moon date. To interpret that date instead as 12 Lamat requires, then, a 1-day decrement to the correlation constant. And similarly, addition of 2600 days to such a new-moon date will usually find another that requires a 1-day increment to the correlation constant in order to make it come out to 12 Lamat in the Mayan calendar. Thus the lunar requirement for any of the three correlation constants under consideration can be satisfied in any century, whether eighth, eleventh, or other. But the nodical requirement of the Maya table can be satisfied only around the eleventh century, whether or not such shortened eclipse cycles are introduced into the interval. Acceptance of that century as contemporaneous with the Codex table, however, does not of itself constrain the choice from among the alternative potential values of the correlation constant. Only if it is required that the "throwback" date of 9.16.4.10 8 precede the historical base by *an integral number* of Maya eclipse cycles (an integral multiple of 11960) does it do so. But since the throwback base of the Venus table was derived from a historical base by going back an integral multiple of the length of the full table, without foreshortening, it is reasonable to expect that the same would have been done for the analogous throwback base of the eclipse table. In that case, acceptance of the artificiality of the 9.16.4.10.8 base, and the historicity of a base such as Makemson proposed ten eclipse cycles later, would determine 584284 as the constant, and would require the second interpretation (1b) of the Landa equation.

Evaluation of possibilities under the third interpretation (1c) and the 584283 value of the constant that it determines will not be undertaken here. It requires not only further consideration of the Maya eclipse table and pertinent astronomy, but also the presentation of another interpretation of the Highland calendrical data that originally motivated the invention of this alternative (LaFarge 1934). I shall not undertake that here. I will only note that, at the present stage in my understanding of the problem, I consider it the least likely of the three. Others, I know, will disagree.

Though the correlation obtained from this exercise is not new, its astronomically based derivation is. I believe that this provides further assurance that one of the Thompson set of values for the correlation constant is correct.

## NOTES

1. See Teeple (1931:94–98) for the derivation of the chronology that is implied by the intervals and dates recorded on p. 24 of the Dresden Codex, and Thompson (1950:224–27) and Lounsbury (1978:776–89, and 1983) for more of the history of these chronological inferences. It should be noted that one of the intervals recorded on this page of the codex is omitted from Table 7.1, viz., the interval 1.5.5.0, the eighth in the series just noted, together with the 1 Ahau indicated as its terminus. Its pertinence is to a problem different from the one under consideration. It is treated in Chapter 8 of this volume.

2. A "ring number" base is a numerologically contrived one prior to the 4 Ahau 8 Cumku epoch of the current chronological era, which, by the 584285 correlation, was −3113 August 13 "seasonal," i.e., retroactive Gregorian. It is designated by a number, in effect negative, with a "ring" encircling its lowest-order digit (see, for example, the one near the foot of the first column in Figure 7.1). For further information on these and their use, see Thompson (1972:20–22) and Lounsbury (1976).

3. For the interpretation of Landa's Maya new-year date see Tozzer (1941:151 n. 748).

4. See LaFarge (1934:115–16); Thompson (1950:303–10). In Thompson's earlier publications on the correlation (1927, 1935), he assumed the first of these interpretations, Eq. (1a).

5. "Julian day number" is used here in its original sense for historical chronology, denoting calendar days. This should not be confused with the later astronomical adaptation of the scheme, in which its "days" run from noon till the next noon.

6. In the Goldstine tables, compiled for use in Old World historical astronomy, this is listed as 8:08 p.m. Babylon time (45 degrees east longitude). This is 5:08 p.m. Greenwich time, and 11:08 a.m. Maya time (90 degrees west).

7. The "throwback" base date, if that is what it is, could have been intended to mark the beginning of the time span during which "12 Lamat"–based cycles were relevant for calculating eclipse times, lunar as well as solar.

## REFERENCES

Goldstine, H. H., 1973. *New and Full Moons, 1001 B.C. to A.D. 1651*, Memoirs of the American Philosophical Society, Vol. 94 (Philadelphia).

Landa, D. de. See Tozzer, 1941.

LaFarge, O., 1934. "Post-Columbian Dates and the Mayan Correlation Problem," *Maya Research* 1:109–24 (New York).

Lounsbury, F. G., 1976. "A Rationale for the Initial Date of the Temple of the Cross at Palenque," in *The Art, Iconography & Dynastic History of Palenque, Part III*, edited by Merle Greene Robertson, pp. 211–24 (Pebble Beach, California: Pre-Columbian Art Research).

—, 1978. "Maya Numeration, Computation, and Calendrical Astronomy," in *Dictionary of Scientific Biography*, edited by Charles C. Gillispie, Vol. 15, pp. 759–818 (New York: Charles Scriber's Sons).

—, 1983. "The Base of the Venus Table of the Dresden Codex, and its Significance for the Calendar-Correlation Problem," in *Calendars in Mesoamerica and Peru: Native American Computations of Time*, edited by Anthony F. Aveni and Gordon Brotherston, pp. 1–26, BAR International Series, 174 (Oxford).

Makemson, M. W., 1943. "The Astronomical Tables of the Maya," *Contributions to American Archaeology*, no. 42, Carnegie Institution of Washington, Publication 546:183–221 (Washington, D.C.).

Meeus, J., 1983. *Astronomical Tables of the Sun, Moon, and Planets* (Richmond, Virginia: Willmann–Bell).

Satterthwaite, L., 1965. "Calendrics of the Maya Lowlands," in *Handbook of Middle American Indians*, Vol. 3, edited by Gordon R. Willey, pp. 603–31; general editor, Robert Wauchope (Austin: University of Texas Press).

Teeple, J. E., 1931. "Maya Astronomy," *Contributions to American Archaeology* no. 2, Carnegie Institution of Washington, Publication 403:29–116 (Washington, D.C.).

Thompson, J. S., 1927. "A Correlation of the Mayan and European Calendars," *Field Museum of Natural History, Publication* 241:1–22, Anthropological Series, Vol. 17, no. 1 (Chicago).

—, 1935. "Maya Chronology: The Correlation Question," *Contributions to American Archaeology*, no. 14, Carnegie Institution of Washington, Publication 456:51–104 (Washington, D.C.).

—, 1950. *Maya Hieroglyphic Writing: An Introduction*, Carnegie Institution of Washington, Publication 589 (Washington, D.C.). Second Edition, 1960, and Third Edition, 1971 (Norman: University of Oklahoma Press).

—, 1972. A *Commentary on the Dresden Codex*, Memoirs of the American Philosophical Society, Vol. 93 (Philadelphia).

Tozzer, A. M., 1941. *Landa's Relacion de las Cosas de Yucatan*, Papers of the Peabody Museum of American Archaeology and Ethnology, Harvard University, Vol. 18 (Cambridge: Peabody Museum).

Villacorta C., J. A. and C. A. Villacorta, 1930. *Codices Mayas Reproducidos y Desarrollados* (Guatemala, C. A.).

# 8

# A Solution for the Number 1.5.5.0 of the Mayan Venus Table

## FLOYD G. LOUNSBURY

### The Problem Number

The originally intended function of the number 1.5.5.0 (9100) from the auxiliary page pertaining to the Venus table of the Dresden Codex (Dresden 24) has until now been a mystery. Many who have puzzled over it have observed that it is equal to the interval between the two days 1 Ahau on the second page of the main Venus table (Dresden 47:A9–C12), which mark a canonical last-of-morning-star date and the sixteenth-next last-of-evening-star date, respectively, and which are the only days 1 Ahau in the entire five-page table other than that all-important first-of-morning-star 1 Ahau at its base (Dresden 50:D13). If this was its only intended significance, and if it was to be added to the first of these to reach the second, or subtracted from the second to reach the first, then it differs in three fundamental respects from the other numbers found in the same tier on that page (Dresden 24), viz., as follows:

1. The others are all of the form

$$N = 37960x - 2340y$$

whereas neither this nor its 2CR complement would require that form.

2. The others are all to be added to a base of the table, whereas this one would be applied to an internal date.

3. The function of all of the others is to derive from the base of an earlier run of the table a new base for a later run, each such base, in principle, approximating a real-time heliacal rising of the morning star,

whereas this number, if the attribute just noted were its raison d'être, would have no such function; it would lead instead from a canonical last-of-morning-star date to a later last-of-evening-star date, or vice versa, a move with neither precedent nor discernable motivation.[1]

An alternative not previously considered, but to be suggested here, would relegate this either to pure coincidence (such as is not uncommon in Mayan calendrics) or to the status of an unanticipated by-product or side effect of an operation that had some other primary goal; it would see the number 1.5.5.0 as intentionally of the same form and with the same kind of function as the other numbers of its tier in the table. In that case its form and its derivation would have to be seen as

$$9100 = 4(37960) - 61(2340)$$

which is the first solution to the above diophantine equation when $N$ is equal to 9100 and $x$ and $y$ are required to be positive integers.[2] It would then be analogous to the others of that tier, viz., 4.12.8.0, 9.11.7.0, and 1.5.14.4.0, which are, respectively:

$$33280 = 1(37960) - 2(2340)$$
$$68900 = 2(37960) - 3(2340)$$
$$185120 = 5(37960) - 2(2340)$$

The function of all of these is to add one or more foreshortened runs of the table to a reckoning base in such a way as to locate a new base, on another day 1 Ahau, for a new run of the table, so as to correct, or partially correct, for an accumulation of drift of the dates of heliacal risings of the morning star away from the canonical dates predicated on the earlier base, such drift having resulted over time from the small difference between the true mean duration of the synodic period of Venus, 583.92 days, and the whole-number reckoning period of 584 days employed in the table. Each 2340-day subtraction effects a 4-day correction, while preserving the *tzolkin* day 1 Ahau, inasmuch as 2340 = 4(584) + 4, and 2340 mod 260 = 0. And the total amount of drift correction effected by any one of the numbers of this tier is thus equal to the coefficient of 2340 multiplied by 4. When those coefficients are 2 or 3, as in the other numbers of this set, the corrections are of 8 or of 12 days and obviously pertained to the then-current or recent periods of historical time; but when the coefficient is 61, as in the case under consideration, it can only have pertained to the much longer passage of time from mythological antiquity to the present.

But why 4, and why 61? The 4 would be simply the result of the arithmetic fact that

$$-61(2340) \bmod 37960 = 4(37960) - 61(2340)$$

That the number is of this form would imply that, while embodying the total correction for runs over a very long span of time (such as from the Old Era base to the then present), it was to be applied to the historical terminus of such a span, rather than to its prehistoric starting point. Remaining to be explained, then, is the 61.

Eric Thompson noted that the optimum mix of corrections is four singles to one double, with six 2340-day subtractions from five lengths of the table, resulting in the assignment of 301 Venus periods to $301(584)-24$ days, and thus making a correction of 24 days to a period in which the accumulated mean error would be 24.08 days, leaving a residual mean error of less than 2 hours in over 481 years, and yielding a mean Venus period of 583.92026 days (Thompson 1950:227a; Lounsbury 1978:788–89). Thompson noted this only to point out that the device invented by the Maya for this purpose was one of *potentially* great precision, but there was no knowing whether the Maya calendar specialists were aware of this ratio or had sufficient information to have deduced it. If the present line of reasoning is correct, we can know now that they did not, for, had they applied this ratio, the crucial coefficient in our formula would probably have been 53, not 61, and the mystery number on p. 24 of the Codex would have been 3.17.5.0 (27820) rather than 1.5.5.0 (9100). The coefficient 61 can have resulted only from application of the ratio of one single to one double correction, that is, of three 4-day corrections, by means of three 2340-day foreshortenings, for every two runs of the table. This is exactly the ratio that is implicit in the number 9.11.7.0 and that is found in the interval from 10.10.11.12.0 (1 Ahau 18 Kayab) to 11.0.3.1.0 (1 Ahau 13 Mac). In other words, their experience up until that time had led them only to this ratio (for reasons I ventured to spell out in a previous publication, 1983), and had apparently led them to assume the validity of this ratio also for very long periods of time.

In applying this ratio and ending up with the number 1.5.5.0, we can imagine that their reasoning went more or less along the following lines.

1. From $-6.2.0$ to 10.10.11.12.0, that is, from the "first" to the last of the 1 Ahau 18 Kayab bases, is 80 calendar-rounds, or 40 lengths of the Venus table:

$$6.2.0 + 10.10.11.12.0 = 10.10.17.14.0$$
$$= (4.0)(2.12.13.0)$$
$$= (2.0)(5.5.8.0)$$

2. We know that two lengths of the table require a triple foreshortening:

$$2(5.5.8.0) - 3(6.9.0) = 9.11.7.0$$

3. Therefore 40 lengths of the table will require one that is 20 times that long:

$$(2.0)(5.5.8.0) - (3.0)(6.9.0) = 9.11.7.14.0$$

4. But here we are now at 1 Ahau 18 Uo (Dresden 48:C12; 10.15.4.2.0), approaching the end of the 41st length of the table. This additional length will require yet another foreshortening, making 61 in all:

$$(2.1)(5.5.8.0) - (3.1)(6.9.0) = 9.16.6.13.0$$

5. Let the total foreshortening now be incorporated into the minimum number of lengths of the table that will contain it, so that it can be applied as an increment to current dates, to show us the next recurrences of their "corrected" positions (where they would have been if reckoned according to present knowledge from that ancient supposedly primal base):

$$4(5.5.8.0) - (3.1)(6.9.0) = 1.5.5.0$$

Translating the arithmetic, these are:

$$
\begin{aligned}
2200 + 1516200 &= 1518400 \\
&= 80(18980) \\
&= 40(37960) \quad \text{(1)}
\end{aligned}
$$

$$
\begin{aligned}
2(37960) - 3(2340) &= 68980 \\
&= \text{Mayan } 9.11.7.0 \quad \text{(2)}
\end{aligned}
$$

$$
\begin{aligned}
40(37960) - 60(2340) &= 20(68980) \\
&= 1378000 \quad \text{(3)}
\end{aligned}
$$

$$41(37960) - 61(2340) = 1413620 \quad \text{(4)}$$

$$
\begin{aligned}
1413620 \bmod 37960 &= 9100 \\
&= \text{Mayan } 1.5.5.0 \quad \text{(5)}
\end{aligned}
$$

I would suggest that something like the above was what lay behind the number 1.5.5.0. If so, we would then ask what use could have been made of it; to what date was it applied, and for what purpose?

## An Unforeseen Consequence

For the other numbers of that tier of the auxiliary table, we have a record of the uses that were made of them: 4.12.8.0 was applied to the last-used 1 Ahau 18 Kayab base, deriving the new base at 1 Ahau 18 Uo; 9.11.7.0 was applied also to that same 1 Ahau 18 Kayab, deriving the next after

1 Ahau 18 Uo in the sequence of bases, viz., at 1 Ahau 13 Mac. It makes perfect sense to have applied these distance numbers, which incorporate 8-day and 12-day timing corrections to the about-to-be-abandoned, or recently abandoned, base at 10.10.11.12.0; but it would make no sense to apply 1.5.5.0, incorporating a 244-day correction, to a recent reckoning base.

A correction that large (244 days) would be applicable only to a remote base, while a number that small (9100 days) would be appropriate as an increment only to a recent date. We are led to assume then, at least as one possibility, that it may have been applied to a recent uncorrected descendant of an ancient base, in order to make up, all at one stroke, for the aggregate accumulation of error over the long span of intervening time.

In that case, we would ask whether it may have been applied to a recent 1 Ahau 18 Kayab, this being seen as a descendant of the ring-number base of that same name at −6.2.0. If it were, it would reveal that the "true" or "corrected" descendant of the ancient 1 Ahau 18 Kayab is a day 1 Ahau 13 Pax, located 14 days after the first-of-evening-star 13 Cimi 19 Muan on the first page of the main table (Dresden 46:B4, B21). But there is no record of any such day to substantiate that hypothetical possibility; besides which, such an application would probably have had little point after the discovery and institution of the corrective devices, for the former ascription of a morning-star heliacal rising to the ancient 1 Ahau 18 Kayab would have been known to be no longer tenable.

A second possibility is that it may have been applied, not as an addition in the usual manner, but as a subtraction from the just instituted or about to be instituted new base at 1 Ahau 18 Uo, in order to determine the calendar-round day and the locus in the current Venus cycle of the pertinent ancient prototype. Or in any case, that is what *we* can do with it. And from that, we can deduce a hypothetical ancient one that takes account of the correction formula implied by 1.5.5.0; thus:

$$
\begin{array}{ll}
10.15.\ 4.\ 2.0, & \text{1 Ahau 18 Uo} \\
\underline{-1.\ 5.\ 5.0} & \\
10.13.18.15.0, & \text{1 Ahau 3 Zotz} \\
\underline{-10.16.\ 3.\ 4.0} & [41(37960),\ =\ 82\ \text{CR}] \\
-\ 2.\ 4.\ 7.0, & \text{1 Ahau 3 Zotz.}
\end{array}
$$

Having that, we can now look at it the other way around, from bottom up (changing the minus signs to plus), as follows.

To a hypothetic pre-Era base, 1 Ahau 3 Zotz, posited to be the date of a heliacal rising of the morning-star Venus, there are added 41 uncorrected lengths of the full Venus table. This leads to the most recent date of the same calendar-round position, which however, cannot possibly be the date of a heliacal rising of Venus, because of its nonrecognition of the accumulation of systematic error. So there is applied then the number that embodies the presumed appropriate correction for 41 lengths of the table, and this leads to the current base, 1 Ahau 18 Uo, again a morning-star heliacal-rising date.[3]

The long first jump in this scheme is pure speculation, of course, without any confirming documentary evidence; there is no record of 1 Ahau 3 Zotz in the role of an ancient base. But the latter and the lesser step can be seen in the Venus table (if one is willing to look at it that way), from the supposed last-of-morning-star 1 Ahau 3 Zotz to the last-of-evening-star 1 Ahau 18 Uo (Dresden 47:A9–C12, reading the *haab* days from the 18 Kayab line at A22 and C22). And then, there is the curious fact that the 244-day correction that is implicit in the number 1.5.5.0 is exactly equal to the sum of the canonical interval provided for the planet's absence at inferior conjunction (8 days) and the strangely short duration of its morning-star apparition (236 days), while the 340-day modular residue from that number is equal to the complementary interval, comprising an overly long absence at superior conjunction (90 days) and a somewhat too short evening-star apparition (250 days). Were it not that these divisions resulted in unrealistic intervals for three of the periods involved, we might be more inclined to write this off as coincidence. But as these intervals are, they beg for explanation. As Aveni has remarked (Chapter 3 of this volume), ". . . who could have imagined the Maya would concoct 236/90/250-day intervals for Venus?"

I think we may have an answer here, though along a line different from the one that Aveni was exploring (possible lunar involvement). It may be that the primary function of the 236-day division was not to express accurately the duration of visibility of the morning star, but rather to locate, within the span of any given synodic period, the "starting point" of the migration of its morning-star-heliacal-rising day. Thus it informs us, for example, that at the beginning of the Era, the day 1 Ahau 3 Zotz would have been the corresponding heliacal-rising day, but that by the time when the 1 Ahau 18 Kayab version of the table was formalized, the heliacal rising had migrated to that day, while the "original" heliacal-rising day had regressed to the position of day 236. Similarly, proceeding to the next version of the table, the numbers show us that the calendar-round day that had been at position 576 (236 + 90 + 250), last of evening star, 1 Ahau 18 Uo, is the one that "now" (10.15.4.2.0) has moved on to be the day of the heliacal rising of the morning star (day 584, or day 0). So also for the critical days of any other synodic period from any page of the table.

If this was the primary function of the number 236, it could still serve its other presumed function as well, merely through informed use of the table. Thus, a user would simply bear in mind that the last of the morning star can be expected about 23 to 27 days later. For the end of evening star, no such supplementary algorithm would be necessary (other than the usual allowance of 2 or 3 days' leeway), since for that position the analogous two functions happen to coincide in their results.

In this connection one may want to ask, "Just when was it that there was a day 1 Ahau 3 Zotz that was 236 days after a heliacal rising of the morning star; or equivalently for present purposes, 240 days after an inferior conjunction of Venus?" And also, for comparison, "When was there a day 1 Ahau 3 Zotz that was actually a date of last visibility of the morning star (or within 2 or 3 days of such a date)?"

Both of these questions can be answered immediately, even without consulting planetary tables. As for the first, it must have been the 1 Ahau 3 Zotz that last preceded the 1 Ahau 18 Kayab of 10.5.6.4.0, namely, the one of 10.3.7.17.0 (27 February A.D. 897, Julian.) This is because 10.5.6.4.0 was the date of the only 1 Ahau 18 Kayab ever that coincided with a heliacal rising of Venus, 4 days after an inferior conjunction, in agreement with the record of the Maya table. And for the second, it must have been five spans of the uncorrected table later, namely the 1 Ahau 3 Zotz of 11.19.5.3.0 (20 October A.D. 1416, Julian), in order to accumulate a shortfall of 26 days to agree with the inherent deficiency in the table's 236-day morning-star period. If day 236 was to be interpreted as "last of morning star," then that was a systematic prediction that always had to wait 5 centuries for its fulfillment! Surely that cannot have been its intended interpretation.

[So as not to leave these assertions without verification, we may consult planetary tables (e.g., Meeus 1983, Tuckerman 1964) or check with a computer program. In respect to the first of these dates, we find that the last inferior conjunction of Venus prior to 27 February A.D. 897 in the Mayan time zone (90 degrees west), was on July 2 of the preceding year, shortly before midnight. The interval from 2 July 896 to 27 February 897 is exactly 240 days. For the second, we find that October 20 of the year 1416 was 25 days before the superior conjunction of 14 November (shortly before midnight, Maya time zone), and that the planet's *arcus visionis* the morning of October 20 (equal to the depression of the sun when the planet is at the horizon just before sunrise) was 6.9 degrees. The last sighting of the morning star was probably that very morning.]

The interpretation that has been put forward here, obviously, is speculative. It will be hard to come to terms with these last suggestions, in view of what we have taken for granted concerning the logical and proper sub-divisions of a Venus ephemeris and what we have supposed to be facts concerning the history of the Maya table. For example, this interpretation implies that the 236-day divider was imposed on the table no earlier than the institution of the 1 Ahau 18 Uo base and the invention of the number 1.5.5.0 for the forty-first span of the table, 82 calendar rounds since the beginning of the Era. (What kind of subdivision, one will wonder, preceded that date?) But the intervals defined by the subdivisions in the Maya table, when given serious attention, have also been hard to come to terms with.

The present interpretation offers, at least, a rationale and a mathe-matical derivation for the number 1.5.5.0. In addition, it may perhaps throw some light on the otherwise puzzling 236-day interval.[4] It does not, however, shed any light on the division of the 340-day residue into periods of 90 and 250 days, which still remains a problem.

NOTES

1. Thompson (1950:226) considered the number 1.5.5.0 to be the result of a scribal error in calculation, and he proposed that it be amended to 1.6.0.0 (= 9360), ascribing to it a hypothetical function that no longer can be entertained as plausible (Lounsbury 1983:10, 17–18). Justeson (1989:92–93, 96–98), following Aveni's inquiry (Chapter 3 of this volume) into possible lunar correlates of the Venus table intervals, has considered the possibility of its having had some function in correlating Venus cycles with eclipse cycles. I have not pursued this lead suffi-ciently far to have formed an opinion as to its potential for solving the 1.5.5.0 puzzle.

2. For methods of solution to diophantine equations, see D. Burton (1976:32–33, 309–10; 1980:42–50, 345–61).

3. There is, of course, an inherent fallacy in the logic of this operation, for the number 1.5.5.0, applied as an increment, embodies not only 61 2340-day foreshor-tenings, but also 4 37960-day lengthenings. This, in effect, changes the ratio for the long span; it is no longer 61 foreshortenings to 41 spans of the table, but rather, 61 to 45. The result is thus closer to 4:3 than to 3:2. The assumption that the Maya astronomers were using a 3:2 ratio (the one implicit in the number 9.11.7.0) requires us to suppose either that they were unappreciative of this fallacy or that they were willing to overlook it. Alternatively, it could be argued that they were really, and intentionally, employing a 4:3 ratio (such as is inherent in the interval from 1 Ahau 18 Kayab, 10.10.11.12.0 to 1 Ahau 3 Xul 11.5.2.0.0, or in that from 1 Ahau 18 Kayab 10.5.6.4.0 to 1 Ahau 13 Mac 11.0.3.1.0). In that case, 61:45 would be seen as 60:45 plus 1:0; whereas 61:41 was seen as 60:40 plus 1:1.

4. The Venus table of the Grolier Codex also has the 236/90/250/8 division of the synodic period. Since it can no longer be doubted that that codex is genuine

(see Carlson 1983), this manner of division marks it as a historical "descendant" of the Dresden Codex table.

## REFERENCES

Burton, D., 1976, 1980. *Elementary Number Theory* (Boston: Allyn & Bacon).

Carlson, J., 1983. "The Grolier Codex: A Preliminary Report on the Content and Authenticity of a Thirteenth-Century Maya Venus Almanac," in A. F. Aveni and G. Brotherston, eds., *Calendars in Mesoamerica and Peru: Native American Computations of Time*, Proceedings, 44th International Congress of Americanists, Manchester 1982; BAR International Series, 174 (Oxford), pp. 27–57.

Justeson, J., 1989. "Ancient Maya Ethnoastronomy: An Overview of Hieroglyphic Sources," in A. F. Aveni, ed., *World Archaeoastronomy*, Proceedings of the Second International Conference on Archaeoastronomy, Merida, 1986 (Cambridge: Cambridge University Press), pp. 76–129.

Lounsbury, F. G., 1978. "Maya Numeration, Computation, and Calendrical Astronomy," in *Dictionary of Scientific Biography*, C. C. Gillispie, general editor, Vol. 15, pp. 759–818 (New York: Charles Scribner's Sons).

—, 1983. "The Base of the Venus Table of the Dresden Codex, and its Significance for the Calendar-correlation Problem," in A. F. Aveni and G. Brotherston, eds., *Calendars in Mesoamerica and Peru: Native American Computations of Time*, Proceedings, 44th International Congress of Americanists, Manchester 1982; BAR International Series, 174 (Oxford), pp. 1–26.

Meeus, J., 1983. *Astronomical Tables of the Sun, Moon, and Planets* (Richmond, Virginia: Willmann-Bell).

Thompson, J. E. S., 1950. *Maya Hieroglyphic Writing: An Introduction.* Carnegie Institution of Washington, Publication 589 (Washington, D.C.). [Second edition, 1960, and third Edition, 1971 (Norman: University of Oklahoma Press)].

Tuckerman, B., 1964. *Planetary, Lunar, and Solar Positions,* A.D. 2 to A.D. 1649, *at Five-day and Ten-day Intervals*, American Philosophical Society Memoirs, Vol. 59 (Philadelphia).

# 9

# The Books of Chilam Balam:
# Astronomical Content
# and the Paris Codex

MERIDETH PAXTON

Written predominantly in the Maya language but almost entirely in European script, the Books of Chilam Balam are post-Conquest counterparts of pre-Columbian hieroglyphic codices. The Books are named for Chilam Balam, a priest of the immediate pre-Conquest period who became famous because he purportedly foretold the arrival of the Spaniards. *Chilam* (*chilan*) is a title meaning "interpreter of the gods." As *Balam* means jaguar, but is also a common family name in Yucatan, the term "Book of Chilam Balam" could be translated as "Book of the Prophet Balam" (Roys 1973:3). These sacred books were compiled in various towns in Yucatan. With one exception, the Chilam Balam of Nah, which was written in Teabo by two scribes with the surname Nah, the works are named for their places of origin.

The exact number of surviving Books of Chilam Balam is uncertain, as some titles referred to in published sources are apparently lost. Eight Books of Chilam Balam are readily accessible to scholars, including those of Chancah, Chumayel, Ixil, Nah, Tekax, Tizimin, and Tusik (Miram 1988). The eighth source, the Pérez Codex (named for the Mexican scholar who assembled it, Juan Pío Pérez), incorporates a now lost Book of Chilam Balam from the town of Maní, possibly a lost Chilam Balam of Oxkutzcab, and a collection of other documents (Gibson and Glass 1975:379–87). Not all of the texts have been fully analyzed, but the manuscripts generally seem to date from the eighteenth and nineteenth centuries. Of course, these books incorporate copies of dated compilations from as early as the sixteenth century, and it has been suggested that some texts are transcriptions from pre-Conquest hieroglyphic codices.

As the subject matter of the Books of Chilam Balam is historical, calendrical, astrological, prophetic, medical, and religious, these works offer promise of broad information on pre-Hispanic Maya practices. There is also, however, an admixture of European content that can be problematic. Helga-Maria Miram (1989) has recently discovered that some sections, on the predictions of the fates of people born on the various days of the *tzolkin*, the *katun* prophecies, the *tun* prophecies, and the language of Zuyua (used in testing the qualifications of rulers), appear to be pre-Columbian in origin. Some portions of the books are a mixture of European and Maya traditions, but the bulk of the material is of European origin. Of the approximately 1000 manuscript pages of the nine surviving books, 600 pages were translated to Maya from European sources. Therefore, caution must clearly be used in consulting the Books of Chilam Balam for information on the pre-Hispanic Maya. Even prior to the Miram study, some of the astronomical content of the Books of Chilam Balam, such as the Ptolemaic conception of the universe diagrammed in the Chilam Balam of Ixil (Figure 9.1), was recognized as entirely European.

In reviewing the astronomical content of the sections of the Books of Chilam Balam identified in the Miram study as generally pre-Columbian in origin, it is evident that some passages contain complex metaphors. Fortunately some of these are explained explicitly, as in the following example from the interrogation in the language of Zuyua.

> "Son, go and bring the flower of the night to me here." This is what will be said. Then let him go on his knees before the head-chief who demands this of him. "Father, here is the flower of the night for which you ask me; I come with it and with the vile thing of the night. There it is with me." These are his words.
>
> . . . This is the flower of the night which is demanded of him: a star in the sky. This is the vile thing of the night: it is the moon.
>
> Roys, 1973, pp. 93–94

Thus it is possible to gain some understanding of the celestial concepts of the ancient Maya from the poetic and esoteric accounts. However, as much of this information may pass unnoticed by non-Mayans, the clearest insights concerning pre-Columbian Maya astronomy come from the sections of the Books of Chilam Balam that are more computational in nature. These are evidently Spanish Colonial counterparts of the calendrical almanacs in the earlier hieroglyphic codices.

*Figure 9.1* The Ptolemaic universe as reproduced in the Book of Chilam Balam of Ixil. (Photograph made from manuscript copy in the Sylvanus G. Morley collection, courtesy of the Laboratory of Anthropology, Museum of New Mexico, Santa Fe.)

## The *Katun* Cycles in the Books of Chilam Balam

The sequence of 13 named Maya *katuns,* or time periods of 7200 days each, which repeated cyclically after intervals equivalent to 256.27 European tropical years (256 years and 98 days), is frequently included in treatments of calendrical subjects in the Books of Chilam Balam. These discussions typically identify each *katun* in the rotation and provide associated prophecies. Historical facts were also often mixed with the predictions, in keeping with the Maya view that such events repeated according to the same cycles. The *katuns* were named for their ending days, as these fell in the 260-day religious cycle (*tzolkin*). As the name of this terminal day was always Ahau ("lord"), it is not surprising that the prophecies were frequently accompanied by portraits of the regents for each *katun*. In examining the *katun* prophecies it is readily apparent that the compilations were made to explain a European concept, the calendar system, to the Maya, as well as to preserve pre-Hispanic ideas.

CORRELATING THE MAYA AND
EUROPEAN CALENDRICAL CONCEPTS

One example that demonstrates the use of the Books of Chilam Balam to incorporate European calendrical concepts in the Maya system can be found in the apparently confused and conflicting accounts of the duration and ordering of the *katuns*. An attempt was clearly being made to relate the century to the existing Maya notion of a repeating cycle of 13 *katuns*. For instance, in the second set of *katun* prophecies in the Chilam Balam of Chumayel (Roys 1973:147–63), the correct length of 20 years was consistently followed, but the ordering appears problematic. The first *katun* to be presented here is Katun 11 Ahau. As one of the entries for this *katun* records the arrival of foreigners, probably Spaniards, an initial date of 1540 would be appropriate for the cycle. This is confirmed by the second prophecy, for Katun 9 Ahau, which includes a portrait drawing of the *katun* regent that also bears a notation of the date 1560. The sequence of prophecies with portraits and dates continues in a routine manner until the sixth *katun* (Katun 1 Ahau), which began in 1640. Because 1640 is one century after the first prophecy, and Katun 1 Ahau is identified in the accompanying text as the first *katun*, it seems that the second hundred-year period was regarded as the beginning of a new cycle. The analogy between the century and the cycle of thirteen *katuns* was further emphasized in the drawing for the final prophecy, Katun 13 Ahau (see Figure 9.2a), beginning in 1780. With the picture of the lord of the thirteenth *katun* appear the years 1780, 1520, and 1599. This thirteenth *katun* was a repetition of the *katun* of the same name that had begun 13 *katuns* before in 1520. Thus 1780 would be equivalent to 1520, the date written below it. In reaching 1780 from 1520 it was necessary to pass through the beginning of the European cycle of time (the century) on New Year's Eve, during 1599 (written on the drawing) and 1699, which are conceptually equivalent in the European system of centuries.[1]

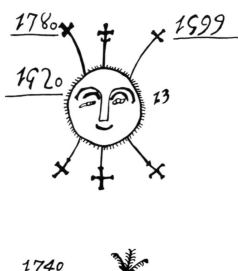

*Figure* 9.2 a. The regent of Katun 13 Ahau, beginning in 1780. b. The regent of Katun 4 Ahau, beginning in 1740. (The drawings, from the Book of Chilam Balam of Chumayel, are based on Roys, 1973, Figures 43 and 41, respectively.)

    Similarly, the Mayan desire to relate the century to *katun* cycles is evident in the confusing statements of the length of the *katun* found in the Codex Pérez (Craine and Reindorp 1979:77–79). Although the Mayan writer began by stating that "There are thirteen Ahau-Katuns of twenty years each" (Craine and Reindorp 1979:77), he continued by including intervals of European dates that define *katuns* of 24-year duration. Perhaps an attempt was being made to associate the divisions of the century with the four-part directional symbolism so important to Maya ritual (Tozzer 1941:135–39). Indeed, a drawing of a wheel showing the sequence of the *katuns* and their associations with directions and the initial days of the 365-day Maya solar year, or *haab*, is included in the Chilam Balam of Ixil (Figure 9.3).

*Figure 9.3* A *katun* wheel from the Book of Chilam Balam of Ixil. Photograph made from manuscript copy in the Sylvanus G. Morley collection, courtesy of the Laboratory of Anthropology, Museum of New Mexico, Santa Fe.

THE KATUN PROPHECIES AND THE CYCLE
OF THE CONSTELLATIONS

The Katun prophecies provide tantalizing suggestions that the Maya some-
how related the lords of these intervals to the planets or constellations.
Returning, for example, to the Chilam Balam of Chumayel, we observe
from the first set of prophecies that during 13 Ahau, "Itzamna, Itzam-tzab,
is his face during its reign" (Roys 1973:134). As Roys noted, Itzam-tzab
could be another name for the constellation entered in the Motul dictionary as *tzab*, or the Pleiades. Further support for relating the lords of the
*katuns* with the constellations comes from the second set of Chumayel
prophecies, where it is recorded that during Katun 12 Ahau

> Yaxal Chuen is his face, Buleu-caan-chac is his face to the rulers. He
> shall manifest himself. He is in the sky by day; he is in the sky by night.
>
> Roys, 1973, p. 158

Moreover, the portrait of the lord of Katun 4 Ahau from the same series of
prophecies is shown with a cluster of four starlike shapes around his head
(Figure 9.2b). But the references to constellations in the *katun* prophecies
of the Books of Chilam Balam are not so explicit as to identify immediately
the star clusters that were of interest to the pre-Hispanic Maya and demonstrate their relationship to the *katun* series. One of the pre-Conquest codices, the Paris Codex, may verify this association and provide further information on how such a system could have operated.

## The Katun Cycles in the Paris Codex

Pages 2–11 of this Codex (Figure 9.4) have long been regarded as a fragment from a complete presentation of the ritual and prophecy for each of
the 13 *katuns* (Gates 1910; Thompson 1950:25). One important indicator
of the content is the sequence of numbered Ahau glyphs illustrated in the
center section of each page, immediately to the left of the serpent/skyband
thrones. Although some of the accompanying numbers have disappeared,
the series can be reconstructed from the remaining examples. From inspec-
tion of p. 5 and the two preceding pages, it is readily apparent that each
coefficient is 2 fewer than the previous entry (Gates 1910:17). This means
that the primary illustration of the first reasonably complete page of the
manuscript must have incorporated 2 Ahau. The text and illustrations for
Katun 4 Ahau could have been placed either on the badly damaged page
preceding the 2 Ahau prophecy, or several pages later, at the other end of
the cycle. As William Gates showed, the complete Ahau series would have

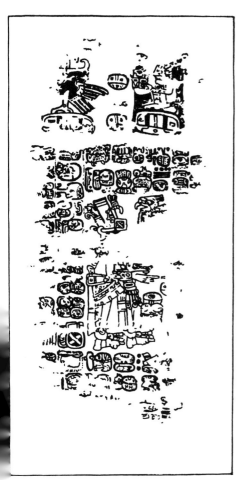

*Figure* 9.4 Paris Codex, pp. 2–11 (based on Villacorta and Villacorta 1976:180–202; and *Codex Peresianus*).

been 4, 2, 13, 11, 9, 7, 5, 3, 1, 12, 10, 8, 6, which exactly follows the pattern of the Katun coefficients.

### THE RELATIONSHIP OF THE PARIS CODEX ZODIACAL ALMANAC AND KATUN PROPHECIES

The information on pp. 23 and 24 of the Paris Codex consists of hiero-glyphic text and a calendrical table that has long been regarded as a proba-ble zodiacal almanac (Spinden 1916). Because there is no demarcation of the two sections, it will be assumed that they are related.[2] Indeed, consider-ation of the text could be helpful to a general understanding of the nature

*Figure 9.4 (Continued).*

and function of the almanac, and could also provide a basis for identifying content shared with the *katun* prophecy pages.

### The Hieroglyphic Text

Damage to the manuscript is such that glyphs are now evident in seven columns and six rows on p. 23, and in six rows and six columns on p. 24. There is ample space at the tops of the pages to allow the inclusion of two more glyph rows. Although it seems unlikely that traces of these hypothetical rows will ever be detected from physical examination of the codex, perhaps some reconstruction of content in this area will be effected when

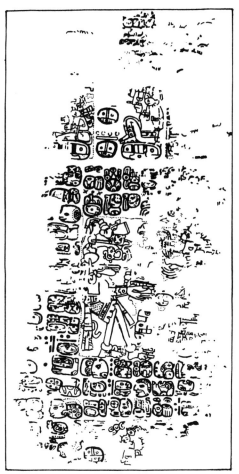

*Figure 9.4 (Continued).*

the remaining text is better understood. Accordingly, the possibility of missing rows will be accommodated here in the glyphic notation, which will follow the standard top-to-bottom and left-to-right convention. The orientation of the individual glyphs on pp. 23 and 24 toward the right has generally been perceived as an indication that the reading order is non-standard, or right to left. This seems correct, as some of the right-facing glyphs painted here are left-facing elsewhere in the codex (see the following).

*The Shared Glyphs.* In view of current uncertainty concerning the significance of the presence or absence of some affixes and main signs in glyphic

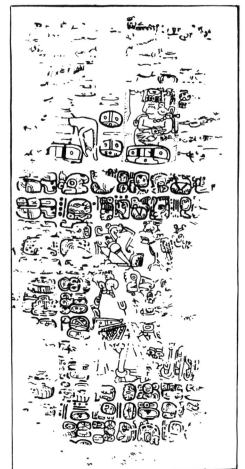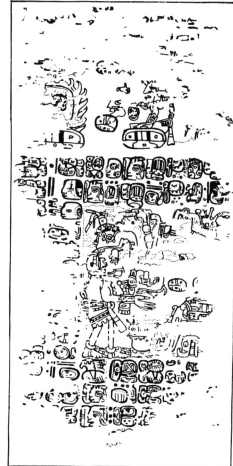

*Figure 9.4 (Continued).*

collocations, the list of glyphs found in both the Paris katun prophecy pages and the zodiacal almanac (Table 9.1) has been compiled conservatively. This study of shared glyphs shows that the common concerns include certain deities, the sky (561c:23),[3] omens or punishment (1.648:25; see Kurbjuhn 1989:91 and Bricker 1986:117–118), a possible milpa glyph (663:23.526:251; see Treiber 1987:67), and a compound that I believe should be read as *"katun."*

*A Reading for the Glyph with Thompson Numbers* 1052.548:24: katunil.— The *katun* glyph is entered in the Paris *katun* prophecy pages as 1052.548:24, appearing at E 1 and G 4 on p. 5, and at G 1 on p. 9. In

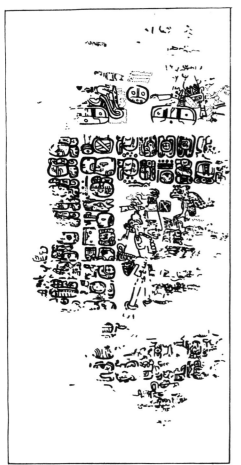

*Figure 9.4 (Continued).*

accordance with the right to left reading order of the glyphs on pp. 23 and 24 of the Paris Codex, the same *katun* glyph is painted on these pages (at 23 E 8 and 24 D 8) as 548:24.1052.[4] While the reading of T548 is widely accepted as *tun*, the decipherment of T1052 (a head, with eyes apparently closed in death) as *k'a* has not previously been proposed (Kurbjuhn 1989:72, 140). Preceding interpretations have seen this combination as simply face-tun (Gates 1910:31), *nup-tun-um* (season of enmity; Knorozov 1982:201), and *tsek tunil* (skull-tun; Treiber 1987:69). One possible reason for the delay in recognizing that the T1052 sign should be read *k'a* is that this explanation is most clearly provided by a glyph illustrating Diego de Landa's *Relación de las cosas de Yucatán*, which is incorrectly drawn in one

*Table 9.1*   Glyphs Common to the Paris Codex *Katun* Prophecy
Pages and the Zodiacal Almanac

| Deities | Thompson number | Paris Codex page | |
| --- | --- | --- | --- |
| God CH or H | 1003.1 | 8 | E 1, 23 B 8 |
| God D | 24.534:24 | 6 | H 4, 23 B 5 |
| | 1009:23.152 | 6 | C 6, 11 C 1, 23 C 5, |
| | | 24 | B 6 |
| God E | 1006.24 | 4 | B 9, 5 E 3, 5 H 3, |
| | | 6 | E 3, 7 H 3, 8 G 2, |
| | | 9 | D 2, 9 F 1, 9 D 4, |
| | | 9 | D 5, 11 E 2, 23 C 3 |
| God G | 168:544.130.172 | 3 | H 3, 7 C 9, 23 D 8 |
| God K | 1020 | 4 | C 2, 5 C 2, 8 I 1, |
| | | 9 | I 2, 10 D 5, 24 C 6 |
| Other | | | |
| | 734:24.115 | 6 | C 9, 7 E 2, 10 C8, |
| | | 23 | B 4, 24 C 8 |
| | 1.648:25 | 4 | (reg. A), 6 C 5, |
| | | 23 | D 3, 24 C 7 |
| | 663:23.526:251 | 3 | C 7, 5 E 2, 23 E 4, |
| | | 24 | D 7 |
| | 526:126.1 | 4 | G 3, 6 G 4, 8 G 5, |
| | | 24 | B 5 |
| | 561c:23 | 8 | C 3, 9 E 3, 23 B 6, |
| | | 24 | C 5 |
| | 548:24.1052 | 5 | E 1, 3 G 4, 9 G 1, |
| | | 23 | E 8, 24 D 8 |

of the most widely cited editions of the work (Tozzer 1941:170). In the
section of the *Relación* that discusses Landa's so-called alphabet and the
general system of hieroglyphic writing, one of the examples of text construction recorded in both Maya glyphs and Spanish script is *Ma in k'ati,* "I
do not wish." The photographic copy of the manuscript shows that the
glyph written below the Spanish *k'a* sound is clearly the T1052 head (see
Figure 9.5).[5] The same head also expresses the second "k" sound in Landa's
alphabet, which differentiates non-glottalized (T25, *ca*) and glottalized
(T1052, *k'*) forms.[6]

Agreement is not unanimous concerning the phonetic reading of the
third sign seen here, the affix T24, but the two most commonly accepted
possibilities are *il* and *ne* (Kurbjuhn 1989:5). Detailed discussion of the
alternatives can not be presented in this study (see Thompson 1950:269–
271; Kelley 1976:192–193; Bricker 1986:92–99; Lounsbury 1984:179,183).
However, if the best reading for this context is *il,* the resulting word, *katunil*
would correspond with the common usage in Classical Yucatecan texts
noted by Bricker (1986:98).

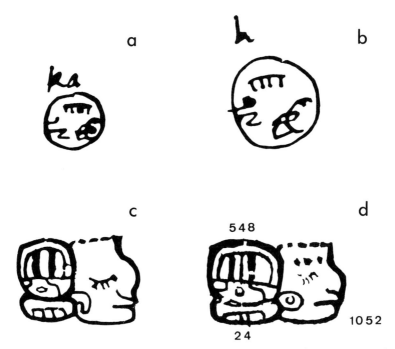

*Figure* 9.5 The reading of a glyph collocation (with Thompson numbers 548:24.1052) as *katunil*. The first drawings (a, b) are from Landa (c.1566:45 recto), photographic copy courtesy of Special Collections, Zimmerman Library, University of New Mexico. See Kelley (1976:Figure 60) for a published version. Parts c and d of the figure are respectively from pp. 23 (position E 8) and 24 (position D 8) of the Paris Codex, based on *Codex Peresianus* (1968).

*The Meaning of the Hieroglyphic Text.* Analysis of the top section of pp. 23 and 24 of the Paris Codex is continuing. However, this preliminary study of the 13 columns of glyphs as pairs ordered from right to left suggests some interpretations. The central concepts evidently include *katuns* (T548:24.1052), omens or evil tidings (T1.648:25), deities, and appearances in the sky. For example, on p. 24 (at C 5), the intransitive verb meaning to appear in the sky (T561c:23; see Schele 1989:9) precedes a compound that probably describes a change of succession (at D 6, T172.168:573b.116; see Riese 1984) involving God K (at C 6, T1020). Lounsbury, Matthews, and Schele (Kurbjuhn 1989:106) have all suggested that T739 (turtle and carapace) is an aspect of God K or a substitute for this deity. Hence, this group of glyphs might be a statement about the change of succession and appearance in the sky of God K, possibly repeated pictorially in the calendrical almanac below by the turtle suspended from a skyband. In other words, this may be a clue pertaining to the possible association of deities, time intervals, and constellations.

### The Function of the Zodiacal Almanac of the Paris Codex

Gates (1931:4–5) noticed that the Ahau coefficients on the *katun* prophecy pages also occur in the center sections of pp. 23 and 24 of the manuscript, as entries (which are blue in the original manuscript[7]) painted both above and below a table of intervals in the 260-day *tzolkin* (Figure 9.6). However, although he was aware that the blue numbers could represent a *katun* series, he was unable to explain the reason for this relationship. Because the accompanying creatures have been interpreted as constellations from a Maya zodiac, the function of the table on pp. 23 and 24 is of particular interest to the present study of possible associations of *katuns* with particular stars. The *katun* interval may have been of special significance to the compiler of this constellation table, as the quarter of the *tzolkin* selected for inclusion contains the day Ahau, for which the *katuns* were named.

As Floyd Lounsbury (1978:760) has commented, gaining an understanding of tables like the almanac on pp. 23 and 24 of the Paris Codex is tantamount to reconstructing the statement of a mathematical problem, as well as the procedure for solving it, by analyzing an answer. Indeed, more than one explanation may be possible. While Harvey Bricker and Victoria R. Bricker (Chapter 6 of this volume) have recently developed one theory, not related to a succession of *katuns*, to explain the two pages, a different view is presented here. For other interpretations of pp. 23–24, see Severin (1981) and Dütting and Schramm (1988).

*Structure.* The complete table of *tzolkin* days, partially lost due to damage to the pages, can easily be reconstructed from the surviving portion (Gates 1910:31–34; Bricker and Bricker, Chapter 6 of this volume: Table 6.1; see Table 9.2 of the present study). There are 13 columns of *tzolkin* days separated by 28-day intervals, and these are arranged to form five rows of 364 days each. The length of the table is 1820 days. The reader should follow a right to left reading pattern for each line, proceeding to the line below when the current line is completed.

It is generally agreed that, although some of these are now missing, the border designs at the top and bottom of the table must have shown a total of thirteen creatures. The figures are suspended from glyphs that are often interpreted as eclipse signs (but see Closs 1983:166). As Harvey and Victoria Bricker (Chapter 6 of this volume) have remarked, the 364-day length of each row of this Paris table is close to the 365.25636-day sidereal year, and

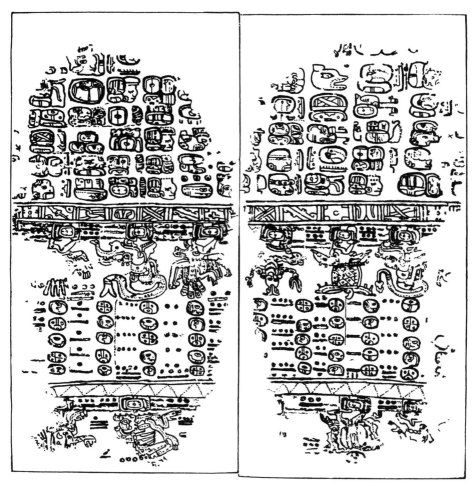

*Figure* 9.6 The Paris Codex, pp. 23–24 (based on Villacorta and Villacorta 1976:220–22; and *Codex Peresianus*).

the 28-day intervals are appropriate to a zodiac with 13 constellations, represented by the creatures along the borders. Hence, it seems quite likely that the main table on pp. 23–24 of the Paris Codex was used to chart the behavior of the 13 constellations in relation to the sun.[8]

*The Katun Cycle and the Calendrical Table of the Zodiacal Almanac.* One obvious use for the Paris table could have been to predict the position of the sun with respect to the constellations at the time of a ritual event marking the end of one *katun* and the beginning of the next. Because the 7200-day length of one *katun* is greater than a single cycle of the 1820-day table,

Table 9.2   The Zodiacal Almanac on Pages 23 and 24 of the Paris Codex[a]

| (13) | (12) | (11) | (10) | (9) | (8) | (7) | (6) | (5) | (4) | (3) | (2) | (1) |
|---|---|---|---|---|---|---|---|---|---|---|---|---|
| 10 Kan | 8 Cib | 6 Lamat | 4 Ahau | 2 Eb | 13 Kan | 11 Cib | 9 Lamat | 7 Ahau | 5 Eb | 3 Kan | 1 Cib | 12 Lamat |
| 10 Lamat | 8 Ahau | 6 Eb | 4 Kan | 2 Cib | 13 Lamat | 11 Ahau | 9 Eb | 7 Kan | 5 Cib | 3 Lamat | 1 Ahau | 12 Eb |
| 10 Eb | 8 Kan | 6 Cib | 4 Lamat | 2 Ahau | 13 Eb | 11 Kan | 9 Cib | 7 Lamat | 5 Ahau | 3 Eb | 1 Kan | 12 Cib |
| 10 Cib | 8 Lamat | 6 Ahau | 4 Eb | 2 Kan | 13 Cib | 11 Lamat | 9 Ahau | 7 Eb | 5 Kan | 3 Cib | 1 Lamat | 12 Ahau |
| 10 Ahau | 8 Eb | 6 Kan | 4 Cib | 2 Lamat | 13 Ahau | 11 Eb | 9 Kan | 7 Cib | 5 Lamat | 3 Ahau | 1 Eb | 12 Kan |
| 4 | 2 | 13 | 11 | 9 | 7 | 5 | 3 | 1 | 12 | 10 | 8 | 6 |

[a] Numbers below the tzolkin positions represent the blue numbers written above (underlined) and below the almanac; entries printed in bold type are clearly legible in the Codex.

some reading method involving recycling would clearly have been required. Damage to the blue numbers written above and below the 28-day *tzolkin* intervals has necessitated reconstruction here also, but as Gates (1931:4–5) has shown, this series must have been 4, 2, 13, 11, 9, 7, 5, 3, 1, 12, 10, 8, 6. Because no day names are written with the blue numbers, the *tzolkin* positions must have been so obvious from the method of use for the table that specification was considered unnecessary. This would have been true if the operation performed were a 20-day advance in the *tzolkin*, since the blue numbers would have formed new coefficients for the same days named in the table. However, this calculation seems so simple as to obviate the need for notation in the almanac. A second possibility, which appears more likely, is that the day was understood to be Ahau. This would have been unambiguous if the numerical sequence given here pertained to *katuns*.

In comparing the red *tzolkin* coefficients with the blue numbers, it can be seen that the order of the coefficients is the same, but that the red numbers follow a shift of three positions to the right. It is possible to think of the blue numbers as an abbreviated form of a table consisting of the same entries as the red table, but starting from a position three 28-day intervals later (Table 9.3 blue and red). The reason for the shift appears to be that this reflects the difference between four complete cycles of the table and the number of days in one *katun*, with a correction included for the difference between the lengths of the lines and the sidereal year.[9]

Assuming for the moment that only the red table existed, and that the user wished to find the position of the sun in the sequence of constellations one *katun* later than 10 Ahau, he probably would have performed a calculation that was equivalent to the following:

$$7200 \div 1820 = 3.396044, \text{ or}$$
three 1820-day cycles plus 1740 days

$$1740 \div 28 = 62.142857, \text{ or}$$
sixty-two 28-day cycles plus 4 days

The addition of 7200 days for the prediction would have required three full cycles of the table and an additional 62 intervals of 28 days, plus 4 days. So from a starting point of 10 Ahau, the reader would have moved through the requisite number of cycles and intervals to an 8 Ahau which fell 4 days to the left of 4 Cib.

A correction would have been necessary due to the difference between the number of days in a line of the table and sidereal year. As noted above, each line of the table represents 364 days, while the length of the sidereal

Table 9.3 Hypothetical Table Showing Recycling of the Paris Codex Zodiacal Almanac[a]

**Blue**

| | | | | | | | | | | | | |
|---|---|---|---|---|---|---|---|---|---|---|---|---|
| 4 Ahau | 2 Eb | 13 Kan | 11 Cib | 9 Lamat | 7 Ahau | 5 Eb | 3 Kan | 1 Cib | 12 Lamat | 10 Kan | 8 Cib | 6 Lamat |
| 4 Kan | 2 Cib | 13 Lamat | 11 Ahau | 9 Eb | 7 Kan | 5 Cib | 3 Lamat | 1 Ahau | 12 Eb | 10 Lamat | 8 Ahau | 6 Eb |
| 4 Lamat | 2 Ahau | 13 Eb | 11 Kan | 9 Cib | 7 Lamat | 5 Ahau | 3 Eb | 1 Kan | 12 Cib | 10 Eb | 8 Kan | 6 Cib |
| 4 Eb | 2 Kan | 13 Cib | 11 Lamat | 9 Ahau | 7 Eb | 5 Kan | 3 Cib | 1 Lamat | 12 Ahau | 10 Cib | 8 Lamat | 6 Ahau |
| 4 Cib | 2 Lamat | 13 Ahau | 11 Eb | 9 Kan | 7 Cib | 5 Lamat | 3 Ahau | 1 Eb | 12 Kan | 10 Ahau | 8 Eb | 6 Kan |

**Red**

| | | | | | | | | | | | | |
|---|---|---|---|---|---|---|---|---|---|---|---|---|
| 10 Kan | **8 Cib** | **6 Lamat** | **4 Ahau** | **2 Eb** | **13 Kan** | 11 Cib | **9 Lamat** | **7 Ahau** | **5 Eb** | **3 Kan** | 1 Cib | 12 Lamat |
| 10 Lamat | **8 Ahau** | **6 Eb** | **4 Kan** | **2 Cib** | **13 Lamat** | 11 Ahau | **9 Eb** | **7 Kan** | **5 Cib** | **3 Lamat** | 1 Ahau | 12 Eb |
| 10 Eb | **8 Kan** | **6 Cib** | **4 Lamat** | **2 Ahau** | **13 Eb** | 11 Kan | **9 Cib** | **7 Lamat** | **5 Ahau** | **3 Eb** | 1 Kan | 12 Cib |
| 10 Cib | **8 Lamat** | **6 Ahau** | **4 Eb** | **2 Kan** | **13 Cib** | 11 Lamat | **9 Ahau** | **7 Eb** | **5 Kan** | **3 Cib** | 1 Lamat | 12 Ahau |
| 10 Ahau | **8 Eb** | **6 Kan** | **4 Cib** | **2 Lamat** | **13 Ahau** | 11 Eb | **9 Kan** | **7 Cib** | **5 Lamat** | **3 Ahau** | 1 Eb | 12 Kan |

**(Yellow)**

| | | | | | | | | | | | | |
|---|---|---|---|---|---|---|---|---|---|---|---|---|
| 3 Kan | 1 Cib | 12 Lamat | 10 Kan | 8 Cib | 6 Lamat | 4 Ahau | 2 Eb | 13 Kan | 11 Cib | 9 Lamat | 7 Ahau | 5 Eb |
| 3 Lamat | 1 Ahau | 12 Eb | 10 Lamat | 8 Ahau | 6 Eb | 4 Kan | 2 Cib | 13 Lamat | 11 Ahau | 9 Eb | 7 Kan | 5 Cib |
| 3 Eb | 1 Kan | 12 Cib | 10 Eb | 8 Kan | 6 Cib | 4 Lamat | 2 Ahau | 13 Eb | 11 Kan | 9 Cib | 7 Lamat | 5 Ahau |
| 3 Cib | 1 Lamat | 12 Ahau | 10 Cib | 8 Lamat | 6 Ahau | 4 Eb | 2 Kan | 13 Cib | 11 Lamat | 9 Ahau | 7 Eb | 5 Kan |
| 3 Ahau | 1 Eb | 12 Kan | 10 Ahau | 8 Eb | 6 Kan | 4 Cib | 2 Lamat | 13 Ahau | 11 Eb | 9 Kan | 7 Cib | 5 Lamat |

[a] Entries printed in bold type in the red table are clearly legible in the codex.

year is 365.25636. So the error, 1.25636 days per line, increases to 6.2818 days per 1820-day cycle, and finally to 24.85107 days after one *katun*. At this point, the table would have been almost one full interval ahead of the stars. Since the Maya did not use fractional values, the correction would have required the reader to move 25 days to the right. However, as finding the location of the proper Ahau day for the end of the *katun* in the red numbers always requires a 4-day shift toward the left, the total adjustment would have been 21 days toward the right. The position of the sun relative to the constellations at the *katun* ending, 8 Ahau, would correspond to a location in the table 21 days to the right of 4 Cib; its location would therefore correspond quite well with the next column to the right of that containing 4 Cib.

A second example will show how such a computation could have been made using both red and blue tables. If the reader were to use the table at the end of Katun 4 Ahau to predict the position of the sun 7200 days later, at the end of Katun 2 Ahau, he could simply have thought of the blue numbers as representing the table for the present *katun* and the red table as the dates for the future one. Reading the 2 Ahau from column 9 of the red table would reach the same corrected constellation position as would result from applying the lengthy calculation described, including the 25-day correction, to the fully expanded table of blue numbers. If the table were to be used for predictions concerning the succeeding *katun*, 13 Ahau, it would have been necessary to create yet a third table, referred to here for convenience as yellow, that followed the same pattern of shifts of 28-day intervals and related stars as is described in Table 9.3 yellow.

In the discussion of the correction for cumulative astronomical error over one *katun*, it was noted that a shift of 21 days toward the right is required. This means that a new source of error, the difference between the correction and the basic 28-day interval of the table, would have been introduced. If the sun were just entering a particular constellation at the beginning of the initial 28-day interval, the pattern of shifts would become inaccurate after four *katuns*. Correction of the accumulated 7-day errors could easily have been made by incorporating a one-interval shift to the left for every four shifts of three intervals to the right in the revision process. Direct observation of the constellations in the sky could also easily have been used to realign a particular position in the table with the appropriate event overhead.

*The Creatures of the Paris Codex Zodiacal Almanac and the* Katun *Prophecies on pp. 23–24.* As mentioned above, the table of red *tzolkin* days and blue numbers is bordered by two bands from which creatures, primarily animals, hang. The upper band is marked with symbols widely accepted as designating the sky, while the lower band has only a zigzagging dotted line.[10] Six reasonably complete animals suspended from eclipse glyphs form the top line; there is space to accommodate a seventh sky beast at the right side of p. 24 where a few traces of painted design remain. A series of bar-and-dot numerals adjacent to the upper row of eclipse glyphs should probably be read as entries of 168, despite the absence of one of the lower bars and one number representing eight days. If the seven animals painted here represent constellations spanning the ecliptic from near the eastern and western horizons, the number of 168 could be explained in terms of the six 28-day intervals, or 168 days, necessary for a constellation to move from rising to setting position at a specific time of day, such as sunrise or sunset.[11] Although the lower constellation band is incomplete, the spacing of the motifs is consistent with recognition of six additional star groups. It is plausible that the ordering of the 13 creatures would reflect the right to left reading pattern of the columns.

While the first constellation on p. 24 is almost entirely missing, and is referred to here simply as *Constellation 1*, the second is widely recognized as a rattlesnake because of the *tzab* (rattle) attachment on its tail. The identity of the third figure is likewise generally accepted as a turtle, and the fourth is clearly a scorpion. Across the line of the screenfold, on p. 23, Constellation 5 is a bird whose precise identification has proved problematic. As summarized in Bricker and Bricker (Chapter 6 of this volume) and Kelley (1976:47), constellation 5 has been regarded as an eagle, a vulture, and a crested guan (*Penelope purpurascens*). Defining the respective limits of naturalistic representation and iconographic convention is certainly challenging in this example, but the head feathers appear to form two distinct units that could be significant. On the basis of these feathers, my own view is that the bird of constellation 5 is probably a harpy eagle (*Harpia harpyja*, Davis 1972:Plate 4, no. 24), as has been suggested, or an owl.[12] The sixth animal is usually thought of as a fish-snake with no counterpart in the real world. The seventh and final animal of the upper band is a bird that may well be a vulture.

Moving to the lower right corner of p. 24, there is an area probably occupied by a single constellation, a frog (Severin 1981:11). This is followed by a bat as the ninth constellation, and damaged spaces on both sides of the screenfold where two constellations were evidently obliterated. The twelfth position is occupied by a death figure, and the thirteenth and final space holds a spotted mammal with claws that is a jaguar.

Because these two pages are linked by the *katun* series to pp. 2–11 of the manuscript, it is possible that further information concerning the missing and damaged constellations is to be gained by examining the latter section. Unfortunately large areas of pp. 2–11 have also been damaged beyond recognition, but such an examination is nevertheless helpful. In reviewing the general scheme of the primary illustrations of the *katun* sequence, located approximately in the centers of the pages, it is apparent that a standing figure on the left side of each scene typically makes offerings to a figure seated on a bench with skyband markings, presumably the regent of the *katun* indicated by the adjacent numbered Ahau glyph (Figure 9.4). Much of the detail for these regents has disappeared. However, it is still possible to relate some features of the designs to the pp. 23–24 constellations. On p. 5, it seems quite likely that the regent of Katun 9 Ahau is posed with the p. 24 scorpion constellation, which possibly served as the main element of a headdress or defined the roof of a house around him. The overall shapes of the motifs are similar, and the p. 5 example has the hooded eye variant of the star symbol as its head, and also as its one remaining claw. A second regent, for Katun 1 Ahau, is shown on p. 9 wearing the fish–snake headdress of the sixth constellation from the upper band of the zodiacal table.

*Tuns and the Constellations.* The illustrations of the upper sections of pp. 2–11 also include creatures, such as the vulture in the top left panel on p. 2 and the death figure in the center panel of p. 4, that resemble the pp. 23–24 constellations. Other animals in these upper panels of the *katun* pages, like the deer in the center of p. 5, could plausibly fill the spaces for the constellations missing from the zodiacal table. Moreover, two lines of numbered Ahau glyphs between the upper left and center illustrations form a two-part series. Understanding the function of the Ahau series might relate the animals to their proper places in the pp. 23–24 table.

In discussing the Ahau series of the upper sections of the *katun* pages, Gates (1910:17–18) proposed two alternative interpretations. One of the Gates options would relate the upper Ahau series to a sequence of *katuns*, and the other would link it to a sequence of *tun* endings. These alternatives are the result of two different reconstructions of the damaged upper areas of the pages (see Table 9.4).

The basic structure of the series is recognizable from the entries of 12 Ahau, 8 Ahau, 4 Ahau, and 13 Ahau surviving on pp. 3–6. From this it is clear that each Ahau number recorded in the lower line of the top sections of the pages is four less than its predecessor on the adjacent page. The pattern for the numbers forming the top line of Ahau glyphs is established by p. 5, where 10 Ahau appears above the 4 Ahau mentioned previously. So one might assume that each Ahau in the upper line is six greater than the

Table 9.4  The Upper Ahau intervals of the Paris Codex, pp. 1–13[a]

| page | 1 | 2 | 3 | 4 | 5 | 6 | 7 | 8 | 9 | 10 | 11 | 12 | 13 |
|---|---|---|---|---|---|---|---|---|---|---|---|---|---|
| (a) The *katun* series | 2 | 13 | 11 | 9 | 7 | 5 | 3 | 1 | 12 | 10 | 8 | 6 | 4 |
|  | 9 | 7 | 5 | 3 | 1 | 12 | 10 | 8 | 6 | 4 | 2 | 13 | 11 |
| (b) The *tun* series | 13 | 9 | 5 | 1 | **10** | 6 | 2 | 11 | 7 | 3 | **12** | 8 | 4 |
|  | 7 | 3 | **12** | 8 | **4** | **13** | 9 | 5 | 1 | 10 | 6 | 2 | 11 |

[a] Entries printed in bold type are clearly legible in the Codex.

238

glyph below. The question of whether the upper Ahau intervals pertain to *katuns* or *tuns* was raised, owing to the damage to the left sides of each of the *katun* pages. Gates noticed that there was sufficient space in front of each of the upper left illustrations to accommodate additional numbered Ahau glyphs, and suggested that these could be intermediate to the Ahau positions recorded in the centers of the pages. If the intermediate Ahau intervals did occur as Gates proposed, the numerical sequence basic to the pp. 23–24 zodiacal almanac would have been repeated along the tops of the *katun* pages. If these intermediate intervals did not exist, the Ahau entries would signify a succession of periods of one *tun*. The *tun* sequence is the most plausible of the Gates interpretations for the upper Ahau series on the Paris *katun* pages. The problem with his proposed *katun* series is that it does not correlate with the *katun* numbers in the primary illustrations on the pages. Moreover, the *tun* sequence would be more consistent with the prominent *tun* glyphs that serve as seats for most of the figures in the upper panels. As Treiber (1987:80–81) has noted, this *tun* series can be linked with the table of 1820 *tzolkin* days on pp. 23 and 24 of the Codex. As mentioned, 1820 days is one complete cycle of this table; it is also 5 *tuns* plus 20 days. So for a user of the pp. 1–13 *tun* table to move forward 1820 days from the 13 Ahau reconstructed in the top row of p. 1, it would be necessary to read through the 5 *tuns* recorded in the upper Ahau row of pp. 2–6 and add the remaining 20 days by dropping to the lower Ahau entry on p. 6. In performing this operation, the reader would have returned to 13 Ahau, as would also have occurred in making a complete cycle through the pp. 23–24 table.

The Books of Chilam Balam support the idea that constellations could be included in illustrations of a *tun* series. In the Chilam Balam of Tizimin, it is recorded that during Katun 3 Ahau

> The four Honored Ones,
> Who come in this *tun*,
> > Or in the eleventh measured *tun* of the *katun*.
> The four Honored Ones having appeared,
> > The four stars having appeared . . .
> They take office,
> > The four Honored Ones
> > > > Edmonson, 1982, p. 90

So it would seem that the illustrations for the *tun* sections running across the tops of pp. 1–13 of the Paris Codex could include constellation symbols associated with the *tuns* named in the Ahau sequence. This possibility is supported by the fact that the numerical sequence of the *tun* coefficients recycles after p. 13, which means that 13 constellations (perhaps those of the pp. 23–24 table) would be the correct number to represent the *tuns*. In such a sequence the vulture illustrated in the upper left corner of p. 2 might be correlated with the *tun* 13 Ahau recorded on the now missing first page. Similarly, the rabbit (?) in the upper left corner of p. 4 might be the constellation for the *tun* 5 probably recorded on p. 3. This further suggests a means of determining additional *katun* constellations. But unfortunately the *tun* constellations cannot be verified through comparison with other illustrations in the Paris Codex. The symbol associated with Katun 1 Ahau in the main section of p. 9 is the fish snake, not the death figure occupying the elaborate seat of the p. 4 *tun* register (1 Ahau, 8 Ahau). Although a death figure could have illustrated the now effaced *katun* prophecy for 8 Ahau on p. 12, the death figure shown on p. 23 of the Paris zodiac is not adjacent to 1 Ahau or 8 Ahau.

*Katuns, Constellations, and the Seasons.* There is other evidence that constellations associated with specific *katuns* would have been important to Maya astronomers using the Paris Codex. During a single cycle of 13

Table 9.5   Seasonal Pairing of *Katuns: Katun* equivalents in the Gregorian calendar (Morley, Brainerd, and Sharer 1983:602)[a]

| Katun | Ending date |
|---|---|
| 4 Ahau | 2 March 1244 |
| 2 Ahau | 18 November 1263 |
| 13 Ahau | 5 August 1283 |
| 11 Ahau | 23 April 1303 |
| 9 Ahau | 8 January 1323 |
| 7 Ahau | 25 September 1342 |
| 5 Ahau | 12 June 1362 |
| 3 Ahau | 27 February 1382 |
| 1 Ahau | 15 November 1401 |
| 12 Ahau | 2 August 1421 |
| 10 Ahau | 19 April 1441 |
| 8 Ahau | 4 January 1461 |
| 6 Ahau | 21 September 1480 |

Table 9.6   *Katun* pairs

| | |
|---|---|
| 4 Ahau and 3 Ahau | 2 Ahau and 1 Ahau |
| 13 Ahau and 12 Ahau | 11 Ahau and 10 Ahau |
| 9 Ahau and 8 Ahau | 7 Ahau and 6 Ahau |
| 5 Ahau is unpaired in this cycle | |

[a] Based on the 584283 correlation constant, this 4 Ahau cycle was selected because it is approximately consistent with the artistic style of Codex Paris.

*katuns*, there would have been seven particularly significant constellations, recalling the arrangement of the upper zodiacal band in the Paris table. Assuming for the moment that Katun 4 Ahau marked the beginning of such a cycle, it may be seen (Table 9.5 and 9.6) that pairing of 12 of the 13 *katuns* would have occurred due to seasonal repetition of the *katun* events. That is, 12 of the 13 *katuns* would have ended with the sun in essentially the same position in which it would have been for another *katun* in the series.[13]

*The Paris Codex Zodiacal Almanac and Astronomical Observation.* Although the Books of Chilam Balam and the Paris Codex indicate that specific asterisms were associated with each *katun*, correlation of the *katun* sequence with historical positions of constellations remains problematic. The ordering of the constellations in the primary illustrations of the *katun* prophecies does not appear to correlate with the pp. 23–24 zodiacal almanac. The scorpion constellation shown in the Katun 9 Ahau illustration of p. 5 is painted above the 9 Ahau column of the almanac, as expected, but the fish-snake associated on p. 9 with Katun 1 Ahau does not appear above the appropriate almanac column.

## Conclusion

Although a substantial portion of the content of the Books of Chilam Balam has been traced directly to European sources, analysis of the remaining sections provides insight into Maya astronomical perspectives. From such study it appears that one purpose of these books was to reconcile unfamiliar European concepts, such as the calendar, with the pre-existing Maya system. A second purpose was evidently to preserve pre-Hispanic ritual knowledge including astronomical concerns; the *katun* prophecies link the cycle of the 13 *katuns* with the constellations. Comparison of these prophecies with the pre-Conquest Paris Codex confirms the association, as pp. 23–24 of this manuscript includes hieroglyphic references to *katuns* (shown herein by the reading of T548:17.1052). Also included in these pages is a recycling zodiacal almanac constructed to include the *tzolkin* days for which the *katuns* were named. This almanac could have been used to predict the position of the sun with respect to the constellations at the beginning of the *katuns*, and on certain other days of the 364-day computing year. Recycling of the table could have corrected for cumulative astronomical error, thereby correlating the almanac with the tropical year. The Paris Codex *katun* prophecy pages incorporate a cycle of *tuns*, suggesting that a further subject of interest to the Maya was the commensuration of the *tun* with the constellation cycles. Perhaps additional study will correlate the constellations used to characterize specific *katuns* in the Paris Codex and the Books of Chilam Balam with specific star groups.

## ACKNOWLEDGMENTS

I would like to thank Anthony F. Aveni for inviting me to contribute this research, and for comments on the manuscript. Contact with the other participants in the symposium has been beneficial as well. Victoria and Harvey Bricker provided a draft of their paper on the Paris Zodiacal almanac and other helpful information. Discussions with Alan Paxton resulted in improvements to this paper. Figure 9.2 was drawn by Laura Donnelly.

## NOTES

1. The Ahau series discussed here corresponds approximately with the European dates given by Roys (1973:205) and Morley, Brainerd, and Sharer (1983:603).

2. A prominent red line divides the almanacs painted on page 69 of the Dresden Codex.

3. Unless otherwise specified, all glyph transcriptions are according to the Thompson (1962) system. Some numbers are preceded by the letter "T" to emphasize that they refer to glyphs.

4. A damaged glyph on p. 24 (at A 7) may provide another example of this combination. The significance of the additional affix in a similar collocation, T548:24.x:1052, on p. 23 (at D 4 and E 6), is unknown.

5. At present I cannot provide a clear justification for the use of the dead head to convey this sound. Most words for *dead*, *death*, *head*, and *face*, compiled in the *Diccionario Maya Cordemex* (Barrera Vásquez 1980) do not incorporate *k'a*. Although *k'alak* ("inert, without life") is included, the stem *kim* is more frequently encountered in the death terms. There is reasonable consensus that T736a and c should be read *cim* or *cimi* (*kim* or *kimi*, according to the Cordemex notation; see Kurbjuhn 1989:106), and that T736b is a separate sign. It seems likely that T736b should be grouped with T1052 and read *k'a*.

6. Schele (1989:6) has noted that the second "k" of the Landa alphabet has the *k'a* pronunciation. However, an association of Landa's examples of *k'a* with T1052 has apparently not been previously made.

7. Although Gates (1910:13–14) was careful to specify that these numbers are distinctly blue, the current scholarly convention is to refer to them as green. This would probably not have been confusing to the pre-Hispanic Maya, who used the same glyph affix (T17) for both colors.

8. Since the 28-day interval charted in the table is also a close approximation of

the sidereal lunar month of 27.32166 days, it is necessary to consider the possibility that the Paris table could have been used to predict the passage of the moon through the various constellations. In fact, this appears unlikely because cumulative astronomical error so rapidly exceeds the length of time spent by the moon in any given constellation. For 13 evenly spaced constellations, the moon would spend just over 2.10 days in each star group. As the difference between the lunar sidereal month and the basic interval of the table is 0.67834 days, the value of 2.10 days would be reached in approximately 3.098 periods of 28 days. To state this more clearly in observational terms, the moon would be off by 9° ([0.67834 days/sidereal month] × 360°), which is 1/3 constellation per period, or one constellation every three periods. This would be the limit of predictive accuracy if the initial position chosen from the table were to fall when the moon had just entered a constellation. Naturally the error would be apparent even more rapidly if the attempt to predict the moon's path were to begin with an interval when it had moved farther through a constellation.

The presence of the eclipse glyphs above the zodiacal beings suggests that the lunar synodic month of 29.53059 days, also close to the 28-day interval of the Paris table, could have been an important subject. Although the table could have been used to predict eclipses on specific occasions (see note 9), it is my view that these eclipse glyphs are probably included here to indicate the general content of the table. The typical lunar intervals useful for predicting eclipses, 163 ± 1, 148 ± 1, 177 ± 1, and 14 or 15 days (see Aveni 1980:79), are not commensurate with the 28-day interval. Rather, the connection of the Paris table with eclipses seems to be through the *tzolkin*. As John Teeple has demonstrated (1930:88–90), these events fit neatly into three concentrations within a double *tzolkin* of 520 days. Anthony Aveni (1980:181–82) has explained that this is because the double *tzolkin* is almost identical in length to three eclipse half years of 173.3 days each. Since the length of one cycle of the Paris table is 1820 days, or 7 *tzolkins*, two cycles correspond to 7 double *tzolkins*, or 21.004 eclipse half-years. Perhaps the table on pp. 23–24 of the Paris Codex was a pre-Columbian counterpart to the *katun* wheels constructed during the Colonial era (Figure 9.3) in that it showed general interrelationships, in this case the meshing of the cycles of eclipses, constellations, and *katuns*. Nevertheless, it would still have been possible to use the table to predict specific astronomical events.

9. It may be noted in passing that a *katun* is 1740 days greater than three of the 1820-day cycles, and that this remainder is close to being an eclipse interval. Aveni (1980:80,177) has commented that 1742 days is one of the intervals reflected both in the observational record and the structure of the eclipse table of the Dresden Codex. Hence, if a user of the Paris Codex table were to experience an eclipse at the end of the third cycle, he could predict that another eclipse might take place two days after a ritual marking the completion of the current *katun*.

10. Because so many of the surviving creatures beneath this band have underworld associations, it is tempting to see it as a representation of the surface of the

earth, transferred to the celestial realm. Perhaps a concept similar to that relating Venus to the underworld (Kelley 1976:Figure 19, Venus god F7; Lounsbury 1982:Fig. 1, d) is represented.

11. The 12 Lamat base for the table may be related to this interval, as it is day number 168 of the *tzolkin*.

12. The Yucatan screech owl cited by Tozzer and Allen (1910:337–38, Pl. 23), *Otus choliba thompsoni*, as the model for numerous examples of birds painted in the codices is described as having two feathered tufts and a rather long beak, short tail, and mottled plumage. Tozzer and Allen further comment that the representational convention was for both feather tufts to be included, even when the bird is shown in profile. In the profile examples one tuft would typically be painted behind the other, as is the case with the bird of the Paris table. The mottled feathers of the Yucatan screech owls are also emphasized in the codex examples, to the point of even being painted on the tufts. Although mottling is not prominent elsewhere on the Constellation 5 bird, it is indicated on the feather tufts.

13. Notations concerning the six constellations not important to the *katun* ritual (or these pairs) were possibly made beneath the lower band of creatures, in an area of the pp. 23–24 painting that is almost entirely destroyed. Three red dots, suggestive of another almanac, remain immediately to the left of the p. 23 skeletal figure.

## REFERENCES

Aveni, A. F., 1980. *Skywatchers of Ancient Mexico* (Austin and London: University of Texas Press).

Barrera Vásquez, A., director, 1980. *Diccionario Maya Cordemex* (Mérida, Yucatán: Ediciones Cordemex).

Bricker, V. R., 1986. "A Grammar of Mayan Hieroglyphs," *Middle American Research Institute, Tulane University,* Pub. 56.

Closs, M. P., 1983. "Were the Ancient Maya Aware of the Precession of the Equinoxes?" *Archaeoastronomy* 6(1–4):164–171.

*Codex Peresianus*, 1968. *Codex Peresianus (Codex Paris): Bibliothèque Nationale Paris.* (Graz: Akademische Druck- und Verlagsanstalt) (Facsimile, with introduction and summary by Ferdinand Anders; Codices Selecti, 9).

Craine, E. R., and R. C. Reindorp (translators and editors), 1979. *The Codex Pérez and the Book of Chilam Balam of Maní* (Norman: University of Oklahoma Press).

Davis, L. I., 1972. *A Field Guide to the Birds of Mexico and Central America* (Austin and London: University of Texas Press).

Dütting, D., and M. Schramm, 1988. "The Sidereal Period of the Moon in Mayan Calendrical Astronomy," *Tribus* 37:139–73.

Edmonson, M. S. (translator and annotator), 1982. *The Ancient Future of the Itza: The Book of Chilam Balam of Tizimin* (Austin: University of Texas Press).

Gates, W. E., 1910. "Commentary upon the Maya–Tzental Perez Codex," *Papers* of the Peabody Museum of American Archaeology and Ethnology, Harvard University, Vol. 6, Number 1.

—, 1931. "The Thirteen Ahaus in the Kaua Manuscript and Related Katun Wheels in the Paris Codex, Landa, Cogolludo and the Chumayel," *Maya Society Quarterly* 1:2–21.

Gibson, C., and J. B. Glass, 1975. "A Census of Middle American Prose Manuscripts in the Native Historical Tradition," in *Handbook of Middle American Indians*, Vol. 15, General Editor, Robert Wauchope, pp. 322–400 (Austin: University of Texas Press).

Kelley, D. H., 1976. *Deciphering the Maya Script*. (Austin and London: University of Texas Press).

Knorozov, Y., 1982. "Maya Hieroglyphic Codices (translated from the Russian by Sophie D. Coe)," *Institute for Mesoamerican Studies, State University of New York at Albany*, Pub. 8.

Kurbjuhn, K., compiler, 1989. *Maya: the Complete Catalog of Glyph Readings*. (Kassel, Germany: Schneider & Weber).

Landa, D. de, c1566. *Relación de las Cosas de Yucatán*. Photographic copy of unpublished manuscript, Special Collections, Zimmerman Library, University of New Mexico.

—, 1941. "Landa's Relación de las Cosas de Yucatán, edited with notes by Alfred M. Tozzer. *Papers of the Peabody Museum of American Archaeology and Ethnology, Harvard University*, Vol. 18.

Lounsbury, F., 1978. "Maya Numeration, Computation and Calendrical Astronomy, in *Dictionary of Scientific Biography*, Vol. 15, Supplement 1, edited by C. C. Gillispie, pp. 759–818 (New York: Scribner's).

—, 1982. "Astronomical Knowledge and its Uses at Bonampak, Mexico" in *Archaeoastronomy in the New World*, edited by A. F. Aveni, pp. 143–68 (Cambridge: Cambridge University Press).

—, 1984. "Glyphic Substutions:Homophonic and Synonymic," in *Phoneticism in Mayan Hieroglyphic Writing*, edited by John S. Justeson and Lyle Campbell, pp. 167–84. *Institute for Mesoamerican Studies, State University of New York at Albany*, Pub. 9.

Miram, H.-M., 1988. *Transkriptionen der Chilam Balames* (3 volumes) (Hamburg: Toro-Verlag).

—, 1989. "The Role of the Books of Chilam Balam in Deciphering the Maya Hieroglyphs: New Material and New Considerations," Paper presented at *Seventh Palenque Round Table*, Palenque, Chiapas.

Morley, S. G., G. W. Brainerd, and R. J. Sharer, 1983. *The Ancient Maya* (Stanford: Stanford University Press) (fourth revised edition of 1946 publication by Sylvanus G. Morley).

Riese, B., 1984. "Hel Hieroglyphs," in *Phoneticism in Mayan Hieroglyphic Writing*, edited by John S. Justeson and Lyle Campbell, pp. 263–86. *Institute for Mesoamerican Studies, State University of New York at Albany*, Pub. 9.

Roys, R. L., 1973. *The Book of Chilam Balam of Chumayel* (Norman: University of

Oklahoma Press). [reprint of second (1967) edition, reproduced from first (1933) edition, published by the Carnegie Institution of Washington].

Schele, L., 1989. *Notebook for the XIIIth Maya Hieroglyphic Workshop at Texas.* (Austin: Art Department, University of Texas at Austin).

Severin, G. M., 1981. "The Paris Codex: Decoding an Astronomical Ephemeris," *Transactions of the American Philosophical Society,* **71,** Part 5.

Spinden, H., 1916. "The Question of a Zodiac in America," *American Anthropologist* n.s., **18**:53–80.

Teeple, J., 1930. "Maya Astronomy," Carnegie Institution of Washington, Publication 403, *Contributions to American Archaeology* 1(2):29–114.

Thompson, J.E.S., 1950. *Maya Hieroglyphic Writing, an Introduction* (Norman: University of Oklahoma Press).

—, 1962. A *Catalog of Maya Hieroglyphs.* (Norman: University of Oklahoma Press).

Tozzer, A. M., and G. M. Allen, 1910. "Animal Figures in the Maya Codices," *Papers of the Peabody Museum of American Archaeology and Ethnology, Harvard University,* Vol. 4, Number 3.

Treiber, H., 1987. "Studien zur Katunserie der Pariser Mayahandschrift," *Acta Mesoamericana,* **2,** edited by Eike Hinz, Ulrich Köhler, Hanns J. Prem, and Berthold Riese (Berlin: Verlag Von Flemming).

Villacorta C., J. A., and C. A. Villacorta, 1976. *Codices Mayas* (second edition of 1930 publication) (Guatemala: Tipografía Nacional).

# IO

# Myth, Math, and the Problem of Correlation in Mayan Books

## DENNIS TEDLOCK

*Nim upeyoxik, utzijoxik puch*
*ta chik'is tzuk ronojel kajulew*[1]

It takes a long performance and account
to complete the lighting of all the sky-earth
Popol Vuh

The book that has come to be known as the Dresden Codex spans a greater reach of time than any other Mayan hieroglyphic text. At the near end, on iconographic grounds, it could date from as late as the fifteenth century (Paxton 1986:169–71), and it contains astronomical tables that were revised at least as late as the fourteenth century (V. Bricker and H. Bricker 1988:59) and possibly as late as the beginning of the sixteenth century (V. Bricker and H. Bricker, Chapter 2 of this volume). At the far end, by means of hypothetical dates in a remote past, it reaches back into the darkness of a mythic world that preceded the creation of human beings.

As a physical object, the Dresden Codex is separated by five centuries from the last known dated inscription of the so-called Classic Maya, which was carved in stone at Toniná on 10.4.0.0.0, or January 13, 909 (Schele and Freidel 1990:392).[2] Lithocentric archaeologists have reported over and over again that Mayan long-count dating came to an end around that time, yet the Dresden Codex contains more long-count dates than any known

Mayan text of whatever period. The latest date written out in full is 10.19.6.1.8, which falls in the year 1210 (Lounsbury 1978:814), and later dates are projected by means of distance numbers. In the middle range are the starting or "base" dates for the tables, typically reaching back into the Classic period. The Mars table (pp. 43b–45b), for example, carries the base date 9.19.7.15.8, which fell in the year 818, while the Venus table (pp. 46–50) is dated to 9.9.9.16.0, falling in 623. Reaching back into a calendrically defined myth age are dates that precede the zero date of what the Maya reckoned as the present era, the so-called "ring" (negative) dates.[3] In the case of the Venus table the ring date is −6.2.0, which would fall, by retrospective Christian reckoning, in the year −3119.

An invisible trail of innumerable texts, written on perishable paper, links the Mayan books known today with the stone monuments of the classic period. Whatever the dates at which the Dresden, Madrid, and Paris Codices passed into European hands, Andrés de Avendaño saw books containing calendars and *katun* prophecies in Yucatán as late as the very end of the seventeenth century, and he even acquired a degree of literacy in the Mayan script (Roys 1967:184). During those same years, in highland Guatemala, Francisco Ximénez saw books he described as containing divinatory calendars "with signs corresponding to each day," and he acquired such a book for his personal library (Ximénez 1967:11). These two sightings occurred nearly seven generations after Diego de Landa's fabled 1562 book burning, which has achieved a sort of ring-date status among Mayanists.

During the decade before the book bonfire in Yucatán, at about the same time de Landa was asking Juan Cocom for the signs of what he took to be the Mayan alphabet (Tozzer 1941:43–44, 169–70), Cristobal Velasco and two other Quiché Maya men of Guatemala were writing a book in the Latin alphabet but in their own language (D. Tedlock 1985:60–61). Their work is based, as they explain in their introduction, on an "original book and ancient writing" called the Popol Vuh. They trace this writing to an ancient city to the east of Santa Cruz Quiché, a city whose insignia, according to the Annals of the Cakchiquels, was a bat (D. Tedlock 1989).[4] That sounds like Copán, and indeed, while the Quiché ancestors were on a pilgrimage there, they burned incense before a "tree-stone," which is what stele are called in the inscriptions of Copán.[5] But once we have traced the paper trail back far enough to find ourselves in the presence of stele, the only books we are likely to catch sight of are the ones that lie open before monkey and rabbit scribes, painted on ceramic vases of the Classic period.

It should not surprise us if there turned out to be intelligible and even systematic links, beyond details of epigraphy and iconography and beyond the mere fact of the use of long-count dates, between the surviving texts on paper and the legible inscriptions on monuments. We are, after all, dealing with a civilization whose scribes did not stop reading and writing just because the erection of dated stele passed out of fashion and the southern lowlands became a poor neighborhood. But there is a problem here: The hieroglyphic books offer idealized charts of recurring astronomical and meteorological events that serve as signs of the mythic deeds of gods, while the stele chronicle the real lives of historical royal personages. The beginning of the solution lies in the fact that there were dates on the Mayan calendar at which ceremonial meetings between gods and rulers could be arranged. The occasion might be an heir designation or an accession to the throne, for example, scheduled so as to become an historic recurrence of a mythic event. The date would be selected by consulting books very much like the Dresden Codex, and at the mythic end of a long interval preceding the ceremony would rest a date at the very dawn of the present era, or all the way back in the darkness of the previous one.

In most Classic inscriptions the mythic roots of history are implicit, as if the scribes had assumed that any serious reader would be in possession of a book. It is only at Palenque, in the inscriptions of the three temples in the Cross group, that a good deal of the sort of information that would normally be kept in books found its way onto stone. Here, myth meets history, and inside the Temple of the Cross the transition between the two takes place in the very middle of a two-part inscription that occupies the opposite ends of a broad stone tablet.[6] At the very beginning of this text is a long-count date, written out in full, that goes back before the present era, and in the narrative that follows are names of the very gods. The date is expressed in positive terms, 12.19.13.4.0, but it does not belong to the chronology of the present Mayan era, which has yet to reach such a large number even in our own times. Instead it refers to the previous era, whose point of contact with the present one was at 13.0.0.0.0. In effect it is a ring date, translatable into the terms of the Dresden Codex as −6.14.0. The initial date in the nearby Temple of the Sun, 1.18.5.3.6, belongs to the present era, but it is still very remote and still refers to events in the lives of gods. Coming just 14 days later is the date in the third temple, that of the Foliated Cross. Taken together, the three dates fall in the years that run from −3119 to −2360 by retrospective Christian reckoning, whereas the Palenque dynasty was founded in 431 and the three temples were dedicated in 690 (Schele and Freidel 1990:217, 242).

The remote events that lie close on either side of 13.0.0.0.0 are hypothetical events, and that is precisely why they offer us an ideal ground for the reconstruction of a conceptual scheme that might join such texts as still cling to paper with those that endure in stone. Just as the actors in these events are divine rather than human, so the astronomy and calendrics ought to be pure rather than applied. Our reconstruction can begin with nothing more complicated than the creation of an experimental chronology that combines early dates from the Cross group inscriptions with others from the Dresden Codex, while at the same time taking account of some of the astronomical intervals given in various Dresden tables and a lunar interval given in the Popol Vuh. What we seek to learn about the Maya is what Aveni (Chapter 3 of this volume) calls "the meter of their celestial harmony."[7]

In the chronology set forth in Table 10.1, the readings of the inscrip-

*Table 10.1*    Combined Chronology for the Cross-Group
Inscriptions, the Dresden Codex, and the Popol Vuh

| Event and source | Long count and calendar round | |
|---|---|---|
| Birth of Hun Hunahpu or senior GI (TC) | −8. 5. 0 | 1 Ahau 8 Muan |
| 819-day rite performed (TC) | −6.15. 0 | 1 Ahau 18 Zotz' |
| Moon begins to wax (TC) | −6.14. 5 | 3 Men 8 Tzec |
| Birth of Lady Egret (TC) | −6.14. 0 | 8 Ahau 13 Tzec |
| First heliacal eastern rise of Venus (DC) | −6. 2. 0 | 1 Ahau 18 Kayab |
| Begin retrograde motion of Mars (DC) | −17.12 | 3 Lamat 1 Uayeb |
| First 0 Zec heliacal western rise of Venus (DC) | 1. 5. 2 | 11 Ik 0 Zec |
| Hun Hunahpu enters sky to set up his 8th house (TC) | 1. 9. 2 | 13 Ik 0 Ch'en |
| 819-day rite; Jupiter resumes forward motion (TS) | 1. 6.14.11. 2 | 1 Ik 10 Tzec |
| Last eastern rise of Venus before triad births (DC) | 1.18. 4. 8. 0 | 7 Ahau 18 Kayab |
| Moon Blood completes 6 moons of pregnancy (PV) | 1.18. 4.16.16 | 1 Cib 9 Mol |
| Venus, after 8 moons in east, begins to disappear (DC) | 1.18. 5. 1.16 | 9 Cib 9 Zac |
| Moon begins to wax (TS) | 1.18. 5. 2. 0 | 13 Ahau 13 Zac |
| Moon Blood harvests maize from a solitary stalk (PV) | { 1.18. 5. 2. 8<br>1.18. 5. 2. 9 | 8 Lamat 1 Ceh }<br>9 Muluc 2 Ceh |
| Birth of Hunahpu or junior GI (TC) | 1.18. 5. 3. 2 | 9 Ik 15 Ceh |
| Birth of Xbalanque or GIII (TS) | 1.18. 5. 3. 6 | 13 Cimi 19 Ceh |
| Moon begins to wax (TFC) | 1.18. 5. 3.10 | 4 Oc 3 Mac |
| Birth of Tahil or GII (TFC) | 1.18. 5. 4. 0 | 1 Ahau 13 Mac |
| Heliacal eastern rise of Venus with Mars nearby (DC) | 10. 5. 6. 4. 0 | 1 Ahau 18 Kayab |
| Heliacal eastern rise of Venus with Jupiter nearby (DC) | 10.15. 4. 2. 0 | 1 Ahau 18 Uo |

*Figure 10.1* The head form of T1030.

tions in the Temples of the Cross (TC), Sun (TS), and Foliated Cross (TFC) generally follow those given by Schele (1987). On the identities of the gods of the Palenque triad (GI, GII, GIII), see Lounsbury (1985), Schele and Miller (1986:48–51), and Schele and Freidel 1990:413–414). In the case of glyph T1030, I follow Stuart (personal communication) in separating the meaning of the head form (Figure 10.1) from that of the full-body form (Figure 10.2). In the Cross-group texts, the former refers to acts of worship timed by the 819-day cycle, while the latter (which is always prefaced by a title) refers to the god Tahil or Kauil (GII or God K).[8] On Lady Egret see Schele and Freidel (1990:468) and D. Tedlock (1990). The astronomical interpretation of the Venus table of the Dresden Codex is standard (see Thompson 1972:66), while other astronomical interpretations follow the recent work of V. Bricker and H. Bricker (1986) for Mars at $-17.12$, Lounsbury (1989) for Jupiter at $1.6.14.11.2$, and Lounsbury (1983) for the joint Venus–Mars and Venus–Jupiter events that conclude the chronology. The dates for events from the Popol Vuh (PV) are inferred from the events that precede and follow them. Palenque dates from before the present era have been converted to the negative ring-date format of the Dresden Codex in order to facilitate comparison.

At the outset, the experimental chronology sheds light on the character of the senior member of a pair of gods, both of them referred to as GI in the Mayanist literature, who are mentioned on the tablet of the Cross. They share a phonetically written name that Lounsbury (1985:56–57) reads as "Hunahpu" (Figure 10.3). As he points out, this name comes from a highland Mayan language (rather than the language of Palenque) and appears in the Popol Vuh, where it is also shared by two different gods. The

*Figure 10.2* The god Tahil or Kauil as the full-body form of T1030, preceded by the rodent-bone title.

*Figure 10.3* The name Hunahpu written phonetically.

senior member of the pair is the father of the junior, implicitly in the Cross text and explicitly in the Popol Vuh. In my own presentation I have followed the practice of the authors of the Popol Vuh, who distinguish the father from the son by naming the former Hun Hunahpu (1 Hunahpu), after the day of the same name. At Palenque the equivalent day (1 Ahau) is given for the birth of the senior Hunahpu.

What is most striking about the first event of the chronology, the birth of Hun Hunahpu, is that it precedes the first recorded rising of Venus as the morning star by 780 days, an interval equivalent to an average Martian synodic period. In the idealized world of mythic time, then, whatever Martian event took place on −8.5.0 must have happened again on −6.2.0. To determine the position of Mars on those two dates we can move forward to −17.12, at which point Mars (by the mythic reckoning of the Dresden Codex) should go into retrograde motion.[9] The distance separating −8.5.0 and −17.12 is 2628 days, which is equivalent to three complete Martian periods (at 780 days each) plus 288 days. Today's astronomers reckon Martian retrograde motion as beginning 292 days (on average) after heliacal rising,[10] which leaves us with 4 extra days to account for. When we consider that the Dresden Mars table treats 78 days as the ideal interval for retrograde motion (V. Bricker and H. Bricker 1986:69) rather than 75 (today's astronomical figure), making that interval a day and a half longer at either end, we can reduce the already small number of extra days to 2 or 3 (depending on which way we round them to whole days). If the mythic event at −8.5.0 is indeed a heliacal rise of Mars, then −17.12 is quite a reasonable date for the onset of retrograde motion in a later Martian period, given an idealized system that was ultimately based on the naked-eye observation of an extremely variable planet.

If there was a mythic rise of Mars on −8.5.0, then there could have been a rise of both Mars and Venus on −6.2.0, the mythic beginning date of the Dresden Venus Table. This finding casts an entirely new light on the event described by Lounsbury (1983:12–16) as taking place on or near 10.5.6.4.0 1 Ahau 18 Kayab, in which Venus underwent a heliacal eastern rise while it was in conjunction with Mars. According to his argument, the 18 Kayab timing for the 1 Ahau starting date of the table was instituted on the basis of this particular occurrence,[11] and the combined 1 Ahau 18 Kayab date was then projected backward, by factors of both 780 and 584 (the periods of Mars and Venus), to the nearest available ring date. In this way, the makers of the table created a mythic precedent that would make an historical rise of Venus in proximity to Mars seem right on schedule. The difficulty with such an interpretation begins with the fact that the resultant ring date is located at an interval of precisely one Martian period after the birth date of Hun Hunahpu. The latter date was carved in stone at Palenque not only before the Dresden Codex was written, but two centuries before 10.5.6.4.0. Furthermore, Lounsbury arrived at this date by adding distance numbers to the 9.9.9.16.0 historical base date specified by the authors of the table, which falls in the year 623. If the table is at least as old as that, then a Venus table with similar characteristics could have been present in the books used by the authors of the Cross-group inscriptions, who finished their work in 690.

There is, of course, the possibility that the Palenque date −8.5.0 appears to have a Martian character solely because of our backward projections from the Dresden Mars and Venus tables, and that the books available at Palenque did not give it a Martian significance. An answer to that objection is given in the inscriptions of the Cross group itself: The interval between the birth of Hun Hunahpu (−8.5.0) and that of Tahil (1.18.5.4.0), who is the youngest member of the Palenque triad and may be one of his sons, is evenly divisible by 780 (see Schele and Freidel 1990:473). That gives −8.5.0 a Martian quality without any help from the Dresden Codex. We are now confronted with the real possibility that the event of 10.5.6.4.0 1 Ahau 18 Kayab, rather than serving as the starting point for retrospective dating by the authors of the Dresden Venus table, might rather have provided an historical commemoration of a joint heliacal rise of Mars and Venus that already had mythic status in the books of Palenque. If so, the commemoration was at best an approximate one, since, as Lounsbury admits (1983:13), Mars did not undergo its own heliacal rise until some days after that of Venus.[12]

There remains the question as to whether the Venus table in use at Palenque, to which we have only indirect clues, might have matched up with the one in the Dresden Codex. Part of the answer will come when we deal with Venus events that occur shortly after the era of ring dates. Even in the present context, however, there is a further significant interval between Palenque events and the ring date of the Dresden Venus table. In the text of the Cross tablet, a rite commemorating an 819-day cycle is performed on −6.15.0. This rite falls on the *tzolkin* date 1 Ahau, and it comes 260 days, or one complete *tzolkin*, before the 1 Ahau heliacal eastern rise of Venus at

−6.2.0. So once again, as in the case of the birth of Hun Hunahpu at −8.5.0, a date at Palenque measures off a meaningful interval with respect to the Dresden Venus table.

The next date on our experimental chronology is the appearance of the thin crescent of the newly waxing moon at −6.14.5, which is cited in the Temple of the Cross as preceding (by 5 days) the birth of Lady Egret.[13] Another such moon, cited in the Temple of the Sun as preceding (by 26 days) the birth of Xbalanque, comes at 1.18.5.2.0. In the Palenque inscriptions in general, 81 moons are reckoned as lasting 2392 days (Aveni 1980:169), yielding a figure of 29.530864 days for an average moon, and indeed 9410 moons of that length bridge the 277885-day interval between the waxing moons of −6.14.5 and 1.18.5.2.0 to the nearest whole day. In the preface of the Dresden eclipse table (pp. 51–58), 405 moons are reckoned as lasting 11960 days (Lounsbury 1978:796), yielding an average moon of precisely the same length as at Palenque.

The 819-day rite performed at −6.15.0 and the waxing of the moon beginning at −6.14.5 set the stage for the birth of Lady Egret at −6.14.0. She is destined to become the mother of two of the gods of the Palenque triad, Hunahpu and Xbalanque, and (though this is not stated explicitly) she may be the mother of Tahil as well (Schele 1987:123). Her name glyph (Figure 10.4) features the head of a heron or egret (Schele and Freidel 1990:468), and if I am correct in reading it as *sak bak' ha'*,[14] it refers specifically to the snowy egret and may be cognate with Xbaquiyalo (D. Tedlock 1990), the name given to the first wife of Hun Hunahpu in the Popol Vuh (D. Tedlock 1985:105). But it is the second wife of Hun Hunahpu who gives birth to Hunahpu and Xbalanque in the Popol Vuh, a goddess we might call Blood Moon. Her name is *xkik'*, which means "little (or precious) blood" but carries a pun on *ik'*, "moon." Lady Egret is also a moon goddess, and on the tablet of the Foliated Cross she performs the first of all bloodletting rituals (Schele and Freidel 1990:227, 245, 255).

All in all, in the period that runs from −8.5.0 to −6.2.0, we have a complete Mars period, an 819-day rite that falls in the right position to mark the start of one complete *tzolkin* that leads to the earliest recorded appearance of Venus, and the birth of a moon goddess. Assembled in this

*Figure 10.4* Lady Egret named as *sak bak' ha'*.

way, the ring dates from Palenque and Dresden give us a considerable foundation for Mayan calendrics in the brief span of 780 days. What is still lacking is any solar presence, beyond the mere fact that each of the *tzolkin* dates is followed by a date from the *haab*, the calendar that measures an invariable solar year of 365 days. The Dresden pages (25–28) that deal directly with the solar year carry no ring date. In the experimental chronology, intervals consisting of multiples of 365 separate the three events occurring on the *haab* date 18 Kayab, but these are accountable to the fact that five Venus periods of 584 days each have the same duration as 8 solar years of 365 days each. During any given passage across the Dresden table commencing on 18 Kayab, only one Venus event occurs on a date that has solar significance in and of itself. The event in question (in the second column on Dresden p. 50) is the western or evening appearance of Venus that falls on a day whose *tzolkin* name is always Ik (but with a variable number) and whose *haab* date is always 0 Zec. *Haab* dates with zero coefficients mark the beginnings (or "seatings") of each of the solar year's nineteen divisions, of which 18 have 20 days each and the last has 5. In the present case we are dealing with a western appearance of Venus that takes place at the beginning of the fifth division of each eighth solar year.

Counting from the Venus table ring date of −6.2.0, the first of all possible 0 Zec evening appearances of Venus takes place, after 2662 days, on 1.5.2 11 Ik 0 Zec. The solar year in question would have begun 80 days earlier, on 9 Ik 0 Pop. Although we have arrived at the eightieth day of this year by means of the Dresden Codex, it has brought us close to a date from the tablet of the Cross, namely 1.9.2 13 Ik 0 Ch'en. In addition to the fact that 0 Ch'en marks the seating of a division of the solar year, the number 1.9.2 (or 542) has a solar dimension all by itself, since it is the sum of the canonical Mayan values for six synodic moons (177 days) and one solar year (365 days). On this date, with the solar year that began on 9 Ik still in progress and the evening appearances of Venus that began on 11 Ik still occurring, Hun Hunahpu enters the sky to set up what the tablet calls his "eighth house" (Schele 1987:69). Among all the gods of the Cross group texts, only Hun Hunahpu does something on a date of unequivocal solar significance. He also has Martian credentials, but he is, at this particular moment in the story, taking a solar role, or at least setting the stage for a future solar deity.

Hun Hunahpu sets up his eighth house while the Dresden Venus calendar is running through the only one of its twenty stages that begins on one of the solar calendar's 19 seating days. Not only that, but the first stage in this particular run begins on 1 Ahau 18 Kayab. Here is further evidence in favor of the notion that this date might have had a Venusian significance not only in the Dresden Codex, but in the books of Palenque as well. In search of still more evidence, we might follow the Dresden table forward to whatever heliacal eastern rise of Venus immediately precedes the birth dates of the gods of the Palenque triad. The required distance from $-6.2.0$ 1 Ahau 18 Kayab (the first such rise) is 277400 days, taking us through seven complete runs of all thirteen rows of the table, plus four rows after that, and arriving at 1.18.4.8.0 7 Ahau 18 Kayab. Here it must be remembered that with a different distance to cover, we might have arrived at 12 Yax, 6 Zip, 5 Kankin, or 19 Xul (the alternative eastern rise dates occurring in the table). Instead we have come to 18 Kayab, which is where we started.

All by itself, finding an 18 Kayab rising of Venus near both ends of the interval between the births of Hun Hunahpu and Lady Egret, on the one hand, and the births of the triad, on the other, lends further support to the idea that it was not the makers of a 10.5.6.4.0 version of the Dresden table who first gave 18 Kayab its importance. The fact that we started off from 1 Ahau and arrived at 7 Ahau is also of interest here, since the Popol Vuh gives Hun Hunahpu a twin brother named Wukub Hunahpu (7 Hunahpu). Following their sacrifice by the lords of Xibalba, the Mayan underworld, they speak with "one mind" from a head that is described as belonging to both of them, the famous head in the calabash tree (D. Tedlock 1985:115). From this head they spit in the hand of Blood Moon, who becomes pregnant with Hunahpu and Xbalanque. The birth of these twins, as reckoned by the Palenque inscriptions, follows a 7 Ahau (or 7 Hunahpu) rising of Venus, as reckoned by the Dresden Codex.

If the merging of the persons of two gods in a single spitting head in a tree is to be understood as taking place on the occasion of the 7 Ahau eastern rise of Venus, it suggests a conjunction between Venus and some other planet.[15] A heliacal rise of Mars is still 280 days away at this point, but there is another planet for which we have a point from which to measure, and that is Jupiter. In the Temple of the Sun, a backward projection very much like those in the Dresden Codex gives 1.6.14.11.2 1 Ik 10 Tzec as a date that not only marks off an 819-day cycle, but the resumption of Jupiter's forward motion after a retrograde interval as well (Lounsbury 1989:246–47). There is no Jupiter table in the surviving codices, but there are enough clues to permit the reconstruction of the sort of table that might have been in use at Palenque, where the periodicity of Jupiter was reckoned at 399 days. Since the behavior of Jupiter is very similar to that of Mars and quite unlike that of Venus, the obvious model for a Jupiter table is the Dresden Mars table, which divides the Martian period into segments of equal length (V. Bricker and H. Bricker 1986:58) and accounts for retrograde motion in the process. In the case of the 399-day period of Jupiter, a division into 19 segments of 21 days each (see Table 10.2) would give this planet a systematic link with the 819-day cycle, which is divisible into 39 such segments. Each successive cycle would then advance with respect to Jupiter's period by one segment. The fact that 819-day intervals ceased to be reckoned after the year 815 (Lounsbury 1978:814) could help explain the absence of a table accounting for Jupiter in post-Classic codices.

As reckoned by our hypothetical Jupiter calendar, heliacal rise would occur within the first few days of the first of 19 segments, retrograde motion would fill segments 7 through 12 (reckoned at a total of 126 days),[16] and heliacal set would occur a few days before the coming of segment 19, leaving Jupiter out of sight for the whole of that segment. Starting from the resumption of Jovian forward motion at 1.6.14.11.2 and counting 82738 days to reach the 7 Ahau eastern rise of Venus at 1.18.4.8.0, we get 207 complete periods of 399 days each with a remainder of 145 days, just 2 days short of advancing Jupiter from segment 13 to segment 1, where its own rise would occur. So it would seem quite plausible that in the mythic astronomical world projected by Mayan books, the morning of 1.18.4.8.0 7 Ahau 18 Kayab saw a joint heliacal rise of Jupiter and Venus. If that is what the Popol Vuh is describing, then the two planets were close enough together to seem, for the moment, to be one. And when Hun Hunahpu and Wukub Hunahpu spoke "with one mind" and spit in the hand of Blood Moon, she conceived twins.

*Table 10.2* Idealized Divisions of Jupiter's Synodic Period

| Division and event | Day |
|---|---|
| 1 Heliacal rise | 0 |
| 2 | 21 |
| 3 | 42 |
| 4 | 63 |
| 5 | 84 |
| 6 | 105 |
| 7 Begin retrograde motion | 126 |
| 8 | 147 |
| 9 | 168 |
| 10 Opposition to the sun | 189 |
| 11 | 210 |
| 12 | 231 |
| 13 Resume forward motion | 252 |
| 14 | 273 |
| 15 | 294 |
| 16 | 315 |
| 17 | 336 |
| 18 | 356 |
| 19 Disappearance | 378 |

Here we must note that in the Dresden Codex the first of the adjustments that shifted the Venus calendar away from an 18 Kayab starting date took effect on 10.15.4.2.0 1 Ahau 18 Uo, which fell on or near a heliacal eastern rise of Venus when it was in conjunction with Jupiter (Lounsbury 1983:16–17).[17] The *tzolkin* date is 1 Ahau rather than 7 Ahau, and the solar date is 18 Uo rather than 18 Kayab, but this event does fall in the same column of the Venus table (the last of twenty columns) as the proposed Jupiter–Venus event of 1.18.4.8.0. We can well imagine that the story of the encounter between Blood Moon (or her Yucatec equivalent) and the two-heads-in-one might have entered into consideration when 10.15.4.2.0 1 Ahau 18 Uo was chosen for the first recorded reform of the Venus calendar.

It remains to be seen whether the moon could have been near Jupiter and Venus on the morning of 1.18.4.8.0, as Blood Moon was near the combined head of Hun and Wukub Hunahpu. Reckoning backward from the newly visible crescent moon at 1.18.5.2.0, we get 8 synodic moons with a remainder of 4 days, placing us (by Mayan reckoning) in the 25th day of a 29-day moon or the 26th day of a 30-day moon. By our own count that could mean a moon age of as many as 27 or 28 days, since the zero point for Mayan moon ages seems to have been the first visibility of the newly waxing crescent rather than conjunction, and since conjunction brings with it a period of invisibility lasting 2 or even 3 days (Aveni 1980:69). A moon that was 28 days past the moment of conjunction would be a very thin crescent (about to go into the dark phase), very close to the eastern horizon when Jupiter and Venus appeared together on the mythic dawn of 1.18.4.8.0 7 Ahau 18 Kayab.

The first of the datable events that take place during the interval between the proposed 7 Ahau 18 Kayab conception of Hunahpu and Xbalanque and their births is related in the Popol Vuh. At 6 months (literally moons), we are told, Blood Moon's pregnancy is discovered by her father (D. Tedlock 1985:115). Six months happens to be the length of the more common of the two types of groups into which lunar synodic periods are arranged in the Dresden eclipse table (the other being five), and the number of days assigned to such a group is nearly always 177 (see Lounsbury 1978:789–95). If we add 176 days to 7 Ahau in order to complete 6 months, we arrive at 1 Cib, or 1 Ajmak in Quiché, on which day the moon would be invisible and on the eve of reappearing. The day name Ajmak means "sinner" in Quiché, in a specifically sexual sense, and indeed Blood Moon is immediately accused of fornication by her father. In a scene following her flight from her father, which takes her out of the underworld (and into visibility as a waxing moon), she herself puns on this day name, saying, "It looks like I'm a sinner [*ajmak*]" (D. Tedlock 1985:118).

At a distance of 236 days from 7 Ahau (or 60 days from 1 Cib) stands the day 9 Cib (Ajmak), which is given in the Dresden Venus table as the date on which Venus shifts into the stage that follows the one that is marked by its heliacal rise on 7 Ahau. Mayanists are in the habit of describing this new stage as a disappearance interval, though on average (as reckoned by today's astronomers) it would begin 27 days too early, which is hardly a matter of a small observational discrepancy. As Aveni (1981:5) has pointed out, the explanation lies in the fact that the values the table gives for three of the four stages of the Venus period have been rounded off to conform with significant lunar intervals. In the case of the morning-star stage, the table is not telling us that Venus disappears after 236 days, but rather that Venus is visible in the east throughout eight lunar synodic intervals and disappears during the ninth interval, which is perfectly true. In our mythic chronology, the ninth interval would begin on 1.18.5.1.16 with a moon of about 26 days (by Mayan reckoning) or as many as 28 days (by our own).

There is one more event of interest before we reach the dates for the births of the gods who may have been conceived on 7 Ahau 18 Kayab, and that is a ritual performed by Blood Moon in the Popol Vuh. After her escape from her father's wrath, she seeks refuge with an old woman named Xmucane, the mother of Hun Hunahpu and Wukub Hunahpu. Xmucane finds it difficult to believe that the children in Blood Moon's womb are her own legitimate grandchildren; so she puts her to a test, sending her off to a field to gather a netful of maize. When Blood Moon finds only a single cornstalk in the entire field, she addresses it with these words:

> *X Toj, x Q'anil,*
> *x Kakaw, ix pu Tziya,*
> *at chajal re kecha Jun B'atz', Jun Chuen.*[18]

> Precious Toj, precious Q'anil,
> precious Cacao, and precious Cornmeal,
> thou guardian of the food of 1 B'atz', 1 Chuen.

The names of the owners of the field, B'atz' and Chuen, are (respectively) the Quiché and Yucatec names for the same day on the *tzolkin* and thus link the Popol Vuh with lowland Maya texts. But the names of interest in the present context are those of the 2 successive days Q'anil and Toj (Lamat and Muluc in Yucatec), whose calendrical order is reversed in Blood Moon's invocation.[19] This reversal is not a matter of a momentary lapse on the part of a scribe, since the order of cacao and cornmeal in the second line fits the order of the day names in the first line. Toj is a day of payment on the Quiché calendar (B. Tedlock 1982:115), and cacao pods once served as currency; Q'anil is a day for the harvest of maize (B. Tedlock 1982:114), and from that harvest comes cornmeal.

The explanation for the apparent reversal of Q'anil and Toj may lie in Blood Moon's lunar character, since by Lounsbury's reckoning (1978:796) the Dresden eclipse table begins on the day 13 Muluc (Toj in Quiché) and then, at the end of an interval of 11959 days, arrives at 12 Lamat (Q'anil in Quiché). In effect, then, Blood Moon might be invoking, by means of metonymy, the calendrical patrons of all possible moons or groups of moons, from the beginning to the end of an eclipse table.[20] Among the intervening dates specified in the Dresden table are Muluc and Lamat days with numbers other than 13 and 12, which helps explain why she invokes Toj and Q'anil in general rather than by specific numbers.

In order to locate Blood Moon's ritual within the interval separating the discovery of her pregnancy on 1 Ajmak (Cib) and the birth of her children, we may first note that if her encounter with the cornstalk is to be anything like her encounter with the calabash tree, it must take place at a time when the moon is reasonably near the horizon rather than high overhead or out of sight beneath the Earth. For other parameters we must appeal to the present-day practices of the Quiché Maya, beginning with the fact that they begin rituals by invoking the name of the current day. Blood Moon's mention of 2 adjacent days indicates that, even as she speaks, Q'anil (Lamat) is in the process of becoming Toj (Muluc), ideally in the middle of the night but in any case after sunset. The Q'anil–Toj pairs of days actually available to her would be numbered 13-1, 7-8, 1-2, and 8-9, in that order. Of these possibilities, the last, 8 Q'anil and 9 Toj, are of paramount importance on the calendar of the contemporary Quiché priest–shaman called *chuchqajaw* or "mother–father," who serves the ritual needs of the members of a lineage (B. Tedlock 1982:74–82, 114–15). On each 8 Q'anil, wherever it might fall during the solar year, the mother–father goes to a shrine at a cornfield to ask for an abundant harvest.[21] The following day, 9 Toj, is for paying up on ritual obligations that may have fallen into arrears during the past 260 days, and it concludes the *tzolkin* ritual cycle.

For Blood Moon (or at least for Lady Egret), the day 8 Q'anil (Lamat) comes 8 days after the newly waxing moon of 1.18.5.2.0, which gives a moon age (by our own reckoning) of 9 or 10 days. Such a moon would set in the west within an hour or so of midnight, nicely placing her ritual at the transition between 8 Q'anil and 9 Toj. The day 9 Toj (Muluc), in its turn, points us back to the Palenque texts in two different ways. First, it comes 249 days after the hypothetical heliacal rise of Jupiter on 1.18.4.8.0, falling just 3 days short of completing the first twelve 21-day segments of the Jovian period. The thirteenth segment is the one in which Jupiter resumes forward motion after a retrograde interval (see Table 2), an event whose importance is reiterated by various historical dates at Palenque (Lounsbury 1989). Second, an explicit mention of the day 9 Muluc appears on the jamb of the sanctuary door of the Temple of the Foliated Cross, where it serves as the name of a house (or temple) where the god Tahil (or an historical human surrogate) takes part in a ritual (Schele 1987:116). Indeed, 9 Muluc may be one of the names of the Temple of the Foliated Cross itself, given that this is the particular temple in which the birth of Tahil is recounted. This potential link between the Popol Vuh narrative and the Palenque inscriptions is strengthened by the probability that Toj (Muluc) was the day on which Tohil, the Quiché equivalent of Tahil, received offerings (D. Tedlock 1985:219, 365).

More striking than the calendrical tie between Blood Moon's ritual and the temple that records the birth of Tahil is the iconographic tie. The "foliated cross" that gives its name to this temple and occupies the center of the tablet inside its sanctuary is a single cornstalk, and its arms are two ears of corn with very long silk hanging down (Figure 10.5). The head at the top of the stalk has a mouth, ear ornaments, and forehead mirror like those associated with Tahil or Kauil, though the volutes of smoke or flame that often come from his forehead appear to have been transformed into the upper foliage and tassel of a cornstalk. [22] This would not be out of character

*Figure 10.5* The cornstalk in the Temple of the Foliated Cross, with the *k'an* sign at its base.

for him, since he is known from other contexts as a god of vegetation and agriculture (Stuart 1987:15–16).

To bring Blood Moon before the cornstalk at Palenque, all we have to do is imagine her pulling on the long silk and magically filling up her net, as she does in the Popol Vuh (D. Tedlock 1985:118–19). She carries this netful of corn back to Xmucane, who immediately runs to the field to see how she could have accomplished such a feat. At the foot of the single cornstalk, Xmucane sees the imprint left in the ground by Blood Moon's net. With great excitement, she reads this as a sign that Blood Moon is just what she claims she is: the legitimate bearer of the successors of Hun Hunahpu and Wukub Hunahpu. To understand Xmucane's interpretation, we must begin with the fact that she is the first of all *ajq'ij* or "daykeepers," which is to say calendrical diviners (D. Tedlock 1985:83). It happens that the Quiché term for the net whose imprint she sees is *k'at*, which is the same as the Quiché day name K'at, equivalent to Yucatec Kan (*k'an*). Written at the foot of the cornstalk in the Temple of the Foliated Cross, in place of the imprint of a net, is the so-called *k'an* cross (Figure 10.5), and *k'an* (in addition to being a day name) can be read in Yucatec as meaning either "maize" or "net" (see Barrera Vásquez 1980). So, whether we read the Popol Vuh or look at the Palenque tablet, we see a cornstalk with a sign at the foot of it, and the sign points to the day K'at/Kan.

What makes Xmucane so excited when she reads the day sign left by Blood Moon may be guessed from a third source, the Dresden Venus table. When Venus is finished with any eastern stage that begins on a day named Ahau (Hunahpu), its first return to the eastern sky always comes on a day named Kan (K'at). When Xmucane sees this day name, she knows, being a daykeeper, that Venus will rise again as the morning star, and that this event will become possible because Hun Hunahpu and Wukub Hunahpu, the sons she lost to the lords of Xibalba, will have legitimate heirs when Blood Moon's children are born. When we combine the legitimizing function of this episode with the Jovian aspect of the night on which it occurred, it helps us understand why Chan-Bahlum, who commissioned the Cross-group inscriptions, repeatedly timed the rites of his kingship (including two rites mentioned on the Foliated Cross tablet) to mark Jupiter's transition from retrograde to forward motion (Lounsbury 1989:248–54). The rhetoric of the inscriptions reveals his great concern to legitimize his line of descent, which had twice passed through women. Instead of attempting to obscure this problem, he enlarged it to mythic proportions, claiming none other than Lady Egret, the Palenque counterpart of Blood Moon, as the founder of his dynasty (Schele and Freidel 1990:252–60). Seen in this light, the cornstalk in the temple, complete with the sign at the foot of it, becomes an evocation of the first of all disputes about descent, a mythic dispute that was doubtless resolved in favor of Lady Egret and her unborn children.

When Blood Moon (or Lady Egret) completes her ritual before the cornstalk on 1.18.5.2.9 9 Muluc 2 Ceh, she is 13 days into the ninth month of the pregnancy that began when she went before the calabash tree on 1.18.4.8.0 7 Ahau 18 Kayab. Hunahpu, the first of her twin sons, is born 13 days after the cornstalk ritual, on 1.18.5.3.2 9 Ik 15 Ceh, or 262 days after his conception. This is close enough to 9 months to lend strong support to the idea that a 7 Ahau heliacal rise of Jupiter and Venus, accompanied by a moonrise, marked the start of Lady Egret's pregnancy, just as the spitting of the single head of 1 and 7 Ahau (Hunahpu) marked the start of Blood Moon's pregnancy in the Popol Vuh. Moreover, 262 days is exactly on target (by the measure of today's astronomy) as the average distance from the first appearance of Venus as morning star to the last, yielding a total of 263 days of visibility.

When we think of Hunahpu as being conceived and born by the exact measure of the visibility of Venus as morning star, he becomes the best candidate, among the members of the triad, for a role as the god (or one of the gods) of Venus. Indeed, among the contemporary Quiché, one of the names for Venus in its eastern appearances is Hunahpu (B. Tedlock, Chapter 1 of this volume). At the very same time, Hunahpu is the only member of the Palenque triad who even comes close, from a calendrical point of view, to having solar credentials. For one thing, he is the namesake of his father, who sets up his house on a day that seats a division of the solar year. For another, the *tzolkin* date of his birth, 9 Ik, is the same as the *tzolkin* date that began the year in which his father acted on 13 Ik. In Fact, Hunahpu is the only member of the triad to be born on one of the 4 *tzolkin* days capable of beginning a new solar year. This day was not the bearer of the particular year in which he was born (that was 8 Manik), but it was the bearer of the year (beginning on 7 Ik) in which he and Xbalanque were conceived.

The calendrical evidence for Hunahpu's solar character, all by itself, might seem merely circumstantial, but the stories told in both the Temple of the Sun and the Popol Vuh bring the matter home quite clearly. The Sun tablet tells us that, in one of the rites of kingship, Chan-Bahlum himself "became the sun," and that he accomplished this through the agency of Hunahpu—not Hun Hunahpu, not Lady Egret, not Xbalanque, not Tahil, but Hunahpu (Schele 1987:96).[23] As for the Popol Vuh, it assigns the role of the sun, on the occasion of the first of all the sunrises of the present era, to this same Hunahpu (D. Tedlock 1985:159–60).

The second member of the Palenque triad, born at 1.18.5.3.6 13 Cimi

19 Ceh, is Xbalanque. Like his brother Hunahpu, he has solar credentials, but they reside in his names rather than in his calendrical connections. On the Sun tablet, his titles and names include Ahau Kin, "Lord Sun"; Balam Ahau, "Jaguar (or Hidden) Lord"; and a possible reference to Xibalba (Schele 1987:91–93). The key to his Popol Vuh name, Xbalanque, lies in the fact that contemporary speakers of Kekchi (a Quichean language) call the sun *b'alamq'e* when it is hidden at night, meaning "jaguar (or hidden) sun," whereas they call the daytime sun *saq'e* ("light, or white, sun") (see Haeserijn 1979).[24] It would seem, then, that if Xbalanque is a solar deity, he is specifically the god of the underworld or nighttime sun. That leaves the sun of the surface of the Earth or the daytime to his brother Hunahpu, who indeed assumes the solar role at sunrise, as we have already seen. Such an interpretation is consistent with the fact that, whenever one of the twins takes the lead in the Popol Vuh, it is Hunahpu who does so when they are on the surface of the Earth, whereas Xbalanque is the one who always knows what to do when they are down below in Xibalba (D. Tedlock 1985:91, 143–45, 153).

Xbalanque also has a lunar aspect to his character, and here again the Palenque inscriptions turn out to be compatible with the Popol Vuh. His birth comes 266 days after his conception on 7 Ahau 18 Kayab, which is the nearest whole-day equivalent of nine synodic moons. His twin brother Hunahpu may have been 4 days premature, but Xbalanque comes right on schedule, the kind of baby who would be a delight to any Quiché midwife (see B. Tedlock 1985:85). Both of them are conceived with a thin crescent moon near Jupiter and Venus on the eastern horizon, but after that, while Hunahpu's gestation is being marked off by Venus, Xbalanque's is meanwhile being marked off by the moon. In this sense Xbalanque has a closer relationship to the moon than the other members of the triad.

As for the Popol Vuh, it goes so far as to give Xbalanque the role of the moon in the same sentence in which it gives the sun to Hunahpu (D. Tedlock 1985:159–60). This has caused much discussion among Mayanists, especially those who expect a list of planets and stars to match up with a list of gods on a 1:1 basis, who expect the moon to be the sole responsibility of a goddess, and who automatically dismiss the Popol Vuh as un-Maya whenever it fails to conform to their preconceived notions as to what is Maya in the pure (and unaffixed) sense. The embarrassing fact is that the idea of a male lunar deity is not a late highland import from Mexico, as some have thought, but is evidenced by an early Classic Mayan conch shell trumpet. Twin brothers are incised on this trumpet, one of them identifiable on iconographic grounds as Hun Ahau (Hunahpu). The other brother is seated within the moon (Figure 10.6), and he is named in

*Figure 10.6* Jaguar Moon Lord, incised on an early Classic conch shell trumpet.

the accompanying inscription as *balam u ahaw*, Jaguar Moon Lord (Schele and Miller 1986:306, 309).[25]

   There remains a question as to precisely how the same god who assumes responsibility for the night (invisible) sun might also take a lunar role. What if this night sun were to become visible, on occasion, over the surface of the Earth? What would it look like at night? During the day? A workable answer to the night question is provided by the contemporary Quiché, who metaphorically refer to the full moon as *q'ij*, "sun" (B. Tedlock 1983:66). They point out that the full moon is like the sun in being a complete disk, in brightly lighting the paths of those who wish to walk about, and in measuring off the whole world in one single and highly visible pass across the sky. As for the daytime appearance of the underworld sun, a possible answer to that question is suggested by the Popol Vuh. When Hunahpu and Xbalanque leap into the fire, preparing themselves for their future solar and lunar roles, they lock their arms together, facing each other (D. Tedlock 1985:149). That suggests a solar eclipse, a notion supported by ethnohistorical evidence for an eclipse agent who is like Xbalanque in taking the form of a jaguar (Closs 1989:411). So the full answer to our double riddle might be this: The night sun seen in the night is a solid disk of white light, and the night sun seen in the day is a solid disk of darkness. As for all the other phases of the moon, which is to say the times of waxing and waning, those can perfectly well continue to be the responsibility of Xbalanque's mother.

   The third member of the Palenque triad, born 14 days after Xbalanque on 1.18.5.4.0 1 Ahau 13 Mac, is Tahil or Smoking Mirror, variously referred to in the Mayanist literature as GII, God K, Kauil, and the Manikin Scepter. Tahil of Palenque (Schele and Freidel 1990:414) is very much like Tohil of the Popol Vuh (D. Tedlock 1985:174–87) in being the god of kingship and blood sacrifice. In contrast with Hunahpu and Xbalanque, whose mother is named at Palenque and whose parentage is completely accounted for in the Popol Vuh, Tahil is like Tohil in having no explicit parentage at all. He is, in fact, a being of a fundamentally different nature from the other two members of the so-called triad. Again and again, the Hunahpu and Xbalanque of Classic art act together in mythic scenes just as they do in the Popol Vuh, and even their head glyphs are homologous (Schele and Miller 1986:50–51). Tahil/Tohil, who is absent from these same scenes, appears in the company of kings, and he takes the form of a physical object in their possession. In the case of Tahil, the object is the Manikin Scepter, and he may also appear on the Double-Headed Serpent Bar that serves the same function as a scepter (Schele and Freidel 1990:414). Tohil, for his part, takes the form of an icon carried in a backpack or set up in a temple by members of the ruling Quiché lineage (D. Tedlock 1985:365).

We might well wonder whether Tahil's "birth," as recorded at Palenque, is of the same nature as the births of Hunahpu and Xbalanque. The sheer spacing of the three events puts Hanahpu and Xbalanque closer to one another than either of them is to Tahil, but a more impressive contrast emerges from the astronomical dimensions of the events. Both Hunahpu and Xbalanque are born when a heavenly body is making a final eastern appearance before an interval of invisibility, Venus in the case of Hunahpu and the moon in the case of Xbalanque. Tahil, on the other hand, appears in the world when Mars rises after a disappearance interval, which raises the possibility that his "birth" is in fact this very rising, as contrasted with the more biological character of the births of Hunahpu and Xbalanque, whose timing fits a term of pregnancy that begins (rather than ends) with rising, specifically the rising of Jupiter and Venus.

Yet another difference between Tahil and what we may well call the twins (rather than calling them the other two members of a set of triplets) emerges from a consideration of the lunar dimension of all three births. Both Hunahpu and Xbalanque are born at the time of a waning moon, almost gone in the case of Xbalanque, whereas Tahil comes into the world with a waxing moon, 10 days old (or 12 by our reckoning) and therefore almost full (see Table 10.1). When we consider this contrast in the light of the contemporary Quiché practice of timing both the planting and harvest of maize so as to reach completion while the moon is waxing but not yet full (B. Tedlock 1985:85–86), we can further understand the contrast between the twins and Tahil. In the Popol Vuh, Hunahpu and Xbalanque are told, "Gardening is not your job" (D. Tedlock 1985:128), and at Palenque their births are indeed related in temples other than the one with the cornstalk, which is where Tahil comes into the world.

Tahil's closest apparent relationships are to Hun Hunahpu, with whom he shares a 1 Ahau birth date marked by a heliacal rise of Mars, and to the object that occupies the central position in his temple, a deified stalk of maize that bears a striking resemblance to himself. That this stalk may be one of his own guises is further suggested by the 9 Muluc (Toj) date on the doorway that leads to it. Days named Toj were sacred to his Popol Vuh counterpart (Tohil), and 9 Toj in particular works well as a date for the ritual Blood Woman performs before a solitary cornstalk. If this stalk, whether at Palenque or in the Popol Vuh, is indeed a manifestation of Tahil/Tohil, then he at least remains in his character as a sacred object.

With all the divine births of the Cross-group inscriptions in place, we may return to the question as to whether the Venus table in the books of Palenque might have been similar to the one in the Dresden Codex, even to the extent of matching heliacal rises of Venus on *tzolkin* days named Ahau with the *haab* date 18 Kayab. We have seen that the birth of Hun Hunahpu on −8.5.0 and the 819-day ritual of −6.15.0 are both separated from the −6.2.0 1 Ahau 18 Kayab ring date of the Dresden table by significant intervals, and that a combination of Palenque and Dresden reckoning produces a joint heliacal rise of Mars and Venus on −6.2.0. Moreover, Hun Hunahpu seats the eighth division of the *haab* while the Dresden Venus calendar is on a run that begins with 1 Ahau 18 Kayab, and he does so during the only Venus stage that begins with a *haab* seating day. Still further, as measured by the Dresden table, the last heliacal eastern rise of Venus before the births of the Palenque triad falls on 7 Ahau 18 Kayab and brings with it, by Palenque reckoning, a heliacal rise of Jupiter and a moonrise as well. And finally, if we assume 7 Ahau 18 Kayab to be the conception date of Hunahpu and Xbalanque, which makes sense in terms of the two heads that appear as one to Blood Moon in the Popol Vuh, then Hunahpu is born by the exact measure of the visibility of the morning-star Venus that appeared at his conception, while Xbalanque is born by the exact measure of nine synodic moons. On all of these points, a Venus table with the ring date −6.2.0 1 Ahau 18 Kayab, as given in the Dresden Codex, makes perfect sense in the context of the Cross-group inscriptions.

On the basis of the evidence presented here, it seems quite unlikely that the heliacal eastern rise of Venus in conjunction with Mars that took place on or near 10.5.6.4.0 1 Ahau 18 Kayab could have served as the foundation date for the Dresden Venus table. That historical event, occurring some days before Mars underwent its own heliacal rise, was at best a rough approximation of a hypothetical event whose mythic value had been established even before the tablets of the Cross group were inscribed. As a consequence, it can no longer serve as the cornerstone of the case in favor

of a Mayan–Julian correlation constant of 584285, as it does for Lounsbury. Indeed, the entire weight of his argument in favor of a 10.5.6.4.0
observational base for the Venus table now shifts to the rises of both Jupiter
and Venus that took place on or near 10.15.4.2.0 1 Ahau 18 Uo (Lounsbury 1983:16–17).[26] On the former date, we may now suggest, the Maya
did absolutely nothing about their Venus calendar, whereas on the latter
date, as Lounsbury has already demonstrated, they took action to bring it
into line with observable phenomena. The canonical table lists 1 Ahau 18
Uo as a date for the disappearance of Venus after an evening-star stage (see
the third column of Dresden p. 47), but on 10.15.4.2.0 the authors of a
revised version reckoned this as the date of a heliacal eastern rise instead
(belonging in the last column of p. 50), thus leaving the overall *tzolkin*
framework of the table undisturbed while altering its relationship to the
*haab*.

Judging from Lounsbury's own graphic presentation of the data
(1983:10), the heliacal rise of Venus corresponding to 10.15.4.2.0 1 Ahau
18 Uo took place on 4 or 5 December, 1129; by Aveni's independent
calculations (Chapter 3 of this volume), it took place on 4 December. Yet
by Lounsbury's 584285 correlation, 10.15.4.2.0 fell on 6 December, which
would mean that Mayan astronomers let their Venus calendar run a day or
two late *even in the act of correcting it*. Such a possibility is all the more
remarkable in the light of his own earlier argument that they favored
"negative errors over positive ones, or early predictions over late ones"
(Lounsbury 1978:789). By such reasoning, even a 584283 correlation figure
would be too large, since (by the calculations of both Lounsbury and Aveni)
it would make the subsequent correction of the Venus calendar on
11.0.3.1.0 right on target rather than early, and the 11.5.2.0.0 correction a
day late. On the other hand, by Lounsbury's later (1983) reasoning, which
is that the Venus calendar must have at least one point of zero observational
error, the best correlation figure is clearly 584283, producing not one but
two heliacal rises of Venus that fall precisely on target, the first on
10.15.4.2.0 1 Ahau 18 Uo (by Aveni's reckoning) and the second on
11.0.3.1.0 1 Ahau 13 Mac (by both their reckonings), with a third rise
falling just one day after 11.5.2.0.0 1 Ahau 3 Xul into the bargain. Revi-
sions of the Venus calendar on these three dates, unlike 10.5.6.4.0 1 Ahau
18 Kayab, are a matter of record rather than supposition.

Thompson, who broadly considered all the evidence available to him
and had a healthy respect for the historical and ethnographic record, finally
came down on the side of 584283 (1960:303–4). Edmonson, after an even
broader survey of the record, has reached the same conclusion (1988:19–

20, 167, 196). As for the ethnographic evidence, there are 57 highland Guatemalan communities, speaking four different Mayan languages belonging to two separate groups (Quichean and Mamean), that keep the *tzolkin* today (Miles 1952; B. Tedlock 1982:92). Their calendars, which are in synchrony with one another, point unanimously to the same figure, 584283. If the higher figure were to be correct, there would have to be a time in the past when some of the Maya, rather than making occasional adjustments to astronomical tables after the manner *actually documented* in the Dresden Codex, instead found it useful to move the foundation upon which all these tables were built, which is to say the *tzolkin*. None of the partisans of the higher correlation figure has even raised this awkward problem, to say nothing of offering a solution.

When it comes to the mythic times that lie close on either side of 13.0.0.0.0, the Palenque texts and the Dresden Codex show a remarkable degree of commensurability, whether at the level of astronomical intervals or at that of the *tzolkin*, and both sources are commensurable, in turn, with *tzolkin* dates from the Popol Vuh and contemporary Quiché practice. As a counterpoint to the ceaseless litany of a narrowly conceived Classic Maya collapse, we may now wish to sing the praises of a single literate and highly coherent tradition that joins the books of Palenque and Copán with the Dresden Codex and the Popol Vuh, a tradition that has been carried forward orally and is currently finding its way back into writing among the Quiché (see B. Tedlock, Chapter 1 of this volume).

As for time in the historical sense, the scheduling of various royal rites at Palenque and other Classic sites, the writing of corrective prefaces for various Dresden tables, and the balancing of observations with formal calendrical concerns in modern Quiché rites (B. Tedlock 1983, 1985) all give ample testimony to a long-standing Mayan concern with actually occurring astronomical events. But as Aveni (1981:13) has pointed out, archaeoastronomical research that centers on observational questions tends to reduce Mayan thought to an approximation of our own. A direct counterbalance to this tendency is offered by the study of the dates Mayans projected backward into mythic times by means of the long count, or fixed within the eternal structure of the *tzolkin*, or both. Such dates open a pathway from practice into theory, from applied astronomy into pure astronomy. What makes Mayan theory most different from ours is that, with the Maya, we are not transported into a lifeless world but rather remain in the realm of beings who think and speak and act, all the way back to the first of all daykeepers, the one the Popol Vuh calls *Ratit Q'ij, Ratit Saq,* "Grandmother of Day, Grandmother of Light."

## NOTES

1. This quotation, which I have emended, is from folio 1r of the Popol Vuh manuscript, which is reproduced in facsimile in Ximénez (1973) and accurately paleographed in Schultze Jena (1944). For these and other italicized words from Quichean languages (including Quiché, Cakchiquel, and Kekchi), I have used the new orthography decided upon by native speakers of those languages (see Academia de las Lenguas Mayas de Guatemala 1988). Sounds are approximately as in Spanish, except that *q* is like Hebrew *qoph*, *tz* is like English *ts*, *x* is like English *sh*, and ' indicates the glottal stop (when it follows a vowel) or glottalization (when it follows a consonant).

2. I follow V. Bricker and H. Bricker (1986:54) in using the Modified Thompson 2 correlation constant of 584283, for reasons which will become obvious. Christian dates are Julian.

3. For evidence that ring dates were intended as statements of long-count positions rather than as mere distance numbers, see Closs (1986:352).

4. Both the Popol Vuh and the Annals of the Cakchiquels call this city Tulan, a name that is both Mexican and (so far as is known at present) post-Classic, but it could have been attributed to a Classic city posthumously, so to speak. Indeed, the name suggests *tolan*, meaning "abandoned place" in both Quiché and Cakchiquel. As to the bat, I read the relevant passage in the Annals of the Cakchiquels (Brinton 1885:par. 5) as *Xa jun chi sotz' chapb'al ru chijol ri Tulan*, "Just a bat was the insignia of the lordship of Tulan."

5. The term in the text of the Popol Vuh is *che' ab'aj*, which I once rendered as "wood and stone" (D. Tedlock 1985:169–70) but would handle differently now. It is an exact translation of the Cholan term for stele, which is given as *te tun* in Copán texts (Schele and Stuart 1986).

6. No one has a better sense of the importance of the tablet in the Temple of the Cross than Linda Schele, and I thank her for insisting that I work on it during the 1989 Advanced Maya Hieroglyphic Writing Workshop at Texas.

7. At the Colgate conference that served as the starting point for the present volume, Aveni specifically urged a closer look at the ring dates in the Dresden Codex, and I am pleased to have followed his suggestion here.

8. All drawings are by Linda Schele.

9. Since the Mars table was aimed primarily at predicting the onset of Martian retrograde motion, and since the earliest historical date of entry into the table is closer to that event than to any other station in the synodic period of Mars (V. Bricker and H. Bricker 1986:57, 61), I reason that the table's mythic ring date also refers to the onset of retrograde motion.

10. These and other contemporary astronomical figures are taken or extrapolated from Aveni (1980:89).

11. Lounsbury (1983:9) considered this to be "a unique event in historical time," but Aveni has pointed out to me that the rarity of an astronomical event is a function of the narrowness with which it is defined. In the present case, Lounsbury (1983:12–13) laid much importance on the closeness of the conjunction between

Mars and Venus, even though it could not have been observed (Mars had not yet completed its disappearance interval at the time).

12. According to the calculations of H. Bricker (personal communication), the gap between these two rises was at least 26 days.

13. Following the initial series date 12.19.13.4.0 (equivalent to −6.14.0), the inscription says that "five days ago (*hobix*) the moon had been born" (Schele 1987:64).

14. For italicized Yucatec words, I follow the orthography of Barrera Vásquez (1980), except for such common Mayanist concepts as *katun*, *tzolkin*, and *haab*.

15. Elsewhere I have argued that this tree was in the west and that the head was the evening star (D. Tedlock 1985:40), but now, for obvious reasons, the tree looks better in the east, though the head remains the planet Venus.

16. Like the interval assigned to Martian retrograde motion by the Dresden Codex, this interval is more generous than the one reckoned by today's astronomers (120 days).

17. The distance between 1.18.4.8.0 and 10.15.4.2.0, because it includes a corrective interval, is neither divisible by the idealized period of Jupiter nor that of Venus. According to H. Bricker (personal communication), Jupiter would not have become visible until several days after the heliacal rise of Venus on 10.15.4.2.0, but Mayan astronomers could have inferred that Jupiter had been very near Venus on that date.

18. This quotation is from folio 17r of the Popol Vuh manuscript and incorporates my own emendations; see Note 1 for sources and orthography.

19. While working on my translation of the Popol Vuh, I discarded the possibility of a calendrical interpretation of Blood Moon's prayer because of this reversal (see D. Tedlock 1985:118 for the result).

20. If this is correct, then the Dresden version of the eclipse table would not be transitional or corrective, as Lounsbury (1978:796) has suggested, but quite possibly canonical.

21. In lowland Maya texts, the maize god is the patron of the number eight (Thompson 1970:289).

22. There is no difference between this head and the glyph Schele (1987:116) identifies as God K at position A-6 on the sanctuary door jamb of the Temple of the Foliated Cross, save that the former is in front view and the latter in profile.

23. To this it may be added that at Quirigua, GI appears as the number four, which is often personified as the sun god (Schele and Miller 1986:306, n. 3).

24. Lounsbury's argument (1985:52–53) that the -*que* in Xbalanque might be *q'e* or "sun" is confirmed by the source cited here, which was not available to him.

25. It should also be noted that the jaguar god appears as the face of the moon on Glyph C of the lunar series (Schele and Miller 1986:306).

26. Lounsbury first made this argument at the 1982 International Congress of Americanists, before he had discovered the Jupiter–Venus conjunction on or near 10.15.4.2.0. He added his new finding to the published version (1983) of his congress paper, but without reconsidering his arguments for the importance of 10.5.6.4.0.

REFERENCES

Academia de las Lenguas Mayas de Guatemala, 1988. *Lenguas mayas de Guatemala: documento de referencia para la pronunciación de los nuevos alfabetos oficiales* (Guatemala: Instituto Indigenista Nacional).

Aveni, A. F., 1980. *Skywatchers of Ancient Mexico* (Austin: University of Texas Press).

—, 1981. "Archaeoastronomy in the Maya Region: A Review of the Past Decade," *Journal of The History of Astronomy* **12**, Archaeoastronomy (3):1–16.

Barrera Vásquez, A., 1980. *Diccionario maya cordemex, maya-español, español-maya* (Mérida: Ediciones Cordemex).

Bricker, V. R., and H. M. Bricker, 1986. *The Mars Table in the Dresden Codex*. Middle American Research Institute Publications **57**:51–80.

—, 1988. "The Seasonal Table in the Dresden Codex and Related Almanacs," *Journal of the History of Astronomy* **19**, Archaeoastronomy (12):1–62.

Brinton, D. G., 1885. *The Annals of the Cakchiquels* (Philadelphia: Library of Aboriginal American Literature).

Closs, M. P., 1986. "The Mathematical Notation of the Maya," in *Native American Mathematics*, edited by Michael P. Closs, pp. 291–369 (Austin: University of Texas Press).

—, 1989. "Cognitive Aspects of Ancient Maya Eclipse Theory," in *World Archaeoastronomy*, edited by A. F. Aveni, pp. 389–415 (Cambridge: Cambridge University Press).

Edmonson, M. S., 1988. *The Book of the Year: Middle American Calendrical Systems* (Salt Lake City: University of Utah Press).

Haeserijn V., E., 1979. *Diccionario k'ekchi' español* (Guatemala: Piedra Santa).

Lounsbury, F. G., 1978. "Maya Numeration, Computation, and Calendrical Astronomy," *Dictionary of Scientific Biography* **25**(1):759–818.

—, 1983. "The Base of the Venus Tables of the Dresden Codex, and its Significance for the Calendar-Correlation Problem," in *Calendars in Mesoamerica and Peru: Native American Computations of Time*, edited by Anthony F. Aveni and Gordon Brotherston, pp. 1–26. BAR International Series 174 (Oxford: British Archaeological Reports).

—, 1985. "The Identities of the Mythological Figures in the Cross Group Inscriptions of Palenque," in *Fourth Palenque Round Table*, edited by Merle Greene Robertson and Elizabeth P. Benson, pp. 45–58 (San Francisco: Pre-Columbian Art Research Institute).

—, 1989. "A Palenque King and the Planet Jupiter," in *World Archaeoastronomy*, edited by A. F. Aveni, pp. 246–59 (Cambridge: Cambridge University Press).

Miles, S. W., 1952. "An Analysis of Modern Middle American Calendars: A Study in Conservation," in *Acculturation in the Americas*, edited by Sol Tax, pp. 273–84 (Chicago: University of Chicago Press).

Paxton, M., 1986. "Codex Dresden: Stylistic and Iconographic Analysis of a Maya Manuscript," Ph.D. dissertation in Art History, University of New Mexico.

Roys, R. L., 1967. *The Book of Chilam Balam of Chumayel* (Norman: University of Oklahoma Press).

Schele, L., 1987. *Notebook for the Maya Hieroglyphic Writing Workshop at Texas* (Austin).

Schele, L., and D. Freidel, 1990. *A Forest of Kings: The Untold Story of the Ancient Maya* (New York: William Morrow).

Schele, L., and M. E. Miller, 1986. *The Blood of Kings: Dynasty and Ritual in Maya Art* (Forth Worth: Kimbell Art Museum).

Schele, L., and D. Stuart, 1986. "Te-Tun as the Glyph for 'Stela,'" *Copán Notes* 1.

Schultze Jena, L. S., 1944. *Popol Vuh: Das heilige Buch der Quiché-Indianer von Guatemala* (Stuttgart: W. Kohlhammer).

Stuart, D., 1987. "Ten Phonetic Syllables," *Research Reports on Ancient Maya Writing* 14 (Washington: Center for Maya Research).

Tedlock, B., 1982. *Time and the Highland Maya* (Albuquerque: University of New Mexico Press).

—, 1983. "Quichean Time Philosophy," in *Calendars in Mesoamerica and Peru: Native American Computations of Time*, edited by Anthony F. Aveni and Gordon Brotherston, pp. 59–72. BAR International Series 174 (Oxford: British Archaeological Reports).

—, 1985. "Hawks, Meteorology, and Astronomy in Quiché Maya Agriculture," *Archaeoastronomy* 8:80–88.

Tedlock, D., 1985. *Popol Vuh: The Mayan Book of the Dawn of Life* (New York: Simon & Schuster).

—, 1989. "Writing and Reflection among the Maya," 1992 *Lecture Series Working Papers* 4 (College Park: University of Maryland Department of Spanish and Portuguese).

—, 1990. "Drums, Egrets, and the Mother of The Gods: Remarks on the Tablet of the Cross at Palenque," *U Mut Maya* 3:13–14.

Thompson, J.E.S., 1960. *Maya Hieroglyphic Writing* (Norman: University of Oklahoma Press).

—, 1970. *Maya History and Religion* (Norman: University of Oklahoma Press).

—, 1972. *A Commentary on the Dresden Codex* (Philadelphia: American Philosophical Society).

Tozzer, A. M., 1941. *Landa's Relación de las Cosas de Yucatán*. Papers of the Peabody Museum of American Archaeology and Ethnology 18 (Cambridge, Mass.: Peabody Museum).

Ximénez, F., 1967. *Escolios a las historias del orígen de los indios*. Sociedad de Geografía e Historia de Guatemala, publicación especial 13 (Guatemala).

—, 1973. *Popol Vuh*. Fascimile edition with paleography and notes by Agustín Estrada Monroy (Guatemala: José de Pineda Ibarra).

# II

# Lessons of the Mayan Sky: A Perspective from Medieval Europe

CHARLES O. FRAKE

*[Kalendarium] est intolerabilis omni sapienti, et horribilis omni astro-nomo, et derisibilis ab omni computista.*

The calendar is intolerable to every scholar, and horrible for every astronomer, and ridiculous to every computationist.

ROGER BACON, *Op. ter.*, cap. 1 xvii[1]

Mayan astronomy and calendrics represent a supreme achievement of the human intellect. To appreciate this achievement we must tax our own minds to comprehend the mathematical complexities of Mayan calendrics and also the astronomy of celestial appearances as the Mayans saw them, then and there. This can only be achieved by painstaking scholarship such as we see in this volume. But the lessons of this work go beyond the Mayan world. Because of the necessary complexity and detail of these chapters, the non-Mayanist may find it difficult to discern the issues of general concern. As a non-Mayanist with a professional interest in the astronomies of other peoples, I argue here that it is precisely because of their careful attention to detail, in their concern to get it right, that these chapters make such powerful arguments relevant to general issues of the human sciences.[2]

A major issue directly addressed in the last section of this volume is the relation between the Mayan tradition of calendric astronomy and that of Western Europe, with which it came in contact in the sixteenth century.

The importance of studying this issue is not simply to disentangle in later documents what is Mayan from what is European. It is also to compare the similarities and differences of two systems developed independently of each other and situated within very different social systems and cultural frameworks. To explore and exploit this connection, I will illustrate some of the specific issues brought up by these Mayanist studies by comparing them with medieval European calendrics.

## Counting and Naming Days

> . . . the calendar is a system of names that have taken on a life of
> their own." J. D. North, 1989, p. 39

The simplest and perhaps most obvious system for naming and counting days has only rarely been employed in world calendars. It would simply count days starting somewhere at day zero. The Mayan "long count," which began on a day in 3114 B.C., long before the first known recorded date, is one example. Another is the Western astronomers' system of Julian day numbers, which begins on 1 January 4713 B.C. This modern scientific system is not without its own peculiar irrationalities. It was originally proposed in 1582 by an Italian Protestant scholar, Joseph Scaliger, as a cycle of 7980 years.[3] The Mayan long count also was set up as a cycle, one of more than 5000 years. A practical disadvantage of long counts is that eventually they require large numbers (I am writing this on Julian Day 2448199). The Mayans had the advantage of a superb number system for concisely representing and calculating large numbers. Their contemporaries in Rome and the medieval West were not so fortunate.

For all its precision, the Mayan long count was only one component in a date. The Mayans, like all calendar-makers, felt the need for more than a single number to accord a day its full identity. A calendar is thus always more than a *count* of days. It is also a *classification* of days, so that any given day is in certain respects the "same" as some other day at some other time. Thus, "Christmas Eve, Tuesday, 24 December 1387 Julian (Figure 11.1) under a full moon," is in some respects like other Christmas Eves, like other holiday eves, other Tuesdays, days in other Decembers, other 24th days of the month, other days in the year 1387 Julian, or other days under a full moon.[4] And it is very much like all Christmas eves that fall on Tuesdays under a full moon. The same point could be made with reference to a Mayan date such as 5 Lamat 1 Mol (9.9.2.4.8.). The way to classify a day, to give it an identity and make it meaningful to human lives, is to

### Dec 1387 JULIAN

| Sun | Mon | Tue | Wed | Thu | Fri | Sat |
|-----|-----|-----|-----|-----|-----|-----|
| 1 | 2 | 3 | 4 | 5 | 6 | 7 |
| 8 | 9 | 10* | 11 | 12 | 13+ | 14 |
| 15 | 16 | 17 | 18 | 19 | 20 | 21 |
| 22 | 23 | **24** | 25 | 26 | 27 | 28 |
| 29 | 30 | 31 | | | | |

*true new moon
+ ecclesiastical new moon

*Figure 11.1* December 1387, Julian. (*) True new moon. (+) Ecclesiastical new moon.

establish its position with respect to a number of differently based counts of days. In both the Mayan and European tradition, days are distinguished by a combination of numbers and sequentially ordered names. In medieval Europe, days were distinguished by weekday name, number, or key letter; by position in relation to a named feast day (such as the eve of Christmas); by its position in the month, either numbered as we do now or, more commonly, following the Roman system of names and backward counts, whereby 24 December becomes 9 Kalendae January. As the dictionary definition of the day called *nonae* suggests, the system is not simple.

> *nonae, -arum,* f. the nones; the fifth day in all the months (except March, May, July, and October, when it was the seventh); so called from being the ninth day (counting inclusively) before the ides.
>
> Cassell's *New Latin Dictionary*

Figure 11.2 shows the Roman days in the common medieval calendar format for the month of January for any Julian year. The cumbersomeness of Roman numerals may well have contributed to the fact that the Roman day count never required a number greater than XVIIII.[5]

As that calendar page informs us, there are yet more ways to name a day. The majority of the days of the year had personal names attached, names of saints whose day of birth, martyrdom, or "translation" were occasions for "feasts," holy days of the church. The few nameless days on the calendar could be identified by their position with respect to a named day. Figure 11.2 lists 21 feasts.[6] The italics represents the red ink of medieval scribes used to mark the "red letter" days of major church holidays. Not only are the days for fourteen Saints celebrated but also the *octava*, the eighth day after (inclusive), of the days of four more Saints are noted. Every Sunday in the year also was a holiday. With 52 Sundays, at least 40 regular

## JANUARIUS
## HABET DIES .XXXI. LUNA .XXX.

| 1 | iii | A | KL | *Circumcisio Domini* |
|---|---|---|---|---|
| 2 | | b | iv Nonas | Octave Sancti Stephani |
| 3 | ii | c | iii Nonas | *Octave Sancti Johannis* |
| 4 | | d | ii Nonas | Octave Sancotrum innocencium |
| 5 | xviiii | e | Nonis | Octave Sancti Thome martiris |
| 6 | viii | f | viii Idus | *Epiphania Domini* |
| 7 | | g | vii Idus | (Claves septuagesime) |
| 8 | xvi | A | vi Idus | (Sancti Inciani sociorum eius) |
| 9 | v | b | v Idus | |
| 10 | | c | iiii Idus | |
| 11 | xiii | d | iii Idus | |
| 12 | ii | e | ii Idus | |
| 13 | | f | Idibus | *Octave Ephiphanie* |
| 14 | x | g | xviiii KL | Sancti Felicis confessoris |
| 15 | | A | xviii KL | Sancti Mauri abbatis |
| 16 | xviii | b | xvii KL | Sancti Marcelli pape |
| 17 | vii | c | xvi KL | Sancti Sulpicii episcopi |
| 18 | | d | xv KL | Sancti Prisce virginis |
| 19 | xv | e | xiiii KL | Sancti Wulfstani episcopi |
| 20 | iiii | f | xiii KL | Sanctorum Fabiani et Sebast. |
| 21 | | g | xii KL | Sancte Agnetis virginis |
| 22 | xii | A | xi KL | *Sancti Vincencii martyris* |
| 23 | i | b | x KL | |
| 24 | | c | ix KL | |
| 25 | viiii | d | viii KL | *Conversio Sancti Pauli* |
| 26 | | e | vii KL | |
| 27 | xvii | f | vi KL | Sancti Juliani episcopi |
| 28 | vi | g | v KL | Sancte Agnetis secunde |
| 29 | | A | iiii KL | |
| 30 | xiiii | b | iii KL | (Sancti Batildis regine) |
| 31 | iii | c | ii KL | |

*Figure 11.2* The format of the medieval perpetual calendar: the month of January in any Julian year.

saints' days, and 30 or more local feasts, there were some 126 days or more during the year when no work was allowed (Cosman 1982–85:33). A major use of a calendar would seem to be to know if the current day happens to be a working day!

Dating by saints' days prevailed in civil legal and business use, whereas the Roman dating was more common in monastic chronicles. Here is an example of a dating typical of medieval English legal records, a

Chelverscoton deed (Warwick County Record Office CR 136 C 756a)
(Gooder 1978:110–12):

> *dat(a) apud Chelverescote die d(o)m(ini)ca p(ro)x(ima) post festum Sancti
> Valentini Anno Regni Reg(is) Edward(i) t(er)cii post conquestum sexto.*
>
> Given at Chelverscote on the Sunday next after the feast of St. Valentine
> in the sixth year of the reign of King Edward the Third after the conquest.
> (Letters in parentheses were represented by abbreviation signs in the
> original document.)

The reign of Edward III began 25 January 1327; its sixth year was 25
January 1332–24 January 1333 (Cheney 1970:20). Saint Valentine's day is
14 February, a Friday in 1332. The next Sunday was 16 February (Figure
11.3).

Although the church practice of counting years, beginning with year 1
(the West as yet had no zero) as the year taken to be that of Christ's birth,
gained favor during the course of the Middle Ages, civil usage in most
places favored counting years from the beginning of the reign of the current
ruler, as this date testifies. Given the political fragmentation of Europe
during this era, as well as the frequent premature demise of many of its
monarchs, the system does not endear itself to historians.

This date also reveals that medieval Europeans counted days in cycles
of 7 using the same weekday names that have persisted since ancient times.
The Roman week now rules the daily lives of nearly everyone in the world.
Whatever its origins as a quarter of a lunar month, the week, since earliest
historical times, makes no pretense of corresponding to any natural cycle,
lunar or solar. Given this obsession in the Western tradition with the
number 7 in counting cycles of days, is there anything strange in the
Mayan attachment to the number 13?

In the Western Julian calendar, there is a 28-year cycle, the "solar
cycle," marking the correspondence of a given day of the week with a given
date. This cycle was incorporated into the medieval perpetual calendar by
marking the days from 1 January to 31 December with the letters *a* through

## Feb 1332 LP YR JULIAN

| Sun | Mon | Tue | Wed | Thu | Fri | Sat |
|-----|-----|-----|-----|-----|-----|-----|
|     |     |     |     |     |     | 1   |
| 2   | 3   | 4   | 5   | 6   | 7   | 8   |
| 9   | 10  | 11  | 12  | 13  | 14V | 15  |
| **16** | 17  | 18  | 19  | 20  | 21  | 22  |
| 23  | 24  | 25  | 26  | 27  | 28  | 29  |

*Figure* 11.3 February 1332, Leap Year, Julian.

*g* in a continuous, repeating series. The letter corresponding to Sunday in a given year is the *Dominical Letter* of that year. One simply notes the letter corresponding to a given date on a calendar page, such as that shown in Figure 11.2.

Apart from being named or numbered in a variety of ways, days take on added meaning when marked by impressive natural events—Venus risings, eclipses, comets, conjunctions, hurricanes, blizzards, earthquakes—keeping in mind the need for cultural definition of the event. For example, the Venus risings noted by the Mayans meant little to the astronomically sophisticated Micronesian navigators, who were more concerned with the positions of the fixed stars at any given time. The power of a calendar and its makers is augmented if natural events can be regarded as an inevitable attribute of a day that incorporates the proper combination of calendric day counts. But even the fundamental task of meshing the cycles of the two most conspicuous objects in the sky, the sun and the moon, has proved difficult for all calendar-makers. The importance to the Maya of lunar–solar correlations, and their success at calculating lunar time, is echoed in the Middle Eastern and Western traditions, intercalculating 19 solar years and 235 synodic months. This cycle has come to be known as *the Metonic cycle*, after an ancient Greek astronomer whose attempts to capture the motions of the moon were long ago satirized by Aristophanes.

## Meshing Celestial Cycles

> The moon by us to you her greeting sends,
> But bids us say that she's an ill-used moon,
> And takes it much amiss that you would still
> Shuffle her days and turn them topsy-turvy:
> And that the gods (who know their feast-days well)
> By your false count are sent home supperless,
> And scold and storm at her for your neglect.
> The Chorus in *Clouds* (Aristophanes 610, 615–19)
> commenting on the Athenian adoption of Meton's cycle[7]

The gods have little right to be angry at human attempts to count moons and days, for in creating heaven and its motions, they have played a terrible trick on us. They tantalize us with cycles of the days, of the moon seasons, planetary and stellar appearances—cycles that sometimes intersect, giving us spectacular conjunctions, oppositions, and eclipses; cycles that always have great real and imagined impact on our lives. A smoothly synchronized meshing of these wheels should not have been too much to ask of the gods.

A random, unrelated, and uninteresting association among them would have been a disappointment, but at least would have sent us on to other things. But the "it-almost-works—if-we-could-only-tinker-with-it-some-more" nature of the cosmic cycles that the gods have given us, has not only consumed endless hours of human mental effort, but, in typical human fashion, has led us into bitter social conflicts.

We know little about the role of the Mayan calendar in political conflicts. We do know that practices, especially with regard to lunar calculations, varied with the political fortunes of different centers (Aveni 1980:169–70). Following the same calendar, and thus celebrating ritual events on the same day, can become a potent symbol of political power. In medieval Europe, we can see how calendric practice become a major instrument of the Roman Church in its establishment of authority well beyond the scope of any one secular political power. After the triumph of Christianity in the Roman world, reckoning the date of Easter became one of the great issues of Western civilization. The heretical Quartodecimans, who would place Easter on the fourteenth moon of the Jewish passover, were a major challenge. The Church turned to the pagan lore of the ancient Greeks for a solution to the problem of assigning Easter to a date that always linked Sunday, the full moon, and the Spring equinox—yet would never fall on passover. The ill-fed ancient gods then had their revenge.[8]

The more computationally difficult the determination of a particular date, the more symbolic power accrued to the achievement of a simultaneous celebration of it throughout the Christian world. As though implicitly realizing this source of power, in their search for the moment when, in the words of the Venerable Bede, "the mutable moon, spotted, vagarious, and oft-dimmed, derives its full light from the eternal sun with which it is, momentarily, in perfect union" (Jones 1943:13), the early Church fathers made a computational nightmare out of determining Easter Sunday. Placing Easter and the "moveable feasts" linked to it on a calendar of the solar year, with its 12 Roman months and 7-day weeks, proved sufficiently thorny that it promoted a whole field of scholarly specialization known as *computus*. This field, which rapidly expanded to include a wide array of computational, calendric, astronomical, and cosmological problems, enlisted talents such as those of the ninth-century Venerable Bede whose *De Temporum Ratione* ("On the Calculation of Time") became a standard text in the Middle Ages. It was Bede who promoted the practice of counting years successively from the year of Christ's birth. By the nineteenth century another scholarly field had developed called by the Germans, who excelled in it, *mathematische und technische Chronologie*, painstaking meta-scholarship devoted to understanding and explaining the calendrical intricacies produced by ancient and medieval computists.[9]

The fundamental cycle of the medieval calendar was the Metonic nineteen-year cycle where the same phase of the moon reoccurs on the same date. In the Julian calendar, this required some manipulations in the counting of the length of lunar months; a simple alternation of 29 and 30 day months does not work (Neugebauer 1983a; van Wijk 1936). Each year was assigned a number, its "Golden Number," in the 19-year cycle. If one knows the Golden Number of a year, one then looks for that number on a monthly calendar page, such as that for January shown in Figure 11.2. There one finds the date of the ecclesiastical new moon. Thus, in 1318 the Golden Number was viii. The number viii is opposite the sixth day, the date of the ecclesiastical new moon. By 1318, the true new moon occurred some 4 days earlier (see Table 11.1). Knowing that difference, one could still predict the date of a true new moon using Golden Numbers, but Easter's date depended not on the phase of the real moon nor the position of the real sun. It was from the conventionally defined ecclesiastical new moon and the ecclesiastical spring equinox that one calculated, by conventions of inclusive counting, the date of Easter.

Golden Numbers and Dominical Letters were just the beginning of the medieval calendricist's inventory of dating devices. It was possible to identify a day by more than its letter, day name, number in the month, month name, year number, and Golden Number of its year. As an indication of

*Table 11.1*   Calendar and Calendric Data for 1318 A.D. Julian[a]

| Jan. 1318 GN = 8 Julian | | | | | | | Feb. 1318 GN = 8 Julian | | | | | | |
|---|---|---|---|---|---|---|---|---|---|---|---|---|---|
| Sun | Mon | Tue | Wed | Thu | Fri | Sat | Sun | Mon | Tue | Wed | Thu | Fri | Sat |
| 1 | 2 | 3* | 4 | 5 | 6+ | 7 | | | | 1* | 2 | 3 | 4+ |
| 8 | 9 | 10 | 11 | 12 | 13 | 14 | 5 | 6 | 7 | 8 | 9 | 10 | 11 |
| 15 | 16 | 17 | 18 | 19 | 20 | 21 | 12 | 13 | 14 | 15 | 16 | 17 | 18 |
| 22 | 23 | 24 | 25 | 26 | 27 | 28 | 19 | 20 | 21 | 22 | 23 | 24 | 25 |
| 29 | 30 | 31 | | | | | 26 | 27 | 28 | | | | |

| Mar. 1318 GN = 8 Julian | | | | | | | Apr. 1318 GN = 8 Julian | | | | | | |
|---|---|---|---|---|---|---|---|---|---|---|---|---|---|
| Sun | Mon | Tue | Wed | Thu | Fri | Sat | Sun | Mon | Tue | Wed | Thu | Fri | Sat |
| | | | 1 | 2 | 3* | 4 | | | | | | | 1* |
| 5 | 6+ | 7 | 8 | 9 | 10 | 11 | 2 | 3 | 4 | 5+ | 6 | 7 | 8 |
| 12 | 13 | 14 | 15 | 16 | 17 | 18 | 9 | 10 | 11 | 12 | 13 | 14 | 15 |
| 19 | 20 | 21 | 22 | 23 | 24 | 25 | 16 | 17 | 18 | 19 | 20 | 21 | 22 |
| 26 | 27 | 28 | 29 | 30 | 31 | | 23 | 24 | 25 | 26 | 27 | 28 | 29 |
| | | | | | | | 30* | | | | | | |

*True new moon.

+Ecclesiastical new moon.

[a]Golden number of 1318 = 8; solar cycle number of 1318 = 11; Dominical letter of 1318 = A; epact of 1318 = 17; concurrent of 1318 = 6; indiction of 1318 = 1; Claves of 1318 = 39; Easter falls on April 23.

the potential, consider a fourteenth-century date taken from the Irish *Annals of Innisfallen:*

> The Kalends of January on Sunday, and the twenty-sixth of the moon thereon. A.D. 1318; Dominical Letter A, and the Tabular Letter O. (*postpuncta*); the second year after the bissextile; the eighth year of the Decemnovennial Cycle; the fifth of the Lunar Cycle; the twenty-fifth of the Solar Cycle according to Gerlandus and the eleventh according to Dionysius; and the first Indiction; has six as the Concurrent is an Embolismal year, has seventeen as epacts, and thirty-nine as Claves.
>
> *Annals of Innisfallen*, Ware, 1976, p. 214[10]

See Table 11.2 for an explanation of each of the components of this date.

If we knew little of medieval European culture beyond dates such as this, we might be tempted, as Mayanists legitimately are, to search for natural or ritual associations for each of its cyclical components. What happened in years of the first indiction? Or in years that were Embolismal? Or in years that had 39 as Claves? Nothing special, actually. In medieval Europe we know that we cannot account for the complexities of the calendar system in this way, for there was an involution of calendric complexity that went far beyond what was needed for any practical purposes, whether for predicting natural events or scheduling cultural ones. The 15-year Indiction cycle provides the most obvious example. It related to nothing, natural or cultural, during the entire medieval era (although it is said to have corresponded to an ancient Roman tax period); yet it was salient enough in the sixteenth century to qualify as one of the three components Scaliger used in his creation of the cycle of Julian days and still used by modern astronomers. In fact it seems as if both nature and culture—and God—were expected to fit their performances to the demands of the calendar. If the god of medieval Christians wanted to attend an Easter service, then he had better consult a human-made calendar made by his worshippers for the dates of the ecclesiastical equinox and ecclesiastical moon rather than looking for the positions of the sun and moon of his own creation. Even the Gregorian reform of 1582 was a dubious victory for this god. The intent was not simply to make the calendar follow nature's order more closely so that the equinox always fell on the same date, but more important, to make that date correspond to 21 March, the ecclesiastical equinox. However, in no time during the history of the medieval church did the true spring equinox actually fall on that date (Newton 1972:22–27). Perhaps even more disappointing to God, the calendric reform became an identity symbol dividing the contesting factions of his church, much as the Easter controversy did a thousand years earlier. The Protestant English did

Table 11.2  Years of the Same Lunar and Solar Cycles as 1318

**19 years before 1318: same date of eccl. moon[a]**
Jan. 1299 GN = 8 Julian

| Sun | Mon | Tue | Wed | Thu | Fri | Sat |
|-----|-----|-----|-----|-----|-----|-----|
|     |     |     |     | 1   | 2*  | 3   |
| 4   | 5   | 6+  | 7   | 8   | 9   | 10  |
| 11  | 12  | 13  | 14  | 15  | 16  | 17  |
| 18  | 19  | 20  | 21  | 22  | 23  | 24  |
| 25  | 26  | 27  | 28  | 29  | 30  | 31* |

**28 years before 1318: same week day and date[b]**
Jan. 1290 GN = 18 Julian

| Sun | Mon | Tue | Wed | Thu | Fri | Sat |
|-----|-----|-----|-----|-----|-----|-----|
| 1   | 2   | 3   | 4   | 5   | 6   | 7   |
| 8   | 9   | 10  | 11* | 12  | 13  | 14  |
| 15  | 16+ | 17  | 18  | 19  | 20  | 21  |
| 22  | 23  | 24  | 25  | 26  | 27  | 28  |
| 29  | 30  | 31  |     |     |     |     |

**532 (19 × 28) years before 1318: same calendar except true and eccl. moons closer[c]**
Jan. 786 GN = 8 Julian

| Sun | Mon | Tue | Wed | Thu | Fri | Sat |
|-----|-----|-----|-----|-----|-----|-----|
| 1   | 2   | 3   | 4*  | 5   | 6+  | 7   |
| 8   | 9   | 10  | 11  | 12  | 13  | 14  |
| 15  | 16  | 17  | 18  | 19  | 20  | 21  |
| 22  | 23  | 24  | 25  | 26  | 27  | 28  |
| 29  | 30  | 31  |     |     |     |     |

[a] Golden number of 1299 = 8; solar cycle number of 1299 = 20; Dominical letter of 1299 = D; epact of 1299 = 17; concurrent of 1299 = 3; indiction of 1299 = 12; Claves of 1299 = 39; Easter falls on 19 April.

[b] Golden number of 1290 = 18; solar cycle number of 1290 = 11; Dominical letter of 1290 = A; epact of 1290 = 7; concurrent of 1290 = 6; indiction of 1290 = 3; Claves of 1290 = 19; Easter falls on 2 April.

[c] All indices repeated except the indication: golden number of 786 = 8; solar cycle number of 786 = 8; dominical letter of 786 = A; epact of 786 = 11; dominical letter of 786 = A; epact of 786 = 17; concurrent of 786 = 6; indiction of 786 = 9; claves of 786 = 39; Easter falls on 23 April.

not accept the Gregorian calendar until the seventeenth century, the Orthodox Russians until the twentieth.

What led to calendric complexity in Europe was not so much a need to predict or schedule events, but rather the dilemmas faced by the Christian church of the early Middle Ages. The core problem was holding together, by means of the symbolic power of a religious ideology, a world that had lost the unifying political power of Rome. In forging its symbols, the church had as raw material portions of two heritages, one the ancient pagan tradition of Rome and Greece and the other the Hebraic tradition of the Jews. Both traditions provided symbolic raw material, but material that required sufficient remolding so as not to remain symbols of pagan or Jewish identity. This need to be identifiably different, while retaining a connection with past traditions, was the major force driving the calculatory involution that marked the construction of the Christian calendar. But the intricate elaborations, like those of a Gothic cathedral's facade, lent to the medieval calendar a symbolic power that made it one of the most effective instruments of Christian unity in belief and practice.[11] In spite of the lack of political unity, the Julian calendar also came to govern civil life throughout Europe. Merchants and rulers everywhere scheduled economic and political life according to the same complicated system that the bishops and monks used to date their holy feasts and to record the deeds of saints, the deaths of kings, the battle of knights, and the eclipses of the sun and moon.

## The Calendar as Text

*Avec ce livre, nous saissons—occasion peu fréquente—certains éléments de "l'outillage mental" des gens de mer.*

With this book we are provided a rare opportunity to grasp something of the mental tool kit of the [medieval] seafarer.
        Michel Mollat on Dujardin-Troadec's study of Breton almanacs.[12]

The several Mayan books that have survived for modern investigation all deal with astronomical and calendrical matters. Sections of them have been appropriately called *almanacs*. The Mayans invented not only a mathematics, an empirical astronomy, and a calendar based on these, but also a medium and a format for the visual display of their science in books. It is difficult to image how, without physical representation in numerals, writing, and graphics, Mayan calendrical astronomy could have progressed so far.

Medieval Europe also had books—painstakingly handwritten and illuminated volumes [that they perhaps valued too much]. C. S. Lewis, the scholar of medieval literature (1964:5), makes much of what he calls "the overwhelmingly bookish or clerkly character of medieval culture." Modern scholars, themselves champions of bookishness, perhaps exaggerate the extent of the same addiction among their medieval subjects. It is probably true that medieval scholars, rather than looking up at the sky, were more likely to seek the position of the sun, moon, and planets in books, copied and recopied from Greek, in Arabic and Latin translations. Despite the vastly greater abundance of material available to the modern scholar, the extent of an observational basis to medieval astronomy seems as difficult to specify as it does for the Maya (see, for example, Goldstein 1972).

Modern scholarship tends to obscure the large quantity of calendars that appear in medieval manuscripts. Scholars concerned with literary texts and artistic illuminations typically ignore the calendar pages that go with them and, although much of medieval art is calendar art, art historians rarely reproduce the calendars themselves.[13] The use of these calendars was not restricted to priests and monks. Calendars were an essential part of the often beautiful "books of hours," produced for lay nobility (Harthan 1977). Chaucer's poetry made extensive use of a calendar written by Nicholas of Lynn (Eisner 1980).

Of special interest are almanacs written by seafarers, who were mostly illiterate (especially in Latin) but, unlike the monks, necessarily attentive to the sky above. A sailor could not predict tides by the ecclesiastical moon. On the other hand, when on shore, he would miss Easter and all the other moveable feasts if he used the real moon as a guide. Sailors' almanacs, produced both by hand on vellum and by woodblock print on paper at the turn of the fifteenth century in Brittany, met these practical needs and were a convenient shirt-pocket size, too. Figure 11.4 is a page from a woodblock print of the early sixteenth century. This page contains all the information of the calendar shown in Figure 11.2, except the days are not consecutively numbered in either the Roman or modern system. Figure 11.5 is a circular tide table from the same book. Its use depends on knowing the age of the true moon. The book also contains a table of moveable feasts, which requires knowing the age of the ecclesiastical moon. Ironically such books, ostensibly for illiterate sailors, today require careful study to understand their use. Latin prose may have been a mystery to the medieval sailor, but he had the knowledge of the graphic and numerical conventions, together with the understanding both of the sea's real time and the church's conventional time to make sense and practical use of his almanac.[14]

Calendar books, whether Mayan or medieval European, give us some grasp of *l'outillage mental* of those who made and used them. It is undoubt-

*Figure 11.4* Breton sailor's calendar. The first column of Roman numerals are the Golden Numbers of the true new moon. The second column are the Golden Numbers for the ecclesiastical moon. Next comes the Dominical Letters and the feast days, both marked by symbols of written names of the saints. The month columns (or rows?—the orientation, if any, is ambiguous) are headed by symbols and initial letters for the month. The circular diagram represents the relative amount of daylight and night during that month—common information in all medieval calendars. *Source:* Howse 1980.

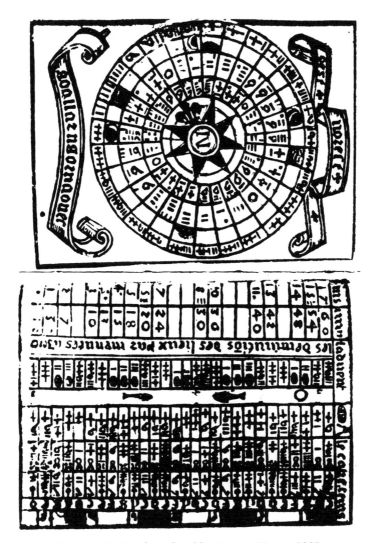

*Figure 11.5* Circular tide table. *Source:* Howse 1980.

edly pernicious, ethnocentric, and otherwise unbecoming an anthropologist to pass judgment on the intellectual merits of the cultural products of human societies. Yet in making a comparison such as this, it is difficult to refrain from expressing admiration for the mental accomplishments of the Mayans, who had none of the advantages of long literary and scientific heritage, not to mention of an incomparably higher level of technological development. Mayan science, in its mathematics, its representation of numbers, and its empirical base is in many respects superior to the science of their European contemporaries. What gave medieval Europe the edge was its love of gadgets, a love that gave birth to the technological development that enabled Europe to conquer the world. There were gadgets like rotating slide rules (*volvelles*) for intercalculating solar and lunar time that are so often bound into medieval manuscripts (North 1976); or the astrolabe Chaucer gave to his son together with an instruction manual, the *Treatise on the Astrolabe* (Skeat 1872; North 1988), the first technical manual in English—a text more understandable and far more enjoyable than my computer manual. But the ultimate medieval gadget was the world's first information-processing and information-producing machine, one that had a practical and symbolic importance comparable to the modern computer. Originally designed to track automatically the motions of the sun, moon, and planets through the celestial sphere as well as to toll the hours of the day, it is the device that you now consult to see if it's finally cocktail time.

## NOTES

1. This epigraph is taken from North 1989:39. The translation is mine.

2. Actually in contemporary, "postmodern" anthropology, the legitimacy of a concern for getting it right has become an issue in its own right. These papers speak indirectly, but eloquently, to that issue as well.

3. In 1582, Scaliger calculated backward to a time when the three great medieval cycles, the 19-year lunar cycle, the 28-year day-of-the-week cycle, and the 15-year "indiction," would have begun together. His result: 4713 B.C. (−4712 BP). He named his cycle after his father Julius. Modern astronomers count their "Julian" (nothing to do with the Julian calendar named after Caesar) dates from January 1, 4713 B.C. The first run of this grand cycle of 19 × 28 × 15 or 7980 (Julian calendar) years is due to end in A.D. 3267 on Julian Day number 2914695 (7980 × 365.25), but astronomers have long forgotten the cyclical intent of the count. The Julian calendar was, in Roman Catholic countries, replaced by the Gregorian calendar in the same year Julian day numbers were born. With the consequent change in the length of the year, the utility of the lunar and solar cycles and thereby the rationale for Scaliger's grand cycle was destroyed (Ginzel 1906–14, I:97–103; Ottewell 1981:23).

4. The calendars and calendric data displayed in the text and in the figures were generated by a computer program, written by the author, using the algorithms for medieval cycles of Ginzel (1906–14) and modern astronomical formulas from Duffett-Smith (1981). Calculated true new moon dates have been checked against Goldstine's (1973) tables.

5. The convention that renders this number as XIX was not commonly used in medieval Europe.

6. There is considerable local and temporal variation in the feast days recognized. Figure 11.2 is based on the fourteenth-century *Kalendarium* of Nicholas of

Lynn, edited and explained by Eisner (1980). Wormald (1934, 1939) has published the saint's days from a long series of English calendars from the entire medieval period.

7. A translation from Jones (1943:3), which omits several lines on the moon's unappreciated service to mankind.

8. On the entangled history of the Easter controversies see Jones (1943), Newton (1972:15–42), Neugebauer (1983b), North (1989:40–44).

9. See Ideler's (1825) pioneering work, Grotefend's (1891) manual, and, especially, Ginzel's (1906–14) three volumes, which cover the world's calendrical systems since ancient times. The tradition of detailed and precise scholarship in this field has been carried on by Otto Neugebauer (1975, 1983a), although with a much narrowed geographical scope and a more judgmental tone than Ginzel's. Other modern studies include Borst (1988) and Cappelli's (1983) handbook. Aveni (1989) provides a rare modern example of an authoritative work that gives balanced treatment to both New and Old World calendrics.

10. Here is an explanation, for example, of the last component of this date: "and thirty-nine as Claves . . ." The Claves or "key" enables one to determine the number of days after its fixed "key date" that a moveable feast will occur in a given year. The key date for the moveable feast of Septuagesima is January 7. For 1318, a Claves of 39 brings one to 15 February, which is Wednesday. The feast will be on the next Sunday, February 19. The key date for Easter is March 11. Thirty-nine days later is 19 April, a Wednesday. The next Sunday, April 23, is Easter.

11. For details of the calendric controversies focused on Easter, see Neugebauer (1975, III; 1983b), Jones (1943), Newton (1972), North (1989).

12. Introduction to Dujardin-Troadec (1966).

13. Pickering's (1980) attempt to educate his colleagues is revealing of the art historians disinterest.

14. Original copies of these almanacs can be found in the Huntington Library, San Marino, California (a manuscript copy); the British Library (including an English copy); the Musée Condeé, Chantilly; the Bodleian Library, Oxford; The National Maritime Museum, Greenwich; the Pepysian Library, Magdalene College, Cambridge; and the Bibliothèque nationale, Paris. A facsimile edition of the Cambridge volume, with explanatory notes by Derek Howse (1980), has been published. Dujardin-Troadec (1965; 1966) has written the authoritative comparative study of the Brouscon almanacs and charts. For explanations of these and similar tidal tables and diagrams, all of which make use of the directional rose of the mariner's compass as a schema for representing and calculating lunar time, see Frake (1985), Howse (1985), and Waters (1967).

## REFERENCES

Aveni, A., 1980. *Sky Watchers of Ancient Mexico* (Austin: University of Texas Press).

—, 1989. *Empires of Time: Calendars, Clocks, and Cultures* (New York: Basic Books).

Borst, A., 1988. "Computus: Zeit und Zahl in Mittelalter," *Deutsches Archiv für Erforschung des Mittelalters* (Köln) **44**(1).

Cappelli, A., 1983. *Cronologie, Cronografia e Calendario Perpetuo* (Milano: Ulrico Hoepli).

Cheney, C. R. (ed.) 1978. *Handbook of Dates for Students of English History* (London: Royal Historical Society).

Cosman, M. P., 1982–85. "Feast and Festivals, European," in Joseph R. Strayer (ed.) *Dictionary of the Middle Ages*, F:33–37 (New York: Scribner).

Duffett-Smith, P., 1981. *Practical Astronomy with your Calculator* (Cambridge: Cambridge University Press).

Dujardin-Troadec, L., 1965. "Calendriers iconographique anglais de 1525 et 1396, inspirateurs probables des cartographers bretons du Conquet (XVIe siecle)," *Actes du quatre-vingt-neuvième Congrès National des Sociétés Savantes, Lyon, 1964, Section de Géeographie,* pp. 167–87. (Paris: Bibliothèque nationale).

—, 1966. *Les cartographes bretons du Conquet: La navigation en images 1543–1650* (Brest: Imprimerie Commerciale & Administrative).

Eisner, S. (ed.), 1980. *The Kalendarium of Nicholas of Lynn* (Athens, Georgia: The University of Georgia Press).

Frake, C. O., 1985. "Cognitive Maps of Time and Tide Among Medieval Seafarers," *Man: The Journal of the Royal Anthropological Institute* **20**:254–70.

Ginzel, F. K., 1906–14. *Handbuch der mathematischen und technischen Chronologie,* 3 vols. (Leipzig: J. C. Hinrichs'sche Buchhandlung).

Goldstein, B. R., 1972. "Theory and Observation in Medieval Astronomy." *Isis* **63**:39–57.

Goldstine, H., 1973. *New and Full Moons* (Philadelphia: American Philosophical Society).

Gooder, E., 1978. *Latin for Local History,* 2nd. ed. (London: Longman).

Grotefend, Hermann, 1891. *Seitrechnung des Deutschen Mittelalters und der Neuzeit* (Hannover: Hahn'sche Buchhandlung).

Harthan, J., 1977. *Books of Hours and Their Owners* (London: Thames and Hudson).

Howse, H. D. (ed.), 1980. *Sir Francis Drake's Nautical Almanack 1546* (with explanatory insert by Derek Howse) (London: Nottingham Court Press).

—, 1985. "Some Early Tidal Diagrams," *Coimbra: Revista de Universidade de Coimbra* **33**:365–85.

Ideler, L., 1825. *Handbuch der mathematischen und technishcen Chronologie,* 2 vols. (Berlin: 2nd ed., 1883, Breslau).

Jones, C. W. (ed.), 1943. *Bedae Opera de Temporibus* (Cambridge, Mass.: Mediaeval Academy of America).

Neugebauer, O., 1975. *A History of Ancient Mathematical Astronomy,* 3 vols. (New York: Springer-Verlag).

—, 1983a. "Astronomical and Calendric Data in the Tres Riches Heures," *Astronomy and History: Selected Essays*, pp. 507–20 (New York: Springer-Verlag).

—, 1983b. "Ethiopic Easter Computus," *Astronomy and History: Selected Essays*, pp. 523–38 (New York: Springer-Verlag).

Newton, R. R., 1972. *Medieval Chronicles and the Rotation of the Earth* (Baltimore and London: Johns Hopkins University Press).

North, J. D. (ed.), 1976. *Richard of Wallingford: An Edition of his Writings with Introductions, English Translation and Commentary*, 3 vols. (Oxford: Clarendon Press).

—, 1988. *Chaucer's Universe* (Oxford: Clarendon Press).

—, 1989. "The Western calendar: intolerabilis, horribilis et derisibilis; four centuries of discontent," in *The Universal Frame: Historical Essays in Astronomy, Natural Philosophy and Science* (London: Hambledon).

Ottewell, G., 1981. *The Astronomical Companion* (Greenville, S.C.: Department of Physics, Furman University).

Pickering, F. R., 1980. *The Calendar Pages of Medieval Service Books: An Introductory Note for Art Historians* (Reading: Reading University Center for Medieval Studies).

Skeat, W. W. (ed.), 1872. *A Treatise on the Astrolabe by Geoffrey Chaucer* A.D. 1391 (Oxford: Oxford University Press) [reprinted 1968].

Ware, R. D., 1976. "Medieval Chronology: Theory and Practice," in James M. Powell (ed.), *Medieval Studies*, pp. 213–38 (Syracuse, N.Y.: Syracuse University Press).

Waters, D. W., 1967. *The Rutters of the Sea: The Sailing Directions of Pierre Garcie, a Study of the First English and French Printed Sailing Directions* (New Haven: Yale University Press).

Wijk, W. E., 1936. *Le Nombre d'or: Étude de Chronologie Technique, Suivie du Texte de la Massa Compoti d'Alexandre de Villedieu* (La Haye: Martinus Nijhoff).

Wormald, F., 1934. *English Kalendars Before* A.D. 1100, vol. 1, texts, Henry Bradshaw Society 72 (London: Harrison & Sons).

—, 1939. *English Kalendars after* A.D. 1100, vol. 1, Abbotsbury–Durham, Henry Bradshaw Society 77 (London: Harrison & Sons).

# INDEX